Wheatley's
Road Traffic
Law in Scotland

Wheatley's
Road Traffic
Law in Scotland

Sixth edition

Andrew Brown QC

Bloomsbury Professional

LONDON • DUBLIN • EDINBURGH • NEW YORK • NEW DELHI • SYDNEY

Bloomsbury Professional
Bloomsbury Publishing Plc
41–43 Boltro Road, Haywards Heath, RH16 1BJ, UK

BLOOMSBURY and the Diana logo are trademarks

of Bloomsbury Publishing Plc

British Library Cataloguing-in-Publication Data

A catalogue record for this book is available from the British Library.

ISBN:	PB:	978 1 52650 648 1
	Epub:	978 1 52650 649 8
	Epdf:	978 1 52650 650 4

Typeset by Evolution Design & Digital Ltd (Kent), UK
Printed and bound by CPI Group (UK) Ltd, Croydon, CR0 4YY, UK

To find out more about our authors and books visit
www.bloomsburyprofessional.com. Here you will find extracts, author
information, details of forthcoming events and the option to sign up for
our newsletters

Preface

Four years after the last edition, much of the impact of the Road Safety Act 2006 is still awaited. However, the range of death by driving offences has been further increased and consideration of extension to reflect cycle caused deaths and serious injuries is underway.

Greater impact has come from changes achieved under devolution, most obviously the introduction of Scottish drink drive limits. These have been welcomed on the safety front, but have inevitably generated sentence appeals.

By contrast, the UK-wide introduction of drug driving provisions, currently in use south of the border, as yet has had no impact in Scotland, due to the absence of equipment and any specified limits which are to be produced by Holyrood. Both, apparently, are due in 2019.

There has, of course, been a wide range of fresh authorities on many aspects of road traffic law. Of particular note might be the review of dangerous driving and the need to focus on driver health, both as a result of the Glasgow bin lorry tragedy. Important clarification of how to approach discount has recently been produced and reflects a pragmatic and, it is suggested, sensible approach to matters. That approach is also to be seen in the recent consideration of, perhaps spurious, challenge to average speed cameras, another advance in road safety.

Reliance on such technology highlights the resourcing issues faced by Police Scotland. While the response to serious accidents is to a high standard and practitioners should note a uniform approach to reports in fatal cases, focusing on what the evidence is, rather than apportioning blame, it appears that preventative road policing has been diminished by the creation of a single force. Unification has led to fewer traffic officers, fewer vehicles and equipment that is either out of date or not replaced. Prosecution of road traffic matters in the Crown Office before and after revealed the differing approaches of the various legacy forces, and the subsequent, and understandable, frustration of those whose standards were lowered.

That problem, and the wider issues of police resource, may be interesting to follow if current moves to reduce the 30 mph speed limit to 20 mph nationally are followed through at Holyrood. Such prosecutions as currently exist for 20 mph limits seem token at best, and the desire by the police to move towards warnings and speed awareness courses, so successfully used south of the border, may be sensible. The focused priorities on mundane road traffic crime referred to in the last edition appear not to have lasted.

Thanks as ever go to many people who have assisted in the preparation of this edition. Paula O'Connell at Bloomsbury Professional demonstrated yet more exemplary patience. So did my family. I am particularly grateful to my wife, Alison Brown, whose experience, and experiences, in the Justice of the Peace Court were extremely helpful. Thanks also to Professor Anthony Busuttil, who very kindly updated his own appendix on "Drugged driving" as well as Prof JK Mason's appendix on statutory defences. Once again, Juliet Petrusev, until recently in the Appeals Unit of the Crown Office, was of great help. Any errors in the book, of whatever kind, are of course mine.

The law is stated up to August 2018.

Andrew Brown QC
Edinburgh

Contents

Chapter 3
Drink and drug related offences

Chapter 4
Preliminary breath tests and provision of specimens for analysis

Chapter 5
Use of specimens and evidence in proceedings under the
Road Traffic Act 1988, sections 3A, 4, 5 and 5A

Chapter 6
Miscellaneous; hospital patients; detention and interpretation

Chapter 7
Other road traffic offences

Chapter 8
Licences, disqualification, endorsement and fixed penalties

Chapter 9
Public service vehicles and carriage of goods by road

Table of Statutes

Table of Statutory Instruments

Table of Cases

Chapter 1

Definitions

1.1 STATUTORY BASIS AND GENERAL DEFINITIONS

Road transport, and the provisions of the Road Traffic Act 1988 and the Road Traffic Offenders Act 1988, remain reserved matters in terms of the Scotland Act 1998.[1] However, since 3 July 2012, and the coming into force of ss 20–22 of the Scotland Act 2012, the Scottish Government now has the power to alter drink driving and speed limits. It did so in relation to the former by lowering the drink drive limits with effect from 5 December 2014 with, it appears, positive impact.[2] UK legislation continues to provide a large number of statutory definitions and descriptions of terms used in road traffic law. (The only addition is reference to a potential 'Scottish national speed limit' in the Road Traffic Regulation Act 1984, which thus far remains window dressing.)

Some of the most important of these have been considered and interpreted by the courts. Section 185 of the Road Traffic Act 1988 (c 52)

---

1   See *Martin & Miller v HMA* [2010] UKSC 10, 2010 SCCR 401, the first true devolution appeal concerning the competence of the Scottish Parliament in introducing 12-month sentences for summary RTA cases involving offences triable either way. This was at odds with the penalty provisions in the Road Traffic Offenders Act 1988, Sch 2. Ultimately, after months of deliberation, and by a majority of three to two, the Court held that the amendments made were principally concerned with penalties and jurisdiction and as a result did not relate to a reserved matter.
2   See the Road Traffic Act 1988 (Prescribed Limit) (Scotland) Regulations 2014, and Chapters 4 and 5.

provides a series of definitions of the term 'motor vehicle' and other expressions relating to vehicles. However, the Road Traffic Act 1991 (c 40) replaces the term 'motor vehicle' with the phrase 'mechanically propelled vehicle' in a number of the principal sections of the 1988 Act.[1] Sections 186–191 of the 1988 Act give a number of supplementary and additional descriptions relating to such vehicles. Section 192 of the 1988 Act (as amended) sets out a number of general interpretations of words and phrases used throughout the Act, and s 194 provides a definition index. Section 11 (as amended) gives a number of particular interpretations relating to ss 3A–10; ss 85 and 86 are respectively an interpretation section and a definition index relative to Pt II of the Act (Construction and Use provisions); s 108 (as amended by the Road Traffic (Driver Licensing and Information Systems) Act 1989) is the interpretation section for Pt III (Drivers' Licences); s 121 (as similarly amended) provides definitions for Pt IV (HGV Drivers' Licences and Passenger-carrying Vehicle Drivers' Licences); and ss 161 and 162 are respectively the interpretation section and definition index for Pt VI (Insurance). Further definition sections are found in ss 136–142 of the Road Traffic Regulation Act 1984 (c 27) and reg 3 of the Road Vehicles (Construction and Use) Regulations 1986, with recent amendments to reflect increasing use of electric vehicles.[2] In addition, other words and phrases associated with driving offences have been the subject of judicial interpretation.

A description of some of the more commonly used statutory and other terms now follows. However, while the definition of a particular term will generally suffice for most of the occasions and purposes of its use in different contexts throughout the legislation, there are certain exceptions to this general rule which are indicated as appropriate in the text. In particular, special significance has been additionally applied to some of these terms in relation to the drink-related offences described in ss 3A–10 of the Road Traffic Act 1988, and this is discussed at 3.3.1 below.

1.2 MOTOR VEHICLES

1.2.1 General

A 'motor vehicle' was originally defined in terms of s 185(1) of the Road Traffic Act 1988 as 'a mechanically propelled vehicle intended or adapted for use on the roads' In other words, the vehicle must be constructed for the purpose of being used on the roads, or alternatively

1   See 1.2.1 below.
2   SI 1986/1078 as amended.

be altered or adapted to make it suitable for that purpose.[1] Whether a vehicle has been 'adapted for use on the roads' will depend on the facts and circumstances in each case.[2] In addition, in terms of the statutory definition it is essential that the vehicle is so constructed that it can be mechanically propelled.

Section 4 of the Road Traffic Act 1991 (which came into effect on 1 July 1992) replaced, in a number of important sections, the term 'motor vehicle' with the words 'mechanically propelled vehicle' The sections of the Road Traffic Act 1988 so affected are ss 1–4 (although not s 5), s 10, s 163, s 168, s 170 and s 181; and also s 11(1) and s 23 of the Road Traffic Offenders Act 1988. The purpose of this amendment is specifically to exclude the qualification of vehicles being 'intended or adapted for use on the road' from these sections, and thus give them a wider application. For example, scrambler motor cycles, some kinds of stock cars, and certain types of building site vehicles could be described as not being intended or adapted for the purpose of being used on the roads, and would not therefore have been caught by the relevant sections as previously described. However, the term 'motor vehicle' is still extensively used in other parts of the legislation.

The words 'mechanically propelled vehicle' therefore now appear in two slightly different contexts in the legislation. Firstly, the words appear, by themselves, and without particular further definition, in the above sections of the Road Traffic Act 1988, as amended by the Road Traffic Act 1991; and secondly they continue to feature in the definition of the term 'motor vehicle' where it appears unaltered elsewhere.

In general, the words 'mechanically propelled vehicle' as used in either context should be interpreted in an ordinary as opposed to a strictly technical sense. Essentially, the phrase means precisely what it says. The definition may be applicable to a vehicle whether that vehicle is moving under its own power, whether it is capable of so moving, or whether it is temporarily out of order. However, if a vehicle is in such a condition that there are no reasonable prospects of it being mobile again, it is no longer a mechanically propelled vehicle.[3] Equally, a vehicle will not qualify for inclusion in the statutory definition if it has reached 'such a state of mechanical or structural decrepitude' that it would offend against common sense to describe it as a mechanically propelled vehicle.[4]

1   *French v Champkin* [1920] 1 KB 76.
2   *Taylor v Mead* [1961] 1 WLR 435, [1961] 1 All ER 626, a case where a commercial traveller adapted a private car to carry goods.
3   *Maclean v Hall* 1962 SLT (Sh Ct) 30; *McNeill v Ritchie* 1967 SLT (Sh Ct) 68.
4   *Tudhope v Every* 1976 JC 42, 1977 SLT 2.

In considering the test to be used in determining whether any particular vehicle falls within these statutory definitions, regard should principally be had to the construction of the vehicle rather than the use to which it is put. In *McEachran v Hurst*,[1] a broken-down moped was being pedalled along a road; it was held that the vehicle was still a moped rather than a cycle. A vehicle, therefore, which is plainly not constructed or adapted or intended for use on the roads will not normally fall within the statutory definition of a motor vehicle. The fact that a vehicle is temporarily broken down or has had its engine removed does not necessarily take the vehicle outwith the statutory definition; even where a vehicle has had its source of motor power removed it can still properly be described as being so constructed as to be mechanically propelled.[2] But if the evidence demonstrates that essential parts of the vehicle, such as the engine or gear box, have been permanently removed and are unlikely to be replaced, then such a vehicle may no longer qualify as a mechanically propelled vehicle. A mechanically propelled vehicle may be in such a dangerous condition that simply by driving it an offence is committed.[3]

A further matter that may also have to be taken into account in considering whether or not a particular vehicle falls within the statutory definition of a motor vehicle in terms of s 185(1) of the Road Traffic Act 1988 is to decide if it can be said, on a reasonable person's view of the facts and circumstances, that one of the uses for which the vehicle was intended was a general use on the road, irrespective of the intention of the manufacturer or the owner.[4] Previous editions have expressed the view that dumper vehicles, for example, being used solely on building sites for construction work, and not in fact used or intended or designed to be used for carrying materials on public roads, would not be classed as motor vehicles. However, this may have been brought into question by the case of *Grant v McHale*.[5] There, a much more simplistic and rigid approach was adopted, concluding, under reference to the wide Scottish statutory definition of 'road' (see 1.8.2 below), that the statutory test was satisfied as the vehicle was mechanically propelled and capable of carrying an adult driver. Nevertheless, while this might be seen as

---

1   *McEachran v Hurst* [1978] RTR 462.
2   *Newberry v Simmonds* [1961] 2 QB 345, [1961] 2 WLR 675, [1961] 2 All ER 318.
3   RTA 1988, s 2A(2); *Carstairs v Hamilton* 1998 SLT 220, 1997 SCCR 311; see also Construction and Use Regulations generally.
4   *Burns v Currel* [1963] 2 QB 433; *Nichol v Heath* [1972] RTR 476; *O'Brien v Anderton* [1979] RTR 388; *Clark v Higson* 2004 SCCR 146.
5   *Grant v McHale* 2005 SCCR 559.

bringing every mechanically propelled vehicle – including those used solely off the public roads and intended only for such use – within the statutory definition, the long line of reasonable person authorities, both north and south of the border was cited, and remain relevant.

In defining the term 'motor vehicle', s 185(1) draws specific attention to the special provision made for invalid carriages in terms of the Chronically Sick and Disabled Persons Act 1970.[1]

Section 185(1), together with s 136 of the Road Traffic Regulation Act 1984, provides further definitions of vehicle types.

1.2.2 Towed vehicles

A motor vehicle does not cease to be classified as such when it is towed by another vehicle.[2] In terms of s 185(1) of the Road Traffic Act 1988, a trailer means a vehicle drawn by a motor vehicle. Any kind of vehicle which is towed is liable to fall within the definition of a trailer; such a vehicle may therefore be at the same time both a motor vehicle and a trailer. Accordingly, the towed vehicle will also require to be covered by insurance, and will be subject to the requirements of the Vehicles (Excise) Act 1971 and the relevant Construction and Use Regulations. This is because the vehicle, although being towed, is still 'used' on the road. Trailers are described at 1.5 below. The position of drivers of towed vehicles is referred to at 1.7.1 and 3.3.2 below.

1.2.3 General application

In terms of s 87 of the Road Traffic Act 1988 (as amended by s 17 of the Road Traffic Act 1991), an appropriate licence is required before any person can drive a motor vehicle of any class on a road; and in terms of s 143 of the 1988 Act there is a requirement that the use of a motor vehicle on a road should be covered by a policy of insurance or other security. In both those instances the definition of a motor vehicle found in s 185 of the 1988 Act should be applied. In terms of s 1(1) of the Vehicle Excise and Registration Act 1994, an excise duty is charged in respect of every 'mechanically propelled vehicle' used or kept on a public road. A 'public road' in this context has the same meaning as in the Roads (Scotland) Act 1984.[3] The phrase 'mechanically propelled vehicle' is not defined in that Act; reference should be made to 1.2.1 above.

1   See 1.6.8 below.
2   *Cobb v Whorton* [1971] RTR 392.
3   Section 62: see 1.8 and 8.15.2 below.

1.2.4 Exceptions

In terms of s 189(1) of the Road Traffic Act 1988, and s 140 of the Road Traffic Regulation Act 1984, certain vehicles such as grass-cutting machines which are controlled by a pedestrian and not capable of being used or adapted for any other purpose, and electrically assisted pedal cycles[1] are not to be considered as motor vehicles. However, this exception might not apply to privately owned grass-mowers with a seat for the driver, which are used on a verge forming part of the road.

A cycle is taken to mean a bicycle, tricycle or a cycle having four or more wheels, and is similarly not to be regarded as a motor vehicle;[2] neither, as indicated above, is an electrically assisted pedal cycle of such a class as is prescribed by regulations. Offences connected with the riding of cycles on the roadway are found in ss 24 and 26; s 28 (as amended by the Road Traffic Act 1991, s 7) and ss 29–32 of the 1988 Act; reference should be made to 2.7, 2.18, 3.18 and 7.2.4 below. A hovercraft is a motor vehicle, whether or not it is adapted or intended for use on the road,[3] but it is not to be regarded as a vehicle of any of the classes as defined in s 185 of the 1988 Act.

Within these general guidelines the question of whether any vehicle does or does not come within the statutory definition of a motor vehicle will depend on the facts and circumstances of each case. In addition to the statutory definition of a motor vehicle, there are numerous regulations governing the construction and use of all kinds of such vehicles. The principal regulations in this respect are the Road Vehicles (Construction and Use) Regulations 1986.[4]

1.3 MOTOR CARS

A 'motor car' is defined in terms of s 185(1) of the Road Traffic Act 1988 as –

> 'a mechanically propelled vehicle, not being a motor cycle or an invalid carriage, which is constructed itself to carry a load or passengers and the weight of which unladen –
>
> (a)   if it is constructed solely for the carriage of passengers and their effects, is adapted to carry not more than seven passengers exclusive

---

1   See Electrically Assisted Pedal Cycles Regulations 1983 (SI 1983/1168).
2   RTA 1988, s 192(1); 1.6.7 below.
3   RTA 1988, s 188.
4   Road Vehicles (Construction and Use) Regulations 1986 (SI 1986/1078).

of the driver, and is fitted with tyres of such type as specified in regulations made by the Secretary of State, does not exceed 3,050 kilogrammes –

(b)   if it is constructed or adapted for the conveyance of goods or burden of any description, does not exceed 3,050 kilogrammes, or 3,500 kilogrammes if the vehicle carries a container or containers for holding for the purpose of its propulsion any fuel which is wholly gaseous at 17.5 degrees Celsius under a pressure of 1.013 bar or plant and materials for producing such fuel –

(c)   does not exceed 2,450 kilogrammes in a case falling within neither of the foregoing paragraphs.'

A similar definition is provided in s 136(2) of the Road Traffic Regulation Act 1984; and reg 3 of the Road Vehicles (Construction and Use) Regulations 1986[1] gives a simpler but essentially identical definition. The significance of the phrase 'mechanically propelled' is discussed at 1.2.1 above.

1.4 GOODS VEHICLES

1.4.1 General

A 'goods vehicle' means a motor vehicle constructed or adapted for the carriage of goods, or a trailer so constructed or adapted.[2] In the Road Vehicles (Construction and Use) Regulations 1986,[3] the definition is 'a motor vehicle or trailer constructed or adapted for use for the carriage or haulage of goods or burden of any description'.

Whether a vehicle has been constructed for the carriage of goods will normally be self-evident. The question of whether a vehicle has been adapted for such use is a question of fact and degree in each case, and is likely to depend chiefly on the nature of the use to which the vehicle is put in its altered state.[4]

There is special provision for the licensing of drivers of large goods vehicles[5] and the licensing of operators of goods vehicles is described at 9.11 below.

---

1   Road Vehicles (Construction and Use) Regulations 1986 (SI 1986/1078).
2   RTA 1988, s 192(1).
3   Road Vehicles (Construction and Use) Regulations 1986 (SI 1986/1078), reg 3(2).
4   *Taylor v Mead* [1961] 1 WLR 435, 1 All ER 626; *Backer v Secretary of State for Environment* [1983] 1 WLR 1485, [1983] 2 All ER 1021.
5   See 9.12 below.

1.4.2 Goods

The term 'goods' includes goods or burden of any description; and the phrase 'carriage of goods' includes the haulage of goods.[1] It is not necessary that the goods carried on the vehicle are for sale; the term can include such diverse matters as workmen's equipment and effluent.[2] However, if a vehicle is fitted with a crane, dynamo, welding plant or other special appliance or apparatus which is a permanent or essentially permanent fixture, the appliance or apparatus shall not be deemed to constitute a load, or goods or burden of any description, but shall be deemed to form part of the vehicle.[3]

1.5 TRAILERS

A 'trailer' is a vehicle drawn by a motor vehicle.[4] This definition is general and extremely wide and includes virtually anything on wheels which is towed or drawn by a motor vehicle. For example, a poultry shed being moved for sale on wheels drawn by a car will be classified as a trailer,[5] as will a wheeled roadman's hut used as an office and taken onto the road.[6]

In *Johnston v Cruickshank*,[7] a case under the Lighting Regulations, it was held that where a mechanically propelled vehicle was drawing a trailer, the vehicle doing the towing, and not the composite vehicle, was to be regarded as the motor vehicle in terms of the requirements of the regulations.

For the purpose of drivers' hours and records, a trailer is defined as any vehicle designed to be coupled to a motor vehicle or a tractor.[8]

It is important to note that for the purpose of drivers' hours and records of work (the tachograph legislation) the total weight of a commercial vehicle is to be calculated on the composite weight of both the towing vehicle and the trailer. If this total weight exceeds the statutory minimum (currently fixed at 3.5 tonnes) then the vehicle will require to be fitted with a tachograph, and the driver will be subject to the regulations

---

1   RTA 1988, s 192(1).
2   *Clarke v Cherry* [1953] 1 WLR 268, [1953] 1 All ER 267; *Sweetway Sanitary Cleaners v Bradley* [1962] 2 QB 108.
3   RTA 1988, s 186(3).
4   RTA 1988, s 185(1). RTA 1988, s 185(1).
5   *Garner v Burr* [1951] 1 KB 31.
6   *Horn v Dobson* 1933 JC 1.
7   *Johnston v Cruickshank* 1963 JC 5, 1962 SLT 409.
8   Regulation (EC) 561/2006.

concerned with the maximum hours which it is permitted to work. Small commercial vehicles below 3.5 tonnes, currently exempt, may therefore fall under these requirements during any periods when a trailer takes the total weight including its load over the statutory minimum.[1] However, this applies only to cases where the trailer is not a 'small trailer' which is defined in the amended terms of s 60(4) of the Transport Act 1968 as one whose unladen weight does not exceed 1,020 kilograms. Such small trailers can therefore be towed without bringing the composite vehicle within the tachograph rules.

A side-car attached to a motor cycle is not normally to be regarded as a trailer (see Road Traffic Act 1988 186(1) and reg 92 Road Vehicles (Construction and Use) Regulations 1986 (SI 1986/1078)

Regulations 83–90 of the same Regulations supply detailed provisions in respect of trailers and side-cars drawn by various kinds of vehicles, and the number of trailers that can be pulled at one time.

A semi-trailer is defined as a trailer which is constructed or adapted to form part of an articulated vehicle.[2]

Towed vehicles are described at 1.2.2 above.

1.6 VARIOUS VEHICLES

1.6.1 Introduction

Throughout the general legislation there are definitions provided of a variety of sorts of vehicles for different purposes. The principal relevance of these definitions is in licensing, weight limits, and construction and use regulations generally. A general description of some of the most commonly used definitions follows.

1.6.2 Articulated vehicles

In terms of s 108(1) of the Road Traffic Act 1988, an 'articulated goods vehicle' means 'a motor vehicle which is so constructed that a trailer designed to carry goods may by partial superimposition be attached thereto in such a manner as to cause a substantial part of the weight of the trailer to be borne by the motor vehicle'. By virtue of the same section, an articulated goods vehicle combination is defined as 'an articulated

---

1   RTA 1988, s 108(1) – definition of 'permissible maximum weight'.
2   And includes a vehicle which is not itself a motor vehicle but which has some or all of its wheels driven by the drawing vehicle – Road Vehicles (Construction and Use) Regulations 1986, SI 1986/1078, reg 3.

goods vehicle with a trailer so attached'. The same definition applies for the purposes of Pt IV of the Act.[1] The context in which these definitions are given in the Act is the licensing of drivers. For the purposes of the Road Vehicles (Construction and Use) Regulations 1986,[2] the term defined is an 'articulated vehicle', which is 'a heavy motor car or motor car, not being an articulated bus, with a trailer so attached that part of the trailer is superimposed on the drawing vehicle and, when the trailer is uniformly loaded, not less than 20 per cent of its load is borne by the drawing vehicle'. An articulated goods vehicle, or an articulated vehicle is therefore regarded, when not divided, as two separate vehicles, namely the drawing vehicle (which is either a motor car or a heavy motor car (depending on the individual weight)), and the trailer. However, in terms of s 186(2), where a vehicle is so constructed that a trailer may by partial superimposition be attached to the vehicle in such a manner as to cause a substantial part of the trailer to be borne by the vehicle, that vehicle shall be deemed to be a vehicle itself constructed to carry a load. Further provision in the definition of articulated passenger vehicles is found in s 187 of the Act.

As indicated at 1.5 above, there are restrictions on the number of trailers that can be drawn by a vehicle and various conditions applicable to their use.

1.6.3 Heavy motor cars

A 'heavy motor car' for the purpose of the Road Traffic Act 1988 means 'a mechanically propelled vehicle, not being a motor car, which is constructed itself to carry a load or passengers and the weight of which unladen exceeds 2,540 kg';[3] a similar definition is provided for the Road Traffic Regulation Act 1984.[4] For the purposes of the Road Vehicles (Construction and Use) Regulations 1986, a heavy motor car is defined as 'a mechanically propelled vehicle, not being a locomotive, a motor tractor, or a motor car, which is constructed itself to carry a load or passengers and the weight of which unladen exceeds 2,540 kg'.[5] Heavy motor vehicles are accordingly the heaviest class of motor vehicle and neither the statute nor the regulations provide an upper limit on their unladen weight. However, other regulations restrict the laden and total weights of such vehicles.

---

1   RTA 1988, s 120.
2   Road Vehicles (Construction and Use) Regulations 1986 (SI 1986/1078), reg 3.
3   RTA, 1988, s 185(1).
4   RTA 1988, s 136(3).
5   Road Vehicles (Construction and Use) Regulations 1986, reg 3(2).

The drawing unit of most articulated vehicles is therefore a heavy motor car, except where it does not exceed 2,540 kilograms, when it is simply a motor car.

1.6.4 Commercial vehicles

A 'heavy commercial vehicle' means any goods vehicle which has an operating weight exceeding 7.5 tonnes.[1]

Goods vehicles generally are described at 1.4.1 above, and the term 'goods' is described at 1.4.2 above.

A 'large goods vehicle' is defined in s 50 and Sch 5 of the Goods Vehicles (Licensing of Operators) Act 1995 for specific purposes of controlled and authorised use within the terms of that Act

A 'medium-sized goods vehicle' means 'a motor vehicle which is constructed or adapted to carry or to haul goods and is not adapted to carry more than nine persons inclusive of the driver and the permissible maximum weight of which exceeds 3.5 but not 7.5 tonnes'.[2]

A 'small vehicle', by virtue of the same section, is 'a motor vehicle (other than a motor cycle or invalid carriage) which is constructed or adapted to carry more than nine persons inclusive of the driver and the permissible maximum weight of which does not exceed 3.5 tonnes'. As indicated at 1.5 above, the permissible maximum weight of 3.5 tonnes is to be calculated by including the weight of any trailer with an unladen weight exceeding 1,020 kilograms and its contents drawn by such a vehicle at the relevant time. This is of particular importance in the drivers' hours of work and tachograph legislation, which comes into effect when a vehicle qualifies as a small goods vehicle. Accordingly, a goods vehicle which is under 3.5 tonnes in weight, and which is not therefore subject to drivers' hours and tachograph requirements, may exceed the minimum weight limit when a trailer in excess of 1,020 kilograms is added; if this happens then the vehicle must be fitted with a tachograph, and the driver and owner of the vehicle are subject to the drivers' hours and record of work legislation. 'Motor vehicle' is defined at 1.2.1 above. The licensing of large goods vehicle drivers and the operators of goods vehicles is discussed in Pt 2 of Ch 9.

---

1   RTRA 1984, s 138(1), (2), wherein also are described the methods of arriving at the operating weight. A similar definition is given in s 20 of the RTA 1988 for the purposes of s 19 of that Act (prohibition of parking on verges, dangerous positions etc). See also 9.12.1 below.
2   RTA 1988, s 108, which also provides a number of definitions concerned with weight considerations relating to commercial vehicles.

1.6.5 Passenger and public service vehicles

A 'passenger vehicle' means a vehicle constructed or adapted for use solely or principally for the carriage of passengers.[1] A passenger vehicle is also defined for the purpose of the Construction and Use Regulations as 'a vehicle constructed solely for the carriage of passengers and their effects.'[2] Distinctions in the same Regulations, subject to numbers of seated passengers, are also drawn between 'bus', 'minibus' and 'large bus'. For the purposes of Pt III of the Road Traffic Act 1988, a 'small vehicle' is defined as set out above at 1.6.4.

A public service vehicle is defined in s 1 of the Public Passenger Vehicles Act 1981 for the purpose of that Act as 'a motor vehicle (other than a tramcar) which – (a) being a vehicle adapted to carry more than eight passengers, is used for carrying passengers for hire or reward; or (b) being a vehicle not so adapted, is used for carrying passengers for hire or reward at separate fares in the course of a business of carrying passengers'. There are further qualifications of this definition within s 1, and the topic is more fully discussed at 9.2.1 below.

The term 'motor vehicle' is discussed at 1.2.1 above.

1.6.6 Motor cycles

A 'motor cycle' is defined as a 'mechanically propelled vehicle, not being an invalid carriage, with less than four wheels and the weight of which unladen does not exceed 410 kg'.[3] The definition of a motor cycle for these purposes includes a variety of vehicles, including three-wheelers, motor bicycles and mopeds, each of which is governed for various purposes by further legislation. For the definition of 'mechanically propelled vehicle', see 1.2.1 above.

'Learner motor cycles' are defined by s 97(5) of the Road Traffic Act 1988 (as amended) and in effect mean either electric motor cycles, those with an engine capacity no greater than 125cc or those with an engine power output which does not exceed 11 kilowatts.

Section 23 of the Road Traffic Act 1988 imposes restrictions on the carriage of persons on motor cycles. The driver is guilty of any offence.

---

1   RTA 1988, s 187(4).
2   Road Vehicles (Construction and Use) Regulations 1986 (SI 1986/1078), reg 3(2).
3   RTA 1988, s 185(1); Road Vehicles (Construction and Use) Regulations 1986 (SI 1986/1078), reg 3(2).

Regulation 102 of the Road Vehicles (Construction and Use) Regulations 1986 requires that footrests are fitted for any passenger. Helmets, or protective headgear, to be used by motor-cyclists are described in ss 16–18 of the Road Traffic Act 1988.

1.6.7 Cycles

A 'cycle' is 'a bicycle, tricycle, or cycle having four or more wheels, not being in any case a motor vehicle'.[1]

The Secretary of State has power to make regulations in respect of brakes, bells, etc on pedal cycles.[2] Regulations made under the corresponding power in prior legislation are the Pedal Cycles (Construction and Use) Regulations 1983.[3]

Reference should also be made to the Electrically Assisted Pedal Cycles Regulations 1983.[4] Offences concerned with the riding of cycles are found in ss 24 and 26; s 28 (as amended by s 7 of the Road Traffic Act 1991); and ss 29–32 of the Road Traffic Act 1988; reference should be made to 2.18, 3.18 and 7.2.4 below.

A police officer has the power to stop any person riding a cycle on a road.[5]

1.6.8 Invalid carriages

An invalid carriage is 'a mechanically propelled vehicle the weight of which unladen does not exceed 254 kg and which is specially designed and constructed, and not merely adapted, for the use of a person suffering from some physical defect or disability and is solely used by such a person'.[6] Special provision for the use of such invalid carriages on the roads is provided by s 20 of the Chronically Sick and Disabled Persons Act 1970;[7] and s 21 of the same Act (as amended by s 35 of the Road Traffic Act 1991) makes provision for the issuing by local authorities of badges for display on motor vehicles used by disabled persons.[8] The Blue Badge scheme is

---

1   RTA 1988, s 192.
2   RTA 1988, s 81.
3   Pedal Cycles (Construction and Use) Regulations 1983 (SI 1983/1176).
4   Electrically Assisted Pedal Cycles Regulations 1983 (SI 1983/1168).
5   RTA 1988, s 163(2).
6   RTA 1988, s 185(1); Road Vehicles (Construction and Use) Regulations 1986 (SI 1986/1078), reg 3(2).
7   As amended by the RTA 1991, Sch 4 para 3.
8   See the Disabled Persons (Badges for Motor Vehicles) (Scotland) Regulations 2000 (SSI 2000/59), as amended by SSIs 2000/170, 2002/450, 2007/162 and 2011/89 and 2011/410.

UK wide but appeals from decisions by Scottish Local Authorities go to the Scottish Ministers. Wrongful use of a disabled person's badge is an offence.[1] Aiding and abetting such an offence is specifically prohibited by s 119. Special parking provisions for the disabled are discussed at 7.9.1 below.

For the phrase 'mechanically propelled vehicle', see 1.2.1 above.

1.6.9 Breakdown and recovery vehicles

These are two distinct categories of vehicle. A recovery vehicle is described in the Vehicles and Excise Registration Act 1994, Sch 1 para 5, and a breakdown vehicle in reg 3 of the Goods Vehicles (Plating and Testing) Regulations 1988.[2]

1.6.10 General

It should be noted in considering the foregoing paragraphs that certain vehicle term definitions are provided for particular purposes such as construction and use regulations, licensing and so on. Care should therefore be taken in considering the context of any definition provided in the legislation. As indicated above,[3] there are a large number of further statutory definitions of various kinds of vehicles and features relating thereto in the definition sections of the principal Acts and Regulations.

1.7 DRIVERS: DRIVING

1.7.1 General

The courts in Scotland have generally held that the driver of a motor vehicle is someone who is either in the driving seat or in control of the steering wheel, and in addition has something to do with (although not necessarily complete control over) the propulsion of the vehicle. In *Ames v McLeod*,[4] a motorist steered his car (which had run out of petrol) down an incline by walking beside it with his hand on the steering wheel, and in these circumstances he was held on appeal to be driving the vehicle at the material time. The Lord Justice-General (Clyde) indicated[5] that it was not

---

1   RTRA 1984, s 117.
2   SI 1988/1478.
3   At 1.1.
4   *Ames v McLeod* 1969 JC 1 (followed in *McArthur v Valentine* 1990 JC 146, 1990 SLT 732, 1989 SCCR 704).
5   At 3.

essential for the purposes of determining whether a person was driving that it is established that the engine was running or that the accused should be sitting in the driving seat. The true test was whether the accused is 'in a substantial sense controlling the movement and direction of the car'; or, in other words, whether the extent of the accused's intervention with the movement and direction of the vehicle was sufficient to establish that he was driving. It should be noted, however, that in almost identical circumstances an opposite conclusion was reached in England.[1] *Ames v McLeod*[2] was followed in *Lockhart v Smith*;[3] in that case a boy who on instruction from the milkman released the handbrake of a milk float so that it rolled downhill, but who did not touch the steering wheel, was held not to be driving.

Motorbikes are perhaps different. Simply pushing and steering one might not obviously be driving. Sitting or being astride one as well as steering it might well be.

Actual movement of the vehicle is not essential albeit it the circumstances in given cases may be unusual. In *Hoy v McFadyen*[4] the appellant was convicted of disqualified driving after sitting in the driver's seat with the engine running. The car was on a hill and since the handbrake was defective it had to be held in position using either the foot brake or the gears when the engine was off. There was slight movement of the car when he engaged the gears having been told to turn the engine off by police officers. Lord Sutherland indicated 'The correct test is to look at what the appellant was doing and not necessarily the result' as 'the question of movement of the car is not essential if the driver's activities have got beyond the stage of mere preparation but have got to the stage when there is active intervention on his part to prevent movement and direction'.[5] This approach has been followed in England.[6]

The person behind the steering wheel of a towed vehicle will in normal circumstances be regarded as driving the vehicle. In *Wallace v Major*[7] it

---

1   *R v MacDonagh (sub nom MacDonald)* [1974] QB 448, [1974] RTR 372, [1974] 2 All ER 257.
2   *Ames v McLeod* 1969 JC1.
3   *Lockhart v Smith* 1979 SLT (Sh Ct) 52.
4   *Hoy v McFadyen* 2000 SCCR 873, followed more recently in *Halliday v PF Paisley* XJ5/09 Decision of 15 May 2009.
5   At p 877E–G.
6   *DPP v Alderton* [2004] RTR 23 where the driver, with the handbrake on, was wheel spinning in his driveway to vent frustration following an argument with his wife.
7   *Wallace v Major* [1946] KB 473.

was observed that such a person might not fall within the definition of a driver because he had no control over the propulsion of the vehicle.[1] However, although this case has not been overturned, in *McQuaid v Anderton*[2] a disqualified driver was held to be driving when steering a towed vehicle. There appears to be no reason why anyone behind the steering wheel of a towed vehicle should not be regarded as driving for most of the purposes of the road traffic legislation.

Whether or not a person is in fact driving at the material time, or is to be regarded as 'the driver' of a vehicle for the purposes of a particular prosecution, will depend on the facts and circumstances of each case, in the context of the particular offence in question.

However, it has been decided that it is possible that, at any one time, more than one person can fall within the definition of being the driver of the vehicle at that time.[3] For example, a learner driver and an instructor may well be regarded as both driving at the same time if in practice both have some measure of control over both the steering and the propulsion of the vehicle.[4]

In *HMA v Cooper*[5] – a case where a couple shared the driver's seat, she sitting on his lap after he had asked if she 'wanted a go' – both were convicted of s 1 (the female accused tendered a plea and gave evidence). The jury appeared to accept the Crown's invitation that a broader view of 'driving' meant that the male accused 'was and continued to be the default driver, allowing some freedom to Ms J under his directions but always ready, he thought, to take over if need be and certainly with the intention that that is how the arrangement should work'. The evidence included apparent efforts by both to operate the brakes and steering before the fatal collision.

Further, where a person acts as a steersman of a motor vehicle, the Road Traffic Act 1988, s 192(1) provides that he is to be included in the term 'driver' as well as any other person engaged in the driving of the vehicle. This provision is specifically excluded from applying to prosecutions under s 1 of the Act. However where a driver has been effectively prevented or dissuaded from driving his vehicle, he can no

---

1   At 477 per LCJ Goddard.
2   *McQuaid v Anderton* [1980] RTR 371 (followed in *Caise v Wright* [1981] RTR 49).
3   *Tyler v Whatmore* [1976] RTR 83.
4   *Langman v Valentine* [1952] 2 All ER 803.
5   2016 SCCR 352.

longer be regarded as driving.[1] In *Farrell v Stirling*,[2] a case involving careless driving under summary procedure, a diabetic experienced for the first time an attack of hypoglycaemia shortly before an accident, and the court there concluded that he could not be described as driving his vehicle at the material time. In *McLeod v Mathieson*,[3] however, this defence was not available to a driver who knew he suffered from such a condition.

The question of whether a motorist was driving or not at any material time may be a relevant issue in many different situations other than those described above, such as where someone is called upon to produce documentation, or to comply with a direction given by a police officer.

Not infrequently the prosecution has to establish that an accused has been driving a vehicle in the absence of direct evidence by reference to the surrounding facts and circumstances.[4]

Further definition of the nature of driving in the context of the drink/driving legislation is found at 3.3.2 below.

1.7.2 Sleeping

Drivers losing control because of fatigue or falling asleep at the wheel has been the source of a number of prosecutions,[5] principally under the heading of dangerous driving in its various forms, though occasionally as careless driving, subject to the circumstances. Shortly put, sleep will not amount to involuntary driving (see below), save perhaps in exceptional circumstances. The approach to such offences is succinctly summed up in *Alexander v Dunn*:[6]

> '[3] The sole question is whether the sheriff was entitled to convict the appellant of dangerous driving by reason of her falling asleep. The test for what constitutes dangerous driving is an objective one (*Allan v Patterson*). It is whether the driving falls far below the standard to be expected of a competent and careful driver and occurs in the face of obvious and material dangers which were or ought to have been observed, appreciated and guarded against (LJG (Emslie) at p.60). It is no defence for a driver to assert that he did not intend to drive in a manner which was dangerous or that he did not intend to fall asleep at the wheel.

1   *Edkins v Knowles* [1973] QB 748 at 757, [1973] RTR 257.
2   *Farrell v Stirling* 1975 SLT (Sh Ct) 71.
3   *McLeod v Mathieson* 1993 SCCR 488.
4   See eg, *Henderson v Hamilton* 1995 SCCR 413.
5   See eg, *Burke v PF Tain* [2016] SAC (Crim) 31; 2016 SCCR 585.
6   2016 JC 125; 2016 SLT 337; 2016 SCCR 305.

[4] The act of driving, which is deemed to be dangerous, still requires to be voluntary. Involuntary actions cannot form the basis for a conviction. Once a driver is asleep, his actions cannot be said to be voluntary, as he lacks consciousness. However, the act of falling asleep, in the absence of special circumstances, is a voluntary act and, when it occurs in the context of driving, will usually be regarded as dangerous. That is because drivers who fall asleep:

> "are always aware that they are feeling sleepy, ... there is always a feeling of profound sleepiness and they reach a point where they are fighting sleep ..."

Although that is a passage of testimony quoted from *R v Wilson* ([2010] EWCA Crim 991; [2011] 1. Cr. App. R. (S) 3,), it coincides with human experience (see *Attorney General's Reference No. 1 of 2009* at p.745 [2009] 2 Cr. App. R. (S.) 742.; *Kay v Butterworth (1945) 61 TLR 452*). It does not require formal proof. A jury are entitled to infer, from the fact that a driver falls asleep, that, prior to falling asleep, he or she was aware of doing so and ignored the obvious dangers in so doing.

[5] There may be special circumstances which make falling asleep involuntary. These include the onset of a medical condition, such as sleep apnoea, narcolepsy or a hypoglycaemic episode (e.g. *Farrell v Stirling 1975 SLT (Sh Ct)71; Macleod v Mathieson 1993 SCCR 488*). However, a driver who knows of his medical condition, and can foresee that he may fall asleep, will be precluded from relying on that condition. It is for an accused to put any special circumstances in issue, and thereafter for the Crown to establish beyond reasonable doubt that the act of driving was nevertheless voluntary because the special circumstance ought to have been foreseen (*Hill v Baxter*).'

1.7.3 Involuntary driving

As noted in the commentary to the SCCR report of *Alexander v Dunn*, supra, the Crown positively libelled that the act of falling asleep was dangerous. An alternative approach would have been simply to libel the driving as dangerous and leave it for the accused to plead that the driving was involuntary, which would be a complete defence to the charge.

Involuntary driving received considerable attention in the cases of *(1) John & Linda Stewart (2) Allan & Aileen Convey v William Payne; (1) Matthew & Jacqueline McQuade and (2) Yvonne Reilly v Henry Clarke*,[1] unsuccessful attempts to raise bills of criminal letters seeking private prosecutions following the Crown's decision not to prosecute either driver. Both had suffered blackouts at the wheel, but the view was taken that there was not

---

1   [2016] HCJAC 122; 2017 JC 155; 2017 SLT 159; 2017 SCCR 56.

sufficient evidence that it was foreseeable that either driver would lose consciousness.

The bills sought to prosecute both men for contraventions of ss 1, 1A and 2 of the Road Traffic Act 1988, or alternatively culpable and reckless driving. However, the Appeal Court, on the particular facts and circumstances of both cases, concluded that the Crown had not erred as a matter of law in either marking decision.

As with *Anderson*, supra, the position was succinctly set out in the decision of the Court:

'**The legal requirements of a charge of dangerous driving**

[82] A person drives dangerously if: (a) the standard of his driving falls far below that which would be expected of a competent and careful driver; and (b) it would be obvious to a competent and careful driver that to drive in such a way would be dangerous. The test for dangerous driving is an objective one, directing attention to the quality of the driving at the time in question. Although the test is an objective one, in determining whether the driving was dangerous regard must be had to circumstances shown to have been within the knowledge of the individual driver (s.2A(3) of the 1988 Act).

[83] A person who falls unconscious at the wheel is, on the face of it, no longer driving voluntarily. However, if the driver is aware that he has a medical condition liable to render him unconscious whilst driving, he may be precluded from relying on that condition as a basis for maintaining that his acts were involuntary. The driver would, however, need to know that he had such a condition. A driver who has been diagnosed with a condition rendering him liable to fall unconscious clearly has that knowledge. Thus a diabetic who knew his condition pre-disposed him to hypoglycaemic episodes rendering him unconscious without warning knew that to drive was to do so in the face of obvious and material danger. The driver in question had suffered such incidents on an increasing basis prior to the accident, including incidents whilst at the wheel (*R v Marison* [1997] RTR 457) – he thus knew that at the material time he was driving in a defective state. The Lord Advocate accepted, correctly, that the knowledge that one is in a defective state rendering it dangerous to drive, need not come from the diagnosis of a condition. Past experience and medical history of the driver might be sufficient to create in him the knowledge that to drive at any given time might be dangerous. Clearly the evidential obstacles in the way of establishing the latter may be greater than in relation to the former, but there is no reason why a driver's general medical history and experience might not be sufficient to create the necessary knowledge in the absence of a diagnosis.

[84] In *Marison* the driving was said to begin at the start of the driver's journey on the day in question and to conclude with the collision. The

critical question in any case such as this is the quality of the driving at the time of the collision. The Crown was thus correct to focus on the day in question in each case. In doing so it was not taking an over-narrow approach to the issue. In particular the Crown did not focus only on the state of health of each respondent on the day in question, or at the start of their journeys. It is clear that the Crown correctly considered that the state of knowledge of each respondent on the day in question had to be assessed in the context of all the information known to each of them, including their medical history and any inferences which might reasonably be drawn therefrom. Accordingly, we do not consider that the Crown made an error of law.'

While both cases, on their particular facts, did not merit prosecution, it may be anticipated that this area of law is likely to become more significant in light of the increasing number of unfit and elderly drivers on the roads. The cases also emphasise the need for a more proactive approach by drivers, medical professionals and the DVLA to the issue of medical fitness (see 8.1.4 and 8.1.5 below).

1.7.4 Attempting to drive

The question of whether a motorist is attempting to drive his vehicle is a question of fact. The phrase has its principal significance in offences under ss 4(1), 5(1) and 6 of the Road Traffic Act 1988, and is more fully described at 3.3.3 below.

1.8 ROAD

1.8.1 General

In the Road Traffic Act 1988 as originally framed, and in earlier legislation, the majority of road traffic offences occurred if the driving or other conduct complained of took place 'on a road'. The principal exceptions to this rule were the drink driving offence sections[1] where the offence occurred if it took place 'on a road or other public place'. Accordingly, two lines of authority developed, namely what was meant by 'a road', and what was to be understood by the phrase 'other public place'. The cases involving the latter normally involved drinking and driving charges; and there were, and are, features common to both definitions.

By virtue of the terms of ss 1, 2 and 3 of the Road Traffic Act 1991, the qualification of the offence taking place 'on a road or other public place'

---

1   RTA 1988, ss 4, 5 and 6.

is extended to cover ss 1, 2, 3 and 3A of the 1988 Act. Accordingly, most offences under ss 1–6 inclusive of the Road Traffic Act 1988 as amended occur if the driving or other conduct complained of takes place 'on a road or other public place'. Sections 3ZA, 3ZB and 3 ZC are 'on a road' only. In the majority of the other sections of the legislation offences are established if the actions of the motorist take place simply 'on a road'.

The legislation therefore seeks to extend the ambit of the most serious driving offences beyond the public roadway, to other places to which the public resort, for example forestry roads. Provision for special events and certain exemptions from prosecution are found in the Road Traffic Act 1988, s 13, and s 13A.[1] The Roads (Scotland) Act 1984 makes a number of provisions in respect of the use of roads and highways, a detailed discussion of which is outwith the scope of this book. However, in general terms the Act gives extensive powers to the roads authority (normally the local council or, in the case of special or trunk roads, the appropriate minister) to control works and excavations, and traffic[2] and to prevent obstruction and interference.[3] Reference should also be made to the New Road and Street Works Act 1991 (c 22). The Road Traffic Act 1988, s 33 controls the use of footpaths and bridleways for motor vehicle trials; and s 34 prohibits the driving of motor vehicles elsewhere than on roads although s 34(3) allows driving within 15 yards of a road for the purpose of parking.

1.8.2 Roads

The statutory definitions of a 'road' are found in the Roads (Scotland) Act 1984, s 151(1),[4] as that definition is amended by the Road Traffic Act 1991, Sch 4 para 78. The definition as contained in the 1984 Act is:

> 'any way (other than a waterway) over which there is a right of passage (by whatever means and whether subject to a toll or not) and includes the road's verge, and any bridge (whether permanent or temporary) over which, or tunnel through which, the road passes; and any reference to a road includes a part thereof.'

To this must be added the further description of the term found in s 192(1) of the Road Traffic Act 1988, as amended by the Road Traffic Act 1991, Sch 4 para 78, which provides: 'and (b) in relation to Scotland, means any road within the meaning of the Roads (Scotland) Act 1984 and any other

1   As introduced by the RTA 1991, s 5.
2   Roads (Scotland) Act 1984, Pt V.
3   R(S)A 1984, Pt VIII.
4   Which is incorporated into the RTA 1988 by s 192(2) of that Act.

way to which the public has access, and includes bridges over which a road passes.'

These additional provisions are not intended to affect the exceptions contained in s 151(3) of the Roads (Scotland) Act 1984, which relate to certain public paths, footpaths and recreational ground.

For convenience the entire collated statutory definition of 'a road' is as follows:

> 'a "road" means ... (a) any way (other than a waterway) over which there is a public right of passage (by whatever means and whether subject to a toll or not) and includes the road's verge, and any bridge (whether permanent or temporary) over which, or tunnel through which, the road passes; and any reference to a road includes a part thereof; ... (and) ... (b) .. means any other way to which the public has access, and includes bridges over which a road passes.'

The definition of a 'road' has therefore gone through three historical stages. Prior to the Roads (Scotland) Act 1984, a number of cases described a road as essentially a highway or other road to which the public had access, or had obtained access thereto without having to overcome a physical obstruction or in defiance of an express or implied prohibition.[1] This reflected the terms of s 121(1) of the Road Traffic Act 1930, which was common to both Scotland and England, and which provided a definition in effect as 'any highway and any other road to which the public has access'. The principal feature of the definition introduced by the Roads (Scotland) Act 1984 was that there should exist a public right of passage over the way in question. The effect of this was to diminish the significance of public access other than by right in any particular case. In *Young v Carmichael*[2] a driver was found on the lawn attached to a private apartment block, onto which he had driven from one of two car parks adjacent to the building. Access to the building was gained from a public road which passed through a gap in the fence surrounding the apartment block and its amenity grounds. The car parks were used by residents, their guests, tradesmen and police. There were signs at the entrance indicating that the car parks were private and for the use of residents only. In the Appeal Court it was held (a) that as the public had no right of access to the car park it was not a road, and (b) that as there was no evidence that members of the public had access to the car parks in the sense that they normally resorted to it and so might be expected to be there, the car park was not 'a public place'. The report also considers the history

---

1   Eg *Harrison v Hill* 1932 JC 13; *Purves v Muir* 1948 JC 122, 1948 SLT 529; *Hogg v Nicholson* 1968 SLT 265.
2   *Young v Carmichael* 1993 SLT 167, 1991 SCCR 332.

of the definition of the terms 'road' and 'other public place' to that date. *Young v Carmichael*[1] therefore concluded that cases decided under earlier legislation which in general terms defined a road as a 'highway or any other road to which the public has access' were of limited value.

However, the additional definition provided by the Road Traffic Act 1991, Sch 4 para 78, passed after the decision in *Young v Carmichael*, seeks to re-introduce the idea of public access into the definition of the term 'road'. Accordingly the case of *Young v Carmichael* is not the final word on this subject and cases decided before the 1984 Act remain of interest. See, for example, *Yates v Murray*[2] which as well as considering more recent cases ultimately applied the test enunciated in *Harrison v Hill*. It is also worth noting that the suggestion that all roads should be seen as public unless there was evidence to the contrary was rejected. The onus remains on the Crown to establish the nature of the road in question. [3]

The importance of public access was emphasised in the unsuccessful Crown appeal in *Teale v Macleod*.[4] There, an existing but damaged road under repair, which was coned off and with signs directing the public to a temporary parallel road, was confirmed not to be a road in terms of the legislation.

A footway associated with a carriageway, or a footpath not so associated, are included in the definition of a road.[5] A lay-by or verge is also part of the road,[6] as is a parking area next to a place of public resort such as an inn, on the basis that it is a way over which there is a public right of passage.[7] The car deck of a ferry was held to be a road when connected to a ramp on the dock in *Dick v Walkingshaw*.[8] The court is entitled to understand that the M9 is a motorway and therefore a road.[9]

In *Adair v Davidson*[10] the drive to a private house was held to be a road, but this was doubted by Lord Guthrie in *Hogg v Nicholson*[11] at 268; see also *Carmichael v Wilson*.[12]

---

1   *Young v Carmichael* 1993 SLT 167, 1991 SCCR 332.
2   *Yates v Murray* 2003 SCCR 727.
3   At para 21.
4   2008 SCCR 12.
5   Roads (Scotland) Act 1984, s 151(2).
6   Roads (Scotland) Act 1984, s 151(1); *MacNeill v Dunbar* 1965 SLT (Notes) 79.
7   *Beattie v Scott* 1991 SLT 873, 1990 SCCR 435.
8   *Dick v Walkingshaw* 1995 SLT 1254, 1995 SCCR 307.
9   *Donaldson v Valentine* 1996 SLT 643, 1996 SCCR 374.
10   *Adair v Davidson* 1934 JC 37, 1934 SLT 316.
11   *Hogg v Nicholson* 1968 SLT 265.
12   *Carmichael v Wilson* 1993 SLT 1066.

1.8.3 Other public places

The phrase 'other public place' means a place to which the public may resort by express or implied permission. The principles which apply are in some respects similar to the question of whether a road is public or not. For example, an isolated farmyard where there were few visitors or passers-by and where in general there would be little if any expectation that the public might be present is not a public place,[1] whereas a private road commonly walked by fishermen and hill walkers is a public place.[2] A field used as a car park at the Highland Show was held to be a public place,[3] as was a spare piece of ground used as an overflow parking area at a cattle mart.[4] The prosecution may have to prove the right to resort to a particular area.[5] In certain circumstances a dock road may be a public place.[6] A driveway from a public road to a hotel, even where the proprietors of the hotel reserved the right to exclude certain members of the public, may still be a public place;[7] similarly, a private camping and caravan site occupied by persons who had gained access through the permission of the site owners was held to be a public place even although other members of the public were effectively excluded from the site.[8] A car park attached to a public house may also be a public place as well as a road.[9] On the other hand, a private car park attached to an apartment block signposted as private was held not to be a public place[10] although in different circumstances a Sheriff's assessment that such a car park was public was upheld.[11]

A garage forecourt is a public place; in *Brown v Braid*[12] it was observed that the test was 'whether the forecourt was a place on which members of the public might be expected to be found and over which they might be expected to be passing, or over which they are in use to have access.'

1   *Alston v O'Brien* 1992 SLT 856, 1992 SCCR 238.
2   *Thomson v MacPhail* 1992 SCCR 466.
3   *Paterson v Ogilvy* 1957 JC 42, 1957 SLT 354.
4   *McDonald v McEwen* 1953 SLT (Sh Ct) 26.
5   *Elkins v Cartlidge* [1974] 1 All ER 829; *Pugh v Knipe* [1972] RTR 286.
6   *Renwick v Scott* 1996 SLT 1164.
7   *Dunn v Keane* 1972 JC 39.
8   *DPP v Vivier* [1991] RTR 205.
9   *Vannet v Burns* 1999 SLT 340, 1998 SCCR 414.
10 *Young v Carmichael* 1993 SLT 167, 1991 SCCR 332; see 1.8.2 above.
11 *McPhee v Maguire* 2001 SCCR 715.
12 *Brown v Braid* 1985 SLT 37, 1984 SCCR 286, 1984 CO Circulars A/22.

Reference should also be made on the question of whether the public has access to a particular place.[1]

1.8.4 Motorways

Driving on motorways is governed by the Motorways Traffic (Scotland) Regulations 1995.[2] The court is entitled to assume from its own knowledge that the M90 is a motorway.[3]

1.9 ACCIDENT

Whether or not an accident has occurred will depend on the facts and circumstances of each case. A satisfactory definition of the word is not easy to provide, having regard to the variety of circumstances under which what might be described as an 'accident' can occur. No definition of the term appears anywhere in the legislation, and the courts have not been anxious to provide a general or all-purpose definition of the word, preferring normally to draw conclusions from the circumstances of each case. It has been suggested that an appropriate test might be to consider whether an ordinary man who witnessed what happened would say that in all the circumstances there had been an accident. It is, however, clear that an accident can arise out of a deliberate act, and need not involve another vehicle. It is also clear that an impact does not have to take place before it can be said there has been an accident.[4]

The matter was considered by the Appeal Court in *Pryde v Brown*,[5] where two pedestrians walking on a main road were obliged to take evasive action when a vehicle came round a bend at speed on the wrong side of the road. In holding that this had been an 'accident', the Appeal Court said:

> 'We do not think that any precise definition of the word "accident" ... can be formulated. We do not think that any of the tests adumbrated in the cases referred to are wholly satisfactory in every circumstance. We do not think that only unintended occurrences can be included in the word "accident", as the word may obviously include occurrences which may have been intended. We do not think it can be limited to untoward

---

1   *Rodger v Normand* 1995 SLT 411, 1994 SCCR 861; *Aird v Vannet* 1999 JC 205, 2000 SLT 435, 1999 SCCR 327; *Vannet v Burns* 1999 SLT 340, 1998 SCCR 414.
2   Motorways Traffic (Scotland) Regulations 1995 (SI 1995/2507).
3   *Donaldson v Valentine* 1996 SLT 643, 1996 SCCR 374.
4   *Bremner v Westwater* 1994 SLT 707, 1993 SCCR 1023.
5   *Pryde v Brown* 1982 SLT 314, 1982 SCCR 26.

occurrences having an adverse physical result, because it is possible to visualise an "accident" having no adverse physical result at all. It seems to us to be more appropriate to proceed on the basis that it will depend on the circumstances of each case whether a happening can properly be described as an "accident" The test is one of common sense rather than conformity with a definition difficult to formulate and providing an exhaustive cover.'

The circumstances in which an accident can be said to have occurred are therefore wide and general. Incidents where a vehicle has been required to take avoiding action as a result of the conduct of another vehicle, where an obstruction or object, as opposed to another vehicle or person, has been struck, or where something has happened as a result of the way a vehicle is being driven completely outwith the awareness of the driver, may all be termed as accidents. Section 170 of the Road Traffic Act 1988[1] envisages that an accident has occurred if injury is caused to any other party or damage is caused to any other vehicle, to specified animals or to any property constructed on, fixed to, growing in or otherwise forming part of the land on which the road is situated or land adjacent thereto. The *de minimis* rule would seem to have very little relevance, if any, in the interpretation of the word.

The question of whether or not an accident has taken place may be of particular importance inter alia in prosecutions under the breathalyser legislation;[2] in charges of failing to stop after an accident;[3] and in respect of prosecution restrictions in terms of s 2(1) of the Road Traffic Offenders Act 1988. The duty on a driver to stop after an accident is discussed at 7.6.3 below.

1.10 USING, CAUSING AND PERMITTING

1.10.1 General

Throughout the legislation there are a number of offences which are committed when an accused person uses a vehicle, or causes or permits a vehicle to be used, in a particular way. The terms 'use' or 'using', 'causing' and 'permitting' have always to be considered in the context in which they are employed; however, certain general observations may be made on these terms.

---

1   As amended by the RTA 1991, Sch 4 para 72.
2   RTA 1988, s 6(2).
3   RTA 1988, s 170.

1.10.2 Using

The most common offences involving use are those which contravene s 143 of the Road Traffic Act 1988 (compulsory insurance), s 87 of the same Act (licensing of drivers) or the use of vehicles in a manner contrary to many of the Road Vehicle (Construction and Use) Regulations 1986.[1] An offence involving 'use' as opposed to 'causing' or 'permitting' normally involves strict liability and the question of *mens rea* is irrelevant. The word has been interpreted in a wide sense and, for example, convictions for using a car without insurance are commonplace where the only use made of the vehicle is to park it on the street. Even if a vehicle is broken down and unable to move by its own power, it will be regarded as being used on the road for the purpose of s 143. 'Driving' involves the use of a vehicle.

A vehicle being towed will also be regarded as being used for all relevant purposes of the legislation.[2] A corporate entity may be guilty of an offence involving use of a vehicle, and because most of such offences carry absolute liability, the employer of a driver who drives or uses a vehicle which contravenes the construction and use regulations may well be guilty of an offence even although the employer had no direct or personal knowledge of the defect which caused the offence.[3] The word 'use' can also mean 'have the use of' and two people may therefore be using a vehicle at the same time.[4]

However, the nature of 'use' has been qualified in certain circumstances. In *Hamilton v Blair and Meechan*[5] it was held that an owner of a vehicle who had hired it out for an excursion to a third party (who was to supply the driver) was not 'using' the vehicle at the material time, nor was the hirer 'using' the vehicle at a time when she was not within the vehicle. In the latter instance, Lord Carmont[6] indicated that the hirer, although not using the vehicle, may have been causing or permitting its use. In *Valentine v MacBrayne Haulage Ltd*[7] (a Sheriff Court case) it was held that where a statute penalised both using and causing as well as permitting use of a vehicle, the category of 'user' should be confined to the driver of the vehicle and his employer at the material time, and should not be extended further. The report usefully considers the principal authorities

1   Road Vehicle (Construction and Use) Regulations 1986 (SI 1986/1078).
2   *Cobb v Whorton* [1971] RTR 392.
3   *Swan v MacNab* 1977 JC 57, 1978 SLT 192, 1978 CO Circulars A/13.
4   *Dickson v Valentine* 1989 SLT 19, 1988 SCCR 325.
5   *Hamilton v Blair and Meechan* 1962 JC 31, 1962 SLT 69.
6   At 76.
7   *Valentine v MacBrayne Haulage Ltd* 1986 SCCR 692.

on the term 'using'. If the vehicle in question is the subject of a hire agreement, then the person who is 'using' the vehicle at the material time is the hirer and not the hire firm.[1]

Whether a vehicle is being 'used' or not may depend upon the particular offence in question. Thus in *Tudhope v Every*[2] it was held that a vehicle which was immobile and parked on a road was being used in terms of s 143 of the Road Traffic Act 1972 (which required vehicles used on a road to be covered by insurance), but was not being used on a road in terms of s 44(1) of the same Act (which requires vehicles used on a road to be covered by an MOT certificate).

The reason for this differing treatment of the same word is that the meaning of the term 'use' contemplated in the two sections of the Act, and the nature of the prohibition involved in each case, is different. A parked car, even when immobile, may cause or be involved in an accident; therefore it must be insured. However, the MOT certificate is designed to cover other areas of use which an immobile vehicle could not perform, and accordingly such a vehicle is not being used for that purpose.

Nothing in the Road Traffic Acts authorises a person to use on a road a vehicle so constructed or used as to cause a nuisance, or affects the liability, under statute or common law of the driver or owner.[3]

1.10.3 Causing or permitting

'Causing' and 'permitting' are two separate ideas. In practice their meanings may overlap. Corporate entities may be guilty of causing or permitting. The principal application of the terms is again in the Road Traffic Act 1988, s 87 (licensing of drivers) and s 143 (compulsory insurance) and in the Construction and Use Regulations.

The two words are used, normally together, in slightly different ways and contexts throughout the legislation, and consideration has to be given to the particular nature of the offence in each case. For general purposes, the term 'causing' involves some measure of direction or control by the accused towards or over a third party in a matter where the accused has the proper capacity to make such a direction or exercise such control. In other words, actual or constructive knowledge of the offence must be established, as well as some measure of participation in allowing the offence to take place, or failing to take reasonable steps to stop it

---

1   *Mackay Brothers & Co v Gibb* 1969 JC 26, 1969 SLT 216; *Farrell v Moggach* 1976 SLT (Sh Ct) 8.
2   *Tudhope v Every* 1976 JC 42, 1977 SLT 2.
3   Road Traffic (Consequential Provisions) Act 1988, s 7.

happening. The most common example of 'causing' in practice is where an employer instructs an employee to drive the employer's vehicle.

For an accused to be convicted of 'causing' a third party to commit an offence, the prosecution will normally have to establish both that the accused directed or controlled the substantive acts complained of, and that he was aware or should have been aware that those acts constituted an offence. In other words, actual or constructive knowledge of the offence must be established, as well as some measure of participation in allowing the offence to take place; a failing to take reasonable steps to stop it happening. This is notwithstanding that most of the offences in which the terms are used involved strict liability.

In *Smith of Maddiston Ltd v Macnab*,[1] a limited company was charged with using, or causing or permitting to be used, a vehicle with an insecure load. The company had hired out to a third party a vehicle and a driver to transport a load. The driver, who was experienced in such matters, elected to secure the load in an ineffective manner although he had been supplied with suitable securing material. The Appeal Court (overruling *Hunter v Clark*)[2] held that the company could not be guilty of the offence as it neither knew nor should have known of the contravention of the relevant regulations, and could not therefore be said to have caused or permitted the use complained of.

In *Macdonald v Wilmae Concrete Co Ltd*,[3] it was held that a company was not guilty of causing or permitting a vehicle to be used with a defective brake in circumstances where it was not proved that any responsible official of the company knew of the defect. In particular, it was held to be insufficient for a conviction simply to show that the company took no action or even that this system of inspection was not perfect. However, in *Brown v Burns Tractors Ltd*,[4] it was held (following *Smith of Maddiston Ltd v Macnab*)[5] that knowledge, in relation to a statutory provision, includes 'the state of mind of a man who shuts his eyes to the obvious and allows another to do something in circumstances where a contravention is likely, not caring whether a contravention takes place or not' In other words, wilful blindness, or culpable ignorance, in respect of the relevant statutory provisions on the part of an accused in a charge of causing or permitting is not a defence. In this context,

1   *Smith of Maddiston Ltd v Macnab* 1975 JC 48, 1975 SLT 86, 1975.
2   *Hunter v Clark* 1956 JC 59.
3   *Macdonald v Wilmae Concrete Co Ltd* 1954 SLT (Sh Ct) 33.
4   *Brown v Burns Tractors Ltd* 1986 SCCR 146.
5   *Smith of Maddiston Ltd v Macnab* 1975 JC 48, 1975 SLT 86.

reference may also be made to *Clydebank Co-operative Society v Binnie;*[1] *Mackay Bros v Gibb;*[2] and *Farrell v Moggach.*[3]

'Permitting' means simply giving permission, or allowing a third party to do something. The permission must, however, be proved to be something which the accused can properly give. In addition, for conviction it must be shown, as in the case of 'causing', that the accused was aware that what was permitted constituted an offence; actual or constructive knowledge of the offence has to be demonstrated, as well as direct or indirect evidence of permission. The same general considerations that apply to 'causing' described above apply also to 'permitting'.

In *MacDonald v Howdle*[4] a driver who offered his car to another on condition that he got it insured was held not to have permitted its use, when the other driver drove without getting insurance. A discussion of what may be meant by the term 'permitting' is found in *Elsby v McFadyen.*[5]

It is competent and common practice for accused persons or corporate entities to be charged with 'using' and 'causing or permitting' as alternatives.

1.11 IDENTIFICATION OF DRIVER

1.11.1 General

Except in some limited cases where there is specific statutory exemption, corroborative evidence of the identity of the driver of a vehicle is still required for the purposes of prosecution of road traffic offences, albeit there has been practical and arguably sensible erosion of the requirement, for example reliance on registered keeper status, and obviously it is under threat of abolition at the time of writing.[6]

Accordingly, if the only evidence of identification is that of two police officers who speak to an admission by the driver that he was driving at the material time, this is insufficient for conviction.[7] Reference in this respect should be made to 7.5.8 below.

---

1   *Clydebank Co-operative Society v Binnie* 1937 JC 17, 1937 SLT 114.
2   *Mackay Bros v Gibb* 1969 JC 26, 1969 SLT 216.
3   *Farrell v Moggach* 1976 SLT (Sh Ct) 8.
4   *MacDonald v Howdle* 1995 SLT 779, 1995 SCCR 216.
5   *Elsby v McFadyen* 2000 SCCR 97.
6   *Mitchell v MacDonald* 1959 SLT (Notes) 74; *Sinclair v MacLeod* 1964 SLT (Notes) 60.
7   *Sinclair v McLeod* 1964 SLT (Notes) 60.

A car driver will not be considered in normal circumstances to be a person in a special capacity in terms of s 255 of the Criminal Procedure (Scotland) Act 1995;[1] however, an accused charged with driving while disqualified will be regarded as being in such a special capacity and so in those circumstances the need for corroborative evidence does not arise.[2] Production of an extract conviction does not amount to waiver by the Crown of the right to rely on this section.[3]

An admission by a driver, made to a police officer or any other person, that he was driving at the time of the alleged offence can be sufficient evidence of identification if the surrounding facts and circumstances confirm that identification.[4]

That can include corroboration by the fact that the accused was the registered keeper,[5] an approach extended in *Coltman v PF Dunoon*,[6] where the relevant VQ5 document showed that the registered keeper was the accused's wife. The court observed: 'corroboration can also be found in the fact that the registered keeper of the car was the appellant's wife, a close family member.' It is worth noting that that information came to hand firstly by inadmissible (Crown concession) hearsay evidence taken from the Police National Computer plus the document itself, produced by the defence during the Crown case. Proximity to the vehicle also provided a sufficiency.

1   *Cruickshanks v MacPhail* 1988 SCCR 165.
2   *Smith v Allan* 1985 SLT 565, 1985 SCCR 190.
3   *Paton v Lees* 1992 SCCR 212; see also *Campbell v HM Advocate* 1999 JC 147, 1999 SLT 399.
4   *Frew v Jessop* 1990 JC 15, 1990 SLT 396, 1989 SCCR 530; *Hingston v Pollock* 1990 JC 138, 1990 SLT 770, 1989 SCCR 697; Fisher v Guild 1991 SLT 253, 1991 SCCR 308; *McClory v McInnes* 1992 SLT 501, 1992 SCCR 319; *Souter v Lees* 1995 SCCR 33); *Henderson v Hamilton* 1995 SCCR 413; *Templeton v Crowe* 1999 JC 47, 1999 SCCR 7).
5   *Elpinstone v Richardson* 2013 JC 29 2012 SCCR 428, which did not follow *Winter v Heywood* 1995 JC 60, 1995 SLT 586, 1995 SCCR 276 (which was authority for the proposition that one source of identification together with the fact that the accused is the registered driver is not enough; although the court's subsequent reliance on a false statement to provide circumstantial sufficiency must be doubted given the court's obiter remarks in *Brown v HMA* 2002 SCCR 1032, paragraph 8); *Henderson v Hamilton* 1995 SCCR 413; *Templeton v Crowe* 1999 JC 47, 1999 SCCR 7).
6   [2018] SAC (Crim) 6.

Likewise, being the registered keeper, allied with surrounding facts and circumstances, may provide sufficient inference that a person is the driver at the material time.[1]

A statement made in reply to a caution, or a caution and charge, if properly administered by a police officer, is competent evidence as to both the identity of the driver and any other relevant matters included in the statement.

1.11.2 Statement made in response to a question

At common law, an admission by an accused that he was the driver at the time of an alleged offence in response to a question from a police officer may be admissible in evidence.[2] The test as to whether such an answer is admissible or not is to be determined having regard, in all the circumstances, to the principle of fairness to the accused. In considering that test, regard must be given to the accused's circumstances and position, and also to the public interest in ascertaining the true facts of each case, and the detection of offences. If, having regard to all these matters, it is decided that the request for information imposes unfairness on the accused, the evidence will generally be inadmissible; equally, if no unfairness is caused to the accused, the evidence will be allowed.[3]

Following the decision in *Cadder v HMA*[4] in relation to the issue of access to legal advice, considerable time and energy has been spent on this area of law. It is perhaps striking that, ultimately, the preceding paragraph, written pre *Cadder*, remains untouched. In relation to roadside cases the most relevant decision is *Ambrose v Harris*.[5] It is, of course, fact specific but emphasises that if not in custody or subject to some element of intimidation, answers to questions are likely to be admissible particularly if a caution has been appropriately given.

1.11.3 Duty to give information to police

In terms of s 172(2) of the Road Traffic Act 1988, as amended by s 21 of the Road Traffic Act 1991, where a driver of a vehicle is alleged to be guilty of any road traffic offence (apart from certain exceptions listed within the section), the keeper of the vehicle or any other person may be required by

---

1   *McCormick v Harrower* 2011 SCCR 710.
2   *Miln v Cullen* 1967 JC 21, 1967 SLT 35.
3   *McClory v McInnes* 1992 SLT 501, 1992 SCCR 319.
4   [2010] UKSC 43, 2010 SCCR 951, 2010 SLT 1125.
5   2012 SCCR 465 post the decision reported at [2011] UKSC 43, 2011 SCCR 651, 2011 SLT 1005.

a police officer to give information as to the identity of the driver at the material time. The phrase 'any other person' includes the alleged driver himself.[1] An admission by the driver under this sub-section is presently admissible in evidence[2] and, as in the case of other forms of admission, can satisfy the test of corroborative evidence if there is supporting evidence from another credible source.[3] The requirement to give this information is not a breach of the European Convention on Human Rights;[4] nor is the use of the admission as evidence in court.[5] The admission can also be used as evidence of identification to a linked non-road traffic charge.[6] Section 172 is discussed in more detail at 7.5.7, 7.5.8 and 7.5.9 below. This and other duties to provide information are described at 2.6 and ch 7 below.

1.11.4 Exceptions

The evidence of a single witness will suffice to establish certain statutory offences.[7] Details of the fixed penalty procedure for traffic light and speeding offences which in the first instance does away with the common law evidential requirements of identification are found at 7.8.3 below.

1   *Foster v Farrell* 1963 JC 46, 1963 SLT 182, overruling *Stewart v McLugash* (1962) 78 Sh Ct Rep 189.
2   *Foster v Farrell* 1963 JC 46, 1963 SLT 182.
3   *Galt v Goodsir* 1982 JC 4, 1982 SLT 94, 1981 SCCR 225.
4   *Jardine v Crowe* 1999 SCCR 52.
5   *Brown v Stott* 2001 SCCR 62.
6   *How v Harvie* 2016 SCCR 435.
7   RTOA 1988, s 21, as amended by the RTA 1991, Sch 4 para 89; ch 7 below, *passim*.

Chapter 2

Dangerous and careless driving

PART 1
DANGEROUS DRIVING

2.1 DANGEROUS DRIVING

Section 1 of the Road Traffic Act 1988,[1] as amended by s 1 of the Road Traffic Act 1991,[2] provides that it is an offence to cause the death of another person by driving a mechanically propelled vehicle dangerously on a road or other public place. Section 2 of the Act (as similarly amended) makes it an offence to drive dangerously and the recently introduced s 1A[3] provides specifically for cases of dangerous driving which causes serious injury to another person, with associated higher penalty provisions.

---

1   c 52.
2   c 40.
3   Introduced by s 143 of the Legal Aid, Sentencing and Punishment of Offenders Act 2012 (c 10), for offences occurring after 3 December 2012.

Section 1 therefore creates a specific and separate offence if death results from such driving. The term 'dangerously' has exactly the same meaning in both ss 1, 1A, and 2. Charges under s 1, however, must be taken on indictment; ss 1A and 2 cases may be taken on summary complaint. Servants of the Crown are not exempted from prosecution under either section, or in respect of other driving offences.[1]

In all statutory dangerous driving cases, it should be noted that an extended sentence is not a competent disposal, given such a conviction cannot be properly categorised as a 'violent offence' in terms of s 210A of the Criminal Procedure (Scotland) Act 1995.[2]

The statutory offence of causing death by dangerous or reckless driving was introduced by the Road Traffic Act 1960.[3] Prior to 1960, the only method open for the prosecution of proceedings against a motorist where death resulted from the driving of a vehicle was to charge him with culpable homicide. However, in many such cases, juries were disinclined to return such a verdict, and a statutory alternative was therefore introduced. The offence of causing death by dangerous or reckless driving again appeared in the Road Traffic Act 1972,[4] s 1; the word 'dangerous' was deleted from the statutory definitions of ss 1 and 2 of the 1972 Act by the Criminal Law Act 1977, s 50(1). Cases prior to this amendment which relied on evidence of 'dangerous driving' are now of limited value in considering current charges. However, by virtue of the Road Traffic Act 1991, s 1, Parliament reverted to describing the offending course of driving as 'dangerous', and abandoned the term 'reckless.' The significance of, and reasons for, this change are given at 2.3.2 below.

2.2 CULPABLE HOMICIDE AND SECTION 1

2.2.1 Procedure and penalties

It is, however, still open to the Crown to bring charges of culpable homicide against a motorist rather than to undertake a prosecution under the Road Traffic Act 1988, s 1. (An unsuccessful attempt, in the case of *HMA v Purcell*,[5] was made by the Crown to libel murder as the principal charge in an undoubtedly dreadful driving case, with s 1 as the alternative. However, neither the circumstances of the case, nor even the

---

1   RTA 1988, s 183.
2   *Crawford v HMA* 2015 SCCR 345.
3   c 16.
4   c 20.
5   2007 SCCR 520.

indictment were found to justify the principal position and ultimately a plea to culpable homicide was accepted. Clearly, use of a vehicle as a weapon could justify a charge of murder).

This procedure is normally adopted only in the most serious cases. It is submitted that the standard of driving to be considered on a charge of culpable homicide should nonetheless be for all practical purposes identical to the standard to be applied in the statutory charge. However, in such a charge there will normally be other features in the circumstances of the case, and in the quality of the driving, which distinguish it from the ordinary case under s 1. A charge of culpable homicide is taken on indictment. The penalties available to the court where culpable homicide is committed by the driver include an unlimited prison sentence, obligatory disqualification for a minimum period of two years,[1] and obligatory endorsement of the driver's licence. In the unlikely event of disqualification not being imposed, 3–11 penalty points must be endorsed on the licence.[2] In terms of s 36 of the Road Traffic Offenders Act 1988, a driver convicted of culpable homicide and thereafter disqualified must re-sit and pass the extended driving test after the period of disqualification has expired before he can apply to have his licence back. The level of custodial sentences is normally those applicable in other forms of culpable homicide.[3]

Similarly, obligatory disqualification and endorsement follow a conviction under s 1 of the Act.[4] The minimum period of disqualification is two years.[5] A sentence of up to 14 years' imprisonment is available.[6] The driver must re-sit and pass the extended test before he can regain his licence.[7] Particularly serious penalties are imposed in s 1 cases if it is shown that the driving may have been affected by the consumption of alcohol.

Statutory offences under s 1 or s 2 of the Act may be separately and alternatively libelled on culpable homicide indictments.[8] A jury is specifically entitled to bring in certain alternative verdicts even where the alternative is not charged.[9] The provisions of s 32 of the Road Safety Act

1   RTOA 1988, s 34(4), as amended by the RTA 1991, s 29(4)(a).
2   RTOA 1988, Sch 2, Pt II, as amended by RTA 1991, Sch 2.
3   *Brodie v HM Advocate* 1992 SCCR 487.
4   RTOA 1988, Sch 2, Pt I, as amended by the RTA 1991, Sch 2 para 5.
5   RTOA 1988, s 34(4), as amended by RTA 1991, s 29(4)(a).
6   Criminal Justice Act 2003, s 285.
7   RTOA 1998, s 36.
8   See, eg, *Dunn v HM Advocate* 1960 JC 55.
9   RTOA 1988, s 23(1), as amended by RTA 1991, Sch 4 para 90; and RTOA 1988, s 24, as amended by the RTA 1991, s 24.

2006 amended s 23 of the Road Traffic Offenders Act 1988[1] and alternative verdicts for 'relevant offences' – under ss 1, 1A, 2 and 3A – are available. Directions to the jury on the alternative verdicts s 2 do not necessarily have to be given in every case.[2]

2.2.2 Warning or notice of intended prosecution: dangerous driving; contents of charge

In respect of an alternative charge in terms of s 2 of the Road Traffic Act 1988 to a charge of culpable homicide, it should be noted that the provisions of s 1 of the Road Traffic Offenders Act 1988, as amended by the Road Traffic Act 1991, Sch 4 para 80, would not apply.[3] The provisions of s 1, which require either that a police officer warns the accused at the time that the offence was committed that a prosecution may follow, or, alternatively, that within 14 days of the incident a notice of intended prosecution should be served on the accused, are pre-requisites of any prosecution under s 2 (though not of s 1) of the Road Traffic Act 1988, and of the other offences specified in Sch 1 to the Road Traffic Offenders Act 1988.[4]

The requirement in such cases for either a prosecution warning or the service of a complaint must be strictly observed; a verbal warning must be given at the time[5] and the warning must be clear and specific.[6] The phrase 'at the time that the offence was committed' was considered by the Sheriff Appeal Court in the case of *Coltman v PF Dunoon*,[7] where the incident of dangerous driving occurred at 6.30 pm and the warning was given at 8.15 pm, after a period of enquiry to find the driver. The court concluded, at para 10, that:

> 'there is one test, which …. is simply whether, applying reasonable latitude, the warning can be said to have been given at the time of the accident. In considering what is reasonable latitude, no doubt regard will be had to whether there was an unbroken chain of circumstances although that can never be the only factor and the passage of time must also be relevant. Were there to be a complicated and unbroken police investigation lasting several days, for example, it is difficult to envisage that any warning given

---

1 As further amended by the Legal Aid, Sentencing and Punishment of Offenders Act 2012 (c 10), Sch 27, para 3 (3 December 2012).
2 *McDonald v HM Advocate* 1999 SLT 243.
3 See RTOA 1988, s 2(4), as amended by RTA 1991, Sch 4 para 81.
4 See eg, *McGlynn v Stewart* 1973 JC 33.
5 *Cuthbert v Hollis* 1958 SLT (Sh Ct) 51.
6 *Watt v Smith* 1942 JC 109, 1943 SLT 101.
7 [2018] SAC (Crim) 6.

thereafter could ever be said to be at the time of the offence. The important point to note however is that it is a question of fact and degree in every case.'

In *Lindsay v Smith*[1] it was held that for police officers to caution and charge the accused was sufficient to comply with the terms of s 1; and that it was desirable that advance notice be given when the accused wishes to rely on a failure to observe this requirement.

Moreover, s 1(3) of the Road Traffic Offenders Act 1988 assumes that the requirements of s 1(1) have been observed in every case until the contrary is proved, and s 2(1) provides exemption from the general requirements in the cases of offences involving accidents. Further, s 2(3) provides that failure to observe the conditions set out in s 1(1) will not bar conviction where the accused cannot be traced despite the exercise of reasonable diligence or where the accused himself contributes to the failure.

The absence of compliance with s 1 does not preclude the possibility of conviction for culpable and reckless conduct given the provisions of the Criminal Procedure (Scotland) Act 1995, Sch 3 para 14.[2]

Any fatal accident inquiry into the circumstances of an incident which subsequently gives rise to a prosecution under s 1 or 2 of the Road Traffic Act 1988 normally takes place after any criminal proceedings have been concluded.

Dangerous driving under s 2 of the Road Traffic Act 1988, if charged alone, is normally taken on summary complaint. The time and place of the alleged offence must be given, but not necessarily the exact nature of the driving.[3]

Differences between the copy of the complaint served on the accused and the court copy will be ignored if there is no prejudice.[4] However, where particular incidents of driving were spoken to in evidence as having taken place on streets not mentioned in the libel, such evidence was held to be inadmissible.[5]

2.3 SECTION 1

Tried on indictment, 14 years' imprisonment, obligatory disqualification (or 3–11 points)

1   *Lindsay v Smith* 1991 SLT 896, 1990 SCCR 581.
2   *Robertson v Klos* 2006 SCCR 52.
3   *Todrick v Dennelour* (1904) 7 F 8, (1904) SLT 573; *Watkin v HM Advocate* 1989 SLT 24, 1988 SCCR 443; see also 2.2.1 above.
4   *Suttenfield v O'Brien* 1996 SLT 198; *Walker v Higson* 1998 SLT 131.
5   *Symmers v Lees* 2000 JC 149, 2000 SLT 507, 2000 SCCR 66.

2.3.1 Ingredients of the offence

Section 1 of the Road Traffic Act 1988 as amended by the Road Traffic Act 1991, s 1, provides: 'A person who causes the death of another person by driving a mechanically propelled vehicle dangerously on a road or other public place shall be guilty of an offence.'

For a conviction against a motorist under s 1 of the 1988 Act as amended, the Crown must prove (i) that the driving complained of was dangerous; (ii) that it was a cause of the death of some other person (who may be a passenger in the car driven by the accused or indeed any other category of person); and (iii) that the driving took place in a 'mechanically propelled vehicle' and on a 'road or other public place'.

In terms of s 24 of the Road Traffic Offenders Act 1988, where a motorist is charged under s 1, alternative verdicts under ss 2, 2B and 3 are also available.[1]

2.3.2 Definitions

'Driving'. See 1.7.1 above.

The definition section of the Road Traffic Act 1988[2] specifically excludes from s 1 prosecutions the extended provision of which includes a steersman in the category of driver, and which otherwise applies for the purpose of the statute. The nature of the driving was considered in the case of *Allan v Patterson*.[3] The full definition given by the Lord Justice-General (Emslie) in the Appeal Court was as follows:

> 'Section 2 [of the 1972 Act] as its language plainly, we think, suggests, requires a judgment to be made quite objectively of a particular course of driving in proved circumstances, and what the court or a jury has to decide using its common sense, is whether the course of driving in these circumstances had the grave quality of recklessness. Judges and juries will readily understand, and juries might well be reminded, that before they can apply the adverb "recklessly" to the driving in question they must find that it fell far below the standard of driving expected of the competent and careful driver and that it occurred either in the face of obvious and material dangers which were or should have been observed, appreciated and guarded against, or in circumstances which showed a complete disregard for any potential dangers which might result from the way in which the vehicle was being driven. It will be understood that in reaching a decision upon the critical issue a judge or jury will be entitled to have

---

1   See 2.2.1 above.
2   RTA 1988, s 192.
3   *Allan v Patterson* 1980 JC 57, 1980 SLT 77, 1979 CO Circulars A/20.

regard to any explanation offered by the accused driver designed to show that his driving in the particular circumstances did not possess the quality of recklessness at the material time.'

The court also approved the description of reckless driving submitted by the Crown. In the Crown's submission, reckless driving meant:

'a piece of driving which, judged objectively, is eloquent of a high degree of negligence – much more than a mere want of due care and attention – and supports the inference that material risks were deliberately courted or that these risks which ought to have been obvious to any observant and careful drivers were not noticed by reason of gross inattention. Driving "recklessly", accordingly, is driving which demonstrates a gross degree of carelessness in the face of evident dangers.'

It is plain from the decision of the Appeal Court that reckless driving was not confined to driving which had been embarked upon wilfully or deliberately in the face of known risks of a material kind. Driving which occurred in circumstances where there were potential dangers, which were only liable to arise, can nonetheless be described as 'reckless'. Further, an examination of the state of knowledge of a driver charged with reckless driving, or of his intentions at the material time, was not relevant. Similarly, the particular skill, capacity or ability of the driver in question was not to be considered. In other words, the tests applied to the driving under consideration had to be regarded objectively in the context of the proved circumstances of the driving; and had to relate purely to the quality of the driving in fact.

A good example may be found from the English authority of Attorney General's Reference (No 4 of 2000), case involving two deaths.[1] The Court of Appeal held:

'that if a driver unintentionally presses the accelerator when he means to press the brake that is no defence to a charge of dangerous driving. Unfortunately, it is all too easy to make a mistake of that nature. The mistake can, as it did in this case, have the most tragic consequences. As we understand the offence of dangerous driving, it is intended to cover occurrences where a driver has made a mistake of this nature. The matters relied upon by the defence in this case did not go to the question of guilt or lack of guilt; they went solely to the question of what would be the appropriate penalty.'

Section 1 of the Road Traffic Act 1991, which provides replacement sections for ss 1 and 2 of the Road Traffic Act 1988, also contains a section

---

1   EWCA Crim 780, [2001] RTR 27.

which defines the meaning of 'dangerous driving'. Section 2A of the Road Traffic Act 1988 provides:

'(1) For the purposes of sections 1 and 2 above a person is to be regarded as driving dangerously if (and, subject to subsection (2) below, only if) –

(a)　the way he drives falls far below what would be expected of a competent and careful driver, and

(b)　it would be obvious to a competent and careful driver that driving in that way would be dangerous.'

The Appeal Court has emphasised on a number of occasions that the court or jury must be satisfied that the driving complained of has failed both parts of the test described in s 2A(1)(a) and (b) before a conviction is possible.[1]

Further on in the same section, additional definition is given:

'(3) In subsections (1) and (2) above "dangerous" refers to danger either of injury to any person or of serious damage to property; and in determining for the purposes of those subsections what would be expected of, or obvious to, a competent and careful driver in a particular case, regard should be had not only to the circumstances of which he could be expected to be aware but also to any circumstances shown to have been within the knowledge of the accused.'

It is submitted that the foregoing statutory definition of what is meant by dangerous driving substantially reflects the essential features of the nature of reckless driving described by the Lord Justice-General in *Allan v Patterson*.[2] Accordingly (and unless and until the Appeal Court decides differently), the standard of dangerous driving, and its necessary ingredients, are for all practical purposes the same as for reckless driving.[3]

The Appeal Court has made it clear that the specific directions contained in *Allan v Patterson* were to be given to juries in all cases of reckless driving.[4] Equally, these directions have to be considered by Sheriffs in considering summary complaints of dangerous driving. It is submitted that the precise terms of the definitions contained in *Allan v Patterson* should be employed, substituting the word 'dangerous' for the word 'reckless' where it occurs.

1　See, eg *Aitken v Lees* 1993 JC 228, 1994 SLT 182, 1993 SCCR 845.
2　*Allan v Patterson* 1980 JC 57, 1980 SLT 77.
3　See *Alexander v Dunn* 2016 JC 125; 2016 SLT 337; 2016 SCCR 305 and *(1) John & Linda Stewart (2) Allan & Aileen Convey v William Payne; (1) Matthew & Jacqueline McQuade and (2) Yvonne Reilly v Henry Clarke* [2016] HCJAC 122; 2017 JC 155; 2017 SLT 159; 2017 SCCR 56.
4　*Crowe v HM Advocate* 1990 JC 112, 1990 SLT 670, 1989 SCCR 681.

Whether or not the tests are met, as referred to by Lord Emslie above, and Lord Carloway more recently, 'just depends on the circumstances'.[1]

Dangerous driving may occur where, although there is no actual danger, the potential for such danger exists.[2]

It may be dangerous driving to drive a vehicle which the driver knows has a dangerous defect.[3]

Reference should also be made to 2.3.4, 2.3.5 and 2.3.6 below. Throughout the rest of the treatment of dangerous driving in this book, references to reckless driving in the cases before the 1988 Act should be regarded for practical purposes as applying equally to dangerous driving. *'Causes the death'*. For a conviction for dangerous driving under s 1, it must also be demonstrated that the death resulted from the driving complained of. The course of driving need not necessarily be the only or indeed the principal cause of the resulting death. Unless the cause or connection between the driving and death is *'de minimis'*, a motorist can be convicted under this section if the driving is shown to be one of several causes which result in the death of the victim.[4] In *McCluskey v HM Advocate*,[5] a driver who caused injuries to an unborn child, which died as a result shortly after birth, was convicted under this section.

In *R v Shelton*,[6] a driver took a lorry which was in a dangerous condition onto the road, where it broke down and blocked the nearside lane of a motorway. Some time later another lorry drove into the back of it and the driver of the second lorry was killed. It was held that there was a sufficient link between the driving and the death to allow the case to go to a jury.

The issue of causation has recently been considered in cases involving s 3ZB. See 8.2.4 below.

'Mechanically propelled vehicle'. See 1.2.1 above.

'Road or other public place'. See 1.8.1, 1.8.2 and 1.8.3 above.

2.3.3 Evidence

It is competent to introduce evidence in the prosecution of a charge of culpable homicide that the motorist had consumed alcohol or drugs such

1   *Craig v HMA* [HCJAC] 116, decision of 4 November 2010.
2   *Mitchell v Lockhart* 1993 SCCR 1070.
3   See 2.3.8 below.
4   *R v Hennigan* [1971] RTR 305, [1971] 3 All ER 133; *Watson v HM Advocate* 1978 SCCR Supp 192.
5   *McCluskey v HM Advocate* 1989 SLT 175, 1988 SCCR 629.
6   *R v Shelton* [1995] Crim LR 635, [1995] RTR 635.

as would be adversely liable to affect his ability to drive. In *McKie v HM Advocate*[1] an accused driver was charged, after an accident, with driving while unfit through drink. Subsequently it was discovered that another person had died as a result of the accident. The driver was charged with culpable homicide and, at his trial, evidence of a medical examination in relation to the drunk driving charge was held admissible. In *Burrell v Hunter*[2] it was held to be competent for a motorist to be charged with dangerous driving whilst suffering 'from a nervous disorder aggravated by the consumption of alcohol'. If such evidence of previous alcohol consumption is adduced, then it must be for the purpose of demonstrating that the consumption of alcohol affected or was liable to affect the driving complained of, or that it was in the circumstances a reasonable inference that the consumption of alcohol had adversely affected the driving. It is of course competent to charge a motorist with further offences in an indictment containing a charge under s 1 or s 2. Additional charges, such as driving a motor vehicle when under the influence of alcohol or drugs in terms of s 4 or 5 of the Act, can, and regularly are, added to such indictments where appropriate. It is submitted that, notwithstanding the rule of evidence in the cases of *McKie v HM Advocate*[3] and *Burrell v Hunter*,[4] it is proper practice for the prosecution to libel such additional offences if reliance is to be placed on the consumption of alcohol in securing convictions under s 1 or s 2 prosecutions.

Amendment of the *locus* of a charge or other matters by the Crown may be allowed at the discretion of the court, especially if there is no prejudice.[5] Reference might also usefully be made to Sch 3 to the 1995 Act.

The manner of earlier driving, and the consequences of a course of driving, are relevant in assessing whether the driving was dangerous, and such consequences may, if appropriate, be libelled in the charge.[6]

If it is not shown that the driving was the cause of death, the driver can still be found guilty of ss 1A, 2, and 3 [7] or even culpable and reckless

---

1   *McKie v HM Advocate* 1958 JC 24, 1958 SLT 152.
2   *Burrell v Hunter* 1956 SLT (Sh Ct) 75.
3   *McKie v HM Advocate* 1958 JC 24, 1958 SLT 152.
4   *Burrell v Hunter* 1956 SLT (Sh Ct) 75.
5   Criminal Procedure (Scotland) Act 1995, s 195; *Craig v Keane* 1982 SLT 198, 1981 SCCR 166; *Brown v McLeod* 1986 SCCR 615; *Fenwick v Valentine* 1993 SCCR 892; *Gullett v Hamilton* 1997 SLT 1207.
6   *McCallum v Hamilton* 1986 JC 1, 1986 SLT 156, 1985 SCCR 368; *Mundie v Cardle* 1991 SCCR 118; *MacDonald v HM Advocate* 1999 SLT 243.
7   s 23 RTA 1988.

conduct or a breach of the peace.[1] Common law alternatives depend upon the provisions of the Criminal Procedure (Scotland) Act 1995, Sch 3 para 14.

Whether or not a jury has to be directed on alternative verdicts will turn on the individual case. It is not essential although if the issue is raised by a party the judge will normally give directions on the matter.[2]

Sentencing for s 1 offences, and other death by driving provisions, has become the focus of much press, political, interest group and judicial attention in the last 15 years. Lengthy sentences of imprisonment have always been imposed where alcohol is involved in dangerous driving cases but it is striking that death by driving cases routinely appeared in the Sheriff Court, and before the progressive increase in Shrieval powers.

How things have changed.[3] In England consideration of sentencing guidelines for s 1 offences – then with a ten-year maximum – were carefully formulated in *Cooksley v R*,[4] a case approved in *HM Advocate v MacPherson*[5] and followed both in terms of length of sentence and disqualification in *Dingwall v HM Advocate*.[6] The guidelines were reconsidered to take account of the increase to a 14-year maximum sentence in *R v Richardson*.[7] It was held that the primary object of the increase was to deal with the most serious cases, and the Court of Appeal accepted the point that there had been no corresponding increase in the penalty for dangerous driving itself. The ranges of sentences considered in Cooksley were nonetheless reassessed upwards to take account of the change although this did not reflect increase on any mathematical basis. Regard was had to *Richardson* in the case of *Wright v HMA*.[8]

In 2008 the Sentencing Guidelines Council in England produced a definitive guideline for cases causing death by driving (ss 1, 2B and 3ZB) to apply to offenders over 18. While applicable only in England and

---

1   *Horsburgh v Russell* 1994 SLT 942, 1994 SCCR 237; *Vannet v Davidson* 1996 JC 17, 1996 SLT 626; *Robertson v Klos* 2006 SCCR 52.
2   *Meyl v HMA* 2005 SCCR 338.
3   See *HM Advocate v Stalker* 2003 SCCR 734 where the Court viewed the case as one that should have been indicted in the High Court. The case arose out of a Crown appeal which included a ground that the Sheriff should have remitted! See also *Sharp v HM Advocate* 2003 SCCR 573 and *Vieregge v HM Advocate* 2003 SCCR 689.
4   *Cooksley v R* [2003] 3 All ER 40; [2003] RTR 483; 2 Cr App R 18 (p 275); [2003] EWCA Crim 996.
5   *HM Advocate v MacPherson* 2004 SCCR 579.
6   *Dingwall v HM Advocate* 2005 SCCR 700.
7   *R v Richardson* [2006] EWCA Crim 3186, The Times January 15 2007.
8   2007 SCCR 139.

Wales, they may be considered in Scotland, and, as a matter of routine, are. See, for example, *HM Advocate v Noche* [2011] HCJAC 108, *HM Advocate v McKay* 2011 SLT 250, and *HM Advocate v McCourt* [2013] HCJAC 114.

However, as noted in *Geddes v HMA*:

> 'It is important to observe that, while the court has encouraged sentencing judges to "have regard" to the English guideline in death by dangerous driving cases, it has not said that it should "be interpreted and applied in a mechanistic way" (*Neill v HM Advocate* [2014] HCJAC 67, Lady Clark of Calton at para.11). In order to ensure a degree of consistency in this jurisdiction, albeit paying due regard to local circumstances, it may be equally important to have regard to existing precedent (e.g. *Neill v HM Advocate* (supra) or *Lynn v HM Advocate* [2008] HCJAC 72). The sentencing judge may wish to consider how a sentence for this type of offence dovetails with modern sentencing developments in relation to Scottish criminal offences generally, including those for, for example, culpable homicide.'[1]

Geddes also provides useful observations on the period of disqualification that may be imposed, noting that while the guideline suggestion of matching disqualification to the length of the custodial term may be reasonable, it is not mandatory, reflecting the court's different and lengthier approach in that case.[2]

HMA v McCourt, which related to a death by careless driving, is of further interest as it revisited the issue of whether factors relating to the deceased can properly form part of the assessment of an appropriate sentence using the guidelines.

In *McCourt*, the absence of a helmet on the part of the deceased cyclist was not mitigatory as there was no evidence before the Sheriff on the matter and his conclusions were speculative. Reference was made to *Wright v HMA*, where the deceased had not been wearing a seatbelt and no evidence was led at trial about alternative outcomes had one been worn. Again, the Court would not entertain speculation.

It may be, therefore, in an appropriately vouched case, that a failure by a deceased to take an obvious safety precaution, such as a seat belt, could amount to a mitigatory factor for an accused.

The Definitive Guideline is set out in full in Appendix E.

2.3.4 Section 1A: causing serious injury by dangerous driving

Tried on indictment, five years' imprisonment, or a fine or both, obligatory disqualification (or 3–11 points)

---

1   2015 SLT 415, 2015 SCCR 230 See also *Milligan v HMA* [2015] HCJAC 84.
2   see para [22].

Tried summarily, 12 months' imprisonment, statutory maximum fine or both, obligatory disqualification (or 3–11 points)

Section 1A of the Road Traffic Act 1988, as introduced by s 143 of the Legal Aid, Sentencing and Punishment of Offenders Act 2012[1] provides: 'A person who causes serious injury to another person by driving a mechanically propelled vehicle dangerously on a road or other public place is guilty of an offence.'

'Serious injury' in Scotland means 'severe physical injury'.[2]

This is another example of Parliament responding to serious consequence cases by introducing a new provision as opposed to simply expanding the range of sentence of the original offence. That might have been seen as more straightforward and obvious, particularly as very serious examples of dangerous driving, without consequence by good fortune alone, still have to be sentenced under reference to a maximum two-year sentence.

As with s 1 offences, sentencing may be guided by reference to the Definitive Guideline issued by the Sentencing Guidelines Council, as happened in *Burke v HMA*,[3] although there is a growing body of both Scottish and English cases, as recognised by the High Court in *Brierley v HMA*.[4] Ultimately, of course, each case will turn on its own facts and circumstances.

In practice, 'serious injury', which does not include injury sustained to the accused, will presumably reflect severe injury as understood by lawyers in the context of assaults.[5] As a result, such offences are most likely to be on indictment.

Consideration of the meaning of 'dangerous' is as considered below under reference to s 2 offences.

There is no requirement to give a warning in terms of s 1 of the Road Traffic Offenders Act 1988 for a charge under this section.

Implied alternatives to the offence are either for dangerous driving, s 2, or careless driving, s 3.[6]

2.3.5 Section 2: dangerous driving

Tried on indictment, two years' imprisonment, or a fine or both, obligatory disqualification (or 3–11 points)

---

1   c 10.
2   See s 1A(2)(b).
3   [2016] SAC (Crim) 31, 2016 SCCR 585.
4   [2016] HCJAC HCA/2016/000450/XC 8 November 2016.
5   See for example *George v HMA* [2011] HJAC 33.
6   S 24 RTOA 1988, as amended.

Tried summarily, 12 months' imprisonment, statutory maximum fine or both, obligatory disqualification (or 3–11 points)

Section 2 of the Road Traffic Act 1988, as amended by s 1 of the Road Traffic Act 1991, provides: 'A person who drives a mechanically propelled vehicle dangerously on a road or other public place is guilty of an offence.'

Dangerous driving is therefore an offence by itself where no fatality occurs. Precisely the same standard and considerations apply in determining whether or not a particular course of driving should be described as dangerous as apply in the cases brought under s 1. A charge under s 2 of the Act may be brought under either solemn or summary procedure, at the option of the Crown. The particular nature of the driving complained of as being dangerous need not be specified in the charge although it is of course necessary to give sufficient details of the time and place of the alleged offence.[1] Careless driving may be and often is charged as an alternative to dangerous driving on the same indictment or complaint. The alternative verdict is always available (Road Traffic Act 1988, s 24 as amended by the Road Traffic Act 1991, s 24), even perhaps to the Court of Appeal in a case where the Crown did not seek it as an alternative in the lower court.[2] Both verdicts will obviously be open to a court in considering the evidence and the appropriate result.[3]

On conviction under s 2 of the Act, the maximum prison sentence in solemn prosecutions is two years, and 12 months in summary cases[4] with obligatory endorsement, and disqualification for a minimum period of 12 months.[5] After the expiry of any period of disqualification the driver must re-sit and pass the extended driving test before getting his licence back.[6] If for any reason disqualification is not imposed, 3–11 penalty points must be endorsed on the licence.[7] For cases where s 2 is charged as an alternative to culpable homicide, reference should be made to 2.2.1 above.

---

1   *Todrick v Dennelar* 1904 7 F (J) 8, (1904) SLT 573; see also *Watkin v HM Advocate* 1989 SLT 24, 1988 SCCR 443.
2   *Angus v Spiers* 2006 SCCR 603.
3   *Wallace v Thomson* 2009 SCCR 421.
4   RTOA 1988, Sch 2, as amended by the RTA 1991, Sch 2 para 6, but affected by s 45 of The Criminal Proceedings (Reform) (Scotland) Act 2007.
5   RTOA 1988, s 34.
6   RTOA 1988, s 36. Failure to impose such a requirement cannot be cured by use of s 299 of the Criminal Procedure (Scotland) Act – see *Iqbal v Harvie* 2016 SCCR 258,
7   RTOA 1988, Sch 2, as amended.

Whether or not driving in a particular case is to be regarded as dangerous will of course depend upon the facts and circumstances that are proved to have prevailed in each case. [1]However, it is not essential for a successful prosecution under this section that there should have been a collision involving another vehicle, or indeed an accident of any sort. Each case will depend on its own facts and all the aspects of the driving complained of require to be considered Dangerous driving may be inferred from a given set of facts and circumstances where, for example, a vehicle behaves in an abnormal fashion without any explanation for that behaviour being proved.

As in cases under s 1, the matter has to be considered objectively, and the ability or state of mind of the motorist is not a relevant consideration. See 2.3.2 above. Driving which can properly be described as dangerous as defined in the case of *Allan v Patterson*[2] is not likely to arise from a momentary lack of attention or a simple error of judgement. Similarly, the intentions of the driver are irrelevant. A test sometimes applied in these circumstances is for the judge or jury to satisfy themselves on the evidence as to what in fact took place, and then put themselves in the position of a bystander and from that viewpoint consider whether the driving proved to have taken place can properly be characterised as dangerous in terms of the definitions found in *Allan v Patterson*.[3] Evidence of driving earlier in the course of a particular journey, prior to the conduct complained of in the indictment or complaint, may be admissible. However, it is considered good practice for the prosecutor to give full notice by way of the description of the *locus* where all of the driving complained of took place.

More than one driver may be guilty of dangerous driving out of the same single incident.[4]

2.3.6 Highway Code

The most readily recognisable tests of dangerous driving may be found within the provisions of the Highway Code. Section 38(7) of the Road Traffic Act 1988 provides in effect that failure to observe the Highway Code may tend to establish liability for reckless driving; however, in terms of the subsection, a violation of any of the provisions of the Highway Code does not necessarily mean that the driver should be

---

1   For a good example of the variety of factors at play see the analysis in *Lizanec v PF Edinburgh* [2016] SAC (Crim) 33.
2   *Allan v Patterson* 1980 JC 57, 1980 SLT 77, 1979 CO Circulars A/20.
3   See 2.3.2 above.
4   See *Watson v HM Advocate* 1979 SCCR Supp 192.

prosecuted. Clearly, therefore, a judge or jury, in considering dangerous driving, may competently have regard to the provisions of the Highway Code in determining whether or not a particular course of driving was dangerous,[1] but equally the fact that a driver has failed to observe a particular rule in the Highway Code does not necessarily mean that he should be convicted. The Highway Code is published by The Stationery Office and is available from its outlets and other bookshops.

2.3.7 Nature of danger

As indicated above, in s 2A(3) of the Road Traffic Act 1988 (introduced by s 1 of the Road Traffic Act 1991), 'dangerous' refers to danger either of injury to any person or of serious damage to property. The prospect of injury to any person includes injury to the driver himself.[2] The subsection does not define what is meant by 'serious damage to property', but any question as to whether serious damage can be distinguished from trivial is almost certainly academic.

2.3.8 Speed in dangerous driving

Excessive speed may be the single most important constituent of a charge of dangerous driving but, if so, it must occur in circumstances which allow the driving to be described as dangerous. In *Frame v Lockhart*,[3] a driver was travelling at 50 mph on an esplanade where the speed limit was 15 mph. Although there was no other traffic, either vehicular or pedestrian, on the esplanade at the material time, the circumstances were such that a large number of pedestrians were in the immediate area and were liable to pass over the esplanade. It was held that, having regard to all the material facts, the speed at which the vehicle was being driven could properly be described as reckless. However, this was a majority decision of the Appeal Court and Lord Robertson's dissenting judgment is worthy of consideration for the contrary view.

Frame v Lockhart was followed in *O'Toole v McDougal*.[4] In that case, a motorist drove for more than 11 miles on the A74 just before midnight at speeds between 100 and 120 mph, the speed limit for that part of the road being 70 mph. The road in question is a dual carriageway with many junctions and gaps in the central reservation and is used by pedestrians and vehicular traffic. While there was no evidence of any actual danger or

---

1   See, eg, *McCrone v Normand* 1989 SLT 332, 1988 SCCR 551.
2   *Fraser v Lockhart* 1992 SCCR 275.
3   *Frame v Lockhart* 1985 SLT 367, 1984 SCCR 377.
4   *O'Toole v McDougal* 1986 SCCR 56.

inconvenience to any other road user, it was held that, in the circumstances, the driver showed a complete disregard for any potential dangers which might have arisen, and that accordingly the speed was so excessive that a conviction for reckless driving was justified. In delivering the opinion of the Appeal Court, the Lord Justice-General (Emslie)[1] said:

> 'If consideration is given to the time at which this chase took place in the hours of darkness, if consideration is given to the character of the roadway and the dangers presented by its particular features of construction which the sheriff has described, if attention is given to the fact that the road was carrying lorry traffic and motor traffic, it appears to us that the sheriff was entitled and indeed well entitled to conclude that anyone who drives on that stretch of road in the face of the potential dangers which it obviously carried at a speed of between 100 and 120 mph is driving recklessly, however skilful he may be in controlling the vehicle at whose wheel he sits. In our judgment the sheriff was perfectly right to be satisfied – not only entitled to be satisfied but we think right to be satisfied – beyond reasonable doubt that in all the circumstances in the findings in fact which are eloquent of potential danger, the appellant's speed was so excessive that it would be regarded as a piece of reckless driving as a whole.'

This case is therefore authority for emphasising that the material risks referred to in the case of *Allan v Patterson*[2] which have to be observed, appreciated and guarded against are not confined to dangers which actually arise during the course of the journey complained of, but include also potential dangers which are likely to or liable to arise. The same point has recently been made in similar circumstances on the same road in *Service v Daldrup*,[3] a successful crown appeal following acquittal.

In *Deans v Skinner*,[4] a driver who had neither a licence nor insurance was driving at an excessive speed. He was pursued by a police car and panicked, going through a red light without being aware of doing so, and passed vehicles halted at traffic lights on the inside. This was considered to be a narrow case, but the driving was judged to be reckless.

It now seems clear that very little is required, in addition to grossly excessive speed, to justify a conviction for dangerous driving[5] However,

1   At p 59.
2   *Allan v Patterson* 1980 JC 57, 1980 SLT 77.
3   *Service v Daldrup* 2005 SCCR 693.
4   *Deans v Skinner* 1981 SCCR 49.
5   *Fraser v Lockhart* 1992 SCCR 275; *Abbas v Houston* 1993 SCCR 1019; *Trippick v Orr* 1995 SLT 272, 1994 SCCR 736; *McQueen v Buchanan* 1997 JC 16, 1997 SLT 765, 1996 SCCR 826; *Howdle v O'Connor* 1998 SLT 94.

excessive speed is not always necessarily sufficient by itself[1] as the Court in *Service v Daldrup* also recognised, observing that 'it may be in most cases speed in itself is not enough'.[2]

Proof of precise speed is not necessary, it being for the Sheriff to interpret the evidence in assessing whether the speed is excessive in the context of s 2 offences.[3]

Where the driving is below the speed limit, it may still be excessive in the light of other factors.[4]

2.3.9 Dangerous defects

Section 2A(2) of the Road Traffic Act 1988[5] specifically provides that a driver may be guilty of driving dangerously if it would be obvious to a careful and competent driver that driving the vehicle in its current state would be dangerous. For example, if a driver takes to the road in the knowledge that his vehicle has defective brakes and an accident occurs as a result of that defect, the driver may be convicted of dangerous driving. This confirms the position which existed previously without particular statutory sanction. In *R v Robert Miller (Contractors) Ltd*,[6] a lorry driver took to the road knowing that one of his tyres was defective. The defect caused an accident which resulted in a death, and the driver was convicted under s 1. Similarly, where a driver embarked upon a journey with an insecure load, knowing that it might fall off, and the load in fact fell off and killed a pedestrian, a conviction for reckless driving followed.[7]

In *Carstairs v Hamilton*,[8] a driver was convicted of dangerous driving when he drove on a public road a go-kart which had no windscreen, roof, suspension and so on, which in effect provided no protection for the driver, and in addition could not easily be seen by other road users. Reference should also be made to *R v Shelton*,[9] where a driver took a defective lorry onto the road and was charged with dangerous driving after it broke down, and another lorry drove into it. For any specific mechanical defect to be

---

1   *Brown v Orr* 1994 SCCR 668; *McQueen v Buchanan* 1997 JC 16, 1997 SLT 765, 1996 SCCR 826.
2   *Service v Daldrup* 2005 SCCR 693 at para 7.
3   *McLean v McLeod* 2002 SCCR 127.
4   *Angus v Spiers* 2006 SCCR 603.
5   As amended by the RTA 1991, s 1.
6   *R v Robert Miller (Contractors) Ltd* [1970] 2 QB 54, [1970] 2 WLR 541, [1970] 1 All ER 577.
7   *R v Crossman* [1986] RTR 49.
8   *Carstairs v Hamilton* 1998 SLT 220, 1997 SCCR 311.
9   *R v Shelton* [1995] Crim LR 635, [1995] RTR 635.

relevant, it must be one which would make it obvious to any competent and careful driver that it was likely to affect the driving of the vehicle.[1]

2.3.10 Jurisdiction

In *R v Robert Millar (Contractors) Ltd*,[2] a lorry was driven in England with a defective tyre, and the driver and the company who employed him and who owned the vehicle were both aware of the defect. An accident was caused by the defective tyre, and the court in England concluded that not only was the driver therefore guilty of dangerous driving, but that the directors of the company, which was situated in Scotland, were equally liable.

2.4 COMMON LAW

At common law any reckless conduct which causes injury or danger is criminal, whether the injury or danger is libelled or not.[3] A charge of this kind is sometimes brought by the Crown where it cannot be proved that the driving took place on 'a road or other public place' or as in *Robertson v Klos*, where notice of intended prosecution requirements were not met;[4] if the driving complained of does not have the necessary ingredients of dangerous driving, the Crown may have recourse to s 34 of the Road Traffic Act 1988.

2.5 DEFENCES

In the case of *Allan v Patterson*[5] it was emphasised that in reaching any decision on whether a particular course of driving should or should not be described as reckless, the judge or jury is entitled to have regard 'to any explanation offered by the accused driver designed to show that his driving in the particular circumstances did not possess the quality of recklessness at the material time'.

---

1   *HM Advocate v Campbell* 1994 SLT 502.
2   *R v Robert Millar (Contractors) Ltd* [1970] 2 QB 54, [1970] 2 WLR 541, [1970] 1 All ER 577.
3   *HM Advocate v Harris* 1993 JC 150, 1993 SLT 963, 1993 SCCR 559, overruling *Quinn v Cunningham* 1956 JC 22, 1956 SLT 55, which had held that any reckless conduct, such as the furious driving of a vehicle, could only be an offence if it was to the danger of the lieges (see also 2.14 below).
4   *Robertson v Klos* 2006 SCCR 52.
5   *Allan v Patterson* 1980 JC 57, 1980 SLT 77, CO Circulars A/20.

A special defence of automatism or the inability of the accused to form the necessary criminal intent is a competent defence to any criminal charge, including driving offences.[1] Three conditions must be satisfied if such a defence is to be successfully established. Firstly, the inability of the accused to form the necessary *mens rea* must be due to some external factor, which was not self-induced.[2] Secondly, the external factor must not be something that the accused was bound to foresee. Thirdly, the external factor must result in a total alienation of reason amounting to a complete absence of self-control on the part of the accused. The standard of proof required to sustain such a defence is high.[3] For example, the defence did not succeed in *Cardle v Mulrainey*,[4] where the accused was aware that he was committing the offences charged but maintained that he was unable to stop himself because of drugs introduced into his drink; nor did it succeed in *Ebsworth v HM Advocate*,[5] where the accused took an excessive amount of prescribed drugs to relieve pain. Reference should also be made to 1.7.3 above and 8.5.4 below.

In summary procedure, the defence of automatism was considered but held not to be established in *Stevenson v Beatson*.[6] In *Farrell v Stirling*[7] a diabetic who went into a state of hypoglycaemia (never having experienced such a condition in the past) just before an accident was held by the court not to be 'driving' and thus not guilty of careless driving. Such a defence could not have succeeded if the accused had had previous experience of the condition and appreciated that it was liable to affect him while he was driving.[8]

It may be possible to put forward a defence of mechanical defect, provided that it is shown that the way in which the vehicle was driven at the material time was due to a complete and unexpected loss of control as a result of some mechanical failure which was not caused in any way by the fault of the motorist. It is therefore considered that such

---

1   *Ross v HM Advocate* 1991 SLT 546, 1991 SCCR 823, partly overruling *HM Advocate v Cunningham* 1963 SLT 345; and affirming *HM Advocate v Ritchie* 1926 SLT 308, where a claim that the accused was suffering from a 'temporary mental disassociation due to toxic factors' was successfully pled.
2   *Finegan v Heywood* 2000 SCCR 460.
3   *Sorley v HM Advocate* 1992 SLT 867, 1992 SCCR 396; *McLeod v Napier* 1993 SCCR 303.
4   *Cardle v Mulrainey* 1992 SLT 1152, 1992 SCCR 658.
5   *Ebsworth v HM Advocate* 1992 SLT 1161, 1992 SCCR 671.
6   *Stevenson v Beatson* 1965 SLT (Sh Ct) 11.
7   *Farrell v Stirling* 1975 SLT (Sh Ct) 71.
8   *McLeod v Mathieson* 1993 SCCR 488; see also 2.3.8 above.

a defence would be unlikely to succeed if the motorist knew, or perhaps should have known by the exercise of reasonable diligence, that the fault existed.[1]

A defence of necessity is competent, and if successful will lead to an acquittal.[2] However, the standard which this defence must reach is high; the defence can only succeed where the driver is found to have acted under an immediate danger of death or great bodily harm to himself, or another, and any reasonable alternative to the offending behaviour must be taken.[3] While the circumstances should not be scrutinised with absolute strictness, it may be difficult to justify driving beyond the point where it is no longer necessary. Examples of cases where this defence was considered are *McLeod v McDougall*;[4] *Hamilton v Neizer*;[5] *Lees v McDonald*[6] and *Dolan v McLeod*.[7]

It would appear to be reasonable to assume that there is also scope for a defence of compulsion or duress along the same lines as the defence of necessity, so that the capacity or intent of the driver is also excluded.

Section 34(4) of the Road Traffic Act 1988 allows a driver to drive off the road, if he does so in order to save a life, put out a fire or deal with a similar emergency.

Emergency services are not excluded from the ambit of ordinary duties applicable to other drivers[8] apart from the regulations concerning speed limits,[9] but drivers of emergency vehicles may be able to plead extenuating or mitigating factors.

Circumstances which do not amount to a special defence of duress may form the basis of mitigating circumstances.[10]

---

1   *R v Spurge* [1961] 2 QB 205, [1961] 3 WLR 23, [1961] 2 All ER 688; *R v Robert Millar Contractors* [1970] 2 QB 54, [1970] 2 WLR 541, [1970] 1 All ER 577.
2   *Tudhope v Grubb* 1983 SCCR 350; *Moss v Howdle* 1997 JC 123, 1997 SLT 782, 1997 SCCR 215.
3   *Dawson v Dickson* 1999 JC 315, 1999 SCCR 698 (sub nom *Dawson v McKay* 1999 SLT 1328); *Dolan v McLeod* 1999 JC 32 1998 SCCR 653.
4   *McLeod v McDougall* 1989 SLT 151, 1988 SCCR 519.
5   *Hamilton v Neizer* 1993 SLT 992, 1993 SCCR 63.
6   *Lees v McDonald* 1997 SCCR 189.
7   *Dolan v McLeod* 1999 JC 32, 1998 SCCR 653.
8   *Husband v Russell* 1997 SCCR 592; see also 2.12 above.
9   RTRA 1984, s 87 as amended.
10   *McLeod v MacDougall* 1989 SLT 151, 1988 SCCR 519; *Connorton v Annan* 1981 SCCR 307.

2.6 DUTY TO GIVE NAME

Any driver of a mechanically propelled vehicle who is alleged to have committed an offence in terms of s 2 or s 3 of the Road Traffic Act 1988 is obliged to give his name and address to any person having reasonable grounds for requiring this information.[1] A failure to provide such information by the driver is an offence, and such a failure will make him liable to arrest without warrant by a police officer who considers that he has committed an offence of reckless or careless driving.[2] Such a request by the police for information, if made in good faith, does not have to be accompanied by an allegation that an offence has taken place.[3] Reference should also be made to 1.11.1 and 1.11.3 above (duty of driver or keeper of vehicle to give information) and to ch 7.

2.7 ART AND PART: AIDING AND ABETTING

That the accused in any case may be guilty either as principal actor or art and part is implied in all charges brought in Scotland whether on indictment or by means of summary complaint, as is aiding and abetting, counselling or procuring or inciting a contravention of any enactment.[4] Any accused found guilty art and part is liable to the same penalties as the principal actor. However, it has been suggested that all members of a gang in a getaway car may not be guilty art and part of all of the offences committed by the driver in attempting to make good his escape.[5]

The offence of aiding and abetting provided by s 176 of the Road Traffic Act 1972 is not repeated in the current legislation, presumably because it is considered to be unnecessary. What constituted the idea of aiding and abetting was discussed in *Valentine v Mackie*[6] and *Manion v Smith*.[7]

Section 176 of the Road Traffic Act 1972 made it an offence to counsel another to commit an offence against the Act. A solicitor advised a client not to report an accident to the police. It was held that in the absence of

---

1   RTA 1988, s 168 as amended by the RTA 1991, Sch 4 para 71.
2   RTA 1988, s 167.
3   *McMahon v Cardle* 1988 SCCR 556; see also *Galt v Goodsir* 1982 JC 4, 1982 SLT 94, 1981 SCCR 225 (followed in *Hingston v Pollock* 1990 JC 138, 1990 SLT 770, 1989 SCCR 697).
4   Criminal Procedure (Scotland) Act 1995, s 293(1)
5   *Webster v Wishart* 1955 SLT 243.
6   *Valentine v Mackie* 1980 SLT (Sh Ct) 122.
7   *Manion v Smith* 1989 SCCR 292.

an averment that by the time the advice was given it would still have been reasonably practicable for the accused to have reported the accident, the complaint was irrelevant.[1] Although s 176 of the Road Traffic Act 1972 has not survived into the Road Traffic Act of either 1988 or 1991, the case of *Martin v Hamilton*[2] may be relevant in common law charges of counselling or incitement, or in cases involving the accused acting art and part.

Section 119 of the Road Traffic Regulation Act 1984 makes it an offence to aid, counsel, procure or incite another to commit an offence against that Act or its relative regulations.

Section 34(5) of the Road Traffic Offenders Act 1988 (which deals with disqualification, for certain offences) applies the preceding provisions of that section to any conviction of an offence committed by aiding, abetting, counselling or procuring, or inciting to the commission of an offence involving obligatory disqualification, as if the offence were an offence involving discretionary disqualification.

2.8 CORPORATE LIABILITY

In *R v Robert Millar Contractors*,[3] a lorry was driven in England with a defective tyre. The driver and the company who employed him and who owned the vehicle were aware of the defect. An accident was caused by the defective tyre, and a court in England concluded that not only was the driver therefore guilty of dangerous driving but that the directors of the company, which was situated in Scotland, were equally liable.

2.9 OVERLOADED VEHICLES

In certain circumstances, rather than prosecute under the foregoing provisions, s 40A of the Road Traffic Act 1988 (as amended) is used when the number of passengers, or the manner in which they are carried, is said to be dangerous. In such cases the risk must arise out of the way the vehicle is actually being used.[4]

---

1   *Martin v Hamilton* 1989 SCCR 292.
2   1989 SCCR 292.
3   *R v Robert Millar Contractors* [1970] 2 QB 54, [1970] 2 WLR 541, [1970] 1 All ER 577.
4   *Akelis v Normand* 1997 SLT 136.

PART 2
CARELESS DRIVING

2.10 CARELESS AND INCONSIDERATE DRIVING (S 3)

Tried summarily, discretionary disqualification, obligatory endorsement (3–9 points) level 5 fine

2.10.1 General

Section 3 of the Road Traffic Act 1988 (as amended by the Road Traffic Act 1991, s 2) provides: 'If a person drives a mechanically propelled vehicle on a road or other public place without due care and attention or without reasonable consideration for other persons using the road or place, he is guilty of an offence.'

Section 3 prosecutions are undertaken summarily; penalties on conviction are again found in Sch 2, P I of the Road Traffic Offenders Act 1988 Disqualification is optional, and normally the disposal involves the imposition of penalty points endorsement of the licence and a fine.

Section 3 provides for two quite separate descriptions of driving either of which, if proved against the motorist, constitute the offence. In the first place it is an offence for a motorist to drive a car on the road without due care and attention; secondly, it is also an offence for a motorist to drive a vehicle on a road without reasonable consideration for other persons using the road. A particular course of driving could conceivably contravene both aspects of the section. The scope of both aspects of this section is extremely wide as reflected in the broad range of penalty points, 3–9 and the option of disqualification. The degree of culpability should determine the sentence imposed, not the consequences.

Prosecution of such offences is now more likely for two reasons. Firstly, the recent guidance of the Lord Advocate is clear that such cases should be prosecuted whereas previously, in large offices at least, they did not receive much attention.

Secondly, as of 16 August 2013, s 3 offences have been added to the list of traffic offences that may be subject to the offer of a fixed penalty either by the police or the Procurator Fiscal. The fixed penalty amount is £100 and 3 penalty points.

2.10.2 Definitions

'Driving'. See 1.7.1 above.

'*Mechanically propelled vehicle*'. See 1.2.1 above.

'*Road*'. See 1.8.2 above.

'*Other public place*'. See 1.8.3 above.

'*Due care and attention*'. A formal definition of these words is not appropriate and has not been attempted by the courts. The question of whether a driver in any particular case has driven without due care and attention is invariably a matter of fact. In general terms the test is concerned with an assessment of whether the driver was exercising the degree of care and attention expected of a reasonable and prudent driver. The circumstances which can produce careless driving are virtually unlimited in nature. The words are therefore to be construed in their ordinary and everyday sense, having regard to the test described at 2.10.3 below.

'*Reasonable consideration*'. Similarly, no formal definition can be given for this phrase; the words must be considered in their normal sense having regard to the test described at 2.10.3 below.

'*Other persons using the road*'. This includes passengers in the accused's vehicle: *Pawley v Wharldall*.[1]

2.10.3 Character of offence: test to be applied

A description of the kind of situations in which careless or inconsiderate driving may arise is virtually unlimited. For example, driving without due care and attention may arise out of simple acts of carelessness or failure to pay sufficient attention in the circumstances, a lack of judgment, momentary inattention or lack of concentration, or a simple mistake, up to and including all cases of extremely bad or objectionable driving which do not attain the high standard required for a charge of dangerous driving.

Typical cases of driving without reasonable consideration for other persons using the road may include (among a wide variety of examples which might be given) driving a vehicle too close to the driver in front thus causing the preceding driver to be distracted, lose concentration and be liable to make driving errors; driving with full beam headlights at night, dazzling and inconveniencing oncoming drivers; driving needlessly in the outside lane of a motorway or dual carriageway, or overtaking in the inside lane, thus inconveniencing other road users; or even driving deliberately at high speed through pools of water causing pedestrians to be splashed with water. It does not appear to have been

1   *Pawley v Wharldall* [1966] 1 QB 373.

established in Scotland whether the prosecution is required to prove that actual inconvenience was caused to other road users, or whether such inconvenience was merely liable to occur. In England, it has been held that actual inconvenience must result.[1] It is submitted that this authority might not be followed in Scotland given, for example, the attitude to actual danger in s 2 cases[2] although this will change once s 3ZA comes into force – see 2.10.4 below.

The test to be applied in all cases is whether the particular course of driving proved in the circumstances, demonstrates that the driver was or was not exercising the degree of care, skill and attention which the reasonable, competent and prudent driver could be reasonably expected to show in the circumstances;[3] driving without reasonable consideration for others involves carelessness.

The same general approach is applied whether the driver is alleged to have driven without due care and attention or without reasonable consideration for other persons using the road. The test as to whether a particular course of driving contravenes this section of the Act therefore involves the application of an objective and fixed standard, which means that the same requirements are imposed on all drivers irrespective of their status, capacity and experience. For example, no distinction is drawn, for the purpose of this section, between a learner driver and a qualified driver.[4]

However, the tests are applied to the facts and circumstances of each case and it therefore follows that it may be appropriate in certain situations to take into account variable factors such as weather and traffic conditions. Driving carelessly, or without reasonable consideration for others, may arise whether the driving complained of was deliberate or unintentional. It is not necessary for there to have been a collision between two vehicles, or contact between a vehicle and some other person or thing, for careless driving to be established; charges may be brought where, for example, the conduct of the accused on the road requires another motorist or road user to take evasive or emergency action. Equally, the fact that two vehicles have been in collision does not necessarily mean that either or both have been guilty of careless driving. Driving deliberately embarked upon to harass or intimidate other motorists or road users may found a contravention of the section.

1   *Dilkes v Bowman Shaw* [1981] RTR 4.
2   Eg *O'Toole v McDougall* 1986 SCCR 56.
3   *Wilson v MacPhail* 1991 SCCR 170.
4   *McCrone v Riding* [1938] 1 All ER 157.

2.10.4 Section 3ZA: Meaning of careless, or inconsiderate, driving

Section 30 of the Road Safety Act 2006 introduced a new s 3ZA to the Road Traffic Act 1988 which is an attempt at clarification. It is in the following terms.

'**3ZA Meaning of careless, or inconsiderate, driving**

(1)   This section has effect for the purposes of sections 2B and 3 above and section 3A below.

(2)   A person is to be regarded as driving without due care and attention if (and only if) the way he drives falls below what would be expected of a competent and careful driver.

(3)   In determining for the purposes of subsection (2) above what would be expected of a careful and competent driver in a particular case, regard shall be had not only to the circumstances of which he could be expected to be aware but also to any circumstances shown to have been within the knowledge of the accused.

(4)   A person is to be regarded as driving without reasonable consideration for other persons only if those persons are inconvenienced by his driving.'

From the Scottish perspective subsection (3) might be seen as arguably allowing greater subjectivity than has previously been understood while subsection (4) shifts the position to the English approach to inconvenience. See 2.10.3 above.

2.10.5 Car telephone cases

In *MacPhail v Haddow*[1] a driver drove off from traffic lights and round a corner while using a car telephone. It was held that no offence had taken place, as no danger or inconvenience was caused to any other road user, and there appeared to be no opportunity for such danger or inconvenience to arise during the course of the journey observed. However, in *Rae v Friel*[2] it was held that where a driver overtook five vehicles at speed while operating his car telephone, he would have been unable to react appropriately to any danger or emergency that arose. Reference may also be made to *Stock v Carmichael*.[3]

While still relevant to careless driving cases the bulk of telephone cases would now be brought under the specific offences created in relation to

---

1   *MacPhail v Haddow* 1990 SCCR 339.
2   *Rae v Friel* 1992 SCCR 688 (distinguishing *MacPhail v Haddow*).
3   *Stock v Carmichael* 1993 SCCR 136.

use of mobile phones[1] – see 7.12.17 below – although it is to be noted that the use of a telephone may also support a common law charge of culpable and reckless conduct.[2]

2.11 CHARGES

In a charge of dangerous driving under the earlier legislation, it was held to be competent for the prosecution to allege that the motorist had committed the offence while suffering from a nervous disorder aggravated by the consumption of alcohol.[3] However, in a case of careless driving, it is not competent to include in the complaint a reference to the effect that the victim has been killed as a result of the driving complained of.[4] In *Sharp v HM Advocate 1987*,[5] the appeal court said it was wrong for a Sheriff to take into account the fatal consequences of a piece of careless driving in considering sentence. However, it is relevant to consider (and libel) other consequences of driving, such as a collision or the vehicle leaving the roadway in order to determine whether the driving was dangerous or careless.[6]

There is no limit to the number of charges which may be included in a complaint, as long as these charges represent distinct and different offences and each can individually be proved on the evidence.[7] It is competent to libel the two alternative offences described in s 3.[8]

No complaint should contain any charge which reveals that the accused has been disqualified by a court order or has any previous convictions.[9] A necessary and solitary exception to this rule is made only in charges of driving or obtaining a licence while disqualified in terms of s 103 of the Road Traffic Act 1988.[10] Reference should also be made to 2.3.3 above.

---

1   Road Vehicles (Construction and Use) Regulations 1986 (SI 1986/1078), reg 110 added by Road Vehicles (Construction and Use) (Amendment) (No 4) Regulations 2003 (SI 2003/2695), reg 2.
2   *Robertson v Klos* 2006 SCCR 52.
3   *Burrell v Hunter* 1956 SLT (Sh Ct) 75.
4   *McCallum v Hamilton* 1986 JC 1, 1986 SLT 156, 1985 SCCR 368.
5   *Sharp v HM Advocate* 1987 SCCR 179.
6   *McCallum v Hamilton* 1986 JC 1, 1986 SLT 156, 1985 SCCR 368; *Mundie v Cardle* 1991 SCCR 118.
7   *Archibald v Keiller* 1931 JC 34, 1931 SLT 560; *Harris v Adair* 1947 JC 116, 1947 SLT 356.
8   *Archibald v Keiller* 1931 JC 1, 1986 SLT 156, 1985 SCCR 368.
9   Criminal Procedure (Scotland) Act 1995, ss 101 and 166.
10   See, for example, *Moffat v Smith* 1983 SCCR 392.

2.12 EVIDENCE: GENERAL RULES

Each case of driving carelessly or without consideration for other road users depends ultimately on its own facts and circumstances. However, there are a number of reported decisions which afford some general assistance by illustrating general rules. Some of these decisions are civil cases.

A driver who makes a signal for a manoeuvre which may lead to another person on the road observing and acting upon that signal may be under a duty to see that his signal has been appreciated and understood by that other person.[1] A motorist who signals to turn and then drives straight on and collides with another vehicle which had relied on that signal may be guilty of careless driving in respect that the other driver was entitled to rely on his false signal.[2] A driver who follows another driver on the road is bound, in so far as is reasonably practicable, to adopt a position on the road and to drive in such a fashion that will allow him to deal successfully with all traffic exigencies reasonably to be anticipated, particularly in relation to the vehicle in front.[3] If a driver turns right into the path of an overtaking car, the test to be applied is whether he ought to have seen the overtaking vehicle.[4] Where a vehicle has skidded, this is not necessarily by itself evidence of carelessness on the part of the driver; however, the skid may well be a factor which has to be considered in all the circumstances of the case.[5] In circumstances where a vehicle went off a stretch of road, then travelled for 120 feet along the roadside verge and thereafter collided with a rock face, it was held, on appeal, that there was on the face of such objective facts, evidence of faulty driving.[6] There is no general rule of law to the effect that a driver requires to drive at night at a speed that will enable him to stop within the limit of vision supplied by his headlights.[7]

If the evidence establishes that traffic lights are showing green in one direction then the court may be entitled, in the absence of any evidence to the contrary, and if it is shown that the light system is working properly, to assume that the traffic lights showing the other way are at red.[8]

1   *Sorrie v Robertson* 1944 JC 95, 1944 SLT 332.
2   *Another v Probert* [1968] Crim LR 564.
3   *Brown & Lynn v Western SMT Ltd* 1945 SC 31.
4   *Millar v Dean* 1976 SCCR Supp 134.
5   *McGregor v Dundee Corpn* 1962 SC 15; *Thomson v Brankin* 1968 SLT (Sh Ct) 2; *Crawford v O'Donnell* 1999 SCCR 39.
6   *Pagan v Fergusson* 1976 SLT (Notes) 44; see also *Ryrie v Campbell* 1964 JC 33.
7   *Morris v Luton Corpn* 1946 KB 114.
8   *Pacitti v Copeland* 1963 SLT (Notes) 52.

However there must be evidence to support this conclusion.[1] There may be circumstances where the driver on a major road may have to take into account the conduct of the driver on a minor road, if the conduct of the latter indicates that he is about to drive his vehicle in such a manner as will affect the driving of the vehicle on the main road, and the driver on the main road has reasonable opportunity to accommodate such interference.[2] This case is of particular interest in this area because in the course of his opinion Lord Robertson considered in detail a number of earlier authorities on the respective duties of drivers on major and minor roads.

Where a driver drove off on his lorry despite the fact that children were playing thereon, he was found guilty of careless driving although not of reckless driving.[3] Again, where the driver of a large articulated vehicle reversed slowly along a road without assistance, using only his mirrors, in an area where he was aware children were playing, and ran over one of the children, he was found guilty of careless driving because he had reversed without having clear vision to the rear, or assistance to allow him to reverse safely. This decision was reached notwithstanding that the lorry was showing a variety of lights, including hazard lights[4]

The ordinary tests which apply to all cases of careless driving apply to a police officer answering an emergency call.[5] The same considerations apply to the driver of an ambulance or others engaged in emergency work although the nature of the work may well be reflected in sentence.[6]

It is not necessary in any charge under s 3 that a collision should have occurred as result of the way in which the offending vehicle has been driven. Moreover, the fact that there has been a collision between the two vehicles does not thereby imply that one of them is necessarily guilty of an offence of careless driving. However, it must be remembered that the facts and circumstances surrounding any particular course of driving may justify the inference that an offence under s 3 has been committed.

---

1   *Inwar v Normand* 1997 SCCR 6.
2   *Ramage v Hardie* 1968 SLT (Notes) 54.
3   *McDonald v Thomson* (1954) 70 Sh Ct Rep 288.
4   *Farquhar v McKinnon* 1986 SCCR 524, followed in *McCrone v Normand* 1989 SLT 332, 1988 SCCR 551.
5   *Wood v Richards* [1977] RTR 201; *Marshall v Osmond* [1983] 2 QB 1034, [1983] 2 All ER 225.
6   *R v Lundt-Smith* [1964] 2 QB 167, [1964] 2 WLR 1063, [1964] 3 All ER 255; *Husband v Russell* 1998 SLT 377, 1997 SCCR 592. In the latter case the driver was given an absolute discharge.

Further, even where there are no eye-witnesses, the facts surrounding an incident may entitle the court to conclude that careless driving has taken place.[1]

For other cases of careless driving for general purposes, see *King v Cardle;*[2] *Sigourney v Douglas;*[3] *Holmes v Stewart;*[4] *Dunlop v Allan;*[5] *Melville v Lockhart;*[6] *McCrone v Normand;*[7] *Brunton v Lees*[8] and *Husband v Russell.*[9]

2.13 HIGHWAY CODE

As in the case of dangerous driving, one of the most easily recognised tests of whether the driving in any particular case has been careless can be ascertained by reference to the provisions of the Highway Code. Section 38 of the Road Traffic Act 1988 provides that failure to observe the Highway Code may tend to establish liability for careless driving.[10] Equally, as in the case of dangerous driving, the fact that the motorist has violated any of the provisions of the Highway Code does not necessarily mean that he should be prosecuted, and if he is prosecuted does not necessarily mean that he should be convicted.

The Highway Code is published by The Stationery Office, and copies of the Code and other driving publications can be purchased at its outlets and some bookshops.

2.14 COMMON LAW

At common law, any reckless conduct which causes injury or inherent danger is criminal.[11] Accordingly the reckless driving of a vehicle may be

---

1   *Ryrie v Campbell* 1964 JC 33; *Pagan v Fergusson* 1976 SLT (Notes) 44.
2   *King v Cardle* 1981 SCCR 22.
3   *Sigourney v Douglas Sigourney v Douglas* 1981 SCCR 302.
4   *Holmes v Stewart* 1983 SCCR 446.
5   *Dunlop v Allan* 1984 SCCR 329.
6   *Melville v Lockhart* 1985 SCCR 242.
7   *McCrone v Normand* 1989 SLT 332, 1988 SCCR 551.
8   *Brunton v Lees* 1993 SCCR 98.
9   *Husband v Russell* 1997 SCCR 592.
10 See, eg, *McCrone v Normand* 1989 SLT 332, 1988 SCCR 551
11 *HM Advocate v Harris* 1993 JC 150, 1993 SLT 963, 1993 SCCR 559, overruling *Quinn v Cunningham* 1956 JC 22, 1956 SLT 55, which had held that any such reckless conduct had to be to the danger of the lieges. See also *Robertson v Klos* 2006 SCCR 52.

an offence and such a charge may be used, for example, where it cannot be proved that the driving took place on a road or other public place.

Offences affecting or relating to traffic on the public roads are not confined to statutory offences. In *MacPhail v Clark*,[1] a farmer was charged at common law with culpable negligence and causing danger to the lieges by recklessly endangering the safety and lives of the occupants of two vehicles travelling on a road next to his farm. The accused had set fire to a quantity of straw, causing thick smoke to drift across the road so that the drivers of the two vehicles, whose vision was obscured, collided. It was held that this was a relevant charge and the accused was convicted and fined.

Driving a vehicle in a disorderly manner likely to create alarm or annoyance may constitute a breach of the peace; also a driver may be charged with assault if he uses his vehicle in a way that constitutes an attack on another person.

2.15 DEFENCES

As in the case of offences under ss 1 and 2 of the Road Traffic Act 1988, the court must always take into account, in assessing whether or not the driving complained of was careless, any explanation tendered by the driver or any other person.

Defences are sometimes raised on the ground that the accused driver was confronted by an untoward incident or unforeseen emergency. Examples of such incidents are that the accused was dazzled by the headlights of an oncoming vehicle, was confronted suddenly by some vehicle, person or object which unexpectedly came into his path, or was stung by a wasp. As in the case of convictions, all such defences depend for their success on a consideration of all the material facts and circumstances. It is submitted that such defences can only succeed when it is shown that the unforeseen circumstances deprived the driver of control or vision and led directly to the accident or other consequences of the driving. Even if it is shown that some sudden or unexpected emergency occurred, the driver still has a duty thereafter, in so far as is reasonably practicable, to drive his vehicle with reasonable care; such emergencies will not necessarily excuse all further driving actions on the part of the driver. Further, it is submitted that an unforeseen emergency brought about by the driver's own negligence, such as carelessly dropping a lighted cigarette into his lap, or stepping on the accelerator rather than the brake, will render a defence of unforeseen emergency extremely difficult to establish. Any

1   *MacPhail v Clark* 1983 SLT (Sh Ct) 37.

contribution to the unforeseen emergency by the accused will therefore proportionately reduce the effectiveness of any such defence. Where a motorist has been placed in a position of emergency or difficulty through circumstances outwith his control, he may be able to argue in his defence that in effect the standard of driving reasonably expected of him in the circumstances is lower than would normally be the case.[1] Reference should also be made to the paragraph on defences to charges of dangerous driving (see 2.5 above) which are also relevant to charges of careless or inconsiderate driving; and also to 3.10 below.

As stated already the driver of an emergency vehicle is not in a special position;[2] however in such a case there may be particular scope for mitigation.[3]

2.16 SECTION 2B: CAUSING DEATH BY CARELESS, OR INCONSIDERATE, DRIVING

Tried on indictment, five years' imprisonment, or a fine or both, obligatory disqualification (or 3–11 points)

Tried summarily, 12 months' imprisonment, statutory maximum fine or both, obligatory disqualification (or 3–11 points)

Section 2B of the Road Traffic Act 1988 is in the following terms:

> **'2B Causing death by careless, or inconsiderate, driving**
>
> A person who causes the death of another person by driving a mechanically propelled vehicle on a road or other public place without due care and attention, or without reasonable consideration for other persons using the road or place, is guilty of an offence.'

Section 24 of the Road Traffic Offenders Act 1988 allows for alternative verdicts under the new s 2B in prosecutions under ss 1 and 3A of the Road Traffic Act. A s 3 conviction will also be an alternative verdict in a s 2B prosecution.

This is a controversial addition and appears to be in response to press and political interest in fatal road traffic incidents. The issue of causation discussed at 2.3.2, and, in relation to s 3ZB at 8.2.4 below, may become much more important and worthy of careful investigation in such cases.

---

1   *Johnston v National Coal Board* 1960 SLT (Notes) 84.
2   Except in the case of adhering to the speed limits: see the RTRA 1984, s 87.
3   *Husband v Russell* 1997 SCCR 592; 2.12 above.

Sentencing will be particularly difficult given the general approach is to reflect the degree of culpability involved – as might be been in s 3A cases – as opposed to the degree of harm. This offence approaches matters from the other direction and if considered in other aspects of life might be seen as Orwellian.

The guidelines from the Sentencing Guidelines Council in England for 'Causing Death by Driving' are reproduced in Appendix E. They have been referred to regularly in Scotland.[1]

2.17 DUTY TO GIVE NAME

See 2.6 above.

PART 3
CYCLING OFFENCES

2.18 OVERVIEW

Whilst cyclists are usually seen as on the receiving end of the dangerous or careless driving of others, the increasing number of cyclists now using roads, and pavements, inevitably means that the misconduct of some is becoming more apparent.

Traditionally, criminal charges have involved breach of local byelaws for riding on the pavement, carrying more than one person under s 24 of the RTA 1988, going through red lights under s 36 or occasionally furious cycling.

However, following the interest provoked south of the border in 2017 by the case of Charlie Alston, who was sentenced to 18 months in custody after being convicted of wanton and furious driving under the 1861 Offences Against the Person Act (having been acquitted of a charge of manslaughter), a consultation process has begun to consider introducing new crimes of causing death by dangerous and careless cycling, conceivably with similar penalties to s 1 and s 2B.

Whether that happens remains to be seen. Meantime, common law charges, for example culpable and reckless conduct, or even culpable homicide, would seem the most obvious option in a serious case. Certainly,

---

1   See eg, *HM Advocate v Noche* [2011] HCJAC 108; *HM Advocate v McKay* 2011 SLT 250; and *HM Advocate v McCourt* [2013] HCJAC 114. 2014 JC 94; 2013 SLT 1081; 2013 SCCR 646.

the current provisions under the Road Traffic Act 1988 are inadequate for such a purpose.[1]

2.19 DANGEROUS CYCLING (S 28)

Tried summarily, level 4 fine

It is an offence to ride a cycle dangerously on a road.[2] The term 'dangerously' has the same meaning as in s 2 of the Road Traffic Act 1988.[3] The word 'cycle' is defined at 1.6.7 above, and the word 'road' is defined at 1.8.2 above. Sections 167 and 168 of the 1988 Act apply in respect of such charges. Cycling at night without lights is an obvious example.

The notice of intended prosecution provisions apply to prosecutions under s 28.[4] The alternative verdict to a charge of dangerous cycling is careless cycling.[5]

2.20 CARELESS CYCLING (S 29)

Tried summarily, level 3 fine

It is an offence to drive a cycle on a road carelessly or without reasonable consideration for other persons using the road.[6] The terms 'without due care and attention' and 'without reasonable consideration for other persons using the road' have the same meaning as in motor vehicle offences.[7] An obvious example might be ignoring traffic signals though this could equally fall under dangerous cycling or a non-endorsable s 36 offence depending on the circumstances. The word 'cycle' is defined at 1.6.7 above, and the word 'road' is defined at 1.8.2 above. Sections 167 and 168 of the Road Traffic Act 1988 apply in respect of such charges.[8] The notice of intended prosecution provisions apply to prosecutions under s 29.[9]

---

1   See also 3.19 below for drink-related cycle offences.
2   RTA 1988, s 28 as amended by the RTA 1991, s 7.
3   See 2.3.2 above.
4   RTOA 1988, s 1.
5   RTOA 1988, s 24(1).
6   RTA 1988, s 29.
7   See 2.11.2 and 2.11.3 above.
8   See 2.6 above.
9   RTOA 1988, s 1.

Chapter 3

Drink and drug related offences

PART 1
INTRODUCTION AND SPECIAL DEFINITIONS

3.1 INTRODUCTION

Sections 4–11 of the Road Traffic Act 1988 (as amended by the Road Traffic Act 1991) deal with drinking and driving offences. These sections have generated a considerable number of reported cases and this area of law in particular is constantly being considered and revised, all the more so given the divergence of approach to drink drive levels introduced in December 2014 by the Road Traffic Act 1988 (Prescribed Limit) (Scotland) Regulations 2014 (SSI 2014/328).

There is sometimes a marked difference in the development of case law in Scotland as distinct from England. For example, there have been a number of English cases following upon *DPP v Warren*,[1] which was concerned with what a police officer should tell a driver about whether there are any medical reasons for not giving blood samples for analysis after arrest. These cases have wrestled with a number of problems which have simply not troubled the Scottish courts to anything like the same extent.[2] Drinking and driving offences are among the most numerous of contested cases dealt with in the Sheriff and Justice of the Peace Courts, and are usually regarded as the most important and contentious of road traffic matters.

---

1   *DPP v Warren* [1993] AC 319, [1992] 4 All ER 865, [1992] WLR 884, [1993] RTR 58.
2   See *McLeod v McFarlane* 1993 SLT 782.

Cases are normally taken on summary complaint. The penalties available are found in Sch 2 to the Road Traffic Offenders Act 1988 Reference should be made to 2.3.3 above for conclusions of evidence.

3.2 GENERAL

3.2.1 General scheme

It is helpful to have a general overall view of these eight important sections of the Road Traffic Act 1988. As noted already, since s 22 of the Scotland Act 2012 came into effect on 3 July 2012, amending ss 8 and 11 of the Road Traffic Act 1988, 'the prescribed limit' and the making of regulations are matters for the Scottish ministers.

Section 3A (which was introduced by s 3 of the Road Traffic Act 1991) makes it an offence to cause the death of another person by careless driving when the driver (1) is at the material time unfit to drive through drink or drugs, (2) is above the permitted level in respect of a sample of breath, blood or urine, (3) has in his body a specified controlled drug and the proportion of it in blood or urine exceeds the specified limit,[1] (4) fails to provide a specimen for analysis in terms of s 7 within 18 hours, or (5) fails to provide a specimen of blood as required under s 7A.

Section 4 makes it an offence to drive or attempt to drive, or to be in charge, of a motor vehicle on a road or in a public place while unfit to drive through drink or drugs. In s 4 prosecutions there does not have to be any specimen taken for analysis from the motorist, although such specimens may properly be required during the police investigation of such a case. An offence under this section occurs simply if, in the judgment of others formed at the relevant time, the driver's ability to drive properly is for the time being impaired. It is not therefore necessary, for conviction, to establish the precise level of alcohol or drugs in the accused driver. This section is the only one available meantime (see s 3A above and s 5A below and at 3.18) to the prosecution in respect of a charge of driving while affected by drugs. While technology exists, and has been introduced in England and Wales, which can determine whether various drugs and their levels are present in the system of a motorist, the position remains that there is no approved device for testing for drugs in Scotland. While this was anticipated sometime in 2019, according to an announcement by the then Cabinet Secretary for Justice, Michael Matheson, on 21 April

---

1   Added by Crime and Courts Act 2013 c 22 Sch 22 para 2(2) (1 March 2018: insertion has effect subject to savings and transitional provisions as specified in 2013 c 22 s 15 and Sch 8; as SI2018-161 art 2).

2017, progress seems slow; and in relation to drug driving, Scotland is not 'at the forefront of efforts across the UK'.

Section 5 makes it an offence for a person to drive or attempt to drive, or to be in charge of, a motor vehicle on a road or other public place after consuming so much alcohol that the proportion in his breath, blood or urine exceeds the prescribed limit. This offence is therefore established following the taking of such specimens from the driver.

Section 5A[1] introduces a new offence of 'Driving or being in charge of a motor vehicle with concentration of specified controlled drug above specified limit'. This is in response to the difficulty in establishing impairment under s 4 and the increasing number of accidents caused by those under the influence of controlled drugs and the anticipation is that the limit may be set as low as zero. That, in Scottish terms, will be a matter for the Scottish Government, as will the specification of drugs affected under the section. The new section will lead to amendment of other associated provisions, namely ss 3A, 6C(1), 6D and 10. However, nothing has been achieved thus far, despite much progress south of the border where 'drugalsyers' were introduced in 2015.

Sections 6 and 6A–6C of the Act as substituted now make general provision for preliminary breath, impairment, or drug tests to be required of drivers by a police officer as a first step to further procedure.[2] Section 6D, as amended, relates to arrest, and now detention, in Scotland only.

Sections 7 and 7A[3] of the Act provides in detail for the provision of specimens of breath, blood or urine for analysis in the course of an investigation as to whether a person has committed an offence under s 3A, s 4, s 5 and now s 5A.

It should be noted that the Court of Appeal has repeatedly held, post *Cadder*, that there is no right of access to a solicitor in these preliminary procedures.[4]

Section 8[5] now simply provides that the lower of the two specimens given is to be used. The familiar provision that if that lower specimen contains not more than 50 microgrammes (changed to 31 microgrammes

1   Added by Crime and Courts Act 2013 (c 22), Pt 3, s 56(1).
2   As substituted by the Railways and Transport Safety Act 2003 which introduced new ss 6–6D so far as Scotland is concerned.
3   Added by Police Reform Act 2002 (c 30), Pt 4 c 2, s 56(1) and as subsequently amended by the Deregulation Act 2015 c 20 Sch 11(1) para 1(1) (10 April 2015).
4   XJ275/12 *Luke v PF Edinburgh* 28 August 2012, following earlier decisions in cases of *Guthrie* and *Black* (unreported).
5   As amended by Scotland Act 2012 (c 11), Pt 2, s 20(4) (3 July 2012).

once the new drink levels were introduced) of alcohol in 100 millilitres of blood, then the motorist may require that it be replaced by a specimen taken in terms of s 7(4), was repealed in 2015.

Section 9 contains special provisions for hospital patients in respect of the tests that may be required under ss 6 and 7.

Section 10 allows the police to detain any person required to give a specimen of breath or blood or urine, at a police station, until it appears that such a person would no longer be contravening s 4, s 5 or s 5A.

Section 11 is an interpretation section relating to ss 3A–10.[1] In addition, ss 15 and 16 of the Road Traffic Offenders Act 1988[2] contain significant evidential provisions relating to ss 3A, 4, 5 and 5A of the Road Traffic Act 1988.

3.2.2 General procedure

It is still envisaged that the first step in normal circumstances will be the requirement by a constable for a motorist to take one of the three preliminary tests provided for in ss 6A–6C.

–   Section 6A reflects what was known as the roadside test for alcohol, and is carried out by the motorist blowing into an approved device. The current Breath Test Device Approval Order lists all the approved devices currently available, and is described in Appendix B.

–   Section 6B, the preliminary impairment test, reflects assessment for unfitness either through drink or drugs.

–   Section 6C allows for up to three preliminary drugs test using an approved device to test sweat or saliva.

Thereafter the Act envisages that the principal method of procedure (other than in cases under ss 3A(1)(a), 4 and 5A will be the provision of a breath specimen for analysis by an accused driver. Blood or urine specimens can be taken at either a police station or a hospital, the former subject to the provisions of s 7(3) which include suspicion of an offence under ss 3A, 4 and 5A where medical advice suggests impairment due to drugs.

The current legislation places little emphasis on procedural, technical or formal requirements which were the subject of many reported decisions

---

1   See the RTA 1991, Sch 4 para 44 and as amended by Scotland Act 2012, Pt 2, s 20(7).
2   As amended by RTA 1991, Sch 4 para 87.

under previous law. It must be emphasised that the provision of a positive breath test in terms of s 6 and the arrest of the accused driver is not now a prerequisite before a specimen of blood, breath or urine may be required for the purpose of establishing whether an offence has been committed in terms of s 3A(b), 4 or 5.

3.3 SPECIAL DEFINITIONS

3.3.1 Introduction

Sections 3A(1)(a), 4(1), 5(1)(a) and 5A(1)(a) of the Road Traffic Act 1988 contemplate an offence where a person drives or attempts to drive a mechanically propelled vehicle or a motor vehicle on a road or other public place. Sections 4(2), 5(1)(b) and 5A(1)(b) of the Act provide that an offence may occur if a person is in charge of a mechanically propelled vehicle or a motor vehicle which is on a road or other public place. The definition chapter (ch 1) provides general descriptions of the various terms used in ss 4 and 5, but in addition, for the purpose of these drink driving offences, special consideration has to be given to the words and phrases 'drives', 'attempts to drive', 'in charge of a motor vehicle' and 'road or other public place'.

3.3.2 'Drives'

The reported cases in recent years dealing with the question of whether a person is or is not driving in the context of prosecutions under ss 4 and 5, or their historical equivalents, have been concerned principally with three particular issues: firstly, whether, in the proven circumstances of the case, a motorist was driving or not; secondly, whether the motorist was driving, as opposed to being in charge of, the vehicle; and thirdly, whether a driver in the circumstances was to be regarded as still driving his vehicle or whether his driving had come to an end.

On the first question, as to whether a person is to be held as driving a vehicle as opposed to not driving it, the position for all practical purposes is as outlined in the definition chapter under the heading 'Drivers and driving' (see 1.7.1 above). This means that a person will generally be held to be the driver of a vehicle if he is in the driving seat or in control of the steering wheel, and in addition has some measure of control over the propulsion of the vehicle.[1] More than one person may be driving the

---

1   *Ames v McLeod* 1969 JC 1; *McArthur v Valentine* 1990 JC 146, 1990 SLT 732, 1989 SCCR 704 *Hoy v McFadyen* 2000 SCCR 877.

vehicle at a particular time.[1] The driver of a towed vehicle was convicted of driving while disqualified in *McQuaid v Anderton*.[2] Despite what was said in *Wallace v Major*,[3] there appears to be no reason why the driver of a towed vehicle should not be convicted of any offence arising out of s 3A, 4, 5 or 5A of the Road Traffic Act 1988.

A passenger was convicted in *Valentine v Mackie*[4] of aiding and abetting a driver with excess alcohol in his blood. In *Farrell v Stirling*[5] (a summary case) a driver was held not to be driving at the time he experienced a totally unexpected attack of hypoglycaemia.

It has also been held in England that to pedal a moped is driving, even though the engine was not operating or operational;[6] the moped did not cease to be a motor vehicle merely because there was, or might have been, a temporary loss of engine power.

The second category of cases involving drinking and driving, in which the nature of the driving has been in issue, is concerned with whether the motorist was at the material time driving, as opposed to being in charge. A complaint may libel an offence in the alternative; that is to say, the driver may be charged with driving or alternatively being in charge of a vehicle in contravention of either of these sections. Having regard to the difference in penalties that may be imposed in respect of these alternatives, the distinction between driving and being in charge of a vehicle remains of importance. Accordingly, reference should be made to 1.7.1 above and this paragraph for consideration of the nature of driving, and reference should be made to 3.3.4 below for consideration of what is involved in being in charge. There appears as yet to be no Scottish authority dealing specifically with the distinction between driving and being in charge; the matter is generally one of fact which will be determined by the circumstances in each particular case.

The third question involving the nature of driving, which the courts have considered in the past was whether a driver in the proven circumstances of the case was to be considered as still in the course of his journey, and therefore driving his vehicle, or whether his driving was to be regarded as having come to an end. Under previous legislation, the

1   *Tyler v Whatmore* [1976] RTR 83; *Langman v Valentine* [1952] 2 All ER 803; RTA 1988, s 192(1).
2   *McQuaid v Anderton* [1980] RTR 371 (followed in *Caise v Wright* [1981] RTR 49).
3   *Wallace v Major* 1946 KB 473 (at 477 per LJC Goddard).
4   *Valentine v Mackie* 1980 SLT (Sh Ct) 122.
5   *Farrell v Stirling* 1975 SLT (Sh Ct) 71.
6   *Floyd v Bush* [1953] 1 WLR 242, [1953] 1 All ER 265; *R v Tahsin* [1970] RTR 88.

roadside breathalyser test could only be required of a motorist by a police constable if the constable had reasonable cause to suspect that the motorist had alcohol in his body while the vehicle was in motion and before the motorist had completed his journey. This issue was at the centre of a large number of cases decided between 1972 and 1983.[1] Apart from the question of whether there is reasonable cause for suspicion, these cases now have only marginal relevance, if any, because of the current terms of s 6(3)–(5), as substituted, of the 1988 Act.

In terms of s 6(3), a preliminary test may be required of a person who 'has been driving, attempting to drive or in charge of a motor vehicle on a road or other public place while having alcohol or a drug in his body or while unfit to drive because of a drug, and in terms of s 6(4) where a person 'is or has been driving, attempting to drive or in charge of a motor vehicle on a road or other public place, and has committed a traffic offence while the vehicle was in motion, and where in terms of s 6(5) 'an accident occurs owing to the presence of a motor vehicle on a road or other public place, and a constable reasonably believes that the person was driving, attempting to drive or in charge of the vehicle at the time of the accident'.

It is therefore clear from the terms of the subsections that the question of whether a police officer makes the requirement for a breath test while the motorist is still engaged on his journey, or whether he has completed his journey and is no longer driving, is now entirely academic.[2] The section was specifically framed to exclude the defence, available to a driver before 1983, that he had completed his journey, and therefore could not thereafter be suspected of having alcohol in his body and thus be required to take a breath test. To underline this, the current legislation imposes no time limit of any kind on the right of a police constable in appropriate circumstances to require a roadside breathalyser specimen, except in the case of prosecutions under s 3A(1)(c) of the Road Traffic Act 1988.

Whether a driver can be said to have driven to a place where he is found will depend upon an examination of the facts and circumstances.[3]

3.3.3 Attempting to drive

In terms of ss 4(1), 5(1)(a) and 5A(1)(a) of the Road Traffic Act 1988, it is a separate offence to attempt to drive a motor vehicle while affected

---

1   Eg, *Edkins v Knowles* [1973] 1 QB 748, [1973] RTR 257; *Ritchie v Pirie* 1972 JC 7, 1972 SLT 2.
2   And see *Allan v Douglas* 1978 JC 7.
3   Eg *Henderson v Hamilton* 1995 SLT 968; 1995 SCCR 413.

by drink or drugs. The idea of attempting to drive is also relevant to prosecutions under s 6. It would appear to be the intention of the Act that this offence should cover the position when the vehicle is not in motion. The question of whether a motorist is attempting to drive at the material time is one of fact. In this context, the meaning of the word 'drive' has exactly the same meaning as in 'driving' as described in the preceding paragraph. In assessing the proven facts in any case, regard will be had principally to the actions of the driver and, where appropriate, to his intentions, expressed or implied. Thus, even where a car is *de facto* incapable of being driven through mechanical defect, anyone attempting to drive such a vehicle may be convicted under these subsections.[1] Again, someone attempting to start a car with the wrong key is attempting to drive that vehicle;[2] the fact that the attempt failed because of ineptitude, inefficiency or insufficient means does not mean that the attempt to drive was not made.

In terms of s 24(2) and (3) of the Road Traffic Offenders Act 1988 a charge under s 3A of the Road Traffic Act 1988 will not authorise a conviction of attempting to commit the offence, but charges under ss 4(1), 5(1)(a) and 5A(1)(a) will.

Each case will depend on its own circumstances: in *Guthrie v Friel*[3] it was observed that making preparations for driving may not be the same thing as attempting to drive. Someone trying to repair a broken-down vehicle may not be attempting to drive.[4]

Anyone who has been effectively stopped or dissuaded from driving cannot be considered as still being within the category of persons driving a vehicle,[5] or, it is submitted, of persons attempting to drive a vehicle.

Persons found not to be attempting to drive a car as in the foregoing illustrations may still be in charge of their vehicle.

3.3.4 'In charge'

Sections 4(2), 5(1)(b) and 5A(1)(b) of the Road Traffic Act 1988 provide that offences occur when a motorist, having consumed alcohol or drugs, is 'in charge' of, as opposed to driving, or attempting to drive, his vehicle. Being in charge of a vehicle therefore only arises before driving has started

---

1   *R v Farrance* [1978] RTR 225.
2   *Kelly v Hogan* [1982] RTR 352.
3   *Guthrie v Friel* 1993 SLT 899, 1992 SCCR 932.
4   *Ritchie v Pirie* 1972 JC 7, 1972 SLT 2.
5   *Edkins v Knowles* [1973] QB 748 at 757, [1973] 2 WLR 977.

or after it has ceased. In *Crichton v Burrell*,[1] a motorist who was standing beside his vehicle with the keys in his possession, waiting for an employee to come and drive the vehicle, was held to be not in charge. The appeal court in that case held that to be 'in charge' meant that the motorist must be in some measure in *de facto* control of the vehicle. The circumstances of that case would therefore appear to indicate that by standing outwith the vehicle and making arrangements for another to drive, the accused had effectively surrendered control of the vehicle. In such a case, the statutory defence provided by s 4(3), and now s 5A(6), would also now be available to the motorist.

In England the matter was considered in *DPP v Watkins*[2] where the view was taken that no hard and fast all-embracing test could be propounded. If the accused is the owner, lawful possessor, or recent driver, then he will be in charge unless that has been relinquished with no realistic possibility of it resuming. If the accused is not the owner, lawful possessor, or recent driver, the question is whether he has assumed being in charge of it, either by being in de facto control or by the inference that he expected imminently to assume control.[3] In short and as ever it will be a question of fact turning on the particular circumstances of the given case.

Watkins was applied, as was *Crichton v Burrell*, in the Scottish case of *Kelso v Brown*.[4] The appellant's conviction was quashed as he could not be taken to have assumed control of his wife's car after she had left him asleep in the passenger seat. The Court said it could not be satisfied 'that the appellant was voluntarily in de facto control of the car (applying *Watkins*) or that he was responsible for the control of the car (applying *Crichton*). Moreover since the appellant was fast asleep, there is nothing to suggest that he could have been expected immediately to assume control of the car'.

The following are some other examples of Scottish decisions. The supervisor of a learner driver has been held to be in charge of a vehicle.[5] A driver sitting in his vehicle (a taxi) which had broken down and was waiting for another vehicle to tow him away was held to be in charge.[6] A mechanic repairing a broken-down vehicle by the roadside was held

---

1   *Crichton v Burrell* 1951 JC 107, 1951 SLT 365.
2   *DPP v Watkins* [1989] QB 821, [1989] 2 WLR 966, [1989] 1 All ER 1126, [1989] RTR 324, 89 Cr. App R 122.
3   At 831.
4   *Kelso v Brown* 1988 SCCR 278, 1998 SLT 921.
5   *Clark v Clark* 1950 SLT (Sh Ct) 68.
6   *MacDonald v Crawford* 1952 SLT (Sh Ct) 92.

not to be in charge of the vehicle.[1] A person who was unconscious in the back of the vehicle which had been made mechanically incapable of being driven was held not to be in charge of the vehicle.[2] The owner of a vehicle who was sitting in the passenger seat at a time when the vehicle's engine was running and the person in the driver's seat was unlicensed, was held not to be in charge of the vehicle.[3] A driver who left his vehicle and gave a friend the keys to drive the car home was deemed not to be in charge of his vehicle.[4] Reference may also be made to *MacDonald v Bain*;[5] *McDonald v Kubirdas*;[6] *MacDonald v MacDonald*;[7] and *Thaw v Segar*.[8]

It is not a coincidence, however, that all of these authorities pre-date the amended terms of the Road Traffic Act 1972. Although these cases are still relevant, the extended powers now available to the police to require preliminary tests in terms of s 6 means that the occasions when being in charge of a vehicle is of significance will become less frequent. However, cases of being in charge of a vehicle are by no means rare. In *Lees v Lawrie*,[9] a supervisor of a learner driver was held to be in charge of a vehicle, but obtained an acquittal by proving that there was no likelihood of him driving. *Cartmill v Heywood*[10] contains many of the features of a typical case.

3.3.5 'Road or other public place'

In the Road Traffic Act 1988 as originally framed, and in earlier legislation, the vast majority of offences occurred if the conduct complained of took place on 'a road'. The only exceptions were the principal sections of the drink-driving legislation (then ss 4, 5 and 6, and now s 5A). The terms of ss 1, 2 and 3 of the Road Traffic Act 1991 extend the application of a 'road or other public place' to ss 1, 2, 3 and 3A of the 1988 Act. The general position, and definitions of the terms 'road' and 'other public place', are discussed at 1.8.1, 1.8.2 and 1.8.3 above.

---

1   *Adair v McKenna* 1951 SLT (Sh Ct) 40.
2   *Dean v Wishart* 1952 JC 9, 1952 SLT 86.
3   *Winter v Morrison* 1954 JC 7.
4   *Farrell v Campbell* 1959 SLT (Sh Ct) 43, (1959) 75 Sh Ct Rep 24.
5   *MacDonald v Bain* 1954 SLT (Sh Ct) 30.
6   *McDonald v Kubirdas* 1955 SLT (Sh Ct) 50.
7   *MacDonald v MacDonald* 1955 71 Sh Ct Rep 17.
8   *Thaw v Segar* 1962 SLT (Sh Ct) 63.
9   *Lees v Lawrie* 1993 SCCR 1.
10   *Cartmill v Heywood* 2000 SLT 799.

PART 2
CARELESS DRIVING, DRIVING OR BEING IN CHARGE OF A VEHICLE WHEN UNDER THE INFLUENCE OF DRINK OR DRUGS

3.4 SECTION 3A

Tried on indictment, 14 years' imprisonment or a fine or both, obligatory disqualification (or 3–11 points)

3.4.1 Introduction

Section 3A of the Road Traffic Act 1988[1] provides:

'(1) If a person causes the death of another person by driving a mechanically propelled vehicle on a road or other public place without due care and attention, or without reasonable consideration for other persons using the road or place, and –

(a) he is, at the time when he is driving, unfit to drive through drink or drugs, or

(b) he has consumed so much alcohol that the proportion of it in his breath, blood or urine at that time exceeds the prescribed limit, or

(ba) he has in his body a specified controlled drug and the proportion of it in his blood or urine at that time exceeds the specified limit for that drug, or[2]

(c) he is, within 18 hours after that time, required to provide a specimen in pursuance of s 7 of this Act, but without reasonable excuse fails to provide it,

(d) he is required by a constable to give his permission for a laboratory test of a specimen of blood taken from him under section 7A of this Act, but without reasonable excuse fails to do so,

he is guilty of an offence.

(2) For the purposes of this section a person shall be taken to be unfit to drive at any time when his ability to drive properly is impaired.

---

1   Introduced by the RTA 1991, s 3, and as amended by Road Safety Act 2006 (c 49), s 31(2) (24 September 2007).
2   Added by Crime and Courts Act 2013 c 22 Sch 22 para 2(2) (1 March 2018: insertion has effect subject to savings and transitional provisions as specified in 2013 c 22 s15 and Sch 8; as SI2018-161 art 2).

(3) Subsection (1)(b), (ba), (c), and (d) above shall not apply in relation to a person driving a mechanically propelled vehicle other than a motor vehicle.'[1]

This section was introduced in the Road Traffic Act 1991 to meet a perceived need to cover those cases where death results from a course of driving which could not be described as reckless, as opposed to careless, and where the driver has been drinking. Broadly, s 3A contains an amalgam of existing ideas. Care has been taken to incorporate into the new offence the original notions of careless driving, drinking while unfit to drive through drink or drugs, and consumption of so much alcohol that the proportion of it in the breath, blood or urine exceeds the prescribed limit. The only original concept included in this offence is that there is a time limit of 18 hours from the time of the accident after which the requirement to provide a specimen in pursuance of s 7 of the Act cannot be made. In general, identical considerations are to be applied to the various component parts of this section as are relevant to their source in other parts of the legislation.

The addition of the new subsection (ba) reflects the introduction of the new s 5A. Like the other subsections, save (a), proof of impairment is irrelevant, 'although the extent of any actual impairment will still be a relevant consideration'.[2]

The possible penalties for this offence, which mirror the s 1 penalties and likewise must be taken on indictment, include imprisonment for up to 14 years, and obligatory disqualification.[3]

As with s 1 offences the sentencing approach to s 3A offences can be severe to reflect the particular culpability involved in a given case. Reference should be made to the careful consideration of relevant factors discussed in *R v Cooksley*[4] and referred to in this context in Scotland in *HMA v Roulston*.[5] There, the Court observed 'that in certain circumstances an offence under section 3A may be more serious than an offence at the lower end of culpability under section 1'.[6] As with other sections involving death by driving, guidance is now regularly found in the Definitive

1   Amended by Crime and Courts Act 2013 (c 22), Sch 22 para 2.
2   *R v Mohamed* [2018] EWCA Crim 596.
3   RTOA 1988, Sch 2, as amended by the Criminal Justice Act 2003, s 285.
4   *R v Cooksley* [2003] EWCA Crim 996, [2003] 3 All ER 340, [2003] RTR 482, [2003] Cr App R 18 (p 275).
5   *HMA v Roulston* 2005 SCCR 193.
6   At para 19.

Guideline produced by the English Sentencing Guidelines Council, and which are reproduced at Appendix E.

By virtue of the Road Traffic Offenders Act 1988, s 24, as amended, provision is made for alternative verdicts in terms of ss 2B, 3, 4(1), 5(1), 7(6) and 7A(6) to a charge under s 3A. However, unlike charges libelling offences under ss 4(1) and 5(1)(a), a charge under s 3A cannot authorise a finding that the motorist is found guilty of an alternative verdict of attempting to commit the offence.

3.4.2 Definitions – general

'Causes the death'. See 2.3.2 above.

'Driving'. See 1.7.1 and 3.3.2 above.

'Mechanically propelled vehicle'. See 1.2.1ff above.

'Road or other public place'. See 1.8.1, 1.8.2 and 1.8.3 above.

'Driving without due care and attention or without reasonable consideration'. See Ch 2, Pt 2 above.

'Breath, blood or urine exceeding prescribed limit'. See 3.13 *et seq* above.

'Driving while unfit to drive through drink or drugs'. See 3.18 *et seq* above.

'Reasonable excuse'. See 4.14.3 and 4.14.7 below.

'Without due care and attention'. See 2.10ff above.

'Without reasonable consideration'. See 2.10ff above.

'Unfit to drive'. See s 3A(2) of the Road Traffic Act 1988 and 3.6.1 below.

It will be noted that s 3A(3) maintains the difference that exists between mechanically propelled vehicles in s 4 and motor vehicles in ss 5 and 5A; reference should be made to 1.2.1 above.

3.4.3 Defences

Apart from the usual common law defences, (see 3.10 below) the statutory defence contained in s 15(3) of the Road Traffic Offenders Act 1988, as amended by the Road Traffic Act 1991, Sch 4 para 87 and the Crime and Courts Act 2013, Sch 22, is available in prosecutions under s 3A(1) of the Road Traffic Act 1988. This topic is discussed at 3.9.1 and 3.17.1 below; see also Appendix D.

3.5 SECTION 4(1)

Tried summarily, six months' imprisonment or a level 5 fine or both, obligatory disqualification (or 3–11 points)

3.5.1 Introduction

Section 4(1) of the Road Traffic Act 1988[1] provides:

> 'A person who, when driving or attempting to drive a mechanically propelled vehicle on a road or other public place, is unfit to drive through drink or drugs shall be guilty of an offence.'

This section is generally used in cases where for a variety of reasons it is not possible to determine the proportion of alcohol present in the motorist by reference to the analysis of specimens of breath, blood or urine. It may be that the accused is so drunk that he is incapable of being subjected to the various statutory procedures, or that such procedures, for whatever reason, cannot appropriately be carried out in the circumstances. There is a tendency also for prosecutors to use this section in respect of an accused who appears in custody and who wishes to plead guilty; such a charge can be prepared without first having an analyst's report on specimens which may have been provided. However information from the analysis can competently be placed before the court in s 4 prosecutions if available.

Prosecutions under s 4 are normally taken under summary procedure. The penalties following conviction are found in Sch 2 to the Road Traffic Offenders Act 1988 and include obligatory disqualification for a minimum period of one year,[2] endorsement of the licence (with 3–11 penalty points if disqualification is not imposed), a maximum prison sentence of six months and a fine at level 5, or both. Minimum disqualification rises to three years if within the ten years immediately preceding the commission of the offence there has been a conviction for one of the drink related offences set out in s 34(3) of the Road Traffic Offenders Act 1988

As noted at 3.2.1 above, this section currently remains the only practical provision for charging a motorist with driving under the influence of drugs, while the developments already available in England and Wales are awaited.

3.5.2 Definitions – general

'*Driving or attempting to drive*'. See 1.7.1, 3.3.2 and 3.3.3 above.
'*Unfit to drive*'. See 3.6.1 below.
'*Mechanically propelled vehicle*'. See 1.2.1ff above.
'*Road or other public place*'. See 1.8.1, 1.8.2 and 1.8.3 above.

---

1   As amended by RTA 1991, Sch 2 para 8.
2   RTOA 1988, s 34(1).

3.5.3 Special definitions: drink and drugs

In a prosecution under s 4 of the Road Traffic Act 1988, the issue is whether the motorist is unfit to drive through drink or drugs, as distinct from ss 5 and 5A cases where the issue is whether the motorist exceeds the prescribed limits of alcohol in his breath, blood or urine, or the as-yet unspecified levels of specified drugs in the body. Although there is no definition of the word anywhere in the legislation, it has never been disputed that the word 'drink' means an alcoholic drink.[1] The question of what constitutes a drug is also not comprehensively defined in the legislation and prior to 1983 was not defined at all. In *Armstrong v Clark*[2] it was held that insulin was included in the term 'drug', and that a motorist who had taken the correct and prescribed dose of insulin, but still thereafter became unfit to drive as a result, could properly be convicted in terms of s 5(1). However, in the broadly similar case of *Watmore v Jenkins*,[3] the appeal court declined to interfere with an acquittal in such circumstances imposed by a lower court; and in *Farrell v Stirling*,[4] a driver in similar circumstances to the accused in *Armstrong v Clark* was held not to be driving. In *Armstrong v Clark*,[5] the court decided that a 'drug' meant medicine given for the purposes of treating a medical condition. It appears that the court did not intend that this definition should be exhaustive and it is clear that the meaning of the word is not confined to medicines designed to treat some medical conditions. In *Duffy v Tudhope*,[6] the accused drove while under the influence of toluene, which he had inhaled in the course of sniffing glue. The appeal court, following *Bradford v Wilson*,[7] held that as the substance had a drugging effect, it was clearly a drug and the accused could properly be convicted.

Following all of these cases, the Transport Act 1982, s 25(3) and Sch 8[8] introduced the current interpretation provisions now found in s 11 of the Road Traffic Act 1988. Inter alia, these provide that 'a drug includes any intoxicant other than alcohol'.[9] It has never been doubted that the main types of drug contemplated by this section are those substances which are the subject of the Misuse of Drugs Act 1971.

1   See *Armstrong v Clark* [1957] 2 QB 391 at 394 per LJC Goddard.
2   *Armstrong v Clark* [1957] 2 QB 391.
3   *Watmore v Jenkins* [1962] 2 QB 572.
4   *Farrell v Stirling* 1975 SLT (Sh Ct) 71.
5   *Armstrong v Clark* [1957] 2 QB 391.
6   *Duffy v Tudhope* 1984 SLT 107, 1983 SCCR 440.
7   *Bradford v Wilson* [1983] Crim LR 482.
8   Which came into force on 6 May 1983 by virtue of SI 1983/576.
9   RTA 1988, s 11(2), as amended by the RTA 1991, Sch 4 para 44.

3.5.4 Driving under the influence of drugs: general

Prosecutions where the motorist is said to be under the influence of drugs must meantime be taken under s 4 of the Road Traffic Act 1988, though that will obviously change once s 5A comes into play.[1]

The section therefore caters for the effect on the human metabolism of different kinds of drug, whether they are those mentioned in the schedules to the Misuse of Drugs Act 1971 or whether they are other kinds of drugging agents. The precise quantification of any particular drug present in any case is not a process currently available, and there are no established degrees of intoxication related to drug quantities as there are with alcohol. This position seems likely to continue until 2019 at the earliest. There are devices which can detect the presence of drugs in a driver's system. However, it is not enough for the prosecution to show that the driver has ingested drugs; s 4 requires that the accused is shown to be unfit to drive because of the drugs. Whether or not the accused's ability to drive is impaired is always a question of fact, but in the absence of authority it seems to be accepted that the mere presence, particularly of a controlled substance, goes some way to provide the necessary grounds for conviction. The new provisions substituted in s 6B reflect the previous practice of what was called field impairment tests, which were themselves not dissimilar in character to the old tests for drinking and driving, such as walking along a straight line, to allow investigating officers to reach a conclusion on the question of impairment. Effective devices – 'drugalysers' – to be used as part of the s 6C provisions are now in use in England and Wales. In the meantime reference might be made to 3.6.1 below.

3.5.5 Driving under the influence of drugs: special provision

If a constable arrests a motorist because he suspects that he has been driving or attempting to drive or been in charge of a vehicle while under the influence of drink or drugs, in terms of ss 3A, 4, 5 and 5A of the Road Traffic Act 1988, he may require the provision of a blood or urine sample.[2]

These requirements are competent even where the motorist has already provided, or has been required to provide, two specimens of breath for analysis. While no suitable devices currently exist to allow use of s 6C preliminary tests, the position remains that to take advantage of this power of requirement, the police constable must receive medical advice

---

1   Added by Crime and Courts Act 2013 (c 22), Pt 3, s 56(1), and see 3.18 below.
2   RTA 1988, s 7 as amended.

that the motorist's condition might be due to drugs, and cannot opt to require a blood or urine specimen on his own initiative.[1]

3.6 SECTION 4(1): THE TEST

3.6.1 General

The test of unfitness to drive in terms of this subsection is whether the driver's ability to drive properly is for the time being impaired through drink or drugs.[2] The question is one of fact. The kind of evidence which is used to support such a charge, whether of driving or attempting to drive when under the influence of drink or drugs, is usually that of medical examination and tests.[3] General observations of the motorist's conduct may also be relevant to the charge. In *McEwan v Higson*[4] it was held that a Sheriff was entitled to convict on the basis of police observations in circumstances where a doctor found that on examination ability to drive was not impaired but possibly could have been an hour earlier.

Such an approach was mirrored in *Chowdry v PF Glasgow*[5] where the appellant, having been stopped by police officers who detected a strong smell of cannabis in his car, failed four out of five tests in terms of s 6B and was deemed impaired by the police. An hour and a half later he provided a negative breath test and was found to have no clinical evidence of impairment by a police surgeon, although the doctor added that drugs could be in a person's system for a short period of time. The Sheriff was held to be entitled to repel a no case to answer submission and subsequently convict drawing on the inferences from such evidence.

The results of the analysis of specimens of breath, blood or urine taken in terms of other parts of the procedure may also be used. If the accused provides such a specimen of breath, blood or urine, the results of that analysis must in all cases be taken into account and it shall be assumed that the proportion of alcohol in the accused's breath, blood or urine at the time of the alleged offence was not less than in the specimen.[6] However, in terms of s 4(5) the test is whether the ability to drive is impaired, and, accordingly, it is theoretically possible (although perhaps highly unlikely in practice) that a motorist could be acquitted of the charge even where

---

1 RTA 1988, s 7(3)(c)
2 RTA 1988, s 4(5).
3 *Murray v Muir* 1950 SLT 41.
4 *McEwan v Higson* 2001 SCCR 579.
5 XJ297/12 Decision of 14 June 2012.
6 RTOA 1988, s 15(2).

there is evidence that the results of analysis of a blood or other specimen proved to be in excess of what is permitted in terms of s 5 of the Act. In *McNeill v Fletcher*[1] an accused was found to have nearly four times the permitted maximum of alcohol in his blood, he was unsteady on his feet, his eyes were glazed and his breath smelt of alcohol; nonetheless, the police surgeon refused to certify the driver as unfit to drive. On appeal it was held that he was entitled to do so. However, in *Murray v Muir*,[2] the evidence demonstrated that a motorist had driven along a main road without any cause for criticism shortly before being taken for an examination by a police surgeon, and this was held not to create any presumption of sobriety which could not be overcome by medical or other evidence.

In *Reid v Nixon; Dumigan v Brown*,[3] a Full Bench laid down general guidelines which are to be followed in cases where the evidence turns on a medical examination by a police surgeon. As cases might arise out of a great variety of circumstances it was recognised that rigid rules for universal application could not be imposed; however, any departure from these guidelines normally requires to be justified. The procedure to be adopted in terms of the guidelines is as follows.

Firstly, the suspect should be cautioned in the usual way by the police and invited formally to give his consent to a medical examination. If he is not first cautioned without good reason, the medical evidence is inadmissible.[4] The accused should be advised of his right to refuse to consent to such medical examination, and it is proper practice that this intimation should be established by full corroborative evidence, although the evidence of one witness only on this matter has been held to be sufficient.[5] However, the requirement to advise the accused of his right to refuse to consent to medical examination may be rendered unnecessary when the accused specifically states that he has no objection to undergoing such an examination.[6] It should also be made clear to the accused that the results of such examinations and tests may be used in evidence.

Secondly, the accused should be told that he has the right to summon a doctor of his own choice, and given facilities for doing so.[7] However, the police examination is not to be delayed until this other doctor is present.

1   *McNeill v Fletcher* 1966 JC 18.
2   *Murray v Muir* 1950 SLT 41.
3   *Reid v Nixon; Dumigan v Brown* 1948 JC 68, 1948 SLT 295.
4   *Gallacher v HM Advocate* 1963 SLT 217.
5   *Farrell v Concannon* 1957 JC 12, 1957 SLT 60.
6   *Taylor v Irvine* 1958 SLT (Notes) 15.
7   Overruling *Harris v Adair* 1947 JC 116.

Thirdly, the medical examination should normally proceed outwith the presence of the police officers.

Fourthly, any questioning of the accused by the doctor in respect of recent events must be directed solely to testing the accused's memory and coherence and not to eliciting information bearing on his guilt and any such information incidentally obtained must not be communicated by the doctor to the police officers.

Fifthly, if the accused refuses to consent to the examination, his refusal can be spoken to in evidence, and if the police doctor has been summoned, he should confine himself to observing the accused and should not carry out any examination or tests.

Should a medical examination be carried out in the case of a motorist suspected of having ingested drugs, there appears to be no reason why the same general principles should not be applied.

3.6.2 Evidence

In practice, evidence in support of a prosecution under s 4 is usually given by police and medical evidence. However, there is nothing to prevent such cases proceeding on the basis of lay evidence, provided that such testimony is sufficient in quality and quantity to allow the court to conclude beyond reasonable doubt that the accused's ability to drive at the material time had been impaired through drink or drugs. For cases on the sufficiency of evidence in a charge of this kind, see *Wallace v McLeod*,[1] *Kenny v Tudhope*[2] and *McEwan v Higson*.[3] Evidence of the levels of alcohol in a specimen of blood, breath or urine which subsequently becomes available may be referred to.

3.7 SECTION 4(2): IN CHARGE OF A VEHICLE

Tried summarily, three months' imprisonment or a level 4 fine or both, discretionary disqualification or obligatory endorsement by ten points

3.7.1 General

Section 4(2) of the Road Traffic Act 1988[4] provides:

---

1   *Wallace v McLeod* 1986 SCCR 678.
2   *Kenny v Tudhope* 1984 SCCR 290.
3   *McEwan v Higson* 2001 SCCR 579.
4   As amended by the RTA 1991, s 4.

'Without prejudice to subsection (1) above, a person who, when in charge of a mechanically propelled vehicle which is on a road or other public place, is unfit to drive through drink or drugs, is guilty of an offence.'

The subsection is designed to cover the situation when the vehicle in question is not in motion, and when the driver is not in the process of concluding a driving operation, and does not fall into the category of a person attempting to drive the vehicle. Whether a motorist is in charge of his vehicle, as opposed to not being in charge, or as opposed to driving or attempting to drive, is a matter of fact and evidence.

3.7.2 Definitions

'In charge'. See 3.3.4 above.
'Mechanically propelled vehicle'. See 1.2.1ff above.
'Road or other public place'. See 1.8.1, 1.8.2 and 1.8.3 above.
'Unfit to drive'. See 3.6.1 and 3.6.2 above.
'Drink or drugs'. See 3.5.3 above.

3.7.3 Procedure and penalties

Prosecutions under s 4(2) of the Road Traffic Act 1988 are normally taken summarily, and may be charged as an alternative to s 4(1). Penalties are given in Sch 2, Pt I of the Road Traffic Offenders Act 1988. Disqualification is discretionary, and ten penalty points must be endorsed on the licence if disqualification is not imposed. A maximum prison sentence of three months or a fine at level 4 (or both) is available.

3.8 SECTION 4(3): STATUTORY DEFENCE (1): NO LIKELIHOOD OF DRIVING

3.8.1 General

Section 4(3) of the Road Traffic Act 1988[1] provides:

'For the purposes of subsection (2) above, a person shall be deemed not to have been in charge of a mechanically propelled vehicle if he proves that at the material time the circumstances were such that there was no likelihood of his driving it so long as he remained unfit to drive through drink or drugs.'

Section 4(3) therefore provides a statutory defence in prosecutions under s 4(2). A driver will be regarded as not being in charge of a vehicle if he

---

1   As amended by the RTA 1991, s 4.

proves that at the material time there was no likelihood of him driving during the period that he remained unfit to drive through drink or drugs.

There was considerable anticipation that this reverse onus provision – and similar provisions in s 5(2), and also s 15(3) of the Road Traffic Offenders Act 1988 – would meet with the difficulties arising from the presumption of innocence enshrined in Art 6(2) of the European Convention on Human Rights. Ultimately, however, and as with other Human Rights points, the matter was resolved under reference to the legitimate and acceptable object of the legislation which could not be regarded as placing a burden on an accused which either went beyond reasonable limits or was arbitrary.[1]

Whether such a defence can be successfully established will be a question of fact and evidence. Once a *prima facie* case is made out by the prosecution the burden of proof in this defence rests on the accused, and the standard of proof is on the balance of probabilities.[2]

If this standard is not reached, but the defence case in any way casts a reasonable doubt on the guilt of the accused in the circumstances of the case, the accused will be entitled to an acquittal. Where appropriate, this defence may be established by uncorroborated evidence, including testimony from the accused driver himself.

It should be noted, however, that to establish a defence of this kind successfully, the accused requires to demonstrate that there is no likelihood of him driving so long as he is affected by drink or drugs to the extent that his ability to drive is impaired. Put another way, the accused has to establish when his ability to drive would no longer be impaired in addition to showing that there was no likelihood of him driving up to that point. In considering such a defence, the court will have regard to the accused's intentions, express or implied, in the light of all the other facts and circumstances of the case.[3]

That case-specific approach was considered in the conjoined appeals of *Ludriecus v Thomson* and *Orrock v Nisbet*,[4] and guidance issued on the phrase 'no likelihood'. Lord Wheatley, at paragraphs [11] and [12] said:

> '[It] is significant that what the accused has to show, on the balance of probabilities, is that there was no likelihood that he would drive. As the sheriff noted in the first appeal, this is a formidable hurdle for the defence in any case. What section 5(2) does not mean is that the accused merely has to prove that there was a possibility, or even a likelihood, that he would

1   See *Sheldrake v DPP* [UKHL] 43, [2005] RTR 2.
2   *Neish v Stevenson* 1969 SLT 229.
3   *Morton v Confer* [1963] 1 WLR 763, 2 All ER 765.
4   2009 JC 78, 2008 SCCR 996, 2009 SLT 34.

not drive. Nor is the test whether the accused was more likely to drive than not. On the other hand, the accused may not have to exclude the possibility that he might drive; that could set too high a test. That possibility will often be present, and is not necessarily inconsistent with a successful defence. Against the background of these general considerations, it is perhaps not helpful to provide any further description of what is meant by the phrase "no likelihood of driving". Within the context of the ordinary meaning of those words, it will be a matter of fact and circumstances in each individual case as to whether the court can reach that particular conclusion. It is clear however that the test which Parliament had in mind in relation to this defence is a high one.

[12] What in practice the court will have to do therefore, is to come to a view, on all of the evidence before it, as to whether the appellant has shown, on the balance of probabilities, that at the time of committing the offence there was no likelihood that he would have driven whilst he was still over the legal limit. That exercise will normally involve reaching a conclusion on proven facts as to what the appellant was likely to have done. The distinction between speculation and inference can be a narrow one, but it is unquestionably legitimate and necessary, in considering this defence, for the court to examine in a balanced manner all of the facts it finds proved, and to come to a clear and logical conclusion as to what would have happened. It is particularly desirable in this kind of exercise that the court should indicate precisely what facts are accepted and what are not, the reasons why particular facts are accepted or rejected, and the process by which the appropriate conclusion is drawn from the facts which are found to be proved. In the absence of such a comprehensive exercise, there will always be room for the claim that the conclusions reached by the sheriff, in whole or in part, were a result of speculation. In our view, in both cases, the sheriffs have each correctly understood the appropriate test; the question remains as to whether or not they can be said to have properly applied that test to the circumstances of the cases before them.'

Lord Reed, at paragraph [22] put matters slightly differently and observed that 'the critical consideration is the intention underlying the offence created by section 5(1)(b), to which section 5(2) provides a defence'. He then cited Lord Bingham in *Sheldrake*:

'The defendant can exonerate himself if he can show that the risk which led to the creation of the offence did not in his case exist. "No likelihood" cannot, in this context, mean "a probability of less than 0.5", since the defence could then be established in circumstances where there remained a substantial risk that the person would drive the vehicle while unfit: the very risk which led to the creation of the offence in section 5(1)(b). At the same time, particularly in the context of a criminal provision, "no likelihood" should not be interpreted as meaning "a probability of nil", since the offence could then be committed notwithstanding that the risk of the person driving while unfit was fanciful or theoretical. That conclusion is supported by the ordinary use of "no likelihood" in everyday speech, where it usually carries a meaning similar to "no real risk" (eg "I can leave my umbrella at home today since there is no likelihood of rain"). Like Clarke LJ in *Sheldrake* [[2004] QB 487] in the Divisional Court (at para 56), I would interpret "no likelihood" in section 5(2) as meaning no "risk, that is a real risk which ought not to be ignored, of the accused driving while over the limit".'

The importance of properly considering all the evidence in a no likelihood case, and properly explaining the conclusions reached, was emphasised in *Ambrose v Harris*.[1] Having spent two years unsuccessfully challenging the admissibility of replies to the police, the Sheriff's failure to consider the defence properly resulted in the conviction being quashed.

Reference should be made to 3.9.1 below (defence of post-incident consumption of alcohol in terms of the Road Traffic Offenders Act 1988, s 15(3)) for evidential considerations relating to the time when a driver may be said to be no longer unfit to drive.

The circumstances in which a defence under s 4(3) may be presented can conceivably overlap with some of the earlier cases where it was found that an accused was not in charge of the vehicle (see 3.3.2 and 3.3.4 above), and these authorities may be of assistance in determining whether a motorist can demonstrate that he is not likely to drive while affected by drink or drugs.

In *Lees v Lawrie*,[2] the supervisor of a learner driver was held to be in charge of the vehicle, but established that there was no likelihood of him driving it and was acquitted.

The statutory defence under s 4(3) is only relevant in prosecutions in cases where the accused is in charge of the vehicle under s 4(2), and does not apply to s 4(1) (cases of driving or attempting to drive). In addition, in considering this defence, regard has to be had to s 4(4) (see 3.8.2 below). The s 4(3) defence is similar to that provided by s 5(2).[3]

3.8.2 Section 4(4): Injury and damage to be disregarded

Section 4(4) of the Road Traffic Act 1988 provides:

'The court may, in determining whether there was such a likelihood as is mentioned in subsection (3) above, disregard any injury to him and any damage to the vehicle.'

1   2012 SCCR 465.
2   *Lees v Lawrie* 1993 SCCR 1.
3   See 3.16.1 below, similar considerations will in general apply to both; see also Appendix C.

In determining whether there is any likelihood that the accused will drive his vehicle while his ability to do so is impaired, the court may disregard any injury to the driver or damage to the vehicle. Thus, it is not necessarily fatal to a prosecution if the evidence shows that either the driver or the vehicle in question is not in a condition to proceed further; the accused may in such circumstances still be deemed to be in charge of the vehicle.

3.9 SECTION 15(3): STATUTORY DEFENCE (2): POST-INCIDENT DRINKING

3.9.1 Statutory provisions

Section 15 of the Road Traffic Offenders Act 1988[1] provides:

'(1) This section and section 16 of this Act apply in respect of proceedings for an offence under any of sections 3A to 5A of the Road Traffic Act 1988 (driving offences connected with drink or drugs); and expressions used in this section and section 16 of this Act have the same meaning as in sections 3A to 10.

(2) Evidence of the proportion of alcohol or any drug in a specimen of breath, blood or urine provided by or taken from the accused shall, in all cases (including cases where the specimen was not provided or taken in connection with the alleged offence), be taken into account and—

(a)   it is to be assumed, subject to subsection (3) below, that the proportion of alcohol in the accused's breath, blood or urine at the time of the alleged offence was not less than in the specimen;

(b)   it is to be assumed, subject to subsection (3A) below, that the proportion of a drug in the accused's blood or urine at the time of the alleged offence was not less than in the specimen.

(3) That assumption in subsection (2)(a) above shall not be made if the accused proves –

(a)   that he consumed alcohol before he provided the specimen or had it taken from him and –

(i)   in relation to an offence under section 3A, after the time of the alleged offence, and

(ii)   otherwise, after he had ceased to drive, attempt to drive or be in charge of a vehicle on a road or other public place, and

---

1   As amended by the RTA 1991, Sch 4 para 87 and by the Crime and Courts Act 2013, Sch 22.

(b)   that had he not done so the proportion of alcohol in his breath, blood or urine would not have exceeded the prescribed limit, and, if it is alleged that he was unfit to drive through drink, would not have been such as to impair his ability to drive properly.

(3A) The assumption in subsection (2)(b) above is not to be made if the accused proves—

(a)   that he took the drug before he provided the specimen or had the specimen taken from him and—

in relation to an offence under section 3A, after the time of the alleged offence, and

otherwise, after he had ceased to drive, attempt to drive or be in charge of a vehicle on a road or other public place, and

(b)   that had he not done so the proportion of the drug in his blood or urine—

(i)   in the case of a specified controlled drug, would not have exceeded the specified limit for that drug, and

(ii)   if it is alleged that he was unfit to drive through drugs, would not have been such as to impair his ability to drive properly.'

It is not clear what the phrase 'including cases where the specimen was not provided in connection with the alleged offence' in s 15(2)[1] is intended to mean. One purpose of this provision may be to avoid any difficulty that may arise when a driver is asked to give a specimen in terms of s 7 or s 7A of the Road Traffic Act 1988 in an investigation under s 5 and it is eventually decided to prosecute under s 4; alternatively it may be designed to avoid questions of competency in respect of the requirement of a specimen on the ground that such a general requirement, in line with certain English authorities, might leave the motorist in doubt as to the particular purpose for which the specimen is required and thus render the specimen invalid through uncertainty. As the subsection now reads, however, it would seem to allow a prosecution to be based, for example, on a blood specimen taken at a hospital for the purpose of treating a motorist injured in an accident; but such an interpretation would require to accommodate the provisions for protection of hospital patients provided by s 9. A further reason for, and consequence of, this amendment may be to cure procedural defects which occur before, as opposed to after, the specimen has been taken. It is also always open to the court to discount such evidence if, for example, it is established that the specimen has been

---

1   Introduced by RTA 1991, Sch 4 para 87.

obtained illegally, by deception or under duress, or not in accordance with the provision of the Act.[1]

The terms of this amendment make it plain that Parliament wishes to diminish even further the technical prerequisites for obtaining specimens for analysis.

Further discussion on the evidential implications of s 15(2) is found at 5.3–5.3.5 below, to which reference should also be made.

Section 15(3) therefore furnishes the guidelines for what is often referred to as the defence of post-incident or post-driving drinking. In English authorities, this has sometimes been described as the 'hip-flask defence', although this can be an inappropriate title. Unlike s 4(3) of the Road Traffic Act 1988, which provides a defence only to s 4(2) prosecutions, a s 15(3) defence can be applied in charges under both sub-ss (1) and (2) of s 4, as well as to charges under s 5(1)(a) and (b) Accordingly, this defence is available in all cases where the prosecution relies in any way on the results of an analysis of breath, blood or urine specimens. Although such specimens are normally used as the basis of prosecutions in terms of s 5, they can be, and sometimes (for the purposes of particular cases) are, used in s 4 cases. The subsection in addition specifically contemplates the possibility of such a defence in s 4 cases generally. The defence is also available in charges taken under s 3A.

The assumption contained within s 15(2) that the proportion of alcohol or drugs at the time of the alleged offence was not less than in the specimen is compatible with the European Convention on Human Rights.[2]

The introduction of s 15 (3A) now provides a similar defence in relation to drug related charges under ss 3A, 4 and 5A.

3.9.2 Onus and standard of proof in defence of post-incident drinking or drug taking

The onus of proof in establishing any offence remains on the Crown. However, in order to overcome the assumption referred to in s 15(3) of the Road Traffic Offenders Act 1988 there has to be evidence that a certain amount of alcohol or drug had been consumed after driving and that this was such as to cast reasonable doubt as to the validity of the assumption.[3] This reversal of onus is compatible with the European Convention on

---

1   *R v Fox* (sub nomine *Fox v Chief Constable of Gwent*) [1985] RTR 337 (at 343 per Lord Fraser), [1985] WLR 1126, [1986] AC 281.
2   See *Parker v DPP* [2001] RTR 16.
3   *Ritchie v Pirie* 1972 JC 7, 1972 SLT 2; *Campbell v Mackenzie* 1982 JC 20, 1982 SLT 250, 1981 SCCR 341.

Human Rights.[1] However, because of the powerful evidential value given to the assumption made in the section, the quality of the evidence required to establish this defence successfully is high. At the same time, in appropriate circumstances, the accused may not have to prove the exact amount of alcohol subsequently consumed.[2]

It is submitted that in the normal case in prosecutions under s 4(1) or (2) where the accused seeks to establish this defence, the following considerations will apply. Firstly, the accused will have to show in evidence, with a substantial degree of accuracy, the amount and nature of the alcohol or drug, if any, that has been consumed prior to the time when, in terms of the section, he ceased to drive, attempt to drive or be in charge of the vehicle. In particular, it will normally be of considerable importance for the accused to provide detailed information as to exactly when or over what period any such alcohol was consumed. Alternatively, if it is claimed that no alcohol or drug was consumed prior to the cessation of any driving operation, this too will have to be proved. The accused will then have to demonstrate that he ceased to drive, attempt to drive or be in charge of his vehicle and when this cessation took place. Next, the accused will require to prove the amount and nature of the alcohol or drug which he thereafter consumed before the specimen was given or the observations on the impairment of his ability to drive occurred, and the period of time over which this consumption took place. Finally, the accused will have to demonstrate, on the balance of probabilities, that but for the intake of the alcohol or drug subsequently consumed, his ability to drive, attempt to drive or be in charge of the vehicle would not have been impaired at the material time. In most cases in practice, it will be essential that expert evidence be given on the effect and consequences of the subsequent drinking proved to have taken place. It is possible to envisage circumstances where the accused can establish that he had consumed no alcohol or drug at all prior to the material time, and that his subsequent condition was wholly accounted for by post-incident drinking or drug taking, but in practice such cases might be relatively unusual. However, reference should be made to *Hassan v Scott*.[3]

In such cases, expert evidence is usually adduced in respect of a number of aspects. The effect of the consumption of alcohol, for example, varies significantly depending on the amount and nature of the alcohol consumed, the height and weight of the motorist, and other factors. Expert witnesses have recourse to tables indicating the given effect of given

1   See *R v Drummond* [2002] EWCA Crim 527, [2002] RTR 21.
2   *Hassan v Scott* 1989 SLT 380, 1989 SCCR 49.
3   *Hassan v Scott* 1989 SLT 380, 1989 SCCR 49.

quantities and types of alcohol on persons of differing physiques. Further, once consumed, alcohol begins thereafter to metabolise within the body and the level of alcohol therefore reduces, after the consumption of alcohol has ceased. Again, expert witnesses have recourse to tables which indicate in general terms the rate at which the body absorbs alcohol and levels reduce accordingly. These tables have not apparently been challenged by the Crown when produced by the defence, on the basis that such evidence is given by properly qualified experts who are entitled to consult such tables as being referable to their particular expertise. The tables, which are produced by the British Medical Association, have been judicially endorsed in England,[1] and are partly reproduced in Appendix A.

A successful defence of post-incident drinking therefore depends on the consideration of a number of matters which, taken together, will establish that at the material time an offence in terms of the Act has not been committed. Careful preparation and proper presentation of this evidence are essential, and each case will depend upon its own facts and circumstances. It should also be remembered that even in cases where a motorist successfully establishes that he has consumed alcohol after he has ceased to drive or attempt to drive a motor vehicle on a road or other public place, he may well, if he is still in the vicinity of his vehicle, be regarded as 'in charge' of that vehicle.

The presumption raised by s 15(2) (as amended) can be overcome by, for example, leading evidence that the accused has in fact consumed no alcohol.[2]

All of these considerations will no doubt apply in cases involving drugs when using s 15(3A).

Evidence of post-driving drinking, where it does not go sufficiently to provide a defence, is competent as evidence in mitigation.[3] Presumably, this might also apply in drug cases.

This defence can be established on the evidence of a single witness only,[4] though this may be rare.[5]

3.9.3 Level of alcohol or drug higher than reading: back calculation

The way in which s 15(2) of the Road Traffic Offenders Act 1988 is phrased suggests that, while it may be open to an accused to establish

---

1   *R v Somers* [1963] 3 All ER 808.
2   *Cracknell v Willis* 1988 RTR 1.
3   *Lees v Gilmour* 1990 SCCR 419.
4   *King v Lees* 1993 SLT 1184, 1993 SCCR 28.
5   See *DPP v Dukolli* [2009] EWHC 3097 (Admin).

that subsequent consumption of alcohol or a drug demonstrates that the level in his body did not exceed the permitted level, it is also possible for the prosecution to establish, on the same principles, that a specimen analysis which was taken some time after driving had ceased, and was at that time lower than the permitted levels, could nonetheless demonstrate that the level of alcohol or drug in the accused's body at the material time exceeded the permitted level. This would be proved by a process sometimes known as 'back calculation'. In other words, the Crown would base its calculations on the levels observed in the specimen analysis; and thereafter, by computing the time between the provision of the specimen and the metabolic rate of reduction, demonstrate that the true level of alcohol in the body exceeded the permitted level at the time the accused was driving the vehicle. It will be recalled that s 15(2) assumes that the level of alcohol or drug in the accused's breath, blood or urine at the time of the alleged offence is 'not less' than in the subsequently taken specimen; it is obvious therefore that the levels at the time of the alleged offence could be significantly more. The courts have been very reluctant to endorse this process and appear to be prepared to countenance 'back calculation' only in exceptional circumstances.[1] However, prosecutors may argue that the terms of s 3A of the Road Traffic Act 1988[2] suggest that Parliament has now specifically endorsed the principle of back calculation by contemplating, in s 3A(1)(c), the provision of specimens for analysis up to 18 hours after the driving which is concerned in the charge.

In *Hain v Ruxton*,[3] the Crown proposed to lead evidence that the level of alcohol in the accused's breath was 39mg. The sample, taken over four hours after he had stopped driving, demonstrated by back calculation that his breath alcohol level at the time he was driving might have been 67mg.

3.9.4 Level of alcohol higher than reading: back calculation and sentence

In *Buglass v Stott* 2001 SCCR 692 the appellant had been sentenced on the basis that when driving she 'had considerably more alcohol in her bloodstream than what was measured'. This approach was not accepted by the Court of Appeal and the view was expressed that a Sheriff 'is not entitled to proceed on a basis of guilt more serious than the Crown had chosen to charge'.

---

1   *Gumbley v Cunningham* [1989] RTR 49; *Millard v DPP* [1990] RTR 201.
2   Introduced by the RTA 1991, s 3.
3   *Hain v Ruxton* 1999 JC 166, 1999 SLT 789, 1999 SCCR 243.

3.10 DEFENCE AT COMMON LAW

Apart from the normal non-statutory defences (which usually are concerned with an error or failure in the procedure, or with an error or failure in the identification of the driver), coercion, or necessity, where a driver is genuinely compelled to drive where otherwise he would not have done so, may provide a successful defence to a charge of driving while unfit through drink or drugs.[1] In the latter case it was held that a defence of duress or necessity was available where a driver acted under immediate danger of death, or serious bodily harm to himself or another. The standard of such a defence is therefore particularly high. Any reasonable alternative to the offending behaviour must be taken accordingly. This sort of defence is not available indefinitely.[2] However, even where a defence of duress or necessity is not fully made out, the circumstances may produce useful mitigation. Equally, driving in a medical or other emergency may provide a defence, but again normally the court will have to be satisfied that no other reasonable alternative method of dealing with the emergency has been ignored; alternatively, such a crisis may allow the court not to disqualify the driver.[3] Reference may also be made to 2.5 and 2.15 above.

3.11 SECTION 4(5): DEFINITION OF UNFITNESS TO DRIVE

Section 4(5) of the Road Traffic Act 1988 provides:

> 'For the purposes of this section, a person shall be taken to be unfit to drive if his ability to drive properly is impaired.'

The test of whether the ability to drive is impaired is therefore a question of fact to be determined by the court on the evidence. Reference should be made to 3.6.1 above for the circumstances under which a medical examination should be conducted. In arriving at its conclusions, the court may properly have regard to the subjective opinion of witnesses, whether police, medical or anyone else. The phrase 'for the time being' means the time at which the driving took place; however, evidence of the driver's conduct before and after the driving occurred is both competent and relevant.

---

1   *Moss v Howdle* 1997 JC 123, 1997 SLT 782, 1997 SCCR 215.
2   *MacLeod v MacDougall* 1989 SLT 151, 1988 SCCR 519.
3   *Watson v Hamilton* 1988 SLT 316, 1988 SCCR 13.

3.12 POWER OF ARREST AND SEARCH

Sections 4(6)–(8) of the Road Traffic Act 1988 were repealed by the by Serious Organised Crime and Police Act 2005 (c 15), Sch 17(2) para 1.

Powers of arrest and search are now provided in ss 6D and 6E of the Road Traffic Act 1988, as substituted for the original s 6 by Railways and Transport Safety Act 2003 (c 20), Sch 7 para 1, and amended by the Crime and Courts Act 2013 to allow for arrest post preliminary drug tests, are considered further in ch 4. These reflect the change in approach to preliminary tests under ss 6 and 6A–C which now focus on drink and drugs as opposed to simply alcohol under the previous s 6. Like the earlier provisions, the powers of search under s 6E do not apply to Scotland, presumably because it was again considered by Parliament that the police in Scotland already have such powers at common law. This view was given substantial support in the case of *Cairns v Keane*,[1] where the police entered the accused's home without invitation and in pursuit of the accused, whom they suspected of having driven while under the influence of alcohol. The court held that the urgency of the situation justified the invasion or trespass of the accused's house. This decision was upheld on appeal, although the appeal court declined to deliver any opinion on the matter.

Reference may also be made to *Binnie v Donnelly*[2] where Scottish police officers followed a suspect vehicle over the border into England, and were held to be then entitled to require him to give a breath specimen, and to *Mackenzie v Hingston*[3] where, similarly, police officers followed a suspect onto a boat moored in a harbour.

PART 3
DRIVING OR BEING IN CHARGE OF A MOTOR VEHICLE WITH ALCOHOL OR A DRUG CONCENTRATION ABOVE PRESCRIBED OR SPECIFIED LIMIT (SS 5 AND 5A)

3.13 SECTION 5

3.13.1 General

The broad purpose of this part of the present legislation is to provide a method of ascertaining the proportion of alcohol present in a specimen

---

1   *Cairns v Keane* 1983 SCCR 277.
2   *Binnie v Donnelly* 1981 JC 92, 1981 SLT 294, 1981 SCCR 126
3   *Mackenzie v Hingston* 1995 SLT 966, 1995 SCCR 386.

of breath, blood or urine. Underlying all of the current provisions is the intention that the principal method of determining the proportion of alcohol should be by way of a specimen of breath at a police station in terms of s 7(1)(a) of the Road Traffic Act 1988.[1] The wording of s 7, read as a whole, makes it clear that a police officer must always, in the first instance, require a breath specimen, save for the five situations envisaged in s 7(3). Parliament, in considering the present terms of ss 7, 7A[2] and 8 of the Act, was intent on diminishing the previous significance of procedural and technical requirements which were features of earlier legislation and which had proved to be a fruitful source of contention in drink-driving prosecutions. The current terms of ss 7 (as amended), 7A and 8 mean that case law in respect of formal requirements concerning s 5 prosecutions, certainly before 6 May 1983, is of limited relevance.

3.13.2 Preliminary test

The provision of a preliminary breath test in terms of s 6A of the Road Traffic Act 1988 (the preliminary breath test and conducted by means of a breathalyser) is still seen as being normally the first step in the statutory procedure. However, it should be emphasised that, in terms of the current provisions, such a roadside test is by no means an essential prerequisite for a prosecution in terms of s 5. A description of what is involved in the preliminary tests is described in ch 4 below.

3.13.3 Section 5(1)

Section 5(1) of the Road Traffic Act 1988 provides:

'If a person –
(a)   drives or attempts to drive a motor vehicle on a road or other public place, or
(b)   is in charge of a motor vehicle on a road or other public place,

after consuming so much alcohol that the proportion of it in his breath, blood or urine exceeds the prescribed limit he is guilty of an offence.'

3.13.4 Special definitions

'Drives'. See 1.7.1 and 3.3.2 above.
'Attempting to drive'. See 3.3.3 above.
'Motor vehicle'. See 1.2.1 above.

1   As amended by the RTA 1991, Sch 4 para 42.
2   Added by Police Reform Act 2002 (c 30), Pt 4 (c 2), s 56(1).

'Road or other public place'. See 1.8.1, 1.8.2 and 1.8.3 above.
'In charge'. See 3.3.4 above.

3.13.5 The prescribed limits

The prescribed limits are a matter for the Scottish Ministers, since s 11(2ZA) now provides that regulations under subsection (2) may be made: '(b) by the Scottish Ministers, in relation to driving or attempting to drive, or being in charge of a vehicle, in Scotland.'[1]

Such regulations, the Road Traffic Act 1988 (Prescribed Limit) (Scotland) Regulations 2014 SSI 2014/328, took effect on 5 December 2014, with the effect that the prescribed limit under s 11(2) of the Road Traffic Act 1988 is now:

(a)   22 microgrammes of alcohol in 100 millilitres of breath;

(b)   50 milligrammes of alcohol in 100 millilitres of blood; or

(c)   67 milligrammes of alcohol in 100 millilitres of urine.

The rules governing the provision of specimens of breath, blood or urine for analysis are found in ss 7 and 7A of the Road Traffic Act 1988, and are discussed more fully in ch 4. These rules should be read in the context of the evidential provisions of ss 15 and 16 of the Road Traffic Offenders Act 1988, which are discussed in ch 5.

3.13.6 Procedure and penalties

These offences are normally prosecuted summarily. Penalties for s 5(1)(a) offences, include obligatory disqualification for a minimum of 12 months, a prison sentence of up to six months and a fine at level 5 (or both). Three to 11 penalty points must be endorsed if for any reason disqualification is not imposed.

For s 5(1)(b) offences disqualification is discretionary, and a prison sentence of up to three months or a fine on level 4 of the standard scale, or both, may be imposed. Ten penalty points are obligatory where there is no disqualification. Reference may be made to the Road Traffic Offenders Act 1988, s 34 and Sch 2, as amended by Sch 2 to the Road Traffic Act 1991.

The introduction of the lower limits caused some issues with sentencing, given the potential tensions between different parts of the UK, and with levels that had been previously at the lower end leading to minimum driving bans.

---

1   Added by Scotland Act 2012 (c 11) Pt 2, s 20(7) (3 July 2012).

The Sheriff Appeal Court provided guidance in the case of *Jenkins v Harvie*,[1] after the sentencing Sheriff had approached matters including by reference to the appellant's reading of 87/22 as now equating to an English reading of 138/35. The court observed that:

> '[8] We consider that the sheriff's approach is erroneous. The gravity of a drink driving offence should be measured in objective, absolute terms rather than by considering the number of times by which a driver exceeds the limit. It is fallacious to equate a reading of 87 in Scotland with one of 138 in England and Wales, when one driver is likely to be considerably more impaired than the other. The fallacy of the sheriff's approach can perhaps also be seen by considering what the approach would be were the limit to be reduced to zero (as some advocate). In that event, it would be mathematically impossible to view any transgression as being a certain number of times more than the limit.

> [9] In our opinion, the proper approach to sentence in a drink driving offence is to consider the alcohol reading together with any aggravating and mitigating circumstances relating to the offence, such as the quality of the driving; and the offender, which must include consideration of his record or lack of record. Disqualification is intended to be a penalty. It should reflect the gravity of the offence; however it is also a deterrent measure and for public protection. A minimum disqualification of one year is obligatory for a contravention of s.5(l)(a) of the 1988 Act. Where the court is sentencing with public safety and protection in mind it is necessary to consider the risk posed by the offender. The level of the alcohol reading together with the offender's antecedent behaviour especially for drink driving offences form two important factors in assessing risk. That is why the minimum period of disqualification for a second drink driving offence within ten years is three years.

> [10] In our opinion the significance of the lower "prescribed limit" in this jurisdiction relates not to the level of risk posed by the offender but rather the importance of the limit is that it now makes it an offence to drive a motor vehicle after consuming lower levels of alcohol in excess of that limit. The offence threshold is thereby lowered in Scotland.

> [11] Section 5(l)(a) of the 1988 Act and therefore the law on drink driving applies throughout the UK. The difference between this jurisdiction and England and Wales relates only to the lower "prescribed limit" by virtue of the Road Traffic Act 1988 (Prescribed Limit) (Sc) Regs 2014 which prescribe lower limits in breath, blood and urine for the purpose of the definition of "the prescribed limit" in s.11(2) of the Road Traffic Act 1988.

---

1   2016 SCCR 268, [2016] SAC (Crim) 14.

[12] Drivers who breach the lower limit will face an obligatory one year disqualification. The risk presented by drivers committing a first drink driving offence is not increased by virtue of the lower limit. A driver who has a reading of 87 micrograms of alcohol in 100 millilitres of breath is clearly guilty of an offence and also poses a risk to public safety but that risk is no greater than it was when the prescribed limit was the previous higher breath alcohol limit of 35.'

The Sheriff's headline disqualification of three years was reduced to two years.

The need to approach the question of risk properly was followed in *Docherty v McPherson*,[1] where an 18-year-old first offender with a reading of 44/22 had a disqualification of two years reduced to 16 months, and thereafter 12 months allowing for discount, which the court observed, 'happens to equate to the statutory minimum period in this context'.[2]

3.14 PUBLIC POLICY

In 1983, and later,[3] the Crown Office indicated publicly that prosecutions would not be taken in cases where the level of alcohol determined by a breath test in terms of s 6 of the Road Traffic Act 1988 did not exceed 40 mg of breath.

With the introduction of the lower limits in December 2014, the Crown Office and Procurator Fiscal Service indicated that it would no longer be bound by such an approach, but rather that: 'Where there is sufficient and reliable evidence, and where it is in the public interest to do so, the Crown will prosecute drink drive cases in contravention of law.'[4]

3.15 SECTION 5(2): STATUTORY DEFENCE (1): NO LIKELIHOOD OF DRIVING

3.15.1 General

Section 5(2) of the Road Traffic Act 1988 provides:

'It is a defence for a person charged with an offence under subsection 1(b) above to prove that at the time he is alleged to have committed the offence,

---

1   2016 SLT 397, [2016] SAC (Crim) 21.
2   At para [7]. See also 8.13 below in relation to discount.
3   *Lockhart v Deighan* 1985 SLT 549; 1985 SCCR 204.
4   Letter dated 27 November 2014 from Cath Dyer, then Crown Agent, to the President of the Law Society of Scotland.

the circumstances were such that there was no likelihood of his driving the vehicle whilst the proportion of alcohol in breath, blood or urine remained likely to exceed the prescribed limit.'

Section 5(2) therefore provides a statutory defence to a charge under s 5(1)(b). It will be noted that the defence is not available in charges under s 5(1)(a). If a driver who is proved to have been, or accepts that he has been, in charge of a vehicle after consuming so much alcohol that the proportion of it in his blood, breath or urine exceeds the prescribed limit, he is entitled to escape conviction if he proves that at the time the offence alleged against him was committed, there was no likelihood of his driving the vehicle whilst the proportion of alcohol in his breath, blood or urine remained likely to exceed the prescribed limit.

This reversal of onus – as with similar provisions in s 4(3), and also s 15(3) of the Road Traffic Offenders Act 1988 – is not incompatible with the presumption of innocence enshrined in Art 6(2) of the European Convention on Human Rights, standing the legitimate and acceptable object of the legislation which could not be regarded as placing a burden on an accused which either went beyond reasonable limits or was arbitrary.[1]

Whether such a defence can be successfully established will in each case be a question of fact and evidence. It is submitted that such a defence, where appropriate, may be established by uncorroborated evidence, including testimony from the accused driver himself. It should be noted, however, that for a successful defence of this kind to be established, the accused requires to demonstrate that there is no likelihood of him driving, so long as the proportion of alcohol in his body exceeds or remains likely to exceed the prescribed limit. The accused therefore has to demonstrate when the proportion of alcohol in his body would have diminished to below the prescribed limit, as well as proving that there was no likelihood of him driving up to that point. In virtually all cases of this kind, proof of when the level of alcohol in the accused's body decreased to a point below the prescribed limit will depend on expert evidence, the general nature of which is discussed at 3.9 above and 3.16 below. In this type of defence equal care may have to be taken in establishing, so far as possible, the point in time when the accused would next have driven.

In *Lees v Lawrie*[2] a supervisor of a learner driver was held to be in charge of a vehicle but not in any way likely to drive the vehicle; whereas in *Williamson v Crowe*[3] a driver in similar circumstances failed to establish

1   See *Sheldrake v DPP* [UKHL] 43, [2005] RTR 2.
2   *Lees v Lawrie* 1993 SCCR 1.
3   *Williamson v Crowe* 1995 SLT 959.

a s 5(2) defence when it was accepted that he might have taken the wheel as a last resort.

Regard must be had to actual likelihoods. In *Brown v Higson* 2000 SLT 994, a conviction was quashed on the basis that while it could be said that the appellant was able to drive, the actual likelihood of him doing so was not present given findings in fact as to his previous behaviour in similar situations, all of which should have led a reasonable Sheriff to the conclusion that the statutory defence had been made out.

It is submitted that the standard of proof on the accused in these circumstances is on the balance of probabilities.[1] In considering this defence, the court will have regard to the accused's intentions, express or implied, in the light of all the other circumstances of the case.[2] In deciding the issue, the court may disregard any injury to the driver or damage to the vehicle.[3] Thus it is not necessarily fatal to a prosecution if the evidence shows that either the driver of the car, or the car itself, was not in a condition to proceed further; the accused even in those circumstances may still be deemed to be in charge of the vehicle.

The circumstances in which a defence under s 5(2) may be presented can conceivably overlap with some of the earlier cases where it was found that the accused was not in charge of the vehicle (see 3.3.2 and 3.3.4 above). The s 5(2) defence is similar to that provided by s 4(3) (see 3.8 above) and similar considerations will in general apply to both. Reference should also be made to Appendix C.

3.16 SECTION 15(3): STATUTORY DEFENCE (2): POST-INCIDENT DRINKING

Section 15 of the Road Traffic Offenders Act 1988[4] provides:

'(1) This section and section 16 of this Act apply in respect of proceedings for an offence under any of sections 3A to 5A of the Road Traffic Act 1988 (driving offences connected with drink or drugs); and expressions used in this section and section 16 of this Act have the same meaning as in sections 3A to 10.

(2) Evidence of the proportion of alcohol or any drug in a specimen of breath, blood or urine provided by or taken from the accused shall, in all

---

1   *Neish v Stevenson* 1969 SLT 229.
2   *Morton v Confer* [1963] 1 WLR 763, [1963] 2 All ER 765.
3   RTA 1988, s 5(3).
4   As amended by the RTA 1991, Sch 4 para 87 and by the Crime and Courts Act 2013, Sch 22.

cases (including cases where the specimen was not provided or taken in connection with the alleged offence), be taken into account and—

(a) it is to be assumed, subject to subsection (3) below, that the proportion of alcohol in the accused's breath, blood or urine at the time of the alleged offence was not less than in the specimen;'

In other words, such readings, irrespective of how they are obtained, must be considered and accordingly, it is in general open for the court in a prosecution under s 5 to ignore any defects, omissions or failures in any procedural aspect of the Act involving the taking of the specimens. It is not clear what the phrase 'including cases where the specimen was not provided in connection with the alleged offence'[1] is intended to mean. This topic is more fully discussed at 3.9.1 above. The assumption contained within s 15(2) that the proportion of alcohol at the time of the alleged offence was not less than in the specimen is compatible with the European Convention on Human Rights.[2]

However, sub-s (3) then provides:

(3) That assumption in subsection (2)(a) above shall not be made if the accused proves –

(a)   that he consumed alcohol before he provided the specimen or had it taken from him and –

  (i)   in relation to an offence under section 3A, after the time of the alleged offence, and

  (ii)   otherwise, after he had ceased to drive, attempt to drive or be in charge of a vehicle on a road or other public place, and

(b)   that had he not done so the proportion of alcohol in his breath, blood or urine would not have exceeded the prescribed limit, and, if it is alleged that he was unfit to drive through drink, would not have been such as to impair his ability to drive properly.'

This topic has already been dealt with at 3.9.1 and 3.9.2 above but is repeated here for convenience.

Section 15(3) of the Road Traffic Offenders Act 1988 furnishes the guidelines for what is often known as the defence of post-incident drinking. In English authorities this has sometimes been referred to as the 'hip-flask defence', although this may be an inappropriate and misleading title. Unlike s 5(2) of the Road Traffic Act 1988, which provides a statutory defence only to s 5(1)(b) prosecutions, a defence under s 15(2) of the Road Traffic Offenders Act 1988 can be applied to charges under both sub-s (1)

1   Introduced by RTA 1991, Sch 4 para 87.
2   See *Parker v DPP* [2001] RTR 16.

(a) and (1)(b), as well as to a prosecution under s 4 of the Road Traffic Act 1988 where that prosecution relies in any way on the results of specimen analysis.

The onus of proof in establishing any offence remains on the Crown. However in order to overcome the assumption referred to in s 15(3) there has to be evidence that a certain amount of alcohol had been consumed after driving and that this was such as to cast reasonable doubt as to the validity of the assumption.[1] This reversal of onus is compatible with the European Convention on Human Rights.[2] Given the powerful evidential value given to the assumption made in the section, the quality of the evidence required to establish this defence successfully is high. At the same time, in appropriate circumstances, the accused may not have to prove the exact amount of alcohol subsequently consumed.[3] Corroboration of this evidence by the defence is not necessary.[4]

It is submitted that in the normal case in prosecutions under s 4(1) or (2) where the accused seeks to establish this defence, the following considerations will apply. Firstly, the accused will have to show in evidence, with a substantial degree of accuracy, the amount and nature of the alcohol, if any, that has been consumed prior to the time when, in terms of the section, he ceased to drive, attempt to drive or be in charge of the vehicle. In particular, it will normally be of considerable importance for the accused to provide detailed information as to exactly when or over what period any such alcohol was consumed. Alternatively, if it is claimed that no alcohol was consumed prior to the cessation of any driving operation, this too will have to be proved. The accused will then have to demonstrate that he ceased to drive, attempt to drive or be in charge of his vehicle and when this cessation took place. Next, the accused will have to prove the amount and nature of the alcohol which he thereafter consumed before the specimen was given or the observations on the impairment of his ability to drive occurred, and the period of time over which this consumption took place. Finally, the accused will have to demonstrate on the balance of probabilities, that but for the intake of the alcohol subsequently consumed, his ability to drive, attempt to drive or be in charge of the vehicle would not have been impaired at the material time. In most cases in practice, it will be essential that expert evidence be given on the effect and consequences of the subsequent drinking proved

---

1   *Ritchie v Pirie* 1972 JC 7, 1972 SLT 2; *Campbell v Mackenzie* 1982 JC 20, 1982 SLT 250, 1981 SCCR 341.
2   See *R v Drummond* [2002] EWCA Crim 527, [2002] RTR 21.
3   *Hassan v Scott* 1989 SLT 380, 1989 SCCR 49.
4   *King v Lees* 1983 SLT 1184.

to have taken place. It is possible to envisage circumstances where the accused can establish that he had consumed no alcohol at all prior to the material time, and that his subsequent condition was wholly accounted for by post-incident drinking, but in practice such cases appear to be relatively unusual. However, reference should be made to *Hassan v Scott*.[1]

In such cases, expert evidence is usually adduced in respect of a number of aspects. The effect of the consumption of alcohol varies significantly depending on the amount and nature of the alcohol consumed, the height and weight of the motorist, and other factors. Expert witnesses have recourse to tables indicating the given effect of given quantities and types of alcohol on persons of differing physiques. Further, once consumed, alcohol begins thereafter to metabolise within the body and the level of alcohol therefore reduces, after the consumption of alcohol has ceased. Again, expert witnesses have recourse to tables which indicate in general terms the rate at which the body absorbs alcohol and levels reduce accordingly. These tables have not apparently been challenged by the Crown when produced by the defence, on the basis that such evidence is given by properly qualified experts who are entitled to consult such tables as being referable to their particular expertise. The tables, which are produced by the British Medical Association, have been judicially endorsed in England.[2]

A successful defence of post-incident drinking therefore depends on the consideration of a number of matters which, taken together, will establish that at the material time an offence in terms of the Act has not been committed. Careful preparation and proper presentation of this evidence are essential, and each case will depend upon its own facts and circumstances. It should also be remembered that even in cases where a motorist successfully establishes that he has consumed alcohol after he has ceased to drive or attempt to drive a motor vehicle on a road or other public place, he may well, if he is still in the vicinity of his vehicle, be regarded as 'in charge' of that vehicle.

It is also important to note that while it may be open to an accused to establish a defence on the basis as above described, there would appear to be nothing to prevent the Crown from proving, on the same principles that a specimen analysis which was taken some time after a driving operation has ceased and which was lower than the permitted limit, could nonetheless demonstrate that at the time the motorist was driving, attempting to drive or was in charge of his vehicle he had more than the permitted level of alcohol, and is thus liable to conviction (see 3.9.2 above).

1   *Hassan v Scott* 1989 SLT 380, 1989 SCCR 49.
2   *R v Somers* [1963] 3 All ER 808; see Appendix A.

Evidence of post-driving drinking, where it does not go sufficiently far to provide a defence, is competent in mitigation.[1] Reference should also be made to Appendix C.

This defence can be established on the evidence of a single witness.[2]

3.17 DEFENCE AT COMMON LAW

See 3.10 above, and Appendix C.

3.18 SECTION 5A: DRIVING OR BEING IN CHARGE OF A MOTOR VEHICLE WITH CONCENTRATION OF SPECIFIED CONTROLLED DRUG ABOVE SPECIFIED LIMIT

Section 5A(1)(a) – To be tried summarily, six months' imprisonment or a level 5 fine or both, obligatory disqualification (or 3–11 points)

Section 5A(1)(b) – To be tried summarily, three months' imprisonment or a level 4 fine or both, discretionary disqualification or ten points.

This provision, added by the Crime and Courts Act 2013,[3] Pt 3, s 56(1) anticipates better detection of drugs in a driver's system. It mirrors in many respects the existing provisions in s 5. As with the current drink drive limits, the selection of any limit under this provision, which may be zero, will be a matter for the Scottish Ministers.

The section reads as follows:

'(1) This section applies where a person ("D") –

(a)   drives or attempts to drive a motor vehicle on a road or other public place, or

(b)   is in charge of a motor vehicle on a road or other public place,

and there is in D's body a specified controlled drug.

(2) D is guilty of an offence if the proportion of the drug in D's blood or urine exceeds the specified limit for that drug…

(8) In this section, and in sections 3A, 6C(1), 6D and 10, "specified" means specified in regulations made –

---

1   *Lees v Gilmour* 1990 SCCR 419.
2   *King v Lees* 1993 SLT 1184, 1993 SCCR 28.
3   c 22.

(a)   by the Secretary of State, in relation to driving or attempting to drive, or being in charge of a vehicle, in England and Wales;

(b)   by the Scottish Ministers, in relation to driving or attempting to drive, or being in charge of a vehicle, in Scotland.

(9) A limit specified under subsection (2) may be zero.'

As noted already, this provision awaits regulations by the Scottish Government before it can have effect. As announced, these, and the necessary equipment, are due in place sometime in 2019. Whether that is achieved will be interesting to follow, given the ever more limited resources of Police Scotland, let alone the enthusiasm of Holyrood.

Looking south of the border, specified drug limits were introduced by the Drug Driving (Specified Limits) (England and Wales) Regulations 2014 (SI 2014/2868), and have already been amended to include amphetamine by SI 2015/911.

Guidance to healthcare professionals was also issued in July 2014 to assist discussion with patients of possible medicinal impairment of driving.

'Drugalysers' are in use and can detect heroin, cocaine and cannabis from saliva.

3.18.1 Sections 5A(3)–(7): statutory defences

'(3) It is a defence for a person ("D") charged with an offence under this section to show that –

(a)   the specified controlled drug had been prescribed or supplied to D for medical or dental purposes,

(b)   D took the drug in accordance with any directions given by the person by whom the drug was prescribed or supplied, and with any accompanying instructions (so far as consistent with any such directions) given by the manufacturer or distributor of the drug, and

(c)   D's possession of the drug immediately before taking it was not unlawful under section 5(1) of the Misuse of Drugs Act 1971 (restriction of possession of controlled drugs) because of an exemption in regulations made under section 7 of that Act (authorisation of activities otherwise unlawful under foregoing provisions).

(4) The defence in subsection (3) is not available if D's actions were –

(a)   contrary to any advice, given by the person by whom the drug was prescribed or supplied, about the amount of time that should elapse between taking the drug and driving a motor vehicle, or

(b)   contrary to any accompanying instructions about that matter (so far as consistent with any such advice) given by the manufacturer or distributor of the drug.

(5) If evidence is adduced that is sufficient to raise an issue with respect to the defence in subsection (3), the court must assume that the defence is satisfied unless the prosecution proves beyond reasonable doubt that it is not.

(6) It is a defence for a person ("D") charged with an offence by virtue of subsection (1)(b) to prove that at the time D is alleged to have committed the offence the circumstances were such that there was no likelihood of D driving the vehicle whilst the proportion of the specified controlled drug in D's blood or urine remained likely to exceed the specified limit for that drug.

(7) The court may, in determining whether there was such a likelihood, disregard any injury to D and any damage to the vehicle.'

Subsection (3) is novel and inevitably limited by subsection (4). It is striking, however, that distinct from the reverse onus approach taken with the other provisions mentioned above, the terms of subsection (5) are explicit that if the defence is sufficiently evidenced raised, it is to be assumed satisfied unless the prosecution proves beyond reasonable doubt that it is not.

Subsections (6) and (7) mirror the defences available under ss 4(3), 4(4) and 5(2) and reference is made to paras 3.8, 3.9 and 3.15 above.

3.18.2 Section 15(3): statutory defence: post-incident drug taking

Reference should be made to paras 3.9 and 3.16 above (s 4(3)).

Section 15 of the Road Traffic Offenders Act 1988[1] provides:

'(1) This section and section 16 of this Act apply in respect of proceedings for an offence under any of sections 3A to 5A of the Road Traffic Act 1988 (driving offences connected with drink or drugs); and expressions used in this section and section 16 of this Act have the same meaning as in sections 3A to 10.

(2) Evidence of the proportion of alcohol or any drug in a specimen of breath, blood or urine provided by or taken from the accused shall, in all cases (including cases where the specimen was not provided or taken in connection with the alleged offence), be taken into account and— ...

(b)   it is to be assumed, subject to subsection (3A) below, that the proportion of a drug in the accused's blood or urine at the time of the alleged offence was not less than in the specimen.

---

1   As amended by the RTA 1991, Sch 4 para 87 and by the Crime and Courts Act 2013, Sch 22.

(3A) The assumption in subsection (2)(b) above is not to be made if the accused proves—

(a)   that he took the drug before he provided the specimen or had the specimen taken from him and—

   (i)   in relation to an offence under section 3A, after the time of the alleged offence, and

   (ii)   otherwise, after he had ceased to drive, attempt to drive or be in charge of a vehicle on a road or other public place, and

(b)   that had he not done so the proportion of the drug in his blood or urine—

   (i)   in the case of a specified controlled drug, would not have exceeded the specified limit for that drug, and

   (ii)   if it is alleged that he was unfit to drive through drugs, would not have been such as to impair his ability to drive properly.'

In order to overcome the assumption referred to in s 15(3A), there has to be evidence that an amount of drug had been consumed after driving and that this was such as to cast reasonable doubt as to the validity of the assumption.[1] This reversal of onus is compatible with the European Convention on Human Rights.[2] Given the powerful evidential value given to the assumption made in the section, the quality of the evidence required to establish this defence successfully will be high. Corroboration of this evidence by the defence will not be necessary.[3]

3.19 CYCLING UNDER THE INFLUENCE OF DRINK OR DRUGS (S 30)

Section 30 of the Road Traffic Act 1988 provides that:

(1)   A person who, when riding a cycle on a road or other public place, is unfit to ride through drink or drugs (that is to say, is under the influence of drink or a drug to such an extent as to be incapable of having proper control of the cycle) is guilty of an offence.

(2)   In Scotland a constable may arrest without warrant a person committing an offence under this section. The procedures under ss 6, 7 and 9 do not apply to s 30 offences. Penalty is a level 3 fine on the standard scale.

---

1   *Ritchie v Pirie* 1972 JC 7, 1972 SLT 2; *Campbell v Mackenzie* 1982 JC 20, 1982 SLT 250, 1981 SCCR 341.
2   See *R v Drummond* [2002] EWCA Crim 527, [2002] RTR 21.
3   *King v Lees* 1983 SLT 1184.

Chapter 4

Preliminary breath tests and provision of specimens for analysis

PART 1
PRELIMINARY TESTS

4.1 SECTIONS 6 AND 6A–6D GENERAL

The introduction of the new ss 6 and 6A–6D by the Railways and Transport Safety Act 2003 was on the face of it a major change in the approach to initial testing of those suspected of committing a drink or drug related offence. Instead of the previous regime of preliminary breath tests relating to alcohol, there is now scope under the new s 6 for a constable to require a person to cooperate with one or more of the new preliminary test introduced by ss 6A–6C, namely preliminary breath tests, impairment tests and drugs tests.

The change reflects the need to detect increasing amounts of drug related offending. In real terms, certainly in the short term, the majority of tests will still be breath tests and currently there is no approved device with which to implement the s 6C test. The situations where the preliminary tests may be used broadly repeat the earlier provisions save that of course they refer both to alcohol and drugs. Likewise the powers of arrest under s 6D largely mirror the original s 6(5) while again the powers of entry provision under s 6E are expressly excluded for Scotland, just as with the earlier s 6(7).

In short therefore, s 6 of the Road Traffic Act 1988 allows a police constable to require cooperation with one or more of the preliminary tests and in a wide variety of circumstances.

In full the section now reads:

'6 Power to administer preliminary tests

(1) If any of subsections (2) to (5) applies a constable may require a person to co-operate with any one or more preliminary tests administered to the person by that constable or another constable.

(2) This subsection applies if a constable reasonably suspects that the person –

(a)   is driving, is attempting to drive or is in charge of a motor vehicle on a road or other public place, and

(b)   has alcohol or a drug in his body or is under the influence of a drug.

(3) This subsection applies if a constable reasonably suspects that the person –

(a)   has been driving, attempting to drive or in charge of a motor vehicle on a road or other public place while having alcohol or a drug in his body or while unfit to drive because of a drug, and

(b)   still has alcohol or a drug in his body or is still under the influence of a drug.

(4) This subsection applies if a constable reasonably suspects that the person –

(a)   is or has been driving, attempting to drive or in charge of a motor vehicle on a road or other public place, and

(b)   has committed a traffic offence while the vehicle was in motion.

(5) This subsection applies if –

(a)   an accident occurs owing to the presence of a motor vehicle on a road or other public place, and

(b)   a constable reasonably believes that the person was driving, attempting to drive or in charge of the vehicle at the time of the accident.

(6) A person commits an offence if without reasonable excuse he fails to co-operate with a preliminary test in pursuance of a requirement imposed under this section.

(7) A constable may administer a preliminary test by virtue of any of subsections (2) to (4) only if he is in uniform.

(8) In this section –

(a)   a reference to a preliminary test is to any of the tests described in sections 6A to 6C, and

(b)   'traffic offence' means an offence under –

(i)   a provision of Part II of the Public Passenger Vehicles Act 1981 (c 14),

(ii)   a provision of the Road Traffic Regulation Act 1984 (c 27),

(iii)   a provision of the Road Traffic Offenders Act 1988 (c 53) other than a provision of Part III, or

(iv)   a provision of this Act other than a provision of Part V.'

4.2 DEFINITIONS

'A constable'. A constable means any member of the police force irrespective of rank, and includes a special constable.

'A constable in uniform'. This phrase has not been judicially considered in terms in Scotland. However, it is submitted that the matter is essentially one of fact. In English cases, a constable otherwise in uniform but without his helmet;[1] and an officer with a raincoat over his uniform[2] were both held to be entitled to make the requirement. If the question of whether the constable was in uniform is not raised specifically in the evidence, there must be facts and circumstances from which the court can infer that the constable was in uniform.[3] In a case under s 2 of the Road Safety Act 1967 it was held that a uniformed constable could make the requirement on the basis of information supplied by a plain clothes officer.[4]

In *Orr v Urquhart*[5] there was no evidence that the constable who required the specimen was in uniform. This was held not to invalidate further procedure under s 7, although in such circumstances no conviction could follow under s 6. The fact that the constable was in uniform does not have to be corroborated.[6] There is no need for uniform in terms of s 6(5).

'Reasonably suspects'. Subsections (2)–(4)

It has to be established that the constable has a reasonable suspicion as set out before requiring cooperation for a preliminary test. Whether or not such reasonable suspicion exists is a matter of fact in each case and depends upon the proven facts and circumstances. Reference can be made to the authorities considering the earlier 'reasonable cause to suspect' of the original s 6(1). In the case of *Copeland v McPherson*,[7] the suspicion

---

1   *Wallwork v Giles* [1970] RTR 117.
2   *Taylor v Baldwin* [1976] RTR 265.
3   *Richards v West* [1980] RTR 215; *Cooper v Rowlands* [1971] RTR 291.
4   *Copeland v McPherson* 1970 SLT 87; *Allan v Douglas* 1978 JC 7.
5   *Orr v Urquhart* 1993 SLT 404, 1992 SCCR 295.
6   *MacLeod v Nicol* 1970 JC 58, 1970 SLT 304.
7   *Copeland v McPherson* 1970 SLT 87.

was held to be reasonable when it arose out of information given to the constable by another officer. In *Dryburgh v Galt*,[1] the information came from an anonymous phone call. The suspicion may arise from the way in which the vehicle is being driven, but it is clear that obviously erratic conduct of the vehicle is not the only method by which such suspicions may arise.[2] In particular, the suspicion in the constable's mind may arise after the vehicle has been stopped for whatever proper and legal purpose. The suspicion must relate to at least one of the three situations covered by the section.

A police constable has wide powers to stop motor vehicles in terms of s 163 of the Road Traffic Act 1988 and the only qualification on these powers would seem to be that they are not exercised capriciously or oppressively. It would therefore seem to be in order that a constable may stop a motorist purely with the intention of seeing whether or not he had been drinking[3] so long as there is no question of mispractice, malice or caprice. Random checks, such as those undertaken during Christmas drink drive campaigns, do not possess such qualities, and in *Miller v Bell* 2004 SCCR 534, were held to be compatible with Art 8 of the European Convention on Human Rights as such use of s 163 'represented a necessary and proportionate response to prevent the commission of crime'. However, once the vehicle has been stopped, the constable must then have reasonable cause to suspect that the motorist has alcohol in his body. The usual reasons given are that alcohol is smelt on the motorist's breath, or that his speech is slurred, his eyes are glazed or his movements are uncoordinated. However, in *Thomson v Ritchie*,[4] it was observed that the reasonable cause for suspicion may arise before the vehicle has been stopped. A constable need not indicate to the motorist the reason for his suspicions; and if in all the circumstances the requirement is legally and properly made, it does not matter if a constable claims to have relied at the time upon grounds for his suspicion that subsequently proved to be improper.[5] It therefore follows that the constable's suspicion, whatever it may be, does not have to be subsequently confirmed as accurate or justified; all that has to be established is that the constable's suspicions were at the material time reasonable in the circumstances. It would accordingly not be a defence to a charge of failing to provide a specimen in terms of this section that the driver has not been drinking or even that he was not

1   *Dryburgh v Galt* 1981 SLT 151, 1981 SCCR 26.
2   *Sinclair v Heywood* 1981 SCCR 63.
3   *Chief Constable of Gwent v Dash* [1986] RTR 41, [1985] Crim LR 674; *Normand v McKellar* 1995 SLT 798; *Stewart v Crowe* 1999 SLT 899, 1999 SCCR 327.
4   *Thomson v Ritchie* 2000 SLT 734, 2000 SCCR 38.
5   *McNaughton v Degnan* 1981 SLT (Notes) 105, 1981 SCCR 97.

the driver at the material time, provided that the constable's suspicions are reasonable.[1] If the constable purports to make the requirement on an unjustified basis but proper grounds exist, then the requirement will be held to have been properly made.[2]

'Reasonably believes'. Subsection (5)

It should be noted that in terms of this subsection the requirement imposed on the constable is significantly higher than in s 6(2)–(4) of the Road Traffic Act 1988 where he simply needs to reasonably suspect. In terms of s 6(5), however, the constable must reasonably believe that the accused was driving or attempting to drive or be in charge of a vehicle at the time of an accident. It is submitted that clearly the word 'believes' is intended to convey a higher standard of conviction on the part of the police constable than the word 'suspects'. While there has been slight change in the form of words used in this section, it is submitted that these do not lead to any material change and again earlier authorities remain relevant. In *Merry v Docherty*,[3] the appeal court discussed in some detail both the need for the prosecution to establish that an accident has taken place as a result of the presence of the vehicle on the road, and further what has to be established in order that it can be shown that a constable has reasonable cause to believe that the accused was driving at the time. In particular, in view of the way in which the section is now phrased, it would seem to be essential for any requirement under this particular subsection that the constable knows of the accident in question at the time when he makes the requirement for the preliminary test. In other words, there has to have been an accident, and a police constable's suspicion or belief that there has been one may not be enough. However, the nature and extent of the constable's knowledge of the accident need not be prescribed in any way, and in a case where police officers had received an anonymous call describing the circumstances of the accident, and the accused's vehicle was found to be in a condition consistent with that description, it was held that the police could have reasonable cause to believe that the accused had been driving his motor vehicle at the time of the accident.[4] English cases that may be of assistance in comprehending

1   See *McNaughton v Degnan* 1981 SLT (Notes) 105, 1981 SCCR 97; and *McNicol v Peters* 1969 SLT 261.
2   *McNaughton v Degnan* 1981 SLT (Notes) 105, 1981 SCCR 97. *McNaughton v Degnan* 1981 SLT (Notes) 105, 1981 SCCR 97.
3   *Merry v Docherty* 1977 JC 34, 1977 SLT 117.
4   *Glass v Milne* 1977 CO Circulars A/7; *Topping v Scott* 1979 SLT (Notes) 21; but see also *Breen v Pirie* 1976 JC 60, 1976 SLT 136.

this phrase are inter alia *Baker v Oxford;*[1] *Moss v Jenkins;*[2] and *Johnson v Whitehouse.*[3]

The constable does not have to be in uniform; nor does he have to have any suspicion that the accused has had alcohol in his body. As with the other s6 requirements, there are no time limits imposed by the subsection on when the requirement must be made.

In *Binnie v Donnelly,*[4] a motorist was involved in an accident on the Scottish side of the Scotland/England border, then drove his car across the border to where he was involved in a further accident. In these circumstances it was decided that there was nothing to stop Scottish police officers pursuing the accused over the border and requiring a breath specimen when he was apprehended. In *MacKenzie v Hingston*[5] police officers similarly pursued a suspect onto a fishing boat.

'*Traffic offence*'. See definition provided in s 6(8)(b).

'*Accident*'. See 1.9.1 above.

'*Driving or attempting to drive*'. See 1.7.1, 3.3.2 and 3.3.3 above.

'*In charge*'. See 3.3.4 above.

'*Motor vehicle*'. See 1.2.1ff above.

'*Road or other public place*'. See 1.8.1, 1.8.2 and 1.8.3 above.

'*Require*'. To require means to ask.[6] The requirement must be corroborated;[7] however, the other points of the procedure need not.[8]

'*Fails to co-operate*'. In terms of s 11(3) of the Road Traffic Act 1988, a person does not co-operate with a preliminary test or provide a specimen of breath for analysis unless his co-operation or the specimen is (a) sufficient to enable the test or the analysis to be carried out, and (b) is provided in such a way as to enable the objective of the test or analysis to be satisfactorily achieved.

1   *Baker v Oxford* [1980] RTR 315.
2   *Moss v Jenkins* [1975] RTR 25.
3   *Johnson v Whitehouse* [1984] RTR 38.
4   *Binnie v Donnelly* 1981 SLT 294, 1981 SCCR 126.
5   *MacKenzie v Hingston* 1995 SLT 966, 1995 SCCR 386.
6   *Milne v McDonald* 1971 JC 40 (per Lord Justice-Clerk Clyde at p 42), 1971 SLT 291 *Milne v McDonald* 1971 JC 40 (per Lord Justice-Clerk Clyde at p 42), 1971 SLT 291.
7   *Carmichael v Gillooly* 1982 SCCR 119.
8   *MacLeod v Nicol* 1970 JC 58, 1970 SLT 304 *MacLeod v Nicol* 1970 JC 58, 1970 SLT 304.

4.3 THE PRELIMINARY TESTS (SS 6A–6C)

The three tests are set out as follows:

'6A Preliminary breath test

(1) A preliminary breath test is a procedure whereby the person to whom the test is administered provides a specimen of breath to be used for the purpose of obtaining, by means of a device of a type approved by the Secretary of State, an indication whether the proportion of alcohol in the person's breath or blood is likely to exceed the prescribed limit.

(2) A preliminary breath test administered in reliance on section 6(2) to (4) may be administered only at or near the place where the requirement to co-operate with the test is imposed.

(3) A preliminary breath test administered in reliance on section 6(5) may be administered –

(a)   at or near the place where the requirement to co-operate with the test is imposed, or

(b)   if the constable who imposes the requirement thinks it expedient, at a police station specified by him.

6B Preliminary impairment test

(1) A preliminary impairment test is a procedure whereby the constable administering the test –

(a)   observes the person to whom the test is administered in his performance of tasks specified by the constable, and

(b)   makes such other observations of the person's physical state as the constable thinks expedient.

(2) The Secretary of State shall issue (and may from time to time revise) a code of practice about –

(a)   the kind of task that may be specified for the purpose of a preliminary impairment test,

(b)   the kind of observation of physical state that may be made in the course of a preliminary impairment test,

(c)   the manner in which a preliminary impairment test should be administered, and

(d)   the inferences that may be drawn from observations made in the course of a preliminary impairment test.

(3) In issuing or revising the code of practice the Secretary of State shall aim to ensure that a preliminary impairment test is designed to indicate –

(a)   whether a person is unfit to drive, and

(b)   if he is, whether or not his unfitness is likely to be due to drink or drugs.

(4) A preliminary impairment test may be administered –

(a)   at or near the place where the requirement to co-operate with the test is imposed, or

(b)   if the constable who imposes the requirement thinks it expedient, at a police station specified by him.

(5) A constable administering a preliminary impairment test shall have regard to the code of practice under this section.

(6) A constable may administer a preliminary impairment test only if he is approved for that purpose by the chief officer of the police force to which he belongs.

(7) A code of practice under this section may include provision about –

(a)   the giving of approval under subsection (6), and

(b)   in particular, the kind of training that a constable should have undergone, or the kind of qualification that a constable should possess, before being approved under that subsection.

6C Preliminary drug test

(1) A preliminary drug test is a procedure by which a specimen of sweat or saliva is –

(a)   obtained, and

(b)   used for the purpose of obtaining, by means of a device of a type approved by the Secretary of State, an indication whether the person to whom the test is administered has a drug in his body and if so—

    (i)   whether it is a specified controlled drug;

    (ii)   if it is, whether the proportion of it in the person's blood or urine is likely to exceed the specified limit for that drug.

(2) A preliminary drug test may be administered –

(a)   at or near the place where the requirement to co-operate with the test is imposed, or

(b)   if the constable who imposes the requirement thinks it expedient, at a police station specified by him.'

(3) Up to three preliminary drug tests may be administered.'[1]

4.3.1 Procedural nature of tests

The administration of a preliminary breath test will be essentially a procedural matter, and can therefore be spoken to in evidence by one

1   As amended by the Crime and Courts Act 2013 (c 22), Sch 22 para 3.

witness only.[1] However, a charge of failing to co-operate with a preliminary test will have to be supported by corroborated evidence.

Where a device is used in either the breath or the drug test, the evidence should indicate that the device is approved; however, in the absence of challenge, this may be presumed.[2] In relation to the impairment test, compliance with code of practice will be likewise presumed unless subject to challenge.

4.3.2 The limits; time and place where tests to be given

Once a constable meets the reasonably suspects or believes requirements of s 6 there is no time limit within which either the requirement be made, or the test administered. Normally the requirement will be made when the suspicion in the constable's mind is formed but given the breadth of scenarios provided for in section, the belief or suspicion may arise in very different situations. For example the requirement may be made where the constable has reasonable cause to suspect that the motorist has been driving, in the absence of direct evidence on that matter, as well as having reasonable cause to suspect that the motorist has alcohol in his body.

Section 6A preliminary breath tests which arise out of reasonable suspicion in terms of s 6(2)–(4) may only be administered at or near the place where the requirement to co-operate is made.

The position is different in the s 6(5) scenario and the test may either be administered at or near the place where the requirement is made or at a police station specified by the constable if he thinks that expedient.

That same choice arises in terms of both the impairment and drug tests under ss 6B and 6C.

The phrase at or near the place where the requirement to co-operate does not appear to have been judicially considered in Scotland; it is thought that the subsection will be construed with reasonable strictness, and if the specimen is provided at a place which is in any way significantly distant from the place where the requirement is made, then the specimen will be regarded as invalid.

4.3.3 Approved devices

A variety of devices have been approved by the Secretary of State for use and reflect new and progressive updating of existing machines. With

---

1   *McLeod v Nicol* 1970 JC 58, 1970 SLT 304; *Wither v McLennan* 1978 CO Circulars A/30.
2   *McIlhargey v Herron* 1972 JC 38, 1972 SLT 185.

ss 5A and 6C in mind, the Home Office has approved two drug testing devices: the Securetec DrugWipe 3S S303G (mobile use) and the Draeger DrugTest 5000 (mobile and station use).

In respect of these devices, the constable must explain clearly to the motorist the method by which the test is to be administered, in accordance with the manufacturer's instructions. Any failure in respect of the foregoing matters will invalidate the test.[1] However, if the instructions have been complied with, the motorist must properly and correctly carry through the test, unless he has a reasonable excuse for not doing so (see 4.4.2 below). An offence under s 6(6) of the Road Traffic Act 1988 will accordingly be committed if the motorist fails to co-operate with the request to provide a specimen in any material way or if he fails to comply with the manufacturer's instructions in respect of the particular device used at the material time.

The evidence should indicate that the device is approved; however, in the absence of challenge, this may be presumed.[2] The approval order in respect of such a device does not have to be produced;[3] and the working of such devices is normally within judicial knowledge.[4]

The test must be carried out in accordance with the device manufacturer's instructions (see 4.10.3 and 4.13.4 below). However, the provision of a specimen is not a prerequisite of further procedure under s 4 or s 5, and any failure in the procedure, either by the constable or the motorist, has relevance only in a charge of failing to provide a specimen in terms of s 6(6).

4.3.4 Safeguards for hospital patients

The preliminary test provisions are subject to the safeguards for hospital patients described in s 9 (see 6.1.1ff below.)

4.4 FAILURE TO CO-OPERATE WITH A PRELIMINARY TEST (S 6(6))

Section 6(6) of the Road Traffic Act 1988 now provides:

> 'A person commits an offence if without reasonable excuse he fails to co-operate with a preliminary test in pursuance of a requirement imposed under this section.'

1 *Jeffrey v MacNeill* 1976 JC 54; see also cases at 4.11.4 below.
2 *McIlhargey v Herron* 1972 JC 38, 1972 SLT 185.
3 *Lee v Smith* 1982 SLT 200, 1981 SCCR 267.
4 *Valentine v MacPhail* 1986 JC 131, 1986 SLT 598, 1986 SCCR 321; however see also 7.8.2 below.

There is no requirement on the constable administering the test to advise the motorist that failure to comply with the procedure may result in prosecution; however the appeal court, in relation to the breath test, has recommended that such a warning be given.[1] Such a warning must be given under s 7 procedure.

A driver may refuse a test even though the equipment is not yet readily available.[2] Reference should also be made to s 11(3) of the Act – see 4.2 above.

4.4.1 Procedure and penalties

A charge of failure to provide a specimen of breath in terms of s 6(6) of the Road Traffic Act 1988 is normally taken on summary complaint and the penalties are found in Sch 2 to the Road Traffic Offenders Act 1988. Unlike s 7(7) of the Act, there is no provision in s 6 which requires the constable administering the test to warn the motorist that failure to comply with the procedure may lead to prosecution. Penalties include a fine up to level 3, discretionary disqualification, or endorsement with four penalty points.

As *Smith v Gibson*[3] makes plain, sentencing in s 6 offences "does not fall within the sentencing regime applicable to drink and substance related driving offences", and "a failure to cooperate with the preliminary breath test, does not relate directly to the quality of the appellant's driving and accordingly does not automatically engage the safety of other road users".

In the result, an eight-year headline disqualification – reflecting previous record and perceived risk – was reduced to four points and a requirement to resit the extended test was quashed.

4.4.2 Reasonable excuse

The majority of cases about reasonable excuse for failing to provide a specimen relate to the provision of a specimen for analysis in terms of s 7(1) of the Road Traffic Act 1988 rather than to the roadside test. What follows is a general statement based in part on those cases that would also seem relevant to the provision of s 6(6).

It can in general terms be a reasonable excuse to fail to provide such a specimen only if the person concerned is physically or mentally

---

1   *O'Sharkey v Smith* 1982 SLT 91, 1981 SCCR 189.
2   *R v Wagner* [1970] RTR 422, [1970] Crim LR 535.
3   2017 SCCR 373, [2017] SAC (Crim) 10, at paras [7] and [10].

unable to provide it, or if to do so would involve a substantial risk to his health.[1] Once the prosecution has established that the accused has failed to provide a specimen, and there were no, or insufficient, reasons for the refusal, it is for the accused to demonstrate that his failure was justified. However, once the issue of reasonable excuse has been sufficiently raised by the defence, it is for the prosecution to rebut it, and in that event the court will have to determine, on the basis of all the evidence led, whether or not it has been established beyond reasonable doubt that the motorist failed to provide the specimen without reasonable excuse.[2] In the normal case, the accused may well have to lead medical or other evidence in support of his claim that he had a reasonable excuse to refuse to take the test. However, the uncorroborated evidence of the accused, if accepted, can be sufficient to establish a defence. In exceptional cases it may be possible to proceed on the basis of a statement of facts agreed between the prosecution and defence, preferably by way of a joint statement of admissions.

It must be emphasised that the reasonable excuse claimed by the accused must relate to the taking of the test, and not to any other matter. It is therefore not a reasonable excuse for the driver to maintain that he has not in fact consumed alcohol as a reason for refusing to take the test,[3] or that he was not in fact the driver at the material time.[4] Nor is it a reasonable excuse that an earlier requirement to give a specimen was made but properly withdrawn.[5] Further, the fact that the reasonable cause of suspicion or belief entertained by the constable turns out in the event to be unjustified, unfounded or inaccurate, this will not invalidate the request to justify the refusal on the grounds of reasonable excuse. Reference may also be made to the cases described at 4.13.3 and 4.13.7 below which deal with the onus of proof and reasonable excuse in charges of failing to provide a specimen for analysis in terms of s 7(6). The circumstances of the latter offence usually involve different consideration to an offence under s 6(6), but there may be general similarities in cases under these two sections.

1   *R v Lennard* [1973] 1 WLR 483, [1973] RTR 252; *Williams v Critchley* [1979] RTR 46; *McGregor v Jessop* 1988 SLT 719, 1988 SCCR 339.
2   *Earnshaw v HM Advocate* 1982 JC 11, 1982 SLT 179, 1981 SCCR 279; *McGregor v Jessop* 1988 SLT 719, 1988 SCCR 339; *Pringle v Annan* 1988 SLT 899, 1988 SCCR 423.
3   *McNicol v Peters* 1969 SLT 261.
4   *McGrath v Vipas* [1984] RTR 58.
5   *Nelson v McGuillivray* 1981 SCCR 70.

In *Duncan v Normand*[1] a driver initially agreed to provide a specimen and then refused to co-operate; it was held that he could not then argue that the prosecution had not established that his failure to provide a specimen was without reasonable excuse. In *Lorimer v Russell*,[2] a driver deliberately failed to give a sample into the Camic machine, but then gave a blood sample. The following day she gave a satisfactory breath sample to get her car back. In these circumstances it was held that she could be charged with failing to give a breath sample even although she had given a blood sample; and that the court could consider the successful subsequent breath test in considering the failure to give the first one.

4.5 ARREST (S 6D)

Section 6D of the Road Traffic Act 1988, as amended, provides:[3]

'(1) A constable may arrest a person without warrant if as a result of a preliminary breath test or preliminary drug test the constable reasonably suspects that—

(a)   the proportion of alcohol in the person's breath or blood exceeds the prescribed limit, or

(b)   the person has a specified controlled drug in his body and the proportion of it in the person's blood or urine exceeds the specified limit for that drug.[4]

(1A) The fact that specimens of breath have been provided under section 7 of this Act by the person concerned does not prevent subsection (1) above having effect if the constable who imposed on him the requirement to provide the specimens has reasonable cause to believe that the device used to analyse the specimens has not produced a reliable indication of the proportion of alcohol in the breath of the person.

1   *Duncan v Normand* 1995 SLT 629, 1994 SCCR 508.
2   *Lorimer v Russell* 1996 SLT 501.
3   Section 6D is to be amended, once the provision contained within the Crime and Courts Act 2013 (c 22), Sch 22 para 4 take effect, as follows: 'In section 6D (arrest), in subsection (1), for the words after "preliminary breath test" substitute 'or preliminary drug test the constable reasonably suspects that— (a) the proportion of alcohol in the person's breath or blood exceeds the prescribed limit, or (b) the person has a specified controlled drug in his body and the proportion of it in the person's blood or urine exceeds the specified limit for that drug.'
4   As amended by the Crime and Courts Act 2013 c 22 Sch 22 para 4.

(2) A constable may arrest a person without warrant if –

(a)   the person fails to co-operate with a preliminary test in pursuance of a requirement imposed under section 6, and

(b)   the constable reasonably suspects that the person has alcohol or a drug in his body or is under the influence of a drug.

(2A) Instead of, or before, arresting a person under this section, a constable may detain the person at or near the place where the preliminary test was, or would have been, administered with a view to imposing on the person there a requirement under section 7.[1]

(3) A person may not be arrested under this section while at a hospital as a patient.'[2]

This section gives a police officer the power to arrest an accused if he *reasonably suspects*, as defined at 4.2 above, that the person has alcohol or a drug in his body or is under the influence of a drug or has failed to co-operate with a s 6 requirement. It should be noted, however, that neither the provision of a preliminary test, nor the failure to co-operate, nor the arrest itself is now a necessary prerequisite of further procedure in prosecutions under s 4, s 5 or s 5A of the Act. The officer who effects the arrest is usually, but need not necessarily be, the same officer who required the specimen of breath; but if a different officer arrests the accused, then that officer must have been in a position to have observed the requirement taking place.[3]

In the latter case, one constable administered a breath test to a motorist and the procedure was observed by another constable who then arrested the motorist. It was held that in fact the test had been carried out by both constables within the meaning of the Act as they were both clearly acting together, and it was observed that the underlying purpose of the section is to give power of arrest only to a constable who observed the test and its positive result.

In the absence of evidence that the constable was in uniform (which will invalidate procedures under s 6(2)–(4)), further procedure under s 7 will not be affected.[4]

---

1   As amended by the Criminal Justice (Scotland) Act 2016 asp 1 (Scottish Act) Sch 2(2) para.36.

2   However, that does not render unlawful subsequent testing carried out under s 9. See *DPP v Wilson* [2009] EWHC 1988 (Admin), [2009] RTR 29 and see 6.1 below.

3   *Stewart v Fekkes* 1977 JC 85.

4   *Orr v Urquhart* 1993 SLT 406, 1992 SCCR 240.

In *Goodson v Higson, 2001 SCCR 88*, the Court of Appeal expressed the obiter view that an off-duty police officer who merely requested a drunk driver to await the arrival of unformed colleagues would have been entitled to make a citizen's arrest in the circumstances of that case.

4.6 POWERS OF ENTRY (S 6E)

Section 6E(1) of the Road Traffic Act 1988 gives a police constable in England the power to enter (if need be using reasonable force) any place for the purpose in imposing a s 6(5) requirement or where he wishes to arrest a person under s 6D, both in situations following accident where the constable reasonably suspects the accident involved injury to a person.

Section 6(E)(2) specifically excludes this provision from applying to Scotland, presumably on the grounds that in Scotland a police constable already has common law powers to effect such entry in these circumstances.[1] Whether the use of such powers, or the powers used in the simple exercise of their duties, is reasonable or not will be case specific. Even if not, that may be excused if the police were acting in good faith.[2]

PART 2
PROVISION OF SPECIMENS FOR ANALYSIS UNDER SECTIONS 7 AND 7A

4.7 SECTION 7

Section 7 of the Road Traffic Act 1988[3] provides as follows:

'(1) In the course of an investigation into whether a person has committed an offence under section 3A, 4 or 5 of this Act a constable may, subject to the following provisions of this section and section 9 of this Act, require him –

(a)   to provide two specimens of breath for analysis by means of a device of a type approved by the Secretary of State, or

(b)   to provide a specimen of blood or urine for a laboratory test.

---

1   *Cairns v Keane* 1983 SCCR 277; *MacKenzie v Hingston* 1995 SLT 966, 1995 SCCR 386.
2   *Paton v Dunn* 2012 SCCR 441.
3   As amended by the RTA 1991, Sch 4 para 42, the Criminal Procedure and Investigations Act 1996, s 63(1), the Police Reform Act 2002, s 55, the Serious Organised Crime and Police Act 2005 (c 15), Pt 5, s 154(6)(b), the Crime and Courts Act 2013 c 22 Sch 22 and the Deregulation Act 2015 c 20 Sch11.

(1A) In the course of an investigation into whether a person has committed an offence under section 5A of this Act a constable may, subject to subsections (3) to (7) of this section and section 9 of this Act, require the person to provide a specimen of blood or urine for a laboratory test.

(2) A constable may make a requirement under this section to provide specimens of breath only if—

(a) the requirement is made at a police station or a hospital,

(b) the requirement is imposed in circumstances where section 6(5) of this Act applies, or

(c) the constable is in uniform.

(2C) Where a constable has imposed a requirement on the person concerned to co-operate with a relevant breath test at any place, he is entitled to remain at or near that place in order to impose on him there a requirement under this section.

(2CA) For the purposes of subsection (2C) "a relevant breath test" is a procedure involving the provision by the person concerned of a specimen of breath to be used for the purpose of obtaining an indication whether the proportion of alcohol in his breath or blood is likely to exceed the prescribed limit.

(2D) If a requirement under subsection (1)(a) above has been made at a place other than at a police station, such a requirement may subsequently be made at a police station if (but only if) –

(a)   a device or a reliable device of the type mentioned in subsection (1)(a) above was not available at that place or it was for any other reason not practicable to use such a device there, or

(b)   the constable who made the previous requirement has reasonable cause to believe that the device used there has not produced a reliable indication of the proportion of alcohol in the breath of the person concerned.

(3) A requirement under this section to provide a specimen of blood or urine can only be made at a police station or at a hospital; and it cannot be made at a police station unless –

(a)   the constable making the requirement has reasonable cause to believe that for medical reasons a specimen of breath cannot be provided or should not be required, or

(b)   specimens of breath have not been provided elsewhere and at the time the requirement is made a device or a reliable device of the type mentioned in subsection (1)(a) above is not available at the police station or it is then for any other reason not practicable to use such a device there, or (bb)   a device of the type mentioned in subsection (1)(a) above has been used (at the police station or elsewhere) but the constable who required the specimens of breath has reasonable cause to believe that the device has not produced a reliable indication of the proportion of alcohol in the breath of the person concerned, or

(bc)   as a result of the administration of a preliminary drug test, the constable making the requirement has reasonable cause to believe that the person required to provide a specimen of blood or urine has a drug in his body, or

(c)   the suspected offence is one under section 3A, 4 or 5A of this Act and the constable making the requirement has been advised by a medical practitioner or a registered health care professional that the condition of the person required to provide the specimen might be due to some drug;

but may then be made notwithstanding that the person required to provide the specimen has already provided or been required to provide two specimens of breath.

(4) If the provision of a specimen other than a specimen of breath may be required in pursuance of this section the question whether it is to be a specimen of blood or a specimen of urine and, in the case of a specimen of blood, the question who is to be asked to take it shall be decided (subject to subsection (4A)) by the constable making the requirement.

(4A) Where a constable decides for the purposes of subsection (4) to require the provision of a specimen of blood, there shall be no requirement to provide such a specimen if –

(a)   the medical practitioner who is asked to take the specimen is of the opinion that, for medical reasons, it cannot or should not be taken; or

(b)   the registered health care professional who is asked to take it is of that opinion and there is no contrary opinion from a medical practitioner; and, where by virtue of this subsection there can be no requirement to provide a specimen of blood, the constable may require a specimen of urine instead.

(5) A specimen of urine shall be provided within one hour of the requirement for its provision being made and after the provision of a previous specimen of urine.

(5A) A constable may arrest a person without warrant if—

(a)   the person fails to provide a specimen of breath when required to do so in pursuance of this section, and

(b)   the constable reasonably suspects that the person has alcohol in his body.

(6) A person who, without reasonable excuse, fails to provide a specimen when required to do so in pursuance of this section is guilty of an offence.

(7) A constable must, on requiring any person to provide a specimen in pursuance of this section, warn him that a failure to provide it may render him liable to prosecution.'

4.7.1 General application

Section 7 (subject to the provisions of the Road Traffic Act 1988, ss 8 and 9) governs the provision of specimens for analysis in the course of an investigation as to whether a person has committed an offence under s 3A, 4, 5 or 5A of the Act.

Firstly, under s 7(1) by the provision of two breath specimens into an approved device situated in a police station. The higher of these two readings is to be disregarded.[1] Only where any one of the five sets of circumstances described in s 7(3) applies does the situation arise where the requirement of the breath specimens cannot be satisfied, and the constable in charge of the procedure must turn instead to the alternative requirement of a specimen of blood or urine.

Secondly, under s 7(1)(A) by the provision of blood or urine for laboratory testing in relation to s 5A offences.

Unlike the provision of a preliminary test under s 6 of the Act, the constable making the requirement must warn the accused that failure to provide a specimen in terms of this section may render him liable to prosecution.[2] The Crown cannot amend at the end of the case to alter a charge of failing to supply a specimen of breath to one of failing to supply a specimen of blood.[3] However, amendment will be allowed if there is no significant change to the essence of the charge.[4] The additional subsections reflect the greater anticipated use of preliminary drug tests and also the scope to test under s 7 at places other than the police station.

The choice of which alternative specimen to choose remains with the police save in s 7(4A) situations where taking blood is ruled out for medical reasons.

The use of evidence of samples does not breach the right to a fair trial under Art 6(1) of the European Convention on Human Rights because of the right against self incrimination. In *Brown v Gallagher* 2002 SCCR

---

1   RTA 1988, s 8(1).
2   RTA 1988, s 7(7).
3   *McArthur v MacNeill* 1987 SLT 299, 1986 SCCR 552.
4   *Fenwick v Valentine* 1994 SLT 485, 1993 SCCR 892; see also 2.3.3 above.

943, the Appeal Court took the view that breath specimens, like blood and urine, were material distinct from the person concerned and so the right not to self incriminate was not interfered with, notwithstanding that failure to do so might lead to prosecution. The Court also expressed the view that even if the right against self incrimination was involved in the process, they would have come to the view that the legislation was a proportionate response to the problem of maintaining road safety.

4.8 PROVISION OF SPECIMENS FOR ANALYSIS (SS 7(1) AND (1A))

4.8.1 Section 7(1)

Section 7(1) of the Road Traffic Act 1988 (as amended) provides:

> 'In the course of an investigation into whether a person has committed an offence under section 3A, 4 or 5 of this Act a constable may, subject to the following provisions of this section and section 9 below, require him –
>
> (a)   to provide two specimens of breath for analysis by means of a device of a type approved by the Secretary of State, or
>
> (b)   to provide a specimen of blood or urine for a laboratory test.'

Section 7(1A) provides:

> 'In the course of an investigation into whether a person has committed an offence under section 5A of this Act a constable may, subject to subsections (3) to (7) of this section and section 9 of this Act, require the person to provide a specimen of blood or urine for a laboratory test.'

4.8.2 Definitions

'In the course of an investigation'. This phrase has not come to the notice of the courts; it is submitted that the question is one of fact and that the meaning of the words is plain.

'A constable'. See 4.2.2 above. For the purpose of administering the provision of breath specimens into an approved device, only certain police officers have been trained in the use of such devices and are authorised by the Chief Constable for the area to use them. There is nothing in s 7 or s 8 which says that the officer administering the test and requiring the two specimens of breath has to be appropriately trained or authorised; however, if the evidence indicates that the operator of the device is unskilled or unauthorised, the Crown may have difficulty in proving, for example, that the device was unreliable. There is no requirement that the constable supervising the procedure be in uniform.

To 'require'. To require means to ask.[1] The requirement of a specimen is something different from the provision of a specimen. The requirement must be corroborated.[2]

'Specimen of breath'. Section 11(3) of the Road Traffic Act 1988 provides that a person does not provide a specimen of breath for a breath test or for analysis unless the specimen (a) is sufficient to enable the test or analysis to be carried out, and (b) is provided in such a way as to enable the object of the test to be satisfactorily achieved.

Section 7(2) as amended makes clear that a specimen of breath can be provided at places other than a police station. That remains theoretical, meantime, as no approved portable device yet exists.

'An approved device'. The Intoximeter EC/IR, approved in terms of the Breath Analysis Devices (Scotland) Approval Order 1998 as from 31 July 1998, now enjoys widespread currency. The prosecution is entitled to a presumption that the device is approved within the meaning of the section, but there must at least be oral evidence that the device was used;[3] and it is unnecessary to produce the relevant Approval Order.[4] Further, where the device has done what it should have done if it was in proper working order, there is a presumption that the machine is in proper working order and has been correctly maintained.[5] In *Brown v Gallagher* 2002 SCCR 415, where challenge was made to the admissibility of a breath alcohol reading relying on non-conformity with the relevant Approval Order in terms of manufacture, and doubt as to the reliability, accuracy and consistency of the device, a robust and practical approach was taken by the Court of Appeal. In particular, the fact that the device reacted inconsistently to mouth alcohol on biological testing did not deprive it of type approval, nor did it mean that the device was not functioning properly given there were two samples and safeguards built in to both the device and the now repealed legislation in the form of s 8(2).

'Specimen of blood'. Section 11(4) of the Road Traffic Act 1988 provides:

---

1   *Milne v McDonald* 1971 JC 40 at 42 (per LJC Clyde), 1971 SLT 291.
2   *Carmichael v Gillooly* 1982 SCCR 119.
3   *Knox v Lockhart* 1985 JC 32, 1985 SLT 248, 1984 SCCR 463; *Davidson v Aitchison* 1986 SLT 402, 1985 SCCR 415; *Valentine v Macphail* 1986 SLT 598, 1986 SCCR 321; but see also *Pickland v Carmichael* 1995 SLT 675, 1995 SCCR 76.
4   *Lee v Smith* 1982 SLT 200, 1981 SCCR 267.
5   *Tudhope v McAllister* 1984 SLT 395, 1984 SCCR 182.

'A person provides a specimen of blood if and only if – (a) he consents to the taking of such a specimen from him; and (b) the specimen is taken from him by either a medical practitioner or …a registered health care professional.'

This definition is applied for the interpretation of ss 4–10 of the Act.[1]

Section 15(4) of the Road Traffic Offenders Act 1988[2] provides:

'A specimen of blood shall be disregarded unless –

(a) it was taken from the accused with his consent by a medical practitioner or a registered health care professional;

(b) it was taken from the accused by a medical practitioner or a registered health care professional under section 7A of the Road Traffic Act 1988 and the accused subsequently gave his permission for a laboratory test of the specimen.'

This definition is provided for the purposes of proceedings under ss 3A–5A of the Road Traffic Act 1988.[3]

Section 16(2) of the Road Traffic Offenders Act 1988 provides:

'Subject to subsections (3) and (4) below, evidence that a specimen of blood was taken from the accused with his consent by a medical practitioner or a registered health care professional may be given by the production of a document purporting to certify that fact and to be signed by a medical practitioner or a registered health care professional.'

Subsections (3) and (4) are concerned with the requirements of service.

Section 11(3) of the Road Traffic Act 1988 provides that a specimen for analysis must be sufficient and provided in a way to enable the objective of the analysis to be satisfactorily achieved. A blood specimen will be inadmissible if the court is satisfied that full and proper consent has not been given to the taking of the specimen.[4]

'Specimen of urine'. The procedure for the provision of a specimen of urine is described in s 7(5) of the Road Traffic Act 1988.

'Laboratory test'. Although this phrase is not defined in the legislation, s 16(1)(b) of the Road Traffic Offenders Act 1988 describes the evidential procedure in respect of findings of the proportion of alcohol or any drug found by an authorised analyst in a specimen of blood or urine; and s 16(7) gives a definition of an authorised analyst.

---

1   RTA 1988, s 11(1).
2   As amended to reflect the terms of the RTA 1988, s 7A (inserted by Police Reform Act 2002, s 56).
3   RTOA 1988, s 15(1).
4   *Friel v Dickson* 1992 SLT 1080, 1992 SCCR 513.

4.8.3 Previous procedure unnecessary

It is not necessary that the procedural requirements of the preliminary tests under s 6 of the Road Traffic Act 1988 (including the power of arrest) be observed before this section can apply, although in practice such a test normally will and should be taken. If not, the court will no doubt look closely into the circumstances of why these preliminary steps were not followed in the light of any defence offered by the accused. However, it is submitted that even an illegal arrest will not make the provision of the specimens obtained under this section inadmissible in evidence; the arrest of the motorist in terms of s 4(6) or 6(5) is not required before the procedure under s 7 is embarked upon.[1] In *Orr v Urquhart*[2] there was no evidence that the police constable who required the preliminary breath specimen was in uniform; it was held that this did not invalidate the procedure under s 7.

4.8.4 Where only one breath specimen given

Although the requirement in terms of s 7(1)(a) of the Road Traffic Act 1988 is to provide two breath specimens, in Scotland, in the case of *Reid v Tudhope*, a conviction was upheld on the strength of one only, where the accused, in a considered attempt to frustrate the procedure, failed to provide a second specimen.[3] That approach was briefly followed in England[4] where it was suggested that in such circumstances the driver could be charged under s 5(1), and with failing to provide a specimen under s 7(6) (but could not be found guilty of both) but was overruled by the House of Lords in *Cracknell v Wilks*;[5] where specific mention was made of the statutory safeguards, which sits well with the line taken later in *Brown v Gallagher*.[6]

The tension between the different approaches in the two jurisdictions remained unresolved until the five-bench decision in *Barclay v Richardson*.[7] A majority of the Court approved the approach taken in *Cracknell v Willis* and disapproved *Reid v Tudhope* in part.

---

1   *Carmichael v Wilson* 1993 SLT 290.
2   *Orr v Urquhart* 1993 SLT 406, 1992 SCCR 295.
3   *Reid v Tudhope* 1986 SLT 136, 1985 SCCR 268.
4   *Burridge v East* [1986] RTR 328.
5   *Cracknell v Wilks* [1988] RTR 1.
6   2002 SCCR 415.
7   2013 SCCR 35. All opinions are worth reading, if nothing else, to demonstrate the tensions present.

The Crown argument that the second sample was a safeguard which could be waived by an accused was rejected by the majority, on the basis of statutory interpretation and 'giving the language of the relevant sections of the 1988 Act its ordinary meaning'.[1] In the same vein, s 15 of the Road Traffic Offenders Act did not somehow qualify or contradict the clear terms of ss 7 and 8 of the Road Traffic Act.

Likewise, the suggestion that surrounding facts and circumstances, such as obvious intoxication, could provide sufficiency for a charge under s 5 was contrary to the structure and scheme of the Act and the allegation of a specific proportion of alcohol in breath.

The fact that one reading has been provided may, however, provide assistance in determining the appropriate level of sentence in a s 7(6) prosecution. Clearly, offences under these two subsections are mutually exclusive. On the other hand, where a driver gave a successful first specimen at the first attempt, but was refused a second chance after failing in his first attempt to give a second specimen in circumstances where both failures were genuine, it was held that in declining to give the accused a second chance to provide the second specimen the police had not given him a fair opportunity for the provision of the specimen.[2] In this respect the relevant test as to whether a proper opportunity has been given to the accused to provide a specimen is considered to be that of fairness to the accused in the light of his own actings.

Where there has been failure to provide the specimen there is no reason why the police should not make a further request.[3]

4.9 WHERE REQUIREMENT FOR A BREATH SPECIMEN MAY BE MADE (SS 7(2)–(2D))

Section 7(2) as amended now allows the requirement to be made at a police station or a hospital.

'Relevant breath test' is defined (s 7(2CA)) as a procedure involving the provision by the person concerned of a specimen of breath to be used for the purpose of obtaining an indication whether the proportion of alcohol in his breath or blood is likely to exceed the prescribed limit. In other words, a preliminary breath test under s 6A.

The possibility of administration of the requirement other than at a police station or hospital is restricted by s 7(2B) to situations where the

1   Lord Bonomy at paragraph 72.
2   *Douglas v Stevenson* 1986 JC 178, 1986 SCCR 519.
3   *Reid v Tudhope* 1986 SLT 136, 1985 SCCR 268.

constable making it is in uniform or has already required a person to cooperate with a relevant breath test in circumstances in which s 6(5) of this Act applies (post accident investigation) The officer is entitled to remain at or near the place where the relevant breath requirement was made – s 7(2C).

If the requirement to provide to provide a specimen has been made other than at a police station, it can subsequently be made at a police station only if a device or a reliable device of the type mentioned in s 7(1) (a) sub-s (1)(a) was not available at that place or for any other reason it was not practicable to use such a device there, or because the constable who made the previous requirement has reasonable cause to believe that the device used there has not produced a reliable result – s 7(2D).

Where the requirement is made at a police station that does not necessarily mean that both the requirement and the subsequent provision of the specimens need be made at the same police station; where the requirement was made at one station and it was then discovered that the approved device was not working there, it was held to be in order to take the specimens at another station.[1]

4.10 CIRCUMSTANCES WHERE A BREATH TEST IS NOT APPROPRIATE (S 7(3))

4.10.1 General

This important subsection in effect prescribes the only circumstances under which breath specimens are not to be provided; in other words, unless one of the circumstances described in the subsection applies, the provision of breath specimens must be required.

The first situation described in the subsection is where the constable making the requirement has reasonable cause to believe that for medical reasons a specimen of breath cannot or should not be provided – s 7(3)(a).

The second situation is where an approved device is not present in the particular police station or alternatively where there is such a device but it is not reliable or it is not for any other reason practicable to use the device – s 7(3)(b).

The third situation is where a device has been used at a police station or elsewhere but the officer has reasonable cause to believe that the machine has not produced a reliable result – s 7(3)(bb).

---

1   *Milne v McDonald* 1971 JC 40, 1971 SLT 291; *Tudhope v Fulton* 1987 SLT 419, 1986 SCCR 567.

The fourth situation is where following a preliminary drug test under s 6C, the constable making the requirement has reasonable cause to believe that the person has a drug in his body – s 7(3)(bc).

Finally, a fifth situation exclusively relates to ss 3A, 4 and 5A prosecutions and arises where the constable making the requirement had been advised by a medical practitioner that the accused's condition might be due to some drug.

All these situations, however, are subject to the important proviso that if they arise after the provision of two breath specimens or after just the requirement to provide them has been made, the police constable making the requirement is not precluded from then requiring a specimen of blood or urine.

4.10.2 Medical reasons (s 7(3)(a))

A breath specimen will not be required if the constable making the requirement has reasonable cause to believe that the specimen cannot or should not be provided for medical reasons.

Firstly, the test is that the constable must have reasonable cause to believe that the medical reasons do exist, not simply that he may have reasonable cause to suspect that such medical reasons may exist. The decision of the constable is intended to be an entirely subjective one and the Road Traffic Act 1988 does not require him to consult medical advice (*Dempsey v Catton*).[1] However, there do have to be grounds for the constable's decision. The term 'medical reasons' is therefore thought to be subject to a reasonably broad interpretation, and can include physical causes such as asthma, and psychological causes such as repugnance.[2] The responsibility of the motorist to reveal any medical condition which may preclude the provision of a specimen is described at 4.13.3 below.

This provision has now been considered in Scotland in the case of *Ritchie v Bainbridge*.[3] Initially the Sheriff acquitted on the basis that where an asthmatic driver could not provide the sample without using his inhaler, the police had no factual basis for any concern under s 7(3)(a) and no reasonable cause to believe that the inhaler would interfere with the use of the Camic machine. The Appeal Court, in allowing a crown appeal, emphasised that the police were entitled to be concerned given their lack of medical training and applied the reasoning of *Davies v DPP*[4]

1   *Dempsey v Catton* [1986] RTR 194.
2   *Johnson v West Yorkshire Metropolitan Police* [1986] RTR 167.
3   *Ritchie v Bainbridge* 2000 SCCR 472 2000 SLT 909.
4   *Davies v DPP* [1989] RTR 391.

that medical reasons could include the concern that a specimen might prove unsatisfactory as evidence.

4.10.3 No device or reliable device available (ss 7(3)(b)–(3)(bb))

Secondly, the requirement to provide two specimens of breath is set aside when there is not an approved device at a particular station, or where at the material time the device is not 'reliable', or where it is for any other reason not practicable to use the device, or where the constable in charge of the test has reasonable cause to believe that the device has not produced a reliable indication of the proportion of alcohol in the breath of the person concerned.

Not all police stations are currently equipped with a breath analyser device. Further, only certain officers in any police force are trained in and authorised to work the device, and it appears that if no such officer is on duty at the material time then that will constitute 'any other reason' that it is not practicable to use the device and the alternative procedure should be adopted.[1]

Alternatively, it may be that the device in the particular station is not 'reliable', usually because at the material time it is not properly operational or functioning. Whether the device is or is not reliable will be a question of fact decided by the court. In terms of the proviso to this section, it may be that the fact that the machine is not functioning correctly will become evident while the two specimens of breath are being provided and, if this is so, it will not preclude a further requirement to provide a specimen of blood or urine. However, the prosecution has to prove that the machine is not reliable in the course of evidence if it is to rely on the alternative procedure. The principal issue in such circumstances, as demonstrated by the reported cases, is whether the information shown within the statement or print-out automatically produced by the device is of such a character that, by virtue of that information alone, the device can be considered not reliable. The question of the reliability of the device is to be assessed at the time the requirement to give a specimen is made.[2]

Whether the machine is reliable or not may have to be considered in the light of the manufacturer's instructions.[3]

---

1   *Chief Constable of Avon & Somerset v Kelliher* [1987] RTR 305, [1986] Crim LR 635.
2   *Ramage v Walkingshaw* 1992 SCCR 82; see also *Wilson v Webster* 1999 SCCR 747.
3   *Jeffrey v MacNeill* 1976 JC 54; *Sloan v Smith* 1978 SLT (Notes) 27; *Hogg v Smith* 1978 CO Circular A/37 (all cases involving the roadside breathalyser device); and *Allan v Miller* 1986 SLT 3, 1985 SCCR 227; *Fraser v Mcleod* 1987 SCCR 294 (cases where observation of the manufacturer's instructions was not required).

If the Crown claims that the device is unreliable, it also has to show that it is the only device available in the police station.[1] The fact that the device is the only one available may be inferred from the circumstances of the procedure.[2] If there is no device, or no reliable device, available at one police station, the accused may be taken to another station and required to give a specimen there.[3]

In a case where the accused failed to give a specimen, the Crown did not have to prove that the Camic device was working properly.[4]

The question of informalities in the print-out and whether the machine is in the circumstances reliable or unreliable, and the relevant cases thereon, are dealt with at 5.8.5ff below.

Section 7(3)(bb) of the Road Traffic Act 1988 has been introduced to anticipate projected developments in breath analyser devices which can detect the substances which interfere with the true analysis of the proportion of alcohol in the motorist's breath, a situation not covered by s 7(3)(b). However, having regard to the broad terms of this subsection, it may be used more freely by prosecutors.

4.10.4 Sections 7(3)(bc)–(3)(c)

These subsections have not so far come to the attention of the court, and their application is essentially a matter of fact. It should be noted that these subsections are restricted to prosecutions under ss 3A, 4 and 5A of the Road Traffic Act 1988. In s 7(3)(c) the situation can arise only once a medical practitioner has suggested that the accused's condition may be due to some drug. The Act appears to impose no obligation on the constable to seek such medical advice; however, once the constable has received such advice from a medical practitioner, he must act on that advice whatever the circumstances, and has no discretion to do otherwise.

4.10.5 Definition: medical practitioner or registered health care professional

It is submitted that a medical practitioner is an appropriately qualified doctor who is authorised to be in medical practice in this country. There appears to be no reported Scottish case where the status of the medical practitioner has been challenged.

---

1   *Houston v McLeod* 1986 JC 96, 1986 SCCR 219; *Walker v Walkingshaw* 1991 SCCR 695.
2   *Welsh v McGlennan* 1992 SCCR 379.
3   *Tudhope v Fulton* 1987 SLT 419, 1986 SCCR 567.
4   *Simpson v Lowe* 1992 SLT 425, 1991 SCCR 728.

In the interpretation section, s11(2) provides that:

'registered health care professional" means a person (other than a medical practitioner) who is—

(a)   a registered nurse; or

(b)   a registered member of a health care profession which is designated for the purposes of this paragraph by an order made by the Secretary of State.'

Section 11(2A) provides that:

'A health care profession is any profession mentioned in section 60(2) of the Health Act 1999 (c. 8) other than the profession of practising medicine and the profession of nursing.'

4.11 PROVISION OF SPECIMEN OF BLOOD OR URINE (SS 7(4) AND (4A))

4.11.1 Sections 7(4) and (4A)

Sections 7(4) and (4A) provide that:

'(4) If the provision of a specimen other than a specimen of breath may be required in pursuance of this section the question whether it is to be a specimen of blood or a specimen of urine and, in the case of a specimen of blood, the question who is to be asked to take it shall be decided (subject to subsection (4A)) by the constable making the requirement.

(4A) Where a constable decides for the purposes of subsection (4) to require the provision of a specimen of blood, there shall be no requirement to provide such a specimen if –

(a)   the medical practitioner who is asked to take the specimen is of the opinion that, for medical reasons, it cannot or should not be taken; or

(b)   the registered health care professional who is asked to take it is of that opinion and there is no contrary opinion from a medical practitioner;

and, where by virtue of this subsection there can be no requirement to provide a specimen of blood, the constable may require a specimen of urine instead.'

4.11.2 Definitions

See 4.8.2 and 4.10.5 above.

In terms of s 11(4) of the Road Traffic Act 1988 as amended:

'(4) A person provides a specimen of blood if and only if—

(a)   he consents to the taking of such a specimen from him; and

(b)   the specimen is taken from him either by a medical practitioner or by a registered health care professional.'

4.11.3 General application

It is clear from the terms of s 7(4) of the Road Traffic Act 1988 that the option of which specimen (either blood or urine) the accused is to provide in circumstances where a breath specimen is not to be taken rests entirely within the discretion of the constable making the requirement. There is no provision for the motorist's preference or view to be taken into account by the constable. *McLeod v MacFarlane*[1] contradicts earlier authorities which suggested that for the provision of the specimen under this section to be properly made the constable making the requirement must tell the motorist of the choice that he has to make and then come to an informed decision about which specimen to require.[2] These cases are now specifically overruled.[3]

The officer who makes the requirement does not have to be the same constable who required any previous breath specimen under s 7(3).

The only qualification to the constable's power is under s 7(4A) when a medical practitioner or registered health care professional expresses the opinion that for medical reasons a blood sample should not be required. There is, however, again no apparent obligation on the constable to seek out such a medical opinion in this matter. Neither does the Act require a constable to justify his choice of the specimen required. Unless a breath specimen cannot or should not be taken for medical reasons, the constable has complete discretion as to whether the motorist should in these circumstances be required to provide a sample of blood or urine.

If a motorist cannot provide a blood or urine sample when required the police can competently go on to require the alternative specimen.[4]

Reference should also be made to 4.13.3 below.

4.11.4 Other provisions

Section 7(4) of the Road Traffic Act 1988 has to be read in the context of the other provisions of s 7, and is subject to the provisions of ss 11(3) and

---

1   *McLeod v MacFarlane* 1993 SCCR 178, overruling *Carmichael v MacKay* 1991 SCCR 953.

2   See eg, *Hobbs v Clark* [1988] RTR 36; *DPP v Byrne* [1991] RTR 119; *Carmichael v MacKay* 1991 SCCR 953.

3   *McLeod v MacFarlane* 1993 SCCR 178; *DPP v Warren* [1992] 3 WLR 884.

4   *McGregor v Jessop* 1988 SLT 719, 1988 SCCR 339.

(4) of the Road Traffic Act 1988 and ss 15(4) and 16(2) of the Road Traffic Offenders Act 1988.

4.12 PROVISION OF URINE SPECIMEN (S 7(5))

4.12.1 Section 7(5)

Section 7(5) of the Act provides:

> 'A specimen of urine shall be provided within one hour of the requirement for its provision being made and after the provision of a previous specimen of urine.'

4.12.2 General application

In terms of this subsection, two specimens of urine have to be given within one hour of the requirement. While the two samples have to be given within an hour of the requirement, there is no stipulation as to when, during the hour, the samples must be given. For practical reasons, the first sample is usually given at the beginning of the period, and the second one towards the end. Unlike the previous legislation, there is no express provision that the first specimen shall be discarded.

The terms of this subsection are simpler than under the previous legislation which also required the provision of two samples of urine and described the circumstances under which a failure would arise.

In a prosecution under the former legislation, where the second urine specimen was provided just over an hour after the requirement, but exactly an hour after the first specimen was provided, it was held to be competent to convict the accused on the basis of the second specimen.[1] However, the accused was convicted on the basis of the specimen which he had provided, not on his failure to provide a specimen within the terms of s 9(5) of the former [1972 Act] legislation. As the present subsection requires that both specimens shall be given within an hour, it may be that the particular circumstances of *Tudhope v Stevenson*[2] would lead under the present law to an acquittal.

In *MacDougall v MacPhail*,[3] the accused was asked to give a urine specimen, but police officers gave evidence that insufficient was produced to divide the specimen into two parts. It was held that the duty on the

---

1   *Tudhope v Stevenson* 1980 SLT (Notes) 94 (following *Roney v Matthews* [1975] RTR 273).
2   *Tudhope v Stevenson* 1980 SLT (Notes) 94.
3   *MacDougall v MacPhail* 1991 SLT 801, 1991 SCCR 358.

accused was to provide a specimen of sufficient quantity to be divided into two parts; and that while the sufficiency of a specimen for analysis can be spoken to only by an analyst, the best evidence as to whether the specimen could be divided into two was that of the supervising police officers. In particular, although s 15(5) of the Road Traffic Offenders Act 1988 provides that the specimen is divided into two parts only when the accused requests a specimen at the time, any specimen given must obviously be capable of division; accordingly[1] the question of sufficiency of the specimen does not depend on a request by the accused for a part of the specimen.

4.13 FAILURE TO PROVIDE A SPECIMEN (S 7(6))

4.13.1 Section 7(6)

Section 7(6) of the Road Traffic Act 1988 provides as follows:

'A person who, without reasonable excuse, fails to provide a specimen when required to do so in pursuance of this section is guilty of an offence.'

4.13.2 General application

Failure includes refusal.[2] The specimens provided must be sufficient to enable the analysis to be carried out. Section 11(3) of the Road Traffic Act 1988 makes clear that a person does not co-operate with a preliminary test or provide a specimen of breath for analysis unless his co-operation or the specimen is (a) sufficient to enable the test or the analysis to be carried out, and (b) provided in such a way as to enable the objective of the test or analysis to be satisfactorily achieved.

If a reliable device is not available at the police station to which the accused is first taken, the test can competently be carried out at another police station.[3]

The prosecution does not have to prove that the device is working properly where it is alleged that the accused has refused to give a specimen.[4]

Where an accused was unable to provide a second specimen of urine, the police are entitled to require a blood specimen, and should do so.[5]

---

1 Overruling *Aitchison v Johnstone* 1987 SCCR 225.
2 RTA 1988, s 11(2).
3 *Tudhope v Fulton* 1987 SLT 419, 1986 SCCR 567.
4 *Simpson v Lowe* 1992 SLT 425, 1991 SCCR 728.
5 *McGregor v Jessop* 1988 SLT 719, 1988 SCCR 339.

4.13.3 Reasonable excuse: onus of proof

The Crown must prove that the motorist had no reasonable cause for refusing to provide the specimen of whatever kind.[1] This is normally done by police officers testifying that no apparent cause existed for the refusal. Alternatively, the officers may describe the reasons, if any, given by the accused for declining to give the sample and thereafter the Crown requires to justify the proposition that such reasons did not amount to a reasonable excuse in the circumstances.[2] At the same time, while it is for the prosecution to demonstrate that no reasonable excuse exists for the refusal, if the accused wishes the court to consider the question of whether he has a reasonable excuse, or whether his excuse is reasonable, then he may have to raise the issue and put it properly into evidence at the appropriate time.

The position is possibly different in England and Scotland. In England it has been held that the duty to give a specimen includes a duty to advise the police of any reason why the specimen cannot be given, although these observations were made obiter.[3] Such a view was specifically rejected in *Pringle v Annan*.[4] In that case the motorist suffered from injuries in a car accident that precluded him from giving a breath specimen, and these injuries were not obvious to the police officer making the requirement. The appeal court held that if the motorist had been asked if there was any reason for his inability to provide a breath specimen he would have been obliged to answer, but that there was no general duty on a motorist to inform the police of any reason for his inability to provide a specimen. In *McClory v Owen-Thomas*[5] it was observed that there was nothing in the section which required the motorist to disclose anything to the police, or which relieves the Crown of the burden of proving the absence of reasonable excuse if the motorist fails or refuses to provide a specimen without explanation, even where the condition which justifies the failure is well known and of long standing.

4.13.4 Instructions to provide specimen

The Act does not indicate what instructions are to be given by the police officers to the motorist to enable him to provide the specimens properly.

---

1   *Stewart v Aitcheson* 1984 SCCR 357.
2   *Earnshaw v HM Advocate* 1982 JC 11, 1982 SLT (Notes) 179, 1981 SCCR 279; *McLeod v Murray* 1986 SCCR 369; *McGregor v Jessop* 1988 SLT 719, 1988 SCCR 339; *Milne v Westwater* 1990 JC 205, 1990 SCCR 46.
3   *Teape v Godfrey* [1986] RTR 213 at 221.
4   *Pringle v Annan* 1988 SLT 899, 1988 SCCR 423.
5   *McClory v Owen-Thomas* 1990 SLT 323, 1989 SCCR 402.

However, it seems clear that sufficient and proper instructions should be given, and whether or not that is done in any case is a matter of fact for the court to decide on the evidence;[1] it therefore appears to follow that, if inadequate instructions are given, and this can be related to the failure to provide a specimen, the accused may be able to claim that he had a reasonable excuse for not providing the specimen required. Cases which feature instructions in respect of particular devices are *Jeffrey v MacNeill;*[2] *Sloan v Smith;*[3] *Hogg v Smith;*[4] *Allan v Miller;*[5] and *Fraser v McLeod.*[6]

4.13.5 Agreement to provide sample

An accused must unequivocally agree to provide a specimen or sample, otherwise he will be deemed to have failed to comply with the provisions of the Act. It is therefore insufficient for the accused, in response to a request for a sample, merely to say 'please yourself' and such an answer will constitute the offence of failure to provide a specimen.[7] Which part of the body a sample of blood is taken from is at the discretion of the doctor.[8]

A conditional acceptance is also not sufficient and will be deemed to be a refusal;[9] eg *Rushton v Higgins*, a case where the driver agreed to give a sample but insisted that it be taken from his big toe.[10] Immediately a failure or refusal occurs, the offence is committed and complete, and the situation cannot be redeemed by the accused changing his mind and offering subsequently to comply with the request to provide a specimen.[11] Moreover the accused cannot complain if he is given further opportunity to provide a specimen after he has initially failed to do so.[12]

1   *Kelly v McKinnon* 1985 SLT 487, 1985 SCCR 97; *Fleming v Tudhope* 1987 CO Circulars A/16.
2   *Jeffrey v MacNeill* 1976 SLT 134.
3   *Sloan v Smith* 1978 SLT (Notes) 27.
4   *Hogg v Smith* 1978 CO Circulars A/37.
5   *Allan v Miller* 1986 SLT 3, 1985 SCCR 227.
6   *Fraser v McLeod* 1987 SCCR 294.
7   *MacPhail v Forbes* 1975 SLT (Sh Ct) 48; *Milne v Elliot* 1974 SLT (Notes) 71; *MacDonald v MacKenzie* 1975 SLT 190; *Beveridge v Allan* 1986 SCCR 542, *Lorimer v Russell* 1996 SLT 501.
8   *Cader v Galt* 1976 SCCR Supp 116.
9   *Solesbury v Pugh* [1969] 1 WLR 1114; [1969] 2 All ER 1171.
10   *Rushton v Higgins* [1972] RTR 456 and *Pettigrew v Northumbria Police Authority* [1976] RTR 177.
11   *Harris v Tudhope* 1985 SCCR 305; *Beveridge v Allan* 1986 SCCR 542; *Thomson v Allan* 1989 SLT 868, 1989 SCCR 327; *Duncan v Normand* 1995 SLT 629, 1994 SCCR 508.
12   *Thomson v Allan* 1989 SLT 868.

The prosecution must prove that the accused has given his full consent to the test.[1]

Where an accused failed to give a breath specimen, and then agreed to provide a blood sample, it was held that it is still possible for a charge of failing to provide a specimen to be made, and evidence of a successful breath specimen given the following day for the purpose of retrieving the car from the police could competently be referred to in evidence.[2] In *Brannigan v McGlennan*[3] it was held to be appropriate for the police to require a specimen of blood after an accused had been charged with failure to supply a specimen of breath.

4.13.6 Reasonable opportunity to provide specimen

The accused motorist must be given a fair and reasonable opportunity of providing the specimens required. What is a fair and reasonable opportunity is a matter for the court. In *Douglas v Stevenson*[4] a driver failed at his first attempt to provide a breath specimen into a Camic device, but succeeded at his second attempt. He then failed at his first attempt at providing a second specimen, and was not given a second chance to provide the second specimen. It was held that the police had not acted fairly in refusing the accused a second opportunity to provide the second specimen, and he was acquitted. Equally, the police may give the motorist several opportunities to provide a specimen.[5]

4.13.7 Reasonable excuse

Section 7(6) of the Road Traffic Act 1988 makes it an offence to fail to provide a specimen for analysis without reasonable excuse. The courts have traditionally taken a narrow view of what is to be regarded as a reasonable excuse. The failure to give proper instructions might justify a refusal,[6] or might be regarded as a failure properly to require a specimen in the first place. In *McLeod v Murray*[7] the accused had been assaulted by the police and refused to give a specimen for analysis because he could not trust the police not to tamper with it; this was held to be a reasonable

---

1   *Friel v Dickson* 1992 SLT 1080, 1992 SCCR 513, [1992] RTR 366.
2   *Lorimer v Russell* 1996 SLT 501.
3   *Brannigan v McGlennan* 2000 SCCR 12.
4   *Douglas v Stevenson* 1986 SCCR 519.
5   *Thomson v Allan* 1989 SLT 868, 1989 SCCR 327.
6   *Kelly v MacKinnon* 1985 SLT 487, 1985 SCCR 97, (although it did not do so in that case).
7   *McLeod v Murray* 1986 SCCR 369.

excuse. However, not every apprehension about the conduct of the police will justify a refusal.[1]

The majority of cases involving reasonable excuse have been concerned with the question of whether the accused is physically or mentally able to give a specimen: or whether the provision of a specimen will involve a serious risk to the accused's health. The courts have normally regarded the standard of evidence and proof that the accused has to produce in order to demonstrate that he was not capable of giving a sample to be a high one. In *Hogg v Lockhart*[2] it was established that the accused had a very powerful repugnance to blood and hypodermic needles and in those circumstances the court held that his refusal to give a blood specimen was reasonable. In *McGregor v Jessop*[3] it was held that a motorist who made several genuine attempts to provide a second urine sample but was unable to do so could be said to have a reasonable excuse for failing to provide a specimen. However, that case was distinguished in *McGuckin v O'Donnell*[4] where the conduct of a motorist who repeatedly said he was unable to provide a second urine sample but made no actual attempt justified the Sheriff's conclusion that he was in effect refusing. In *Lockhart v Stanbridge*[5] it was held that a mental condition of a very extreme character which rendered the accused unable to provide a specimen was a reasonable excuse; in that case medical evidence from a specialist in clinical psychology was led. In *Pringle v Annan*[6] an accused was physically unable to give a specimen of breath because of chest injuries he had just received in a car crash. Reference should also be made to 4.4.2 above and 8.5.3 below.

On the other hand, a mere fear of needles is not a sufficient excuse,[7] even where the fear amounts to a phobia which does not amount to an invincible repugnance.[8] Nor is embarrassment a reasonable excuse.[9] Where an accused had a medical condition but deliberately declined to give a specimen he was held not to have a reasonable excuse.[10] In *Milne*

---

1   *Gallacher v Scott* 1989 SLT 397, 1989 SCCR 61.
2   *Hogg v Lockhart* 1973 SLT (Sh Ct) 40.
3   *McGregor v Jessop* 1988 SLT 719, 1988 SCCR 337.
4   *McGuckin v O'Donnell* 2001 SLT 768.
5   *Lockhart v Stanbridge* 1989 SCCR 220.
6   *Pringle v Annan*1988 SLT 899, 1988 SCCR 423.
7   *Glickman v McKinnon* 1981 JC 81; see also *R v Lennard* [1975] RTR 252.
8   *McIntosh v Lowe* 1991 SCCR 154.
9   *Palmer v Killion* [1983] RTR 46.
10   *Singh v McLeod* 1986 SCCR 656

v Westwater[1] the accused's claim that he was terrified of needles was disbelieved.

It is not a reasonable excuse that the accused was not in fact driving or in charge of the vehicle.[2] However, in such a case disqualification is not obligatory (see 4.13.3 above). Nor is a refusal justified because the accused wishes to wait until his solicitor arrives.[3] It would appear from the terms of this section that a failure to arrest the accused under s 6D would not constitute a reasonable excuse for the accused to provide a specimen. However, if the requirement to provide a sample of blood or urine is refused following what the police consider was a failure by the accused to provide a proper second breath specimen, the Crown will be required to prove that the breath analyser device is unreliable before it can proceed to hold that the accused refused to provide a specimen of blood or urine.[4] In that case, police officers considered that the accused had failed to provide a proper specimen, and charged him under s 7(6). Thereafter, they discovered that the breath analysis device had produced proper readings, but the print-out was inaccurate in other respects. It was held that before the Crown could secure a conviction in these circumstances, it was necessary to prove that the machine was unreliable before it could properly require a blood or urine sample. As the Crown had not proved this, the accused was acquitted. On the other hand, where an accused only pretended to blow into the Camic device, and the machine produced a 'breath invalid' print-out, the prosecution does not require to show that the device was reliable.[5]

The Crown does not have to prove that the other breath analyser device is working properly if the court is satisfied that the driver has deliberately failed to provide a specimen.[6] A driver cannot claim that he has a reasonable excuse if he first agreed to give a sample and then refused to co-operate.[7] Reference should also be made to 4.4.2 above.

It should be noted that if, in terms of ss 6(4) and 7(6), a motorist has a reasonable excuse for failing to supply one or other of a specimen of blood or urine, then it is still open for the police to further require a specimen of

1   *Pringle v Annan* 1990 JC 205, 1990 SCCR 46.
2   *McLellan v Tudhope* 1984 SCCR 397.
3   *Manuel v Stewart* 1986 SLT 593, 1986 SCCR 121.
4   *Tudhope v Quinn* 1984 SCCR 255.
5   *Simpson v Lowe* 1992 SLT 425, 1991 SCCR 728.
6   *Simpson v Lowe* 1992 SLT 425, 1991 SCCR 728; see also *Brannigan v McGlennan* 2000 SCCR 12.
7   *Duncan v Normand* 1995 SLT 629, 1994 SCCR 508.

the remaining alternative.[1] What may be a reasonable excuse for failing to provide one kind of specimen will not necessarily (or indeed normally) be a reasonable excuse for failing to provide a different kind of specimen.

What duties are incumbent upon a motorist to reveal the nature of any disability to provide a specimen are described at 4.13.3 above.

4.13.8 Procedure and penalties

Proceedings for refusal to provide a specimen are taken summarily, and the penalties are given in Sch 2 to the Road Traffic Offenders Act 1988.

Obligatory disqualification only applies in cases where the accused was driving or attempting to drive. In such cases should disqualification not follow endorsement is in the range of 3–11 points. The maximum sentence is six months or level 5 fine or both.

If it is established that the accused was not in fact driving or attempting to drive, disqualification is discretionary.[2] Endorsement is set at ten penalty points. The maximum sentence is three months or level 4 fine or both.

Where the charge libelled is a failure to provide a specimen of breath, the Crown cannot amend the complaint at the end of its case to a charge of failure to supply a specimen of blood.[3] However, where an accused was taken to a police station where it was discovered that the Camic device was not working, and was then taken to another police station, the Crown was allowed to amend the *locus* in the complaint to include the second police station.[4] Similarly, amendment to the complaint will be allowed if the alteration is not material.[5]

4.14 WARNINGS (S 7(7))

4.14.1 Section 7(7)

Section 7(7) of the Road Traffic Act 1988 provides as follows:

'A constable must, on requiring any person to provide a specimen in pursuance of this section, warn him that a failure to provide it may render him liable to prosecution.'

---

1   *Hall v Allan* 1984 SLT 199, 1983 SCCR 520.
2   See also *Aird v Valentine* 1986 SCCR 353.
3   *McArthur v MacNeill* 1986 JC 182, 1987 SLT 299, 1986 SCCR 552.
4   *Tudhope v Fulton* 1987 SLT 419, 1986 SCCR 567; see also *Belcher v MacKinnon* 1986 CO Circulars A/55.
5   *Fenwick v Valentine* 1994 SLT 485, 1993 SCCR 892; see also 2.3.3 above.

4.14.2 General application

It seems clear that the Road Traffic Act 1988 intends that the accused will be warned at the same time as the requirement is made that failure to provide the specimen in terms of the requirement may result in prosecution. The Act, however, provides no sanction in the event of such a failure. It must be assumed that if the constable making the requirement fails to give a clear and unequivocal warning that such failure to provide a specimen may lead to prosecution, then this will invalidate the entire procedure and lead to the specimen being considered inadmissible in evidence. This is despite the terms of s 15(2) of the Road Traffic Offenders Act 1988 which provides that evidence of the proportion of alcohol or any drug in a specimen of breath, blood or urine provided by the accused shall be taken into account 'in all cases'. The provisions of s 15(2) must presumably be construed as meaning that such specimens will be taken into account in all cases so long as the specimens are taken in accordance with the provisions of the Act.[1]

4.15 SPECIMENS OF BLOOD TAKEN FROM PERSONS INCAPABLE OF CONSENTING (S 7A)

Section 7A of the Road Traffic Act 1988[2] provides as follows:

'7A Specimens of blood taken from persons incapable of consenting

(1) A constable may make a request to a medical or health care practitioner for him to take a specimen of blood from a person (`the person concerned') irrespective of whether that person consents if –

   (a)   that person is a person from whom the constable would (in the absence of any incapacity of that person and of any objection under section 9) be entitled under section 7 to require the provision of a specimen of blood for a laboratory test;

   (b)   it appears to that constable that that person has been involved in an accident that constitutes or is comprised in the matter that is under investigation or the circumstances of that matter;

   (c)   it appears to that constable that that person is or may be incapable (whether or not he has purported to do so) of giving a valid consent to the taking of a specimen of blood; and

---

1   *R v Fox [1985] RTR 337 at 343, per Lord Fraser; [1985] 1 WLR 1126, Murray v DPP [1993] RTR 209*, Simpson *v Spalding* [1987] RTR 221.

2   Inserted by the Police Reform Act 2002, s 56 and amended by The Deregulation Act 2015

(d) it appears to that constable that that person's incapacity is attributable to medical reasons.

(2) A request under this section –

(a) shall not be made to a medical or health care practitioner who for the time being has any responsibility (apart from the request) for the clinical care of the person concerned; and

(b) shall not be made to a practitioner other than a police medical or health care practitioner unless –

  (i) it is not reasonably practicable for the request to made to a police medical or health care practitioner; or

  (ii) it is not reasonably practicable for such a practitioner (assuming him to be willing to do so) to take the specimen.

(3) It shall be lawful for a medical or health care practitioner to whom a request is made under this section, if he thinks fit –

(a) to take a specimen of blood from the person concerned irrespective of whether that person consents; and

(b) to provide the sample to a constable.

(4) If a specimen is taken in pursuance of a request under this section, the specimen shall not be subjected to a laboratory test unless the person from whom it was taken –

(a) has been informed that it was taken; and

(b) has been required by a constable to give his permission for a laboratory test of the specimen; and

(c) has given his permission.

(5) A constable must, on requiring a person to give his permission for the purposes of this section for a laboratory test of a specimen, warn that person that a failure to give the permission may render him liable to prosecution.

(6) A person who, without reasonable excuse, fails to give his permission for a laboratory test of a specimen of blood taken from him under this section is guilty of an offence.

(7) In this section

'medical or health care practitioner' means a medical practitioner or a registered health care professional

'police medical or health care practitioner' means a medical practitioner, or a registered health care professional who is engaged under any agreement to provide medical or health care services for purposes connected with the activities of a police force.'

4.15.1 General application

Section 7A introduces the potential, subject to s 9, of taking blood samples from those who are or appear incapable of consenting, and who, in the view of the constable, appear to have been involved in an accident that is or related to the matter being investigated. The person must be someone the constable would ordinarily be able to make the s 7 requirement of, but appears to the constable to be incapable because of medical reasons.

The request to take a specimen is not made to the medical practitioner responsible for the clinical care of the person but, in terms of s 9(1A), they must be consulted and may object under s 9(2) if it would be prejudicial to their patient's proper care and treatment. Instead it is to be made to a police medical practitioner, as defined in s 7A(7), save where it not reasonably practical to do so or for a police medical practitioner to take the specimen. Another medical practitioner will then suffice.

A blood sample taken and passed on to the constable under s 7A shall be lawful even though consent is absent. However, it is only done if the medical or health care practitioner thinks it fit to do so – s 7A(3) – and accordingly the request may be refused irrespective of concerns as to proper care and treatment.

If a specimen is taken it cannot be subjected to laboratory testing unless the person it was taken from knows that has been taken, and has thereafter given permission for testing, having been required to do so by a constable – s 7A(4).

Section 7A(6) introduces a new offence of subsequently failing, without reasonable excuse to give permission for a laboratory test of a specimen of blood taken. As with s 7, a warning must be given that a failure to give the permission may lead to prosecution – s 7A(5)

The use of evidence of samples does not breach the right to a fair trial under Art 6(1) of the European Convention on Human Rights because of the right against self incrimination. In *Brown v Gallagher* 2002 SCCR 943, the Appeal Court took the view that breath specimens, like blood and urine, were material distinct from the person concerned and so the right not to self incriminate was not interfered with, notwithstanding that failure to do so might lead to prosecution. The Court also expressed the view that even if the right against self incrimination was involved in the process, they would have come to the view that the legislation was a proportionate response to the problem of maintaining road safety.

4.15.2 Definitions

'An accident that constitutes or is comprised in the matter that is under investigation or the circumstances of that matter.' This is a question of fact.

'*A constable*'. See 4.2 above. There is nothing in the section requiring specialist training for the purpose of requesting a sample. The provision that appearance of medical reason for incapacity is a matter for the constable must presume that the assessment is based on medical advice, if only arising from the protection of s 9(1A). Otherwise the Crown might have difficulty in proving the point.

To 'require'. To require means to ask. The requirement of a specimen is something different from the provision of a specimen.

'*Laboratory test*'. Although this phrase is not defined in the legislation, s 16(1)(b) of the Road Traffic Offenders Act 1988 describes the evidential procedure in respect of findings of the proportion of alcohol or any drug found by an authorised analyst in a specimen of blood or urine; and s 16(7) gives a definition of an authorised analyst.

4.15.3 Previous procedure unnecessary

By the nature of the section this is self-evident.

4.16 FAILURE TO PROVIDE A SPECIMEN (S 7A(6))

4.16.1 Section 7A(6)

Section 7A(6) of the Road Traffic Act 1988 provides as follows:

> 'A person who, without reasonable excuse, fails to give his permission for a laboratory test of a specimen of blood taken from him under this section is guilty of an offence.'

4.16.2 General application

Failure includes refusal.[1]

4.16.3 Reasonable excuse: onus of proof

The Crown must prove that the motorist had no reasonable cause for refusing to give permission.[2] This will presumably be done by police officers testifying that no apparent cause existed for the refusal. Alternatively, the officers may describe the reasons, if any, given by the accused for refusing to give permission and thereafter the Crown requires to justify the proposition that such reasons did not amount to

---

1   RTA 1988, s 11(2).
2   *Stewart v Aitcheson* 1984 SCCR 357.

a reasonable excuse in the circumstances.[1] At the same time, while it is for the prosecution to demonstrate that no reasonable excuse exists for the refusal, if the accused wishes the court to consider the question of whether he has a reasonable excuse, or whether his excuse is reasonable, then he may have to raise the issue and put it properly into evidence at the appropriate time. See also 4.13.3.

4.16.4 Agreement to give permission

See 4.13.5.

4.16.5 Reasonable opportunity to give permission

The accused motorist must be given a fair and reasonable opportunity of providing the permission required. What is a fair and reasonable opportunity is a matter for the court. The cases referred to at 4.13.6 provide general guidance.

4.16.6 Reasonable excuse

The cases referred to at 4.13.7 may provide some guidance, although, in fact, reasonable excuse is likely to be a much harder concept to rely on in the context of s 7A.

4.16.7 Procedure and penalties

Proceedings for refusal to provide a specimen are taken summarily, and the penalties are given in Sch 2 to the Road Traffic Offenders Act 1988.

Obligatory disqualification only applies in cases where the accused was driving or attempting to drive. In such cases, should disqualification not follow, endorsement is in the range of 3–11 points. The maximum sentence is six months or level 5 fine or both.

If it is established that the accused was not in fact driving or attempting to drive, disqualification is discretionary. Endorsement is set at ten penalty points. The maximum sentence is three months or level 4 fine or both.

---

1   *Earnshaw v HM Advocate* 1982 JC 11, 1982 SLT (Notes) 179, 1981 SCCR 279; *McLeod v Murray* 1986 SCCR 369; *McGregor v Jessop* 1988 SLT 719, 1988 SCCR 339; *Milne v Westwater* 1990 JC 205, 1990 SCCR 46.

4.17 CHOICE OF SPECIMENS OF BREATH (S 8)

Section 8 of the Road Traffic Act 1988, as amended by the Deregulation Act 2015, now simply provides:

'(1) Of any two specimens of breath provided by any person in pursuance of section 7 of this Act that with the lower proportion of alcohol in the breath shall be used and the other shall be disregarded.'

The previous option in s 8(2) of having blood or urine taken where a reading was under 50 (and prior to the newer lower limits) has been repealed across the UK.

Chapter 5

Use of specimens and evidence in proceedings under the Road Traffic Act 1988, sections 3A, 4, 5 and 5A

5.1 SECTION 15

Sections 15 and 16 of the Road Traffic Offenders Act 1988 provide important evidential considerations in prosecutions under ss 3A, 4, 5 and 5A of the Road Traffic Act 1988.

Section 15 of the Road Traffic Offenders Act 1988[1] reads in full as follows:

'(1) This section and section 16 of this Act apply in respect of proceedings for an offence under any of sections 3A–5A of the Road Traffic Act 1988 (driving offences connected with drink or drugs); and expressions used in this section and section 16 of this Act have the same meaning as in sections 3A to 10 of that Act.

(2) Evidence of the proportion of alcohol or any drug in a specimen of breath, blood or urine provided by or taken from the accused shall, in all cases (including cases where the specimen was not provided or taken in connection with the alleged offence), be taken into account and –

(a),   it is to be assumed, subject to subsection (3) below, that the proportion of alcohol in the accused's breath, blood or urine at the time of the alleged offence was not less than in the specimen;

(b)   it is to be assumed, subject to subsection (3A) below, that the proportion of drug in the accused's blood or urine at the time of the alleged offence was not less than in the specimen.

(3) The assumption in subsection 2(a) above shall not be made if the accused proves –

(a)   that he consumed alcohol before he provided the specimen or had it taken from him and –

(i)   in relation to an offence under section 3A, after the time of the alleged offence, and

---

1   As amended by the RTA 1991, Sch 4 para 87, the Police Reform Act 2002 (c 30), Pt 4 (c 2), s 57(3), the Crime and Courts Act 2013 c 22 Sch 22 and the Deregulation Act 2015 c 20 Sch11(1).

    (ii)   otherwise, after he had ceased to drive, attempt to drive or be in charge of a vehicle on a road or other public place, and

(b)   that had he not done so the proportion of alcohol in his breath, blood or urine would not have exceeded the prescribed limit and, if it is alleged that he was unfit to drive through drink, would not have been such as to impair his ability to drive properly.

(3A) The assumption in subsection 2(b) above is not be made if the accused proves –

(a)   that he took the drug before he provided the specimen or had it taken from him and –

    (i)   in relation to an offence under section 3A, after the time of the alleged offence, and

    (ii)   otherwise, after he had ceased to drive, attempt to drive or be in charge of a vehicle on a road or other public place, and

(b)   that had he not done so the proportion of drug in his blood or urine–

    (i)   in the case of a specified controlled drug, would not have exceeded the specified limit for that drug, and,

    (ii)   if it is alleged that he was unfit to drive through drugs, would not have been such as to impair his ability to drive properly.

(4) A specimen of blood shall be disregarded unless –

(a)   it was taken from the accused with his consent by a medical practitioner or a registered health care professsional;

    or

(b)   it was taken from the accused by a medical practitioner or a registered health care professsional under section 7A of the Road Traffic Act 1988 and the accused subsequently gave his permission for a laboratory test of the specimen.

(5) Where, at the time a specimen of blood or urine was provided by the accused, he asked to be provided with such a specimen, evidence of the proportion of alcohol or any drug found in the specimen is not admissible on behalf of the prosecution unless –

(a)   the specimen in which the alcohol or drug was found is one of two parts into which the specimen provided by the accused was divided at the time it was provided, and

(b)   the other part was supplied to the accused.

(5A) Where a specimen of blood was taken from the accused under section 7A of the Road Traffic Act 1988, evidence of the proportion of alcohol or any drug found in the specimen is not admissible on behalf of the prosecution unless –

(a)   the specimen in which the alcohol or drug was found is one of two parts into which the specimen taken from the accused was divided at the time it was taken; and

(b)   any request to be supplied with the other part which was made by the accused at the time when he gave his permission for a laboratory test of the specimen was complied with.'

5.2 SECTION 15(1)

Section 15(1) now reads as follows:

'(1) This section and section 16 of this Act apply in respect of proceedings for an offence under any of sections 3A–5A of the Road Traffic Act 1988 (driving offences connected with drink or drugs); and expressions used in this section and section 16 of this Act have the same meaning as in sections 3A to 10 of that Act.'

The terms of this section are self-evident and simply make it clear that the same evidential considerations apply in terms of this and the following section to ss 3A, 4, 5, and 5A prosecutions.

5.3 EVIDENCE OF SPECIMEN TO BE TAKEN INTO ACCOUNT IN ALL CASES, S 15(2)

5.3.1 General

Section 15(2) of the Road Traffic Offenders Act 1988 now provides:

'(2) Evidence of the proportion of alcohol or any drug in a specimen of breath, blood or urine provided by or taken from the accused shall, in all cases (including cases where the specimen was not provided or taken in connection with the alleged offence), be taken into account and –

(a),   it is to be assumed, subject to subsection (3) below, that the proportion of alcohol in the accused's breath, blood or urine at the time of the alleged offence was not less than in the specimen;

(b)   it is to be assumed, subject to subsection (3A) below, that the proportion of drug in the accused's blood or urine at the time of the alleged offence was not less than in the specimen.'

This subsection is clearly designed to diminish the importance of formal or procedural requirements. In particular, notwithstanding the circumstances under which such specimens have been taken, the Act appears to provide that the evidence of the proportion of alcohol or drug in such specimens must be taken into account 'in all cases'. It is, however, not yet entirely clear what the effect of this will be in the variety of situations that will arise in practice. It has been suggested that the effect of this provision will be to render admissible in evidence even specimens which have been unlawfully obtained. However, it is submitted that the effect of this section can only at best cure procedural or technical requirements imposed by other parts of the legislation. Firstly, the Act provides specifically in s 15(4) that a specimen of blood is to be disregarded unless it was taken from the accused with his consent by a medical practitioner or a registered health care professional. Further, s 11(4) of the Road Traffic Act 1988 makes it clear that a specimen of blood is provided only if the accused consents to it being taken, and it is taken by a medical practitioner or a registered health care professional. Clearly, therefore, a specimen of blood taken without the accused's consent, or by someone other than a medical practitioner or a registered health care professional cannot be admissible in evidence and cannot be used in any way or under any circumstances in proceedings under s 4 or 5 of the Road Traffic Act 1988. The additional removal of restriction by the amendment to s 15(2) provided by the Road Traffic Act 1991, Sch 4 para 87(3) allows the Crown to use specimens provided for other purposes. This is more fully discussed at 3.9.1 above. If this is so, it is submitted that nonetheless any specimens always have to be taken in accordance with the other provisions of the Act. Reference is made to the following paragraphs.

5.3.2 Interpretation of s 15(2)

The only direct authority on this matter to date is to be found obiter in the judgment of Lord Fraser in *R v Fox*.[1] In that case the accused was the driver of a motor vehicle involved in an accident. No other vehicle was involved. The accused left the scene and went home. The police, who had no knowledge of his physical condition, went to his house and got no answer to their knock on the door, although they heard voices inside. The police therefore entered the premises and required the driver to give a specimen of breath (the roadside test), which he refused. He was then arrested and taken to a police station where he provided a breath specimen for analysis which exceeded the statutory limit.

It was held that, under English law, the police officers were trespassing at the time they made the first requirement for a breath specimen, and when they purported to arrest the accused.[2] In these circumstances it was

---

1   *R v Fox* [1985] RTR 337, [1985] 1 WLR 1126.
2   It should be noted that in Scotland this conclusion would not have been reached – see *Cairns v Keane* 1983 SCCR 277.

held that neither the provision of a preliminary breath specimen nor the arrest is a necessary precondition of the procedure for the provision of specimens under the equivalent of s 7 of the Road Traffic Act 1988, and that the accused could accordingly be convicted on the basis of these specimens. It was explained that although the police, who were acting in good faith, may have exceeded their common law powers in their alleged arrest of the accused, the evidence subsequently obtained of an offence committed prior to the arrest was admissible and not tainted by the illegality of the arrest itself.

This approach, in terms of good faith, has been reflected in Scotland.[1] In England it has been applied in relation to blood samples taken after an unlawful arrest in hospital.[2]

In discussing the terms of the equivalent of s 15(2) of the Road Traffic Offenders Act 1988, that the proportion of alcohol in a specimen of breath, blood or urine shall 'in all cases' be taken into account (a matter which was not necessary for the decision), Lord Fraser said:[3]

> 'As at present advised, I do not think those words can make evidence admissible if it would not be admissible under the general law. I am inclined to read them as referring only to a specimen "provided pursuant to the provisions of this Act".'

The effect therefore of the terms of s 15(2), it is submitted, is to allow any sample to be considered in evidence even although procedural requirements have not been followed, or some other illegal or improper act is associated with the procedure which does not, however, contravene the provisions of the Act. It is thought, therefore, that failure to observe the following provisions will not render the results of the analysis of the specimen inadmissible.

5.3.3 Circumstances where failure does not render a specimen inadmissible

1. Section 6D of the Road Traffic Act 1988 empowers a constable to arrest a person without warrant if, as a result of a preliminary breath or drug test, the constable reasonably suspects that the proportion of alcohol in the person's breath or blood exceeds the prescribed limit, or the person has a specified controlled drug in his body and the proportion of it in the person's blood or urine exceeds the specified limit for that

---

1   *Paton v Dunn* 2012 SCCR 441.
2   *DPP v Wilson* [2009] EWHC 1988 (Admin), [2009] RTR 29. See also ch 6.
3   At [1985] RTR 343.

drug. A failure to arrest, or an improper arrest, will not invalidate the subsequent provision of a specimen for analysis, as emphasised by the terms of subsections 6D(2) and (2A). The power of arrest is enabling only and does not have to be the prerequisite of the provision of a specimen. See for example, *Orr v Urquhart*[1] and *Carmichael v Wilson*.[2] A police constable has the right to enter any premises in the course of an investigation.[3]

2. Sections 6–6C (preliminary tests). None of the provisions of these sections are required to have been implemented before a specimen of breath, blood or urine is given in terms of s 7(1) or 7(1A). The principal purpose is procedural only; in other words, a constable does not have to administer a breath test before requiring a specimen of breath, blood or urine. Even if a breath test is negative, it would appear to be still open to the constable to require a specimen for analysis. For example, when there was no evidence that the constable who required the roadside test was in uniform this did not invalidate the resulting s 7 procedure.[4] However, the provisions of s 6 are of course relevant in themselves if for any reason the outcome of the test procedure is to be used in any subsequent proceedings, for example if the driver fails to provide such a test contrary to s 6(6) (see 4.5 above). Further, in certain circumstances, the evidence produced as a result of such a test may have evidential significance.[5] In these latter cases, the other provisions of s 6–6C (for example where the test is carried out and if it is in accordance with a code of practice) will have to be observed if the requirement to co-operate with a preliminary test, or the provision of such a test and its result, has to be established in evidence.

5.3.4 Circumstances where failure will render a subsequent specimen inadmissible

On the other hand, it is submitted that the requirements of the following sections do have to be observed if the specimen is subsequently to be admissible in evidence.

1. Section 7 of the Road Traffic Act 1988. This section, which allows for the provision of specimens for analysis, contains within its terms

1   *Orr v Urquhart* 1993 SLT 406, 1992 SCCR 295.
2   *Carmichael v Wilson* 1993 JC 83, 1993 SCCR 290.
3   *Cairns v Keane* 1983 SCCR 277 and as reflected in s 6E specifically not applying to Scotland. See also *Paton v Dunn* 2012 SCCR 441.
4   *Orr v Urquhart* 1993 SLT 406, 1992 SCCR 295.
5   *Gallagher v McKinnon* 1987 SLT 531, 1986 SCCR 704.

a number of requirements which, it is submitted, must be observed before the specimen can be regarded as competent evidence. For example, in terms of ss 7(1) and (2) as amended, breath specimens can only be given into an approved device at the various loci specified. Section 7(3) details in specific terms the circumstances in which a blood or urine specimen is to be taken rather than a breath specimen. Section 7(4A) stipulates *inter alia* that if a medical practitioner or registered health care professional is of the opinion that for medical reasons a blood specimen should not be taken then the specimen shall be one of urine. Section 7(5) defines how a specimen of urine should be given. It is submitted that if any of these specific provisions within s 7 is not observed, then any specimen taken in terms of this section should not be admissible in evidence.

Section 7(7) requires that a constable must warn any person required to give a specimen in terms of this section that failure to provide such a specimen may result in prosecution. Again it is submitted that this requirement is mandatory, and failure to give the warning will invalidate any subsequent proceedings under s 7(6).

2. Section 7A of the Road Traffic Act 1988. As with s 7, it is submitted that the particular requirements of s 7A, for example medical reason for incapacity, which medical practitioner should be asked to take the specimen, and the requirement to give a warning that failure to give permission for laboratory testing may result in prosecution, must be observed before the specimen can be regarded as competent evidence.

3. Section 8 of the Road Traffic Act 1988. The requirement that the lower proportion of alcohol in the breath tests shall be used and the other shall be disregarded must be complied with.

4. Section 9 of the Road Traffic Act 1988. The provisions for the protection of hospital patients require to be observed and failure to do so will render any subsequent specimen inadmissible in evidence.

5. Section 11(4) of the Road Traffic Act 1988 and s 15(4) of the Road Traffic Offenders Act 1988. The requirement that a blood sample can only be taken with the accused's consent and by a medical practitioner or registered health care professional is plainly a prerequisite of allowing that specimen to be admitted in evidence.

6. Sections 15(5) and 15(5A) of the Road Traffic Offenders Act 1988. The requirement to provide part of the specimen to the accused in terms of these subsections, if the accused so claims, must also, it is submitted, be observed before the results of the specimen can be admitted. It would appear that the motorist must expressly indicate that he wishes to take

the divided specimen at the time it is offered to him.[1] Reference should also be made to 5.7 below.

5.3.5 Circumstances where admissibility is a matter of discretion

If the evidence of a specimen in terms of the foregoing paragraphs would normally be admissible, it is submitted that there may still be a residual power to exclude the evidence if the court considered that the specimen had been obtained by fraud or deceit, or if the police had behaved oppressively to the motorist in obtaining the specimen. Reference should again be made to the opinion of Lord Fraser in *R v Fox*.[2] Section 78(1) of the Police and Criminal Evidence Act 1984 gives courts in England a wide discretion to exclude evidence in any case which might cause unfairness. It is submitted that the same consideration applies in Scotland at common law. Reference might usefully be made to *Douglas v Stevenson*;[3] *Woodburn v McLeod*;[4] *Green v Lockhart*,[5] *and Raynor v Cottam*.[6]

5.4 LEVEL OF ALCOHOL HIGHER THAN READING

The way in which s 15(2) of the Road Traffic Offenders Act 1988 is phrased indicates that it is open to the Crown to attempt to prove that the proportion of alcohol in an accused's breath, blood or urine, or drug in blood or urine, was higher at the time of the alleged offence than that provided in the specimen. The assumption provided in the subsection is that the level of alcohol in the accused's body at the time of the alleged offence is to be not less than the proportion indicated in the specimens taken. In other words, the Crown is not precluded from proving that the proportion of alcohol or drug in the accused's breath, blood or urine at the time of the alleged offence was greater than shown in the subsequently taken specimen. It is therefore possible for the Crown to secure a conviction even although the levels demonstrated to be present in the specimen were lower than the legal limit. This subject, sometimes called back calculation, is more fully described at 3.9.3 above.

---

1   *Aitchison v Johnstone* 1987 SCCR 225.
2   *R v Fox* [1985] RTR 337, [1985] 1 WLR 1126.
3   *Douglas v Stevenson* 1986 SCCR 519.
4   *Woodburn v McLeod* 1986 JC 56, 1986 SLT 325, 1986 SCCR 107.
5   *Green v Lockhart* 1986 SLT 11, 1985 SCCR 257.
6   *Raynor v Cottam* 2011 SCCR 119.

5.5 THE STATUTORY DEFENCES (S 15(3) AND S 15(3A))

5.5.1 Section 15(3)

Section 15(3) of the Road Traffic Offenders Act 1988[1] provides as follows:

> (3) The assumption in subsection 2(a) above shall not be made if the accused proves –
>
> (a) that he consumed alcohol before he provided the specimen or had it taken from him and –
>
>   (i) in relation to an offence under section 3A, after the time of the alleged offence, and
>
>   (ii) otherwise, after he had ceased to drive, attempt to drive or be in charge of a vehicle on a road or other public place, and
>
> (b) that had he not done so the proportion of alcohol in his breath, blood or urine would not have exceeded the prescribed limit and, if it is alleged that he was unfit to drive through drink, would not have been such as to impair his ability to drive properly.'

A similar defence, introduced by the Crime and Courts Act 2013, now applies for the proportion of drugs:

> '(3A) The assumption in subsection 2(b) above is not be made if the accused proves –
>
> (a) that he took the drug before he provided the specimen or had it taken from him and –
>
>   (i) in relation to an offence under section 3A, after the time of the alleged offence, and
>
>   (ii) otherwise, after he had ceased to drive, attempt to drive or be in charge of a vehicle on a road or other public place, and
>
> (b) that had he not done so the proportion of drug in his blood or urine–
>
>   (i) in the case of a specified controlled drug, would not have exceeded the specified limit for that drug, and,
>
>   (ii) if it is alleged that he was unfit to drive through drugs, would not have been such as to impair his ability to drive properly.'

The assumption referred to is that contained in s 15(2) of the Road Traffic Offenders Act 1988, namely that the proportion of alcohol or drug at the time of the alleged offence was not less than in the specimen, and is compatible with the European Convention on Human Rights.[2]

1   As amended by the RTA 1991, Sch 4 para 87(4).
2   See *Parker v DPP* [2001] RTR 16.

5.5.2 Onus and standard of proof

The onus is on the accused to establish this defence. This reversal of onus is compatible with the European Convention on Human Rights.[1] The standard of proof which is required is on the balance of probabilities.[2] However, if the circumstances are such that the evidence casts a reasonable doubt on the prosecution case, the accused will be entitled to the benefit of such doubt. In practice, however, this situation is unlikely to occur; the evidence of post-incident drinking, and presumably also specified drugs, has by its nature to be clearly distinguished from what was consumed prior to the driver ceasing to drive, attempting to drive or being in charge of his vehicle, and in most cases it will be for the accused to remove any doubt about the quantity of alcohol or specified drug consumed before and after the material time. The accused will have to establish each part of his defence. Accordingly, he will in normal circumstances require to establish when it was that he stopped driving, attempting to drive or being in charge of the vehicle. He will then require to establish the amount of alcohol or specified drug which he has consumed after that time. Thereafter, the accused will require to show that, but for the consumption of the alcohol or drug, he as an individual would have provided a specimen at the time he ceased to drive, attempt to drive or be in charge which would have been lower than the maximum permitted level prescribed in s 11(2) or regulations as referred to in s 5A(8) of the Road Traffic Act 1988. Alternatively, where it is alleged he was unfit to drive through drink or drugs, he must prove that it would not have been such as to impair his ability to drive properly.

The technical steps in the defence case are usually spoken to in practice by the evidence of an expert analyst.

This defence can be established by the evidence of a single witness,[3] though this may be rare.[4]

This subject is more fully discussed at 3.9 and 3.16 above.

5.6 TAKING OF BLOOD SPECIMENS (S 15(4))

Section 15(4) of the Road Traffic Offenders Act 1988[5] provides as follows:

1   See *R v Drummond* [2002] EWCA Crim 527, [2002] RTR 21.
2   *Neish v Stevenson* 1969 SLT 229, overruling *Thaw v Segar* 1962 SLT (Sh Ct) 63.
3   *King v Lees* 1993 SLT 1184, 1993 SCCR 28.
4   See *DPP v Dukolli* [2009] EWHC 3097 (Admin).
5   As amended by Police Reform Act 2002 (c 30), Pt 4 (c 2), s 57(3).

'A specimen of blood shall be disregarded unless –

(a)   it was taken from the accused with his consent and either –

    (i)   in a police station by a medical practitioner; or a registered health care professional; or

    (ii)   elsewhere by a medical practitioner; or

(b)   it was taken from the accused by a medical practitioner under section 7A of the Road Traffic Act 1988 and the accused subsequently gave his permission for a laboratory test of the specimen.'[1]

Failure to observe the provisions of s 15(4) will make the evidence of the blood specimen and any analysis thereof inadmissible in evidence, notwithstanding the terms of s 15(2). Accordingly, if the specimen is not taken by a medical practitioner, or if it is taken without the accused's consent, the specimen will not be allowed in evidence.[2]

5.7 PART OF SPECIMEN TO BE SUPPLIED TO ACCUSED (SS 15(5) AND (5A))

Sections 15(5) and (5A) of the Road Traffic Offenders Act 1988 provide as follows:

'(5) Where, at the time a specimen of blood or urine was provided by the accused, he asked to be provided with such a specimen, evidence of the proportion of alcohol or any drug found in the specimen is not admissible on behalf of the prosecution unless –

(a)   the specimen in which the alcohol or drug was found is one of two parts into which the specimen provided by the accused was divided at the time it was provided, and

(b)   the other part was supplied to the accused.

(5A) Where a specimen of blood was taken from the accused under section 7A of the Road Traffic Act 1988, evidence of the proportion of alcohol or any drug found in the specimen is not admissible on behalf of the prosecution unless –

(a)   the specimen in which the alcohol or drug was found is one of two parts into which the specimen taken from the accused was divided at the time it was taken; and

(b)   any request to be supplied with the other part which was made by the accused at the time when he gave his permission for a laboratory test of the specimen was complied with.'

1   See also the RTA 1988, s 11(4).
2   *Friel v Dickson* 1992 SLT 1086, 1992 SCCR 513; see 5.3.2ff above.

The intention of both is to allow the accused the right to part of the specimen he has provided, or given permission for laboratory testing of, in order that he may have it independently analysed. Failure to observe the terms of this subsection will mean that the court cannot consider the results of any such analysis, notwithstanding the terms of s 15(2) of the Road Traffic Offenders Act 1988 as amended. Further, if the police do anything which frustrates the purpose of the section a conviction will not follow.[1] Error in detail, such as a mistake in labelling, should not matter if the sample can still be analysed.[2]

The purpose of this subsection is achieved in practice by dividing the specimen of blood or urine into two and handing one of the two parts to the accused, if asked for. It is submitted that, in particular, having regard to the terms of s 11(3)(a) of the Road Traffic Act 1988, each of the two parts of the divided specimen must be sufficient to allow proper analysis to be carried out. In *Gallagher v McKinnon*,[3] it was held that where the analysis of the specimen retained by the police differs from the analysis of the specimen handed to the accused, the court could look at extraneous evidence (but not the readings from the breath analyser device) in deciding which of the two results was accurate. Reference in this respect should also be made to *Jordan v Russell*[4] and *Campbell-Birkett v Vannett*.[5] Whether or not the accused has requested part of the specimen he has provided and such specimen has been given to him are questions of fact. It would appear from the terms of the subsection that the motorist must take the initiative in asking for his part of the specimen.[6]

The part of the specimen given to the accused must be capable of being analysed within a reasonable time. In *Ellis v Cruikshank*[7] the specimen was found to be incapable of analysis some three months after its provision. It was held that any such specimen must be capable of analysis within a reasonable time at the point when it is delivered to the accused.

The supply of part of the specimen to the accused must be unconditional; where a police officer was only prepared to give the accused the specimen on condition that the motorist signed a receipt, this was held to invalidate the prosecution.[8]

---

1   *Perry v McGovern* [1986] RTR 240.
2   *Butler v DPP* [1990] RTR 377 and *DPP v Snook* [1993] Crim L R 883.
3   *Gallagher v McKinnon* 1987 SLT 531, 1986 SCCR 704.
4   *Jordan v Russell* 1995 JC 78, 1995 SLT 1301, 1995 SCCR 423.
5   *Campbell-Birkett v Vannett* 1999 SLT 865.
6   See also *Aitchison v Johnstone* 1987 SCCR 225.
7   *Ellis v Cruikshank* 1973 SCCR Supp 49.
8   *Smith v Skeen* 1974 SCCR Supp 64.

5.8 DOCUMENTARY EVIDENCE OF SPECIMENS (S 16)

5.8.1 Section 16

Section 16 of the Road Traffic Offenders Act 1988 reads in full as follows:

'(1) Evidence of the proportion of alcohol or a drug in a specimen of breath, blood or urine may, subject to subsections (3) and (4) below and to section 15(5) and (5A) of this Act, be given by the production of a document or documents purporting to be whichever of the following is appropriate, that is to say –

(a)   a statement automatically produced by the device by which the proportion of alcohol in a specimen of breath was measured and a certificate signed by a constable (which may but need not be contained in the same document as the statement) that the statement relates to a specimen provided by the accused at the date and time shown in the statement, and

(b)   a certificate signed by an authorised analyst as to the proportion of alcohol or any drug found in a specimen of blood or urine identified in the certificate.

(2) Subject to subsections (3) and (4) below, evidence that a specimen of blood was taken from the accused with his consent by a medical practitioner or a registered health care professional may be given by the production of a document purporting to certify that fact and to be signed by a medical practitioner or a registered health care professional.

(3) Subject to subsection (4) below –

(a)   a document purporting to be such a statement or such a certificate (or both such a statement and such a certificate) as is mentioned in subsection (1)(a) above is admissible in evidence on behalf of the prosecution in pursuance of this section only if a copy of it either has been handed to the accused when the document was produced or has been served on him not later than seven days before the hearing, and

(b)   any other document is so admissible only if a copy of it has been served on the accused not later than seven days before the hearing.

(4) A document purporting to be a certificate (or so much of a document as purports to be a certificate) is not so admissible if the accused, not later than three days before the hearing or within such further time as the court may in special circumstances allow, has served notice on the prosecutor requiring the attendance at the hearing of the person by whom the document purports to be signed.

(5) In Scotland –

(a) a document produced in evidence on behalf of the prosecution in pursuance of subsection (1) or (2) above and, where the person by whom the document was signed is called as a witness, the evidence of that person, shall be sufficient evidence of the facts stated in the document, and

(b) a written execution purporting to be signed by the person who handed to or served on the accused or the prosecutor a copy of the document or of the notice in terms of subsection (3) or (4) above, together with, where appropriate, a post office receipt for the registered or recorded delivery letter shall be sufficient evidence of the handing or service of such a copy or notice.

(6) A copy of a certificate required by this section to be served on the accused or a notice required by this section to be served on the prosecutor may be served personally or sent by registered post or recorded delivery service.

(7) In this section "authorised analyst" means –

(a) any person possessing the qualifications prescribed by regulations made under section 76 of the Food Act 1984 or section 27 of the Food and Drugs (Scotland) Act 1956 as qualifying persons for appointment as public analysts under those Acts, and

(b) any other persons authorised by the Secretary of State to make analyses for the purposes of this section.'

The section, in general terms, provides that the evidence of the proportion of alcohol in a breath test under s 7(1)(a) of the Road Traffic Act 1988 may be proved by a statement produced automatically by an authorised breath analyser device, while evidence of the amount of alcohol or a drug in a specimen of blood or urine provided in terms of s 7(1)(b) or s 7(1A) of that Act may be given by a certificate signed by a certified analyst. There have been a substantial number of cases dealing with the certificates automatically produced by the Camic Breath Analyser Device though these are no longer used. The section also describes the proof of the taking of a blood specimen,[1] and the requirements of service in respect of the service of the certificates described in the section.[2] A definition of the term 'authorised analyst' is also provided.[3]

5.8.2 Statement produced by a breath analyser device (s 16(1)(a))

Section 16(1)(a) of the Road Traffic Offenders Act 1988 reads as follows:

1 RTOA 1988, s 16(2).
2 RTOA 1988, s 16(3), (4), (5) and (6).
3 RTOA 1988, s 16(7).

'Evidence of the proportion of alcohol or a drug in a specimen of breath, blood or urine may, subject to subsections (3) and (4) below and to section 15(5) and 15(5A) of this Act, be given by the production of a document or documents purporting to be whichever of the following is appropriate, that is to say –

(a)   a statement automatically produced by the device by which the proportion of alcohol in a specimen of breath was measured and a certificate signed by a constable (which may but need not be contained in the same document as the statement) that the statement relates to a specimen provided by the accused at the date and time shown in the statement ...'.

5.8.3 Approved breath analyser device

A number of devices are approved by the Secretary of State for use in Scotland. Most, if not all of the case law concerned with the earlier Camic device will apply *mutatis mutandis* to the devices now approved.

If an approved device is not currently available in a police station, or it is not practicable to use it, or if it has been used when there is reasonable cause to doubt the reliability of the results, in terms of s 7(3) of the Road Traffic Act 1988, only specimens of blood or urine can be required of motorists.

The prosecution are entitled to a presumption that the breath analyser is an approved device within the meaning of the section.[1] It is unnecessary for the relevant Approval Order to be produced.[2] Further, when the device has in practice done what it should have done if it was in proper working order, then it is to be presumed that the machine is in proper working order and has been correctly maintained.[3] The court is entitled to use its knowledge of how the device operates (see 4.8.2 above and 5.8.4 below).

In *Brown v Gallagher*,[4] challenge was made to the admissibility of a breath alcohol reading relying on non-conformity with the relevant Approval Order in terms of manufacture, and because of doubt as to the reliability, accuracy and consistency of the device. The Court of Appeal took a robust and practical approach to the case. In particular, the fact that the device reacted inconsistently to mouth alcohol on biological testing did not deprive it of type approval, nor did it mean that the device was

---

1   *Davidson v Aitchison* 1986 SLT 402, 1985 SCCR 415; *Valentine v Macphail* 1986 JC 131, 1986 SLT 598, 1986 SCCR 321.
2   *Lee v Smith* 1982 SLT 200, 1981 SCCR 267.
3   *Tudhope v McAllister* 1984 SLT 395, 1984 SCCR 182.
4   *Brown v Gallagher* 2002 SCCR 415.

not functioning properly given there were two samples and safeguards built in to both the device and the legislation in the form of s 8(2). While that second safeguard has now gone, it might be expected that the same robust approach would still be taken.

A similarly robust and common sense approach to devices that have been modified or upgraded has been taken in England.[1]

5.8.4 Operation of approved devices

Essentially, any approved device must be in operational condition and maintained in accordance with the manufacturer's directions. It should be operated only by a police officer who has been authorised to do so by the Chief Constable. In order to comply with the requirements of the legislation the devices have certain common operational features. A print-out is produced and is considered to contain both a statement and a certificate which is described in the Road Traffic Offenders Act 1988, ss 16(3)(a) and (5), and as such will be admissible in evidence so long as the other provisions of the Act are complied with. The evidence of the officer who signed the certificate is not essential if there is sufficient evidence from other officers of the conduct of the test and its result.[2]

Judicial knowledge, it is submitted, extends to the operation of the approved devices. The prosecution does not have to prove that the print-out and its contents qualify as including both a statement and a certificate as above described.[3]

By way of example, the Intoximeter EC/IR in many respects operates in a similar fashion to the now long obsolete Camic Breath Analyser device. Breath samples are given into the machine which are analysed, and the details of the test are displayed on a display unit. The machine also produces a print-out containing the relevant information and results of the test. However, the technology used in the Intoximeter machine is different. It is operated by an attached standard PC keyboard, which is used for data entry. Once the relevant information has been entered into the machine by way of the keyboard (after the machine has automatically purged itself of alcohol), a mouthpiece is fitted into the breath tube on the machine. The motorist is instructed to take a deep breath and blow into the mouthpiece as steadily and for as long as possible. The breath flow rate is indicated in the display by asterisks. The machine then

---

1   See *Breckon v DPP* [2007] EWHC 2013, [2008] RTR 8, and *Coxon v Manchester City Magistrates' Court* [2010] EWHC 712.

2   *Donoghue v Allan* 1985 SCCR 93.

3   *Annan v Mitchell* 1984 SCCR 32; *Aitchison v Matheson* 1984 SCCR 83.

evaluates the sample and again automatically purges itself of alcohol. If the motorist does not submit a valid breath sample, the unit displays 'specimen incomplete'.

Three minutes are allowed for a valid sample to be provided, failing which the test is aborted. The same procedure is operated for the second test. The operator manual suggests that the machine should not be used in environments with heavy alcohol vapour, cigarette smoke, high levels of radio frequencies, magnetic interference or new paint. It is said that these conditions will not interfere with the results of the test but may affect the useful lifespan of various components. Regard might also be had to the Police Scotland Drink/Drug Driving Standard Operating Procedures (updated 30 July 2018), available online, including the delay required after irritant spray has been used.

It is open to the defence to establish any failure to comply with the manufacturer's instructions, and to argue that such failure should lead to acquittal.[1] Reference should also be made to *Kelly v MacKinnon*[2] and *Fleming v Tudhope*.[3]

5.8.5 Informalities in print-out

There have been a number of cases concerned with informalities connected with the documents automatically produced by the breath analyser devices. The subsection does not indicate any particular formality in respect of the information produced by the machine in the statement or certificate; all that is required is that the statement and certificate should evidence the information required by the Road Traffic Act 1988.[4] Further, apparent defects in the statements are curable by parole evidence from a police officer present at the time the test was taken.[5] For example, when the statement did not indicate the name of the driver, or when the certificate was not signed by the constable supervising the taking of the specimen, the Crown may produce verbal evidence to show that

---

1   *Jeffrey v MacNeill* 1976 JC 54; *Sloan v Smith* 1978 SLT (Notes) 27; *Hogg v Smith* 1978 CO Circulars A/37 (all cases involving the roadside breathalyser device); *Allan v Miller* 1986 SLT 3, 1985 SCCR 227; *Fraser v McLeod* 1987 SCCR 294 (cases where observation of the manufacturer's instructions were not required).
2   *Kelly v MacKinnon* 1985 SLT 487, 1985 SCCR 97.
3   *Fleming v Tudhope* 1987 CO Circulars A/16.
4   *Jones v McPhail* 1984 JC 67, 1984 SLT 396, 1984 SCCR 168; see also *Aitchison v Matheson* 1984 SCCR 83.
5   *Aitchison v Matheson* 1984 SCCR 83.

the statement and certificate relate to the accused and the test which he has taken.[1]

In *Allan v Miller*[2] it was held that where the device appeared to be performing its functions as it was supposed to there was no need to produce specialist evidence that the machine was working properly. There must always be evidence that the print-out relates to the accused.[3]

When the statement gives information which is patently incorrect, then the prosecution may not be able to rely on the evidential presumptions created by this subsection. Nonetheless, it may still be open for the prosecution to establish the results of the test by other evidence, such as testimony from police officers present at the time, of what readings were produced on the visual display when the test was taken.[4]

If the informalities or defects in the print-out are so fundamental as to indicate that the machine's analytical function is unreliable, the police may turn to the alternative procedure of requiring a specimen of blood or urine.

Informalities in the certificates relating to blood or urine specimens are dealt with at 5.8.7 below.

5.8.6 Defects in print-out: reliability of device

In terms of ss 7(3)(b) and (bb) of the Road Traffic Act 1988, the provision of a specimen of breath for analysis must be made into a reliable device. The question of what is meant by a device being at the police station or elsewhere under (bb), or what is meant by it being for any other reason not practicable to use it there, is dealt with at 4.10.3 above. If the device is not reliable, then the alternative requirement of a blood or urine specimen must be made. The device may be properly considered unreliable if for some technical reason it is not working or functioning properly. However, in terms of the reported cases, the circumstances in which the reliability or otherwise of the device has been considered usually relate to the information contained within the statement or print-out automatically produced by the device.

---

1   *NcNamee v Tudhope* 1985 SLT 322, 1984 SCCR 423.
2   *Allan v Miller* 1986 SLT 3, 1985 SCCR 227.
3   See *O'Brien v Ferguson* 1986 JC 82, 1987 SLT 96, 1986 SCCR 155 (a case involving a blood specimen) and 5.8.7 below.
4   *Smith v MacDonald, Smith v Davie* 1984 SLT 398, 1984 SCCR 190; see also *McLeary v Douglas* 1978 JC 57, 1978 SLT 140; *Gunn v Brown* 1987 SLT 94, 1986 SCCR 179.

As indicated in the foregoing paragraph (5.8.5), certain informalities or apparent defects may be cured by parole evidence. However, certain defects may be so fundamental that they must be regarded as indicating that the machine is unreliable. In *Tudhope v Quinn*[1] it was held that what the Crown had to prove was that the analytical or measuring function of the device was unreliable if the primary requirement of a breath specimen was to be set aside and a blood or urine specimen used instead. Although it is good practice to produce the print-out in evidence where the alternative procedure is employed, it is not necessary to do so.[2]

The primary or best evidence that the machine is unreliable comes from the police officers who administered the test, and it has been said that the test of reliability is subjective to the officer carrying out the test; the police are entitled to go to the alternative procedure if they conclude on reasonable grounds that the device was unreliable, even if in the event it is proved to be working properly.[3]

In *Aitchison v Meldrum*[4] and *Tudhope v Craig*[5] relatively minor defects in the operation of the machine evidenced in the print-out were held not to invalidate the results contained in the print-out.

In *Gilligan v Tudhope*[6] the device produced a print-out which gave nonsensical times and dates for the test, but there appeared to be nothing wrong with the analytical function of the machine. It was held that in these circumstances the machine was not unreliable, and that the alternative procedure of the provision of a sample of blood or urine was not open. Presumably the defects described in this case could have been cured by parole evidence from the police officers who administered the test. In *Ross v Allan*,[7] the device gave a reading of 75 microgrammes in 100 millilitres of breath in respect of the first specimen of breath, and a reading of zero for the second. It was held that these readings clearly showed that the analytical function of the machine was not operating properly, that the device should therefore be regarded as unreliable, and that the Crown did not have to provide expert evidence on the question of the unreliability of the machine. In *Lunney v Cardle*[8] the machine gave readings of 92 and 14

1   *Tudhope v Quinn* 1984 SCCR 255.
2   *Houston v McLeod* 1986 JC 96, 1986 SCCR 219.
3   *Burnett v Smith* 1990 JC 119, 1990 SLT 537, 1989 SCCR 628; *Whigham v Howdle* 1996 SLT 1175; *Miller v Dick* 2000 JC 71, 1999 SCCR 919.
4   *Aitchison v Meldrum* 1984 SLT 437, 1984 SCCR 241.
5   *Tudhope v Craig* 1985 SCCR 214.
6   *Gilligan v Tudhope* 1986 JC 34, 1986 SLT 299, 1985 SCCR 434.
7   *Ross v Allan* 1986 JC 49, 1986 SLT 349, 1986 SCCR 100.
8   *Lunney v Cardle* 1988 SLT 440, 1988 SCCR 104.

microgrammes respectively, and the extent of the discrepancy was held to be sufficient to justify the conclusion that the device was unreliable. In *Carson v Orr*[1] the two readings were 87 and 58 microgrammes; it was there considered reasonable for the police officers to decide that the machine was reliable.

In *Hodgkins v Carmichael*,[2] the Camic device calibrated properly but the tape inside was twisted and did not produce a print-out. This was discovered an hour later and the print-out recovered and successfully used, although the machine had been declared at the earlier stage to be unreliable. In *Burnett v Smith*[3] a driver gave a specimen into the Camic device and the print-out gave readings of 39 and 55 microgrammes. The supervising officer considered the readings and also that at an appropriate point in the proceedings a green light flashed on the device, and concluded that the device was unreliable, and turned to the alternative procedure. The appeal court decided that the belief of the supervising officer that the device was unreliable was in fact wrong, but reasonable, and refused to fault the procedure. Further, it was specifically determined in that case that the test of the reliability of the device had to be a subjective one at the instance of the officers conducting the procedure, and in effect the appeal court concluded that the courts should support the conclusions of the supervising officers so long as these were reasonably reached. In *Miller v Dick*[4] it was enough for the prosecution that police officers reasonably believed that the Camic device was faulty because another officer has mistakenly informed them to that effect.

In *Currie v MacDougal*[5] it was decided that a Camic device which was not regularly maintained and was used as a training device was properly regarded as unreliable. However, the Crown will normally have to show that if a device is regarded as unreliable there is no other available and reliable device within the police station.[6] The fact that there is no other such device available may be inferred from the evidence of the procedure.[7] If there is no reliable device at the station where the requirement is made, the accused can be taken to another station where a reliable device is available.[8]

1   *Carson v Orr* 1992 SCCR 260.
2   *Hodgkins v Carmichael* 1989 SLT 514, 1989 SCCR 69.
3   *Burnett v Smith* 1990 JC 119, 1990 SLT 537, 1989 SCCR 628.
4   *Miller v Dick* 2000 JC 71, 1999 SCCR 919.
5   *Currie v MacDougal* 1988 SLT 632, 1988 SCCR 266.
6   *Houston v McLeod* 1986 JC 96, 1986 SCCR 219; *Walker v Walkingshaw* 1991 SCCR 695.
7   *Welsh v McGlennan* 1992 SCCR 379.
8   *Tudhope v Fulton* 1987 SLT 419, 1986 SCCR 567.

The test of whether the machine is reliable is determined at the time the requirement is made.[1] In *Wilson v Webster*[2] the clock on the Camic was faulty, so police officers took a blood sample instead, which proved insufficient for analysis. They went back to the Camic and obtained a reading. This was held to be in order because the analytical function was accurate at the time the request was made, even although the clock was wrong. The blood sample, if insufficient, would therefore have been inadmissible.

If the accused wishes to claim that the device is unreliable, in the face of prosecution evidence that it is reliable, the onus is on him to establish his defence on the balance of probabilities.[3]

In summary, if the Crown seeks to rely on the fact that the machine is unreliable in requiring the alternative procedure of a blood or urine specimen, it must be demonstrated from the print-out that the analytical function of the device is not operating correctly or satisfactorily. If there are other defects in the print-out which do not relate to the analytical function of the device, such defects may be curable by parole evidence. If the print-out is defective and inadmissible in evidence the Crown may rely on the visual testimony of the test from the supervising officers.[4]

It must be remembered in considering all the foregoing cases that they involved the Camic Breath Analyser device which is no longer approved, and care may have to be taken in applying these authorities to other devices. However, as all such devices must have common operational features, most if not all of the cases cited will be directly applicable to any other breath analysis device.

5.8.7 Analyst's certificate (s 16(1)(b))

Under this part of the subsection, evidence of the proportion of alcohol in a specimen of blood or urine may, subject again to the provisions of ss 16(3)–(6) of the Road Traffic Offenders Act 1988, be given by a document purporting to be 'a certificate signed by an authorised analyst as to the proportion of alcohol or any drug found in a specimen of blood or urine identified in the certificate'.

An 'authorised analyst' is defined in s 16(7).

1   *Ramage v Walkingshaw* 1992 SCCR 82.
2   *Wilson v Webster* 1999 SCCR 747.
3   *Aitchison v Matheson* 1984 SCCR 83.
4   *Smith v MacDonald, Smith v Davie* 1984 JC 73, 1984 SLT 398 at 401, 1984 SCCR 190.

As before, the prosecution has to prove that the specimen was taken from the accused and transmitted to the analyst.[1] However, the fact that the specimen has been sent for analysis may be inferred.[2]

In *O'Brien v Ferguson*[3] a specimen taken at the county hospital was wrongly labelled as having been taken at the police station. There was contradictory parole evidence as to whether the specimen was transmitted to a laboratory for analysis. It was held that there was insufficient evidence to link the specimen taken with the specimen analysed, and the driver was acquitted.

In *McKinnon v Westwater*[4] a specimen taken at Tain was wrongly marked as having been taken at Evanton; parole evidence was allowed which linked the specimen to the accused. This was followed in *McPherson v McNaughton*[5] when there was a discrepancy between the motorist's name on the specimen and on the certificate.

The certificate must state that the signatories have themselves carried out the relevant examination, unless the evidence is agreed.[6]

In a case where an analyst was cited to give evidence and had no recollection of the particular analysis in question but refreshed his memory from a register of print-outs which were possibly still extant but which were not produced, it was held that the analyst's evidence was competent and did not breach the best evidence rule.[7]

In a case decided under pre 1972 legislation,[8] it was held that the certificate was intended to vouch the analyst's conclusion and not the provenance of the specimen; accordingly factual errors in the certificate did not make the analyst's conclusions contained therein inadmissible.[9]

5.8.8 Taking of blood specimens (s 16(2))

Section 16(2) of the Road Traffic Offenders Act 1988 provides as follows:

'Subject to subsections (3) and (4) below, evidence that a specimen of blood was taken from the accused with his consent by a medical practitioner or

1   *O'Brien v Ferguson* 1987 SLT 96, 1986 SCCR 155.
2   *McLeary v Douglas* 1978 SLT 140; *Tudhope v Corrigall* 1982 SCCR 558.
3   *O'Brien v Ferguson* 1987 SLT 96, 1986 SCCR 155.
4   *McKinnon v Westwater* 1987 SCCR 730.
5   *McPherson v McNaughton* 1992 SLT 600, 1992 SCCR 434.
6   *Normand v Wotherspoon* 1993 JC 248, 1994 SLT 487, 1993 SCCR 912; *Donnelly v Schrikel* 1995 SLT 537.
7   *McLeod v Fraser* 1987 SLT 142, 1986 SCCR 271.
8   Road Safety Act 1967, s 3(8).
9   *Lawrie v Stevenson* 1968 JC 71, 1968 SLT 342.

a registered health care professional may be given by the production of a document purporting to certify that fact and to be signed by a medical practitioner or a registered health care professional.'

Subsections (3) and (4) are concerned with the requirements of service of certificates. What constitutes a 'medical practitioner' is discussed at 4.10.5 above. Registered health care professional is defined in s 11(2) of the Road Traffic Act 1988 – see 4.10.5 above. Section 16(5) of the Act also applies for the purposes of this subsection.

Section 11(4) of the Road Traffic Act 1988 also provides that a person provides a specimen of blood if, and only if, he consents to its being taken by a medical practitioner or a registered health care professional, and it is so taken.

Accordingly, failure to observe the provisions of s 16(2) will be fatal to any prosecution based on a specimen of blood, notwithstanding the terms of s 15(2) (as amended) of the Road Traffic Offenders Act 1988. If the specimen is not taken by a medical practitioner or registered health care professional, or if the specimen is taken without the accused's consent, the specimen will not be allowed in evidence and evidence of the analysis of the specimen will be inadmissible. The court must be satisfied that full and proper consent has been given by the accused to the taking of the specimen.[1]

Reference should be made to 5.3.2 above.

5.8.9 Service of statement or certificate (s 16(3))

Section 16(3) of the Road Traffic Offenders Act 1988 reads as follows:

'Subject to subsection (4) below –

(a)   a document purporting to be such a statement or such a certificate (or both such a statement and such a certificate as is mentioned in subsection (1)(a) above) is admissible in evidence on behalf of the prosecution in pursuance of this section only if a copy of it either has been handed to the accused when the document was produced or has been served on him not later than seven days before the hearing, and

(b)   any other document is so admissible only if a copy of it has been served on the accused not later than seven days before the hearing.'

This subsection has to be read along with the following subsection (s 16(4)); and with ss 16(5) and (6).

---

1   *Friel v Dickson* 1992 SLT 1086, 1992 SCCR 513.

Section 16(3) provides for the requirements of service in respect of both kinds of certificate described in s 16(1). In particular, s 16(3)(a) refers to the statement and certificate comprised in the print-out automatically produced by the breath analysis device. Service of this statement and certificate can be effected on the accused at the time the device produces the print-out. It is submitted that this means that the document or documents must be given to the accused in the course of the procedure involved in the taking of the specimen, and that, for example, handing the document to the accused after he has left the police station does not comply with the requirement of service. Alternatively, in accordance with the second part of s 16(3)(a), where the accused has not been handed a copy of the document at the time it was produced, service of the document must be made on him not later than seven days before the trial diet. By virtue of s 16(3)(b), the requirement of service is satisfied in the case of an analyst's certificate (in terms of s 16(1)(b) of the Act), or a doctor's or registered health care professional's certificate (in terms of s 16(2) of the Act), by service of such certificates on the accused not later than seven days before the trial diet.[1]

If service of documents or certificates is not effected by either of the methods described in s 16(3), then the documents or certificates are inadmissible in evidence, and the prosecution cannot rely on the evidence contained within the documents or certificates to secure a conviction.[2] However, in the event that the certificate and statement automatically produced by a breath analyser device are not handed to the accused at the time and were not subsequently served on the accused, and thus became inadmissible in evidence, it is still open to the Crown to secure a conviction on the basis of parole evidence from the police officers who administered the test of the readings they observed on the visual display unit of the breath analyser device.[3]

Even if the accused declines to take the copy of the print-out at the time when it is produced by the breath analyser device, in terms of the first part of the subsection, then service of the copy must still be made in terms of the second part of the subsection.[4] If service in terms of this subsection has not been effected, objection to the production of the

---

1   All reference to 'days' in this and the following subsection means clear and full days (*McMillan v HM Advocate* 1983 SLT 24, 1982 SCCR 309).
2   *McLeary v Douglas* 1978 JC 57, 1978 SLT 140.
3   *Gunn v Brown* 1987 SLT 94, 1986 SCCR 179.
4   *Annan v Crawford* 1984 SCCR 382; *McDerment v O'Brien* 1985 SLT 485, 1985 SCCR 50.

principal (which must be lodged) normally requires to be taken before the close of the Crown case.[1]

The fact that certificates were served with a complaint which was dropped and substituted by a fresh complaint which was not accompanied by further certificates does not invalidate the initial service of the certificates, which remain valid for the purposes of the second complaint.[2]

It is not necessary for the prosecution, in a case based on a blood or urine specimen, to produce the specimen on which the certificate is based.[3]

5.8.10 Certificate not admissible in evidence (s 16(4))

Section 16(4) of the Road Traffic Offenders Act 1988 provides:

> 'A document purporting to be a certificate (or so much of a document as purports to be a certificate) is not so admissible if the accused, not later than three days before the hearing or within such further time as the court may in special circumstances allow, has served notice on the prosecutor requiring the attendance at the hearing of the person by whom the document purports to be signed.'

This subsection applies not only to the documents automatically produced by a breath analyser device in terms of ss 16(1)(a) and (3)(a), but also to certificates supplied by analysts or doctors in terms of ss 16(1)(b) and (2) respectively. If the defence wishes to avoid the evidential consequences of s 16(3), then notice must be served on the Crown to this effect not later than three clear days before the trial diet. The court has the discretion to allow later intimation by the accused, but will normally only exercise this discretion on cause shown. The effect of such intimation by the accused is to require the police officer who signs the certificate on the print-out to attend the trial diet to give evidence to the effect that he did so; or more commonly in practice, to require the presence of the authorised analyst who has examined the blood or urine specimen to speak to his findings, usually with a view to establishing one of the statutory defences.

If the accused wishes to challenge the contents of the print-out or the operation of the machine, he must do so by giving notice in terms of this subsection; otherwise the print-out, its contents, and the operation of the device cannot be challenged.[4]

---

1   *Skeen v Murphy* 1978 SLT (Notes) 2; however, reference should also be made to *McLeary v Douglas* 1978 JC 57, 1978 SLT 140 and *Macauley v Wilson* 1995 SLT 1070.
2   *Buonaccorsi v Tudhope* 1982 SLT 528, 1982 SCCR 249.
3   *Williamson v Aitchison* 1982 SLT 399, 1982 SCCR 102.
4   *Annan v Mitchell* 1984 SCCR 32.

5.8.11 Sufficiency of evidence (s 16(5))

Section 16(5) of the Road Traffic Offenders Act 1988 provides:

'(5) In Scotland –

(a) a document produced in evidence on behalf of the prosecution in pursuance of subsection (1) or (2) above and, where the person by whom the document was signed is called as a witness, the evidence of that person, shall be sufficient evidence of the facts stated in the document, and

(b) a written execution purporting to be signed by the person who handed to or served on the accused or the prosecutor a copy of the document or of the notice in terms of subsection (3) or (4) above, together with, where appropriate, a post office receipt for the registered or recorded delivery letter shall be sufficient evidence of the handing or service of such a copy or notice.'

The effect of similar provisions under previous legislation was considered in *MacNeill v Perrie*.[1]

5.8.12 Definition

'Purporting to be signed'. See *Donlon v MacKinnon*.[2]

5.8.13 Evidence

In *Donoghue v Allan*[3] the police officer who signed the certificate part of the print-out was not called as a witness, but it was held that this did not preclude a conviction if there was adequate other evidence vouching the document. In *McLeod v Fraser*[4] the analyst's certificate was not referred to in evidence (although it was a production) but the analyst himself gave evidence. It was held that notwithstanding the terms of this subsection the analyst's testimony could be regarded as satisfying the best evidence rule.

The question of errors and defects in the certificates is discussed at 5.8.5 and 5.8.6 above.

5.8.14 Methods of service (s 16(6))

Section 16(6) of the Road Traffic Offenders Act 1988 provides:

---

1   *MacNeill v Perrie* 1978 CO Circulars A/13.
2   *Donlon v MacKinnon* 1981 SCCR 219.
3   *Donoghue v Allan* 1985 SCCR 93.
4   *McLeod v Fraser* 1987 SLT 142, 1986 SCCR 271.

'A copy of a certificate required by this section to be served on the accused or a notice required by this section to be served on the prosecutor may be served personally or sent by registered post or recorded delivery service.'

This subsection prescribes the methods of service of the certificates, statements and notices referred to elsewhere in the section.

It is submitted that, in Scotland, personal service means that the documents in question must be handed personally to the accused, or to the procurator fiscal or a member of his staff, although in England effective service was held to have taken place where the documents were given to the accused's agent[1] and even, in one case, to the accused's counsel.[2] It is considered doubtful that these last two cases would be followed in Scotland; see *Geddes v Hamilton*.[3]

5.8.15 Qualified analyst (s 16(7))

Section 16(7) of the Road Traffic Offenders Act 1988 provides:

'In this section "authorised analyst" means –

(a)   any person possessing the qualifications prescribed by regulations made under section 76 of the Food Act 1984 or section 27 of the Food and Drugs (Scotland) Act 1956 as qualifying persons for appointment as public analysts under those Acts, and

(b)   any other person authorised by the Secretary of State to make analyses for the purposes of this section.'

This subsection provides the definition of the term 'authorised analyst' referred to in s 16(1)(b) (see 5.8.7 above).

1   *Anderton v Kinnaird* [1986] RTR 11.
2   *Penman v Parker* [1986] RTR 403.
3   *Geddes v Hamilton* 1986 SLT 536, 1986 SCCR 165.

Chapter 6

Miscellaneous; hospital patients; detention and interpretation

6.1	**PROTECTION FOR HOSPITAL PATIENTS**
6.1.1	Section 9
6.1.2	Definitions
6.1.3	General application
6.2	**POWER TO DETAIN PERSONS AFFECTED BY ALCOHOL OR DRUGS**
6.2.1	Section 10
6.3	**INTERPRETATION (S 11)**

6.1 PROTECTION FOR HOSPITAL PATIENTS

6.1.1 Section 9

Section 9 of the Road Traffic Act 1988[1] provides:

'(1) While a person is at a hospital as a patient he shall not be required to co-operate with a preliminary test or to provide a specimen under section 7 of this Act unless the medical practitioner in immediate charge of his case has been notified of the proposal to make the requirement; and –

(a) if the requirement is then made, it shall be for co-operation with a test administered, or for the provision of a specimen, at the hospital, but

(b) if the medical practitioner objects on the ground specified in subsection (2) below, the requirement shall not be made.

(1A) While a person is at a hospital as a patient, no specimen of blood shall be taken from him under section 7A of this Act and he shall not be required to give his permission for a laboratory test of a specimen taken under that section unless the medical practitioner in immediate charge of his case –

---

1 As amended by Police Reform Act 2002 (c 30), Pt 4 (c 2), s 56(1) and the Serious Organised Crime and Police Act 2005 (c 15), Pt 5, s 154.

(a)   has been notified of the proposal to take the specimen or to make the requirement; and

(b)   has not objected on the ground specified in subsection (2).

(2) The ground on which the medical practitioner may object is –

(a)   in a case falling within subsection (1), that the requirement or the provision of the specimen or (if one is required) the warning required by section 7(7) of this Act would be prejudicial to the proper care and treatment of the patient; and

(b)   in a case falling within subsection (1A), that the taking of the specimen, the requirement or the warning required by section 7A(5) of this Act would be so prejudicial.'

6.1.2 Definitions

'*While a person is at hospital as a patient*'. This phrase is to be strictly construed, and does not, for example, include a person in an ambulance waiting to go to hospital. Such a person will not qualify for the protection conferred by this section.[1] The term 'hospital' is defined in s 11 (see 6.3.1 below).

'*Co-operation with a test administered*'. The tests administered are the preliminary tests in terms of ss 6–6C of the Road Traffic Act 1988.

'*Provision of a specimen*'. The specimens referred to are specimens of breath in terms of s 7(1)(a), blood or urine in terms of s 7(1)(b), and blood in terms of s 7A(1).

'*Medical practitioner*'. See 4.10.5 above.

'*In immediate charge has been notified*'. The scope for passage of time between notification and provision of a sample was considered in *Pacitti v Frame*.[2] Immediate charge was interpreted as referring to the doctor in charge of the patient at the time notification was made by the police and not later on, when, as happened in that case, a different doctor had taken charge. There was accordingly no need to repeat the notification

6.1.3 General application

It should be noted that the constable must seek out the medical practitioner's opinion before he can require co-operation or provision of a specimen of a person who is in hospital as a patient. In particular, it is clear that in terms of sub-s (2)(a), the constable must obtain the medical

---

1   *Manz v Miln* 1977 JC 78; see also *MacNeill v England* 1971 SLT 103; and *Watt v MacNeill* 1980 SLT 178.

2   *Pacitti v Frame* 2004 SCCR 487.

practitioner's opinion not only as to whether the patient can co-operate with a preliminary test or to provide a specimen under s 7 but, as a quite separate issue, whether the requirement or request for a specimen, or the warning which must be given in terms of s 7(7) of the Road Traffic Act 1988, to the effect that a failure to provide a blood or urine specimen may render the driver liable to prosecution, would be prejudicial to the proper care and treatment of the patient. Presumably, it is conceivable that one form of specimen might be prejudicial, but another may not. The same approach applies in terms of sub-s (2)(b) so far as the taking of the specimen, and the requirement or the warning required by s 7A(5) of Road Traffic Act 1988.

Failure to observe the requirements imposed by this section will render the specimen inadmissible (see 5.3.4 above). It has not been decided whether a requirement made by a police officer, in the face of an objection by the medical practitioner in charge, will constitute a reasonable excuse for failing to provide a specimen in terms of ss 7(6) and 7A(6), but this point is probably academic. By virtue of s 15(4) of the Road Traffic Offenders Act 1988, and s 11(4) of the Road Traffic Act 1988, any specimen of blood has to be taken by a medical practitioner or a registered health care professional with the accused's consent.

In *DPP v Wilson*[1] a patient was wrongly arrested within a hospital and despite the terms of s 6D(3). Nonetheless, subsequent blood testing carried out in terms of s 9 was not unlawful as a result.

6.2 POWER TO DETAIN PERSONS AFFECTED BY ALCOHOL OR DRUGS

6.2.1 Section 10

Section 10 of the Road Traffic Act 1988, as amended,[2] provides:

'(1) Subject to subsections (2) and (3) below, a person required under section 7 or 7A to provide a specimen of breath, blood or urine may afterwards be detained at a police station (or, if the specimen was provided otherwise than at a police station, arrested and taken to and detained at a police station) if a constable has reasonable grounds for believing that, were that person then driving or attempting to drive a mechanically propelled vehicle on a road, he would commit an offence under section 4, 5 or 5A of this Act.

1 [2009] EWHC 1988 (Admin), [2009] RTR 29.
2 By the Road Traffic Act 1991, Sch 4 para 43, the Railways and Transport Safety Act 2003, s 107 and Sch 7), the Serious Organised Crime and Police Act 2005 and the Crime and Courts Act 2013 (c 22), Sch 22.

(2) Subsection (1) above does not apply to the person if it ought reasonably to appear to the constable that there is no likelihood of his driving or attempting to drive a mechanically propelled vehicle whilst his ability to drive properly is impaired or whilst –

(a)   the person's ability to drive properly is impaired,

(b)   the proportion of alcohol in the person's breath, blood or urine exceeds the prescribed limit, or

(c)   the proportion of a specified controlled drug in the person's blood or urine exceeds the specified limit for that drug.

(2A) A person who is at a hospital as a patient shall not be arrested and taken from there to a police station in pursuance of this section if it would be prejudicial to his proper care and treatment as a patient.

(3) A constable must consult a medical practitioner on any question arising under this section whether a person's ability to drive properly is or might be impaired through drugs and must act on the medical practitioner's advice.'

This section in effect allows a police officer to detain any motorist who has been required to provide a specimen of breath, blood or urine at the police station until he is satisfied either that, in his opinion, the level of alcohol or drugs in the accused's body is such that were he to drive he would no longer be committing an offence, or it ought reasonably appear to the officer that there is no likelihood of him driving. Despite the objective use of 'ought' the decision in these matters is left entirely to the constable in question, and there is no sanction provided by the section in respect of any abuse of power in respect thereof other than by making a complaint in the normal way. However, if the accused's condition arises from the consumption of drugs, the constable is required to seek out a medical practitioner's advice on the question of whether the accused's ability to drive is impaired and, having done so, the constable must act on the advice given.

6.3 INTERPRETATION (S 11)

Section 11 (as amended by the Crime and Courts Act 2013) of the Road Traffic Act 1988 now provides:

'(1) The following provisions apply for the interpretation of sections 3A to 10 of this Act.

(2) In those sections –

"controlled drug" has the meaning given by section 2 of the Misuse of Drugs Act 1971, "drug" includes any intoxicant other than alcohol,

"fail" includes refuse,

"hospital" means an institution which provides medical or surgical treatment for in-patients or out-patients,

"the prescribed limit" means, (in Scottish terms) –

(a)   22 microgrammes of alcohol in 100 millilitres of breath;

(b)   50 milligrammes of alcohol in 100 millilitres of blood; or

(c)   67 milligrammes of alcohol in 100 millilitres of urine.

"registered health care professional" means a person (other than a medical practitioner) who is –

(a)   a registered nurse; or

(b)   a registered member of a health care profession which is designated for the purposes of this paragraph by an order made by the Secretary of State.

"specified", in relation to a controlled drug, has the meaning given by section 5A(8)

(2ZA) Regulations under subsection (2) may be made—

(a)   by the Secretary of State, in relation to driving or attempting to drive, or being in charge of a vehicle, in England and Wales;

(b)   by the Scottish Ministers, in relation to driving or attempting to drive, or being in charge of a vehicle, in Scotland.

(2A) A health care profession is any profession mentioned in section 60(2) of the Health Act 1999 (c. 8) other than the profession of practising medicine and the profession of nursing.

(2B) An order under subsection (2) shall be made by statutory instrument; and any such statutory instrument shall be subject to annulment in pursuance of a resolution of either House of Parliament.

(3) A person does not co-operate with a preliminary test or provide a specimen of breath for analysis unless his co-operation or the specimen –

(a)   is sufficient to enable the test or the analysis to be carried out, and

(b)   is provided in such a way as to enable the objective of the test or analysis to be satisfactorily achieved.

(4) A person provides a specimen of blood if and only if –

(a)   he consents to the taking of such a specimen from him; and

(b)   the specimen is taken from him either by a medical practitioner or, by a registered health care professional.'

The effect of the interpretation section has been referred to *passim* in the preceding chapters on ss 3A–10 of the Road Traffic Act 1988 and ss 15 and 16 of the Road Traffic Offenders Act 1988.

Chapter 7

Other road traffic offences

7.1 GENERAL: HIGHWAY CODE

In addition to the offences covered by ss 1–11 of the Road Traffic Act 1988 and described in the preceding chapters, there are a very large number of further offences, directions and regulations contained in the extensive legislative instruments concerned with road traffic. The Highway Code does not create offences as such; rather it contains a series of directions for the guidance of persons using roads. Although, in terms of s 38(1) of the Road Traffic Act 1988, the Highway Code continues to have effect, a failure *per se* on the part of anyone using the road to observe the provisions of the code does not make that person guilty of a criminal offence. Section 38(7) of the Act provides:

> 'A failure on the part of a person to observe a provision of the Highway Code shall not of itself render that person liable to criminal proceedings of any kind but any such failure may in any proceedings (whether civil or criminal, and including proceedings for an offence under the Traffic Acts, the Public Passenger Vehicles Act 1981 or ss 18 to 23 of the Transport Act 1985) be relied upon by any party to the proceedings as tending to establish or negative any liability which is in question in those proceedings.'

Accordingly, the provisions of the Highway Code may provide useful guidance in determining whether a civil wrong, or an offence in terms of any of the principal Acts described, has or has not been committed.[1] The Secretary of State has the responsibility for issuing the Highway Code and has the power to revise it from time to time as the need arises, although in terms of s 38(5) of the Act he is obliged to consult such representative organisations as he thinks fit. Further, the Secretary of State and local authorities have powers and responsibilities to furnish road safety training and information, in terms of ss 39 and 40 The Highway Code is published by The Stationery Office, and is available from its own and some other bookshops, as are other Department of Transport motoring publications. It is also available online (www.gov.uk/highway-code).

There follows a description of some of the principal traffic offences contained in the legislation, although it must be remembered that there are a very large number of other provisions which do not often feature in practice. The penalties for offences under the Road Traffic Act 1988 (as amended by the Road Traffic Act 1991) are contained in Sch 2 to the Road Traffic Offenders Act 1988 (as amended by Sch 2 to the Road Traffic Act 1991), which also includes penalties in respect of other offences such as those described in the Road Traffic Regulation Act 1984 and

---

1   *McCrone v Normand* 1989 SLT 332.

contraventions of the Construction and Use regulations in terms of s 42 of the Road Traffic Act 1988 (as amended by s 8 of the Road Traffic Act 1991). Schedule 2 does not reflect the change practically achieved by s 45 of the Criminal Proceedings etc (Reform) (Scotland) Act 2007 which led to a maximum 12-month sentence for summary statutory offences triable under both summary and solemn procedure.

Penalties in respect of offences under other Acts and regulations are normally found within the body of such legislation.

7.2 RACES AND TRIALS

7.2.1 Section 12

Tried summarily, obligatory disqualification (or 3–11 points) and level 4 fine

Section 12 of the Road Traffic Act 1988 (as amended)[1] provides:

'(1) A person who promotes or takes part in a race or trial of speed between motor vehicles on a highway is guilty of an offence.

(1A) Subsection (1) is subject to—

(a)   in relation to England and Wales, sections 12A to 12F (which make provision to allow the holding of races or trials of speed between motor vehicles on public ways in England and Wales);

(b)   in relation to Scotland, sections 12G to 12I (which make provision to allow the holding of races or trials of speed between motor vehicles on public ways in Scotland).

(2) In this section "public way" means, in England and Wales, a public highway and, in Scotland, a public road.'

Sections 12G–I envisage either regulations or the making of provision authorisation for the holding of races or trials of speed by the Scottish Ministers.

Under s 12H, the provisions of ss 1, 1A, 2, 2B and 3 of the Road Traffic Act 1988 will not ordinarily apply to such regulated events. Likewise, regulations removing requirements for licence and insurance, speed limits and the like are anticipated. The application of ss 3A to 11 of the Act cannot be disapplied.

7.2.2 Definitions

'*Motor vehicle*'. See 1.2.1 above.

'*Public road*'. See 1.8.1 and 1.8.2 above.

---

1   Added by Deregulation Act 2015 c 20.

7.2.3 General application

For an offence to be committed under this section, it is not necessary that the race or trial of speed should have been pre-arranged. In *Ferrari v McNaughton*[1] the evidence indicated that two vehicles engaged upon a race or trial of speed quite spontaneously. In these circumstances, the appeal court held that a contravention of s 12 of the Road Traffic Act 1988 had occurred. No definition exists within the legislation of what constitutes a race or trial of speed and whether such an event has taken place will depend on the facts and circumstances in each case.

In *Hunter v Frame* 2004,[2] a majority decision of the Court of Appeal, the view was expressed that the absence of authority on the matter was unsurprising given that 'race' must be given its ordinary meaning in the English language, namely that it 'connotes a competition as to speed', whereas trial of speed reflects participants competing against the clock as opposed to each other. In that case evidence of jockeying for position was held not to be capable, without indulging in speculation, of amounting to racing and the convictions were overturned. However, the conduct involved was condemned and described as justifying a conviction for dangerous driving under s 2 which is not an alternative verdict.

Under s 13 of the Road Traffic Act 1988, other competitions or trials, other than a race or trial by speed, may be permitted to take place on the road, provided that they are properly authorised and conducted in accordance with the relevant regulations.[3]

7.2.4 Section 31:4 Regulation of cycle racing on public ways

Tried summarily, level 1 fine

Section 31(1) provides:

> '(1) A person who promotes or takes part in a race or trial of speed on a public way between cycles is guilty of an offence, unless the race or trial –
>
> (a)　is authorised, and
>
> (b)　is conducted in accordance with any conditions imposed, by or under regulations under this section.'

1　*Ferrari v McNaughton* 1979 SLT (Notes) 62, 1979 CO Circulars A/13.
2　*Hunter v Frame* 2004 SCCR 214, 2004 SLT 697.
3　RTA 1988, s 13; reference must also be made to s 13A, added by the RTA 1991, s 5, as well as s 33 of the RTA 1988.
4　As amended by RTA 1991, Sch 4 para 49. As amended by RTA 1991, Sch 4 para 49.

The conditions are set out in the remainder of the section and it is to be noted that 'public way' means, in Scotland, a public road but does not include a footpath.

7.3 SEATBELTS AND PROTECTIVE HEADGEAR

Primary seatbelt legislation is found in ss 14, 15, 15A, and 15B of the Road Traffic Act 1988 as amended. Section 15A was introduced by the Motor Vehicles (Safety Equipment for Children) Act 1991. Section 15B, which concerns the requirement to notify bus passengers to wear seat belts, was added by the Motor Vehicles (Wearing of Seat Belts) (Amendment) Regulations 2006 (SI 2006/1892), reg 4. It does not apply to local bus services in built-up areas nor, obviously, to vehicles constructed or adapted for standing passengers.

In particular, the requirement to wear a seatbelt imposed on the driver and adult passengers is found in s 14, and further described in the Motor Vehicles (Wearing of Seat Belts) Regulations 1993[1] as variously amended by the Motor Vehicles (Wearing of Seat Belts) (Amendment) Regulations of 2006 and 2015, and the Police and Fire Reform (Scotland) Act 2012 (Consequential Modifications and Savings) Order 2013/119 (Scottish SI).

These regulations must be read along with regs 46, 47 and 48 of the Road Vehicles (Construction and Use) Regulations 1986[2] which define the relevant terms and vehicle exemptions. Use exemptions are found in reg 6 of the 1993 Regulations. These exemptions apply chiefly to the driver of, or a passenger in, a motor vehicle constructed or adapted for carrying goods, while on a journey which does not exceed 50 metres and which is undertaken for the purpose of delivering or collecting anything; drivers performing a manoeuvre, including reversing; the holder of a certificate in the prescribed form signed by a medical practitioner that it is inadvisable on medical grounds for the driver to wear a seatbelt; a constable or similar person protecting or escorting another person; firemen; taxi drivers; disabled persons wearing seatbelts; certain processions; and those testing a vehicle under trade plates. It is also an offence to wear a seatbelt which does not comply with the regulations; that in itself, however, may constitute a further offence.

Failing to wear an adult seatbelt by any person over the age of 14 in the front and rear of a motor car is covered by reg 5, and the description of

---

1   Motor Vehicles (Wearing of Seat Belts) Regulations 1993 (SI 1993/176).
2   Road Vehicles (Construction and Use) Regulations 1986 (SI 1986/1078) (as amended by SI 1987/1133; SI 1989/1478; SI 1991/2003); and SI 2001/1043.

child restraints to be worn by children in the rear of a vehicle are covered by reg 8. The interpretation of 'child' is set out in reg 2: a child is a person under 14, and may either be a small child, that is aged under 12 and under 135 cm in height, or in other cases a large child. Exemptions are provided in reg 10 and include carriage of all ages of children in taxis where no appropriate seat belt is available, those with medical certificates, and most practically, in cases of a small child aged three years or more who is wearing an adult belt and who, because of an unexpected necessity, is travelling a short distance in a passenger car or light goods vehicle in which no appropriate seat belt is available for him.

Seat belts to be worn by children in the front of a vehicle are described in the Motor Vehicle (Wearing of Seat Belts by Children in Front Seats) Regulations 1993.[1] The vehicles which are required to have seatbelts fitted are described in regs 46 and 47 (as amended, above) of the Road Vehicles (Construction and Use) Regulations 1986.

The driver is guilty of an offence if he or any child is not wearing a seatbelt; the driver is not guilty of any offence if a seatbelt fails to be worn by an adult passenger.[2] Contraventions of seatbelt provisions attract a variety of penalties ranging from level 2 to level 4 fines. Reference should be made to the Road Traffic Offenders Act 1988, Sch 2. Since s 24 of the Road Safety Act 2006 came into force in September 2007, penalties relating to seat belt offences for children, front and rear, are set at level 2. Level 4 offences related to offences under s 15B and failure by bus operators to take all reasonable steps to ensure that every passenger is notified of the requirement to wear a seat belt at all times.

Protective headgear for motor cyclists is governed by ss 16, 17 and 18 of the Road Traffic Act 1988, and the Motor Cycles (Protective Helmets) Regulations 1998.[3]

7.4 TRAFFIC DIRECTIONS: CONSTABLE'S DIRECTIONS (S 35)

Tried summarily, discretionary disqualification or obligatory endorsement of 3 points, level 3 fine

---

1 SI 1993/31 as amended by the Motor Vehicles (Wearing of Seat Belts by Children in Front Seats) (Amendment) Regulations 2006 (SI 2006/2213) and Motor Vehicles (Wearing of Seat Belts by Children in Front Seats) (Amendment) Regulations 2015 (SI 2015/402).
2 RTA 1988, ss 14(3) and 15(4).
3 SI 1998/1807.

7.4.1 General

By virtue of s 35(1) of the Road Traffic Act 1988, where a constable is engaged in the regulation of traffic in a road, a person who, while driving or propelling a vehicle, neglects or refuses to stop the vehicle or make it proceed in or keep to a particular line of traffic when directed to do so by the constable in the execution of his duty shall be guilty of an offence. Section 35(2) gives similar powers to a constable to enable a traffic survey to be carried out. Any vehicle is covered by this section.

Whether an offence under this section has taken place is a matter of fact. A police officer does not have to be specially authorised to regulate traffic; however the Crown must show that the officer was acting in the execution of his duty. The section, however, does not specify that the constable must be in uniform. It is important to note that, in terms of s 21(3) of the Road Traffic Offenders Act 1988, the Crown can secure a conviction under this section on the evidence of only one witness.[1]

It would appear to be a possible defence to a charge of this kind that the constable was acting capriciously.[2] In *Keane v McSkimming*,[3] it was observed that it was sufficient for the prosecution to show that the signal given by the police officer was obvious; it is not necessary for a conviction that it is established in evidence that the driver in fact saw the signal. However, it is also clear from this case that the fact that the driver did not see the signal may in appropriate circumstances be a good defence to the charge.

7.4.2 Traffic signs (s 36)

Tried summarily, discretionary disqualification or obligatory endorsement of three points, for offences involving motor vehicles and signs specified in regulations made under s.36, level 3 fine

It is an offence in terms of s 36 of the Road Traffic Act 1988[4] for a person driving or propelling a vehicle not to comply with a traffic sign of the prescribed size, colour and type or as otherwise authorised by the provisions of the Road Traffic Regulation Act 1984. It is to be noted that this provision applies beyond motor vehicles and does apply to pedal cyclists, as evidenced by the regular placing of advanced stop lines for them.

The sign must indicate a statutory prohibition, restriction or requirement, and must also be properly established in terms of the

---

1   See also *Sutherland v Aitchison* 1970 SLT (Notes) 48.
2   *Beard v Wood* [1980] RTR 454, [1980] Crim LR 384.
3   *Keane v McSkimming* 1983 SCCR 220.
4   As amended by the Scotland Act 2016.

legislation.[1] However, any traffic sign placed at or near a road is presumed to be properly authorised and lawfully placed unless the contrary is proved.[2] At the same time, any traffic sign should conform exactly to the description of that sign given in the appropriate regulations.[3] In *Skeen v Smith*[4] a sign displayed on a pole at a road junction was erected properly, but the corresponding 'stop' sign marked on the road was not entirely clear. It was held that this did not entitle the driver to ignore the sign on the pole. Quite how rigorously exact conformity may be demanded is arguable in light of the more pragmatic and purposive approach to statutory interpretation in recent years.[5]

If traffic lights are showing green in one direction, and there is evidence that the system is working properly, the court may assume that the counter lights are at red,[6] provided that there is some evidence to support that conclusions such as that the lights are working correctly.[7]

Part V of the Road Traffic Regulation Act 1984 gives general provisions to the relevant authority as to traffic signs. In relation to devolved competence, within the meaning of the Scotland Act 1998, that now means the Scottish Ministers.

The principal regulations are now the Traffic Signs Regulations and General Directions 2016, which attempt to simplify matters. Transitional provisions under reg 14 provide for continuing compliance for many pre-existing signs under the earlier 2002 Regulations.[8]

As in s 35, in terms of s 21(3) of the Road Traffic Offenders Act 1988, a conviction for an offence under s 36 may follow from the evidence of one witness only.[9]

Emergency vehicles are exempt from compliance with traffic lights if being used for such a purpose.[10] That said, care must be taken in such

---

1   RTA 1988, s 35(2).
2   *Spiers v Normand* 1995 JC 147, 1996 SLT 78; RTA 1988, s 36(3).
3   *Davies v Heatley* [1971] RTR 145.
4   *Skeen v Smith* 1979 SLT 295.
5   See *Peake v DPP* [2010] EHWC 286 (Admin), 2011 RTR 3, *PF Airdrie v McConnell* 2011 SCCR 32, and *Wilson v PF Kilmarnock* [2012] HCJAC 148 XJ174/12.
6   *Pacitti v Copeland* 1963 SLT (Notes) 52.
7   *Inwar v Normand* 1997 SCCR 6.
8   Traffic Signs Regulations and General Directions 2016 (SI 2016/362) as amended by the Traffic Signs Amendment (Scotland) Regulations and General Directions 2018 (SSI 2018/161).
9   See also *Sutherland v Aitchison* 1970 SLT (Notes) 48.
10   Traffic Signs Regulations and General Directions 2002, reg 36.

circumstances and prosecution under ss 1–3 of the RTA 1988 may follow if it is not.

For the prosecution of traffic light offences using photographic evidence, see 7.8.3 below.

7.4.3 Directions to pedestrians (s 37)

Tried summarily, level 3 fine

A pedestrian proceeding across or along a carriageway in contravention of a direction to stop given by a constable engaged in regulating traffic in the execution of his duty, is guilty of an offence.[1] The constable must be in uniform. Unlike the two preceding sections, s 21(3) of the Road Traffic Offenders Act 1988 does not apply to this offence, and the prosecution must offer full corroborative evidence to secure a conviction.

A constable may also require a person committing an offence under s 37 of the Road Traffic Act 1988 to give his name and address, and if that person refuses to do so, his refusal constitutes a further offence.[2]

For possible defences to a charge under s 37, reference should be made to 7.4.1 above.

7.5 POWERS OF POLICE OFFICERS TO STOP VEHICLES AND REQUIRE INFORMATION

7.5.1 General (s 163)

Tried summarily, level 3 (person riding a cycle) or 5 (person driving a mechanically propelled vehicle) fine

By virtue of s 163 of the Road Traffic Act 1988,[3] a person driving a mechanically propelled vehicle on a road, or riding a cycle on a road, must stop on being required to do so by a police constable in uniform. Failure so to stop is an offence. It is sufficient for a conviction that the Crown proves that the policeman's signal was obvious; it does not have to be proved that the driver saw the signal.[4] This offence is not one provable by the evidence of one witness only in terms of s 21 of the Road Traffic Offenders Act 1988; full corroborated evidence is required for conviction.

1   RTA 1988, s 37.
2   RTA 1988, s 169.
3   As amended by RTA 1991, Sch 4 para 67 and s 27 of the Road Safety Act 2006.
4   *Keane v McSkimming* 1983 SCCR 220.

7.5.2 Duty to give information and documents (s 164)

Tried summarily, level 3 fine

By virtue of s 164 of the Road Traffic Act 1988,[1] a police constable or vehicle examiner may require certain classes of person to produce their driving licence. The express purpose of this production of the licence is to enable the constable to ascertain the name and address of the holder of the licence, and its date and authority of issue.

The classes of person of whom this requirement can be made are: a person driving a motor vehicle on a road; a person whom a constable has reasonable cause to believe was driving a motor vehicle on a road when it was involved in an accident or who has committed a motor vehicle offence; a person who is supervising a provisional licence holder, or who was supervising a provisional driver when an accident or a suspected offence occurred. If the driver is not able to produce his licence at the material time when he is required to do so, he can escape conviction in terms of sub-s (7) and (8). Subsection (7) arises when a driver has previously surrendered his licence to a police officer or other authorised person in terms of the fixed penalty procedure and s 56 of the Road Traffic Offenders Act 1988. Subsection (8) covers the normal situation where a driver does not have his licence with him at the time the requirement was made. In those circumstances, the driver can escape conviction if (a) he produces his licence personally within seven days at a nominated police station, or (b) if he produces it at the police station as soon as reasonably practicable, or if he proves that it was not reasonably practicable for him to produce it to the police station before the day on which proceedings were commenced by the service of the complaint. In association with the requirement to produce a licence at a nominated police station, the police officer will normally issue a standard form (HORT 1) to the driver.

It should be noted that in certain circumstances the officer may seize a licence produced to him.[2]

7.5.3 Duty to give name and address and certain documents (s 165)

Tried summarily, level 3 fine

By virtue of s 165 of the Road Traffic Act 1988,[3] broadly the same categories of person as are described in s 164 (apart from the drivers of invalid

---

1   As amended by RTA 1991, Sch 4 para 68 and the Road Safety Act 2006.
2   RTA 1988, s 164(3) and (5).
3   As amended by RTA 1991, Sch 4 para 69.

carriages) may also be required by a constable or vehicle examiner to give their name and address, and the name and address of the owner of the vehicle. In addition, holders of a full licence may be required to produce certain documents relevant to the vehicle for examination, namely the insurance certificate, the MOT certificate and any relevant goods vehicle test certificate. In relation to insurance certificates, this may be done electronically.[1]

There may be further duties to provide information in terms of s 171 (see 7.5.9 below). Again, it is a defence to a charge under this section if the driver produces the document or any other required evidence to a nominated police station within seven days, or as soon as reasonably practicable, or if he proves that it was not reasonably practicable for him to have presented the necessary information to the police station before the day on which any complaint was served.

7.5.4 Powers to seize and retain vehicles driven without licence and insurance (s 165A and s 165B (inserted by s 152 of the Serious Organised Crime and Police Act 2005))

There has been ever increasing concern as to the number of unlicenced and uninsured drivers on the roads, perhaps best reflected in the harsher sentencing policy for contraventions of s 143 of the Road Traffic Act 1988 (although the recent provision of fixed penalties for such offences does not sit well with the general approach). Home Office figures also suggest that drivers without a valid licence commit almost 10 per cent of recorded traffic offences and are nine times more likely to be involved in accidents.[2]

Given advances in technology, in particular automatic number plate recognition, and immediate access to the DVLA and the Motor Insurance Databases, it is now possible, thanks to the new provisions contained in ss 165A and 165B for the police to act swiftly and meaningfully to prevent continued illegal driving, as opposed to the earlier position of issuing HORT 1 forms, or simply reporting matters to the Procurator Fiscal.

The provisions were effective from 6 July 2005 when the regulations referred to in s 165B, the Road Traffic Act 1988 (Retention and Disposal of Seized Motor Vehicles) Regulations 2005 (SI 2005/1606), came into force.

---

1   Motor Vehicles (Electronic Communication of Certificates of Insurance) Order 2010/1117.
2   Letter from Home Office to Chief Officers of Police dated 30 June 2005.

Section 165A[1] provides:

'165A Power to seize vehicles driven without licence or insurance

(1) Subsection (5) applies if any of the following conditions is satisfied.

(2) The first condition is that –

(a) a constable in uniform requires, under section 164, a person to produce his licence for examination,

(b) the person fails to produce them, and

(c) the constable has reasonable grounds for believing that a motor vehicle is or was being driven by the person in contravention of section 87(1).

(3) The second condition is that –

(a) a constable in uniform requires, under section 165, a person to produce evidence that a motor vehicle is not or was not being driven in contravention of section 143,

(b) the person fails to produce such evidence, and

(c) the constable has reasonable grounds for believing that the vehicle is or was being so driven.

(4) The third condition is that –

(a) a constable in uniform requires, under section 163, a person driving a motor vehicle to stop the vehicle,

(b) the person fails to stop the vehicle, or to stop the vehicle long enough, for the constable to make such lawful enquiries as he considers appropriate, and

(c) the constable has reasonable grounds for believing that the vehicle is or was being driven in contravention of section 87(1) or 143.

(5) Where this subsection applies, the constable may –

(a) seize the vehicle in accordance with subsections (6) and (7) and remove it;

(b) enter, for the purpose of exercising a power falling within paragraph (a), any premises (other than a private dwelling house) on which he has reasonable grounds for believing the vehicle to be;

(c) use reasonable force, if necessary, in the exercise of any power conferred by paragraph (a) or (b).

---

1   As amended by the Road Safety Act 2006 (Consequential Amendments) Order 2015/583.(e

(6) Before seizing the motor vehicle, the constable must warn the person by whom it appears that the vehicle is or was being driven in contravention of section 87(1) or 143 that he will seize it –

(a)   in a section 87(1) case, if the person does not produce his licence immediately;

(b)   in a section 143 case, if the person does not provide him immediately with evidence that the vehicle is not or was not being driven in contravention of that section.

But the constable is not required to give such a warning if the circumstances make it impracticable for him to do so.

(7) If the constable is unable to seize the vehicle immediately because the person driving the vehicle has failed to stop as requested or has driven off, he may seize it at any time within the period of 24 hours beginning with the time at which the condition in question is first satisfied.

(8) The powers conferred on a constable by this section are exercisable only at a time when regulations under section 165B are in force.

(9) In this section –

(a)   a reference to a motor vehicle does not include an invalid carriage;

(b)   a reference to evidence that a motor vehicle is not or was not being driven in contravention of section 143 is a reference to a document or other evidence within section 165(2)(a);

(c)   and "licence" has the same meanings as in section 164;

(d)   "private dwelling house" does not include any garage or other structure occupied with the dwelling house, or any land appurtenant to the dwelling house.'

As can be seen, seizure of the vehicle can occur if any one of the three conditions are satisfied, namely failure to produce documents under the powers provided by ss 164 and 165 and the associated reasonable grounds for believing that the driver is contravening either s 87 or s 143(1), or where there is a failure to stop in breach of s 163 and the same reasonable grounds for belief exist.

Reasonable grounds for belief will no doubt stem from the officer's own knowledge but will presumably principally derive from information contained within the databases referred to above. The officer must be in uniform and a warning must be given 'unless circumstances make it impracticable for him to do so' that seizure will take place unless the relevant documentation or supportive evidence is produced immediately. This will be a matter of fact and degree in each case.

Where a driver has failed to stop or subsequently drives off, the power to seize runs for 24 hours from the time of the condition being satisfied.

In order to seize and remove a vehicle, the officer may enter any premises save a private dwelling house but that does exception does not include any garage, other building or land associated with the dwelling house.

Section 165B provides:

'165B Retention etc of vehicles seized under section 165A

(1) The Secretary of State may by regulations make provision as to –

(a) the removal and retention of motor vehicles seized under section 165A; and

(b) the release or disposal of such motor vehicles.

(2) Regulations under subsection (1) may, in particular, make provision –

(a) for the giving of notice of the seizure of a motor vehicle under section 165A to a person who is the registered keeper, the owner or the driver of that vehicle;

(b) for the procedure by which a person who claims to be the registered keeper or the owner of a motor vehicle seized under section 165A may seek to have it released;

(c) for requiring the payment, by the registered keeper, owner or driver of the vehicle, of fees, charges or costs in relation to the removal and retention of such a motor vehicle and to any application for its release;

(d) as to the circumstances in which a motor vehicle seized under section 165A may be disposed of;

(e) as to the destination –

(i) of any fees or charges payable in accordance with the regulations;

(ii) of the proceeds (if any) arising from the disposal of a motor vehicle seized under section 165A;

(f) for the delivery to a local authority, in circumstances prescribed by or determined in accordance with the regulations, of any motor vehicle seized under section 165A.

(3) Regulations under subsection (1) must provide that a person who would otherwise be liable to pay any fee or charge under the regulations is not liable to pay it if –

(a) he was not driving the motor vehicle at the time in question, and

(b) he did not know that the vehicle was being driven at that time, had not consented to its being driven and could not, by the taking of reasonable steps, have prevented it from being driven.

(4) Regulations under subsection (1) may make different provision for different cases.

(5) In this section –

"local authority" –

(a)   in relation to England, means –

    (i)   a county council,

    (ii)   the council of a district comprised in an area for which there is no county council,

    (iii)   a London borough council,

    (iv)   the Common Council of the City of London, or

    (v)   Transport for London;

(b)   in relation to Wales, means the council of a county or county borough; and

(c)   in relation to Scotland, means a council constituted under section 2 of the Local Government etc. (Scotland) Act 1994;

"registered keeper", in relation to a motor vehicle, means the person in whose name the vehicle is registered under the Vehicle Excise and Registration Act 1994.'

The Road Traffic Act 1988 (Retention and Disposal of Seized Motor Vehicles) Regulations 2005 (SI 2005/1606), as amended by SI 2008/2097, provides the detail of what is anticipated in s 165B.

Regulation 4 provides that seizure notices must be given by the officer to the driver unless circumstances man that is not practicable. The vehicle is then passed into the custody of an authorised person (either an officer or other authorised under reg 3(1) by the local Chief Officer of Police) and he must take such steps as are reasonably practicable to give a seizure notice in accordance with this regulation to the person who is the registered keeper and to the owner, where that appears to be someone different.

'Registered keeper', in relation to a motor vehicle, means the person in whose name the vehicle is registered under the Vehicle Excise and Registration Act 1994.

'Owner' includes (a) the person by whom, according to the records maintained by the Secretary of State in connection with any functions exercisable by him by virtue of the 1994 Act, the vehicle is kept and used; (b) in relation to a vehicle which is the subject of a hiring agreement or a hire-purchase agreement, the person entitled to possession of the vehicle under the agreement.

Provisions of service of the seizure notice are set out in reg 4(5) and principally include leaving it at, or sending it by registered post to, the address held for the keeper on the register or the owner's usual or last known address.

The seizure notice sets out where the vehicle was seized, where it is now being kept, and that to claim back the vehicle the registered keeper or owner of the vehicle is required to claim the vehicle from the authorised person on or before the date specified in the notice, which will be a date not less than seven working days from the day when the notice is given to the registered keeper or owner. Otherwise the vehicle will be disposed of.

Charges arise from the seizure and retention of the vehicle – see reg 6. These have to be paid to have the vehicle released, though not where the person liable to pay was not driving the vehicle at the time it was seized under section and did not know that the vehicle was being driven at that time, had not consented to its being driven and could not, by the taking of reasonable steps, have prevented it from being driven – see reg 5(5).

Likewise, the registered keeper or owner must either produce at a specified police station a valid certificate of insurance covering his use of that vehicle and a valid licence authorising him to drive that vehicle or nominate a third person who produces at a specified police station a valid insurance certificate and licence covering that person's use of that vehicle – see reg 5.

Disposal of the vehicles is provided for in regs 7 and 8 allows for any proceeds of sale to be paid to the owner net of any charges arising from seizure and retention.

7.5.5 Duty to give name and address in dangerous and careless driving or cycling (s 168)

Tried summarily, level 3 fine

By virtue of s 168 of the Road Traffic Act 1988,[1] the driver of a mechanically propelled vehicle who is alleged to have committed an offence under s 2 or 3 of the Act (dangerous or careless driving) or the rider of a cycle who is alleged to have committed an offence under s 28 or 29 of the Act must give his name and address to any person (not just a police officer) having reasonable grounds for requiring that information. Failure so to give the name and address, or the giving of a false name and address, is an offence. What constitutes reasonable grounds for making the requirement is a matter of fact in each case. The same requirement can be made in a case of dangerous or careless cycling in terms of ss 28 and 29 of the Act. Any person who fails to give his name and address or to produce his licence in these circumstances may be arrested without warrant.[2] In a prosecution

---

1   As amended by the RTA 1991, Sch 4 para 71.
2   RTA 1988, s 167.

under s 168, evidence identifying a driver who claimed he did not know who was driving at the material time is admissible.[1]

7.5.6 Duty on pedestrian to give name and address (s 169)

Tried summarily, level 1 fine

A constable may require a person who is committing an offence under s 37 of the Road Traffic Act 1988 (failure by a pedestrian to comply with a direction to stop given by a constable) to give his name and address, and failure to do so will constitute a further offence[2] (see 7.4.3 above).

7.5.7 Duty to give information as to identity of driver (s 172)

Tried summarily, discretionary disqualification or obligatory six penalty points3 (save for bodies corporate under s 172 (5) and (11)), and level 3 fine

Section 172 of the Road Traffic Act 1988,[4] requires the keeper or driver of a vehicle, or any other person, to give information to a duly authorised police officer as to the identity of the driver of the vehicle at any time the driver is alleged to have been guilty of most road traffic offences. The section is frequently used in the course of police investigations and reads in full as follows:

'(1) This section applies –

(a) to any offence under the preceding provisions of this Act except –

  (i) an offence under Part V, or

  (ii) an offence under section 13, 16, 51(2), 61(4), 67(9), 68(4), 96 or 120,

  and to an offence under section 178 of this Act,

(b) to any offence under sections 25, 26 or 27 of the Road Traffic Offenders Act 1988,

(c) to any offence against any other enactment relating to the use of vehicles on roads, and

(d) to manslaughter, or in Scotland culpable homicide, by the driver of a motor vehicle.

1　*Clark v Allan* 1988 SLT 274, 1987 SCCR 333.
2　RTA 1988, s 169.
3　Penalty increased from 3 to 6 points by s 29 of the Road Safety Act 2006 as of 24 September 2007 (SI 2007/2472, art 2(g)).
4　As amended by RTA 1991, s 21 and the Vehicle Excise and Regulation Act 1994, s 63 and Sch 2 and the Statute Law (Repeals) Act 2004 (c 14), Sch 1(14) para 1.

(2) Where the driver of a vehicle is alleged to be guilty of an offence to which this section applies –

(a)   the person keeping the vehicle shall give such information as to the identity of the driver as he may be required to give by or on behalf of a chief officer of police or the Chief Constable of the British Transport Police Force

and

(b)   any other person shall if required as stated above give any information which it is in his power to give and may lead to identification of the driver.

In this subsection references to the driver of a vehicle include references to the person riding a cycle.

(3) Subject to the following provisions, a person who fails to comply with a requirement under subsection (2) above shall be guilty of an offence.

(4) A person shall not be guilty of an offence by virtue of paragraph (a) of subsection (2) above if he shows that he did not know and could not with reasonable diligence have ascertained who the driver of the vehicle was.

(5) Where a body corporate is guilty of an offence under this section and the offence is proved to have been committed with the consent or connivance of, or to be attributable to neglect on the part of, a director, manager, secretary or other similar officer of the body corporate, or a person who was purporting to act in any such capacity, he, as well as the body corporate, is guilty of that offence and liable to be proceeded against and punished accordingly.

(6) Where the alleged offender is a body corporate, or in Scotland a partnership or an unincorporated association, or the proceedings are brought against him by virtue of subsection (5) above or subsection (11) below, subsection (4) above shall not apply unless, in addition to the matters there mentioned, the alleged offender shows that no record was kept of the persons who drove the vehicle and that the failure to keep a record was reasonable.

(7) A requirement under subsection (2) may be made by written notice served by post; and where it is so made –

(a)   it shall have effect as a requirement to give the information within the period of 28 days beginning with the day on which the notice is served, and

(b)   the person on whom the notice is served shall not be guilty of an offence under this section if he shows either that he gave the information as soon as reasonably practicable after the end of that period or that it has not been reasonably practicable for him to give it.

(8) Where the person on whom a notice under subsection (7) above is to be served is a body corporate, the notice is duly served if it is served on the secretary or clerk of that body.

(9) For the purposes of section 7 of the Interpretation Act 1978 as it applies for the purposes of this section the proper address of any person in relation to the service on him of a notice under subsection (7) above is –

(a)   in the case of the secretary or clerk of a body corporate, that of the registered or principal office of that body or (if the body corporate is the registered keeper of the vehicle concerned) the registered address, and

(b)   in any other case, his last known address at the time of service.

(10) In this section –

"registered address", in relation to the registered keeper of a vehicle, means the address recorded in the record kept under the Vehicle Excise and Registration Act 1994 with respect to that vehicle as being that person's address, and

"registered keeper", in relation to a vehicle, means the person in whose name the vehicle is registered under that Act;

and references to the driver of a vehicle include references to the rider of a cycle.

(11) Where, in Scotland, an offence under this section is committed by a partnership or by an unincorporated association other than a partnership and is proved to have been committed with the consent or connivance or in consequence of the negligence of a partner in the partnership or, as the case may be, a person concerned in the management or control of the association, he (as well as the partnership or association) shall be guilty of the offence.'

7.5.8 Definitions (s 172)

'*Keeper of the vehicle.*' This phrase is intended to refer to the person in whose custody the vehicle is, at the time of making the requirement. It is submitted that the keeper of any vehicle is not necessarily confined to the person who is the registered owner. The various parts of the section appear to draw a distinction between the registered keeper and the person keeping the vehicle.

'*Any other person.*' This phrase includes the driver himself.[1] Thus, where a police officer is investigating an alleged offence in terms of s 172(1) of the Road Traffic Act 1988, he is entitled to ask the person who is said to

---

1   *Foster v Farrell* 1963 SLT 182.

have been driving at the material time to confirm whether or not he was driving at the time the alleged offence is said to have been committed.

'By or on behalf of a chief officer of police or the Chief Constable of the British Transport Police Force.' This phrase includes any police officer whom the Chief Constable of the area has authorised to make the requirement on his behalf. The Chief Constable may, but does not have to, make a specific authorisation to each individual officer; a general authorisation may be given to particular officers to exercise this power.[1] A police officer who has not been duly authorised in terms of this section cannot ask the driver or any other person to confirm the driver's identity at the material time in terms of this section.[2]

7.5.9 General application (s 172)

The provisions of s 172 of the Road Traffic Act 1988, as amended by the Road Traffic Act 1991, are significantly widened, and are specifically framed for the purpose of giving police officers the power to carry out the new procedures involved in the automatic detection of road traffic offences. Section 172(2) makes it clear that the requirement to provide information can be made of the keeper of the vehicle or anyone else. In particular, the requirement can be made of officers of a company; this is to allow the identification of the drivers of fleet or hire vehicles. A requirement to furnish the police with the name of the driver is not a breach of the European Convention on Human Rights.[3] Nor is it incompetent to use this information to convict an accused driver as the use of the section is a proportionate response to the public interest in maintaining road safety, was no more objectionable than using breath or other samples, and involved putting a single question the answer to which could not of itself incriminate the suspect and in any event the penalty for refusal was moderate and non-custodial.[4] Admission to being the driver under s 172 is also admissible as evidence of identity in a linked non-road traffic offence.[5]

The offence is not a continuing one but occurs on a particular occasion[6] which is important in terms of the six-month time bar provisions under s 136 of the Criminal Procedure (Scotland) Act 1995. However, that does

1   *Gray v Farrell* 1969 SLT 250.
2   *Foster v Farrell* 1963 SLT 182.
3   *Jardine v Crowe* 1999 SCCR 52.
4   *Stott v Brown* 2001 SCCR 62 overturning *Brown v Stott* 2000 SCCR 314, 2000 SLT 379.
5   *How v Harvie* 2016 SCCR 435.
6   Thomson v Jackson 2010 SCCR 915.

not mean that further requirements may not be made, for example where a written request is ignored, simply that time will have started running after the original requirement.[1]

In situations where the registered keeper is, for example, a company, repeated s 172 requirements may be made as police investigations continue into discovering who was driving at the time. While cumbersome, these do not trigger the time bar against the individual driver. That only commences when he or she is made subject of a s 172 requirement.[2]

It is a defence to an offence charged under this section that the person required to provide the information can demonstrate to the satisfaction of the court that he did not know and could not with reasonable diligence have ascertained who the driver of the vehicle was.[3] This defence is not available to a body corporate, partnership or unincorporated association unless in addition to the matters referred to in s 172(4) the accused shows that no record was kept of the person who drove the vehicle and that the failure to keep a record was reasonable.[4] The powers contained in this section are crucial to the operation of the automatic detection of offences which is described at 7.8.3 below.

The offence of failing to give the required information under s 172 can be proved by the evidence of a single witness.[5]

In requiring information under this section, the police officer in making the requirement does not have to indicate that the person who was driving the vehicle at the material time is alleged to have been guilty of a particular offence.[6] A statement made by a driver in response to a requirement in terms of this section is admissible in evidence in any subsequent prosecution.[7] The officer need not explain that failure to answer is an offence.[8] The police are entitled to make this requirement of

1   Ibid, at paragraph [12].
2   *Coupar v PF Dundee* XJ856/13 (Decision of 22 October 2013). Three s 172 requirements were made against a company, a partnership and ultimately the individual accused. The time bar only commenced 28 days after he was sent a written request.
3   RTA 1988, s 172(4).
4   RTA 1988, s 172(6).
5   RTOA 1988, s 21(3), as amended by RTA 1991, Sch 4 para 89.
6   *McNaughton v Buchan* 1980 SLT (Notes) 100; *McMahon v Cardle* 1988 SCCR 556; *Duncan v McGillivray* 1989 SLT 48, 1988 SCCR 488.
7   See *Foster v Farrell* 1963 SLT 182; *Gray v Farrell* 1969 SLT 250; *Galt v Goodsir* 1982 JC 4, 1982 SLT 94, 1981 SCCR 225; and *Clark v Allan* 1988 SLT 274.
8   *Brown v Frame* 2005 SCCR 400 explaining *Duncan v McGillivray* 1989 SLT 48, 1988 SCCR 488.

any person if they have information to support an allegation against the driver that he has committed a relevant offence.[1]

The impact of s 172 requirements can be seen by reference to s 12(4)[2] of the Road Traffic Offenders Act 1988 which provides:

'(4) In summary proceedings in Scotland for an offence to which section 20(2) of this Act applies, where –

(a)   it is proved to the satisfaction of the court that a requirement under section 172(2) of the Road Traffic Act 1988 to give information as to the identity of a driver on a particular occasion to which the complaint relates has been served on the accused by post, and

(b)   a statement in writing is produced to the court, purporting to be signed by the accused, that the accused was the driver of that vehicle on that occasion, that statement shall be sufficient evidence that the accused was the driver of the vehicle on that occasion.'

7.5.10 Duty of owner of vehicle to give insurance information (s 171)

Tried summarily, level 4 fine

The chief purpose of this section is to allow a police officer to require the owner of a vehicle to give such information as is necessary to determine whether a driver was driving without insurance on any occasion when the driver has been asked to produce a certificate of insurance under s 165(1) or 170 of the Road Traffic Act 1988.

7.5.11 Road Traffic Offenders Act 1988, ss 90A–90F: deposits and prohibition on driving

These provisions, introduced by the Road Safety Act 2006, came into effect on 5 January 2009. Broadly, the aim of the legislation is to stop drivers without a current or satisfactory UK address from avoiding prosecution or payment of a fixed penalty by leaving the country or avoiding contact.

---

1   *Galt v Goodsir* 1982 JC 4, 1982 SLT 94, 1981 SCCR 225; *McMahon v Cardle* 1988 SCCR 556; *Hingston v Pollock* 1990 SLT 770, 1989 SCCR 697.

2   An offence under ss 16, 17 and 88(7) of that Act (temporary minimum speed limits), s 89(1) (speeding offences generally) of the Road Traffic Regulation Act 1984; an offence under s 36(1) of the Road Traffic Act 1988; an offence under Part I or II of the Road Traffic Regulation Act 1984 of contravening or failing to comply with an order or regulations relating to bus lanes or routes; an offence under s 29(1) of the Vehicle Excise and Registration Act 1994 (using or keeping an unlicensed vehicle on a public road); an offence under s 11(1) of the HGV Road User Levy Act 2013 (using or keeping heavy goods vehicle if levy not paid).

Reference should be made to the Road Safety (Financial Penalty Deposit) Order 2009 (SI 2009/491) as amended, most recently by the Community Drivers' Hours Offences (Enforcement) Regulations 2018/24.

Section 90A[1] is in the following terms:

'90A Power to impose financial penalty deposit requirement

(1) A constable or vehicle examiner may impose a financial penalty deposit requirement on a person on any occasion if the conditions in this section are satisfied.

(2) The constable or vehicle examiner must have reason to believe—

(a)   that the person –

   (i)   is committing or has on that occasion committed an offence relating to a motor vehicle or trailer; or

   (ii)   has, within the period of 28 days before the day of that occasion, committed an offence relating to a motor vehicle which is a Community drivers' hours offence, and

(b)   that the person, the offence and the circumstances in which the offence is committed are of a description specified in an order made by the Secretary of State.

(3) The person must be—

(a)   given written notification that it appears likely that proceedings will be brought against him in respect of the offence, or

(b)   (if the offence is a fixed penalty offence) either given such notification or given a fixed penalty notice (or, in Scotland, handed a conditional offer) in respect of the offence.

(4) The person must fail to provide a satisfactory address; and for this purpose "a satisfactory address" is an address in the United Kingdom at which the constable or vehicle examiner considers it likely that it would be possible to find the person whenever necessary to do so in connection with the proceedings, fixed penalty notice or conditional offer.

(5) The person who is to impose the financial penalty deposit requirement—

(a)   if a constable, must be in uniform, and

(b)   if a vehicle examiner, must produce his authority.'

(6) A constable or vehicle examiner may not impose a financial penalty deposit requirement on a person under this section in relation to a Community drivers' hours offence where the constable or vehicle examiner has reason to believe that—

---

1   As amended by the Community Drivers' Hours Offences (Enforcement) Regulations 2018/24 and by the Haulage Permits and Trailer Registration Act 2018.

(a)   a financial penalty deposit requirement has already been imposed on the person under this section in relation to the offence;

(b)   proceedings have already been initiated against the person for the offence; or

(c)   any other penalty has already been imposed on, or other proceedings have already been initiated against, the person in respect of the relevant breach in Northern Ireland, another member State or a contracting third country.

(7) In subsection (6)(c) "relevant breach" means the breach of the applicable Community rules which constitutes the Community drivers' hours offence.'

As can be seen, the scheme applies to vehicle examiners.

Section 90B provides that a financial penalty deposit is the payment of an appropriate amount either immediately or within a relevant period. The amount and the manner of payment are specified in orders made by the Secretary of State. The relevant period is the suspended enforcement period for a fixed penalty, either 28 days or longer period if specified for a conditional offer, or otherwise the period ending with the person being charged with the offence.

Payment is dealt with in s 90C. Receipts will be given and in the event of no prosecution the deposit will be refunded. In the case of a subsequent fine or an unchallenged fixed penalty the deposit is used to pay it and any excess is to be refunded. Interest calculated by the Treasury will be paid on refunds.

Section 90D allows for prohibition on further driving where immediate payment of a deposit is required. Also the police officer or vehicle examiner may give written instruction to remove a vehicle to a particular location subject to specified conditions. Non-compliance with a prohibition or written directions is an offence triable summarily with up to a level five fine.

The prohibition will come to an end on payment of the deposit, payment of the fixed penalty or conditional offer as appropriate, on conviction or acquittal, or on being told that there is to be no prosecution or the expiry of prosecution period.

7.6 DUTIES ON DRIVER IN CASE OF ACCIDENT (S 170)

RTA 1988, s 170(4); tried summarily, six months' imprisonment or level 5 fine or both, discretionary disqualification, obligatory endorsement 5–10 points

RTA 1988, s 170(7); tried summarily, level 3 fine

The clear distinction between the two offences is significant in terms of prosecution. *Wilson v Scott* 2004 SCCR 436 clarified that only offences under s 170(7) would be matters capable of conditional offer under Sch 5 of the Road Traffic Offenders Act 1988. Accordingly, and under reference to s 10 of the 1988 Act, the District Court does not have jurisdiction to try s 170(4) charges.

7.6.1 General

Section 170 of the Road Traffic Act 1988[1] reads in full as follows:

'(1) This section applies in a case where, owing to the presence of a mechanically propelled vehicle on a road, an accident occurs by which –

(a)   personal injury is caused to a person other than the driver of that motor vehicle, or

(b)   damage is caused –

    (i)   to a vehicle other than that motor vehicle or a trailer drawn by that motor vehicle, or

    (ii)   to an animal other than an animal in or on that motor vehicle or a trailer drawn by that motor vehicle, or

    (iii) to any other property constructed on, fixed to, growing in or otherwise forming part of the land on which the road or place in question is situated or land adjacent to such land.

(2) The driver of a mechanically propelled vehicle must stop and, if required to do so by any person having reasonable grounds for so requiring, give his name and address and also the name and address of the owner and the identification marks of the vehicle.

(3) If for any reason the driver of the mechanically propelled vehicle does not give his name and address under subsection (2) above, he must report the accident.

(4) A person who fails to comply with subsection (2) or (3) above is guilty of an offence.

(5) If, in a case where this section applies by virtue of subsection (1)(a) above, the driver of a motor vehicle does not at the time of the accident produce such a certificate of insurance or security, or other evidence, as is mentioned in s 165(2) of this Act –

(a)   to a constable, or

---

1   As amended by RTA 1991, Sch 4 para 72 and Motor Vehicles (Compulsory Insurance) Regulations 2000 (SI 2000/726), reg 2(6)(b).

(b)   to some person who, having reasonable grounds for so doing, has required him to produce it, the driver must report the accident and produce such a certificate or other evidence.

This subsection does not apply to the driver of an invalid carriage.

(6) To comply with a duty under this section to report an accident or to produce such a certificate of insurance or security, or other evidence, as is mentioned in s 165(2)(a) of this Act, the driver –

(a)   must do so at a police station or to a constable, and

(b)   must do so as soon as is reasonably practicable and, in any case, within twenty-four hours of the occurrence of the accident.

(7) A person who fails to comply with a duty under subsection (5) above is guilty of an offence, but he shall not be convicted by reason only of a failure to produce a certificate or other evidence if, within seven days after the occurrence of the accident, the certificate or other evidence is produced at a police station that was specified by him at the time when the accident was reported.

(8) In this section "animal" means horse, cattle, ass, mule, sheep, pig, goat or dog.'

7.6.2 Definitions (s 170)

'Mechanically propelled vehicle'. See 1.2.1 above.
'A road'. See 1.8.1, 1.8.2 and 1.8.3 above.
'Accident'. See 1.9.1 above.
'Personal injury'. It is submitted that the meaning of this phrase is not confined to physical injury, but could include shock or even emotional distress.
'Stop'. The Act does not provide a definition of this word, or a description of the period over which the duty to stop must be exercised. However, it is clear that the driver must stop at, or as near as reasonably practicable to, the locus of the accident, and further that he must remain there for such time, as in the circumstances, gives persons entitled to have the particulars described in the section sufficient opportunity to require them of the driver personally.[1]
'Animal'. For the purposes of this section, 'animal' means a horse, cattle, ass, mule, sheep, pig, goat or dog.[2] Accordingly, no duty to stop

---

1   *Campbell v Copeland* 1972 JC 24; *Singh v McLeod* 1987 SLT 550, 1986 SCCR 656; *Hynd v O'Brien* 1990 JC 252, 1990 SCCR 129; *Percy v Lees* 1992 SCCR 234; *Cunningham v Crowe* 1994 SCCR 330; *Souter v Lees* 1995 SCCR 33.
2   RTA 1988, s 170(8).

is imposed if damage is caused to fowl, deer, or any other wild or domestic animal.

7.6.3 General application (s 170)

The circumstances in which a duty under this section can arise are extremely wide. If an accident which is covered by any of the situations described in sub-ss 1(a) and (b) can be attributed in any way to the presence of a motor vehicle on a road, then the driver of that motor vehicle is under an immediate duty to stop. As indicated in the preceding paragraph, the driver must stop as near as is practicable to where the accident occurred. It will also be noted that the offending vehicle need not necessarily be being driven at the material time; if, for example, an accident happens as a result of a vehicle being dangerously parked, the duty to stop imposed upon the driver of that vehicle by this section will still arise. Even although the driver complies with all other parts of s 170 of the Road Traffic Act 1988, a failure to stop at the material time will nonetheless contravene the provisions of the first part of s 170(2).

In addition to the duty imposed on a driver to stop following such an accident, in terms of the first part of s 170(2), the same section imposes an additional and quite separate duty on the driver in these circumstances to provide his name and address, and the name and address of the owner of the vehicle and the identifying marks of the vehicle, to any person who requires that information from him and who has reasonable grounds for making that requirement. Whether such a person has reasonable grounds for requiring this information will depend on the facts and circumstances of each case. The duty to furnish the required information is personal to the driver and may not be delegated.[1] Again, an offence can be committed under this part of s 170(2) even where all other parts of s 170 are complied with by the offending driver. On the other hand, in the case of *Adair v Fleming*,[2] it was held that where a vehicle had collided with another vehicle and the driver of the offending vehicle had given his name and address to the driver of the other vehicle, the driver of the offending vehicle was not, in the circumstances, thereafter under a duty to report the accident to the police in terms of s 170(3).

If the circumstances of an incident of driving are such that a driver had, or should have had, reasonable cause to suppose that he might have been involved in an accident, then he has a duty in terms of this section

---

1   *Campbell v Copeland* 1972 JC 24.
2   *Adair v Fleming* 1932 JC 51, 1932 SLT 263.

to stop and satisfy himself about what had happened. In *Sutherland v Aitchison*,[1] a driver on a single track road mounted the verge in order to pass a vehicle coming in the opposite direction. As he did so he heard a noise which he thought might have been his exhaust hitting a stone, but which was in fact a collision between the two vehicles. It was held that in these circumstances the driver, having heard some noise, was under a duty to stop and see if he had been involved in an accident. Accordingly, a driver would appear to have a duty to satisfy himself that he has not been involved in an accident, if the circumstances suggest that he might have been. Section 170(2) does not qualify in any way the time limits within which the duty conferred by the section must be discharged and accordingly it is submitted that the duty to stop or to furnish information if properly required to do so, must be discharged as soon as reasonably practicable after the duty has arisen.

Section 170(3) and (6) makes provision for an offence which is quite separate and distinct from the offence described in s 170(2). It is therefore possible, and not unusual, for a driver to contravene both subsections. The duty incumbent upon a driver in terms of s 170(3) and (6) arises in particular if he has failed in any way to discharge his duties under s 170(2). Thus, if a driver has failed to stop at an accident, or has declined to give his name and address to someone having reasonable grounds to require this information, or has not given his name and address because there was no one at the scene of the accident, or no one who had reasonable grounds for requiring the information, then he must discharge the obligation described in s 170(6). It should be emphasised that a driver does not have any kind of discretion to report the matter to the police within the 24 hours following the accident. Rather, he is under an absolute duty to report the matter to the police as soon as reasonably practicable, and in any event within the period of 24 hours. On the other hand, however, a driver who fulfils all of the duties incumbent on him in terms of s 170(2) is under no duty to report an accident to the police in terms of s 170(3) and (6).[2]

In *Wood v McLean*,[3] it was held that it was sufficient for a conviction under an earlier version of the offence described in s 170(3) and (6) for the prosecution to show firstly that the driver's name and address were not given to anyone at the *locus* of the accident, and secondly that the accident was not duly reported to the police. It was also suggested in that case that if the accused sought out a person with an interest in the matter

1   *Sutherland v Aitchison* 1975 JC 1.
2   *Adair v Fleming* 1932 JC 51, 1932 SLT 263.
3   *Wood v McLean* 1947 JC 18, 1947 SLT 22.

and reported the incident within 24 hours, this might provide a defence. However, it is submitted that such a defence could only be successfully pled in only the most exceptional of circumstances.

In effect the prosecution has to prove a negative, and it has been held that, for example, the court may infer from the fact that the police were still making inquiries into an accident a month afterwards that the driver had not complied with the subsection.[1]

Any direct link between the presence of the vehicle on the road and the accident which occurs as a result, such as a passenger falling off the platform of a bus, imposes the duties described in s 170.[2]

Where the accident involves personal injury in terms of s 170(1)(a), the driver must produce a certificate of insurance at the time of the accident, to a constable or to a person who has reasonable grounds for requiring him to produce it. If he does not, he must report the accident to the police as soon as reasonably practicable and in any event within 24 hours, and produce the certificate of insurance within 7 days.[3]

In *Martin v Hamilton*[4] a solicitor advised a client not to report an accident. He was charged with counselling another to commit an offence under s 176 of the Road Traffic Act 1972. It was held that in the absence of an averment that by the time the advice had been given it would still have been reasonably practicable for the motorist to have reported the accident, the charge was not relevant.

When an accused said that he had not stopped because he thought that he might be over the drink-driving limits, the court could legitimately consider this as an aggravation of the offence.[5]

7.6.4 Accident inquiries

The Secretary of State may direct that inquiry be made into the cause of any accident which arises out of the presence of a mechanically propelled vehicle on a road.[6] The inquiry may be public. Such an inquiry, which normally takes place if the accident involves the death of a person who was at the material time in the course of his employment, has the power

---

1   *Walton v Crowe* 1993 SCCR 885, following *Milne v Whaley* 1975 SLT (Notes) 75; see also *Brittan v Mackenzie* 1985 SCCR 114 and *Hornall v Scott* 1993 SLT 1140, 1993 SCCR 65.
2   *Quelch v Phipps* [1955] 2 QB 107.
3   RTA 1988, s 170(5), (6) and (7), as amended.
4   *Martin v Hamilton* 1989 SCCR 292.
5   *Williams v Vannet* 1996 SCCR 16.
6   RTA 1988, s 181.

to inspect any vehicle in connection with that inquiry, but any report made to or by the Secretary of State following such inquiry may not be used in any subsequent legal proceedings. Obstruction of inspection of vehicles after an accident is an offence, tried summarily with a penalty of up to a level 3 fine.

7.7 TAKING AND DRIVING AWAY (S 178)

Summarily: 12[1] months' imprisonment or a fine or both, discretionary disqualification

Indictment: 12 months' imprisonment or a fine or both, discretionary disqualification

7.7.1 Section 178

Section 178 of the Road Traffic Act 1988 provides:

'(1) A person who in Scotland –

(a) takes and drives away a motor vehicle without having either the consent of the owner of the vehicle or other lawful authority, or

(b) knowing that a motor vehicle has been so taken, drives it or allows himself to be carried in or on it without such consent or authority,

is subject to subsection (2) below, guilty of an offence.

(2) If –

(a) the jury, on proceedings under this section on indictment, or

(b) the court, on summary proceedings under this section,

is satisfied that the accused acted in the reasonable belief that he had lawful authority, or in the reasonable belief that the owner would, in the circumstances of the case, have given consent if he had been asked for it, the accused shall not be liable to be convicted of the offence.'[2]

In terms of s 23 of the Road Traffic Offenders Act 1988,[3] if an accused on indictment is charged with stealing a car, a jury is entitled to bring an alternative verdict under this section.

---

1 Given the provisions of s 45 of the Criminal Proceedings etc (Reform) (Scotland) Act 2007.
2 Subsection (3) was repealed by the Criminal Justice (Scotland) Act 2016 (Consequential and Supplementary Modifications) Regulations 2017/452 (Scottish SI) Sch 1(1) para 11 (25 January 2018).
3 As amended by RTA 1991, Sch 4 para 90.

7.7.2 Definitions

'*Drives*'. See 1.7.1 and 3.3.2 above.
'*Motor vehicle*'. See 1.2.1 above.

7.7.3 General application

The offence described in this section was originally created to deal with the offence of joy-riding, which occurs when a vehicle is taken without the permission of its rightful owner for the purposes of a single trip or for a short period, and where the taker of the vehicle does not necessarily have the intention of depriving the owner of his property on a permanent basis. Such cases may cover a variety of situations in practice, and formerly were charged simply as theft. However, because it could be argued in such cases that the intention permanently to deprive the owner of his property (an arguably necessary ingredient of a common law charge of theft) might well be absent, it was considered appropriate to provide a special statutory offence. It is competent to charge an accused with the alternative of a common law charge of theft and an offence in terms of s 178 of the Road Traffic Act 1988.

For a conviction under s 178(1)(a), the prosecution must prove that the accused both took and drove away the vehicle, and that he did so without the owner's permission. In particular, if the owner's permission is only given for a particular journey, but the driver then embarks on a wholly unauthorised journey, an offence may be committed under this section.[1]

For a conviction under s 178(1)(b), the prosecution must show that the accused knew that the vehicle had been stolen.[2] Other cases on this last point are *Hipson v Tudhope*;[3] *Rowley & Davie v Hamilton*.[4] A statutory defence is available in terms of s 178(2), which is sometimes overlooked.

It is competent to libel an attempt to contravene s 178 despite the statute not making reference to it, albeit s 35(5) of the RTOA 1988 does.[5]

---

1   *Barclay v Douglas* 1983 SCCR 224.
2   See, eg *Ashcroft's Curator Bonis v Stewart* 1988 SLT 163.
3   *Hipson v Tudhope* 1983 SLT (Notes) 659, 1983 SCCR 247.
4   *Rowley & Davie v Hamilton* 1989 SCCR 211.
5   And see *Wilson & Forbes v Morton*, High Court 1975, unreported, but referred to in *RCB v HMA* 2016 SCCR 374.

7.7.4 Penalties

The penalties under s 178 of the Road Traffic Act 1988 are found in Sch 2, Pt 1 to the Road Traffic Offenders Act 1988.[1] They include imprisonment, fines (which are not defined) and discretionary disqualification. The power of the court to impose penalty points and order endorsement of the driver's licence has been removed.[2] Similarly, while discretionary disqualification is available to the court for the offence of stealing or attempting to steal a motor car,[3] the same provisions in the 1991 Act also remove the power to impose endorsement and penalty points previously available. The net effect of these provisions is that while the court may disqualify a driver for stealing or attempting to steal a vehicle, or for an offence under s 178, in neither instance can the court order penalty points or any endorsement of the driver's licence.

7.8 SPEED LIMITS

RTRA 89: tried summarily, discretionary disqualification or obligatory 3–6 penalty points (3 for fixed penalties), and level 3 fine (Note: Once s 17 of the Road Safety Act 2006 is brought into force, this will alter to 2–6 including scope for graduated fixed penalties)

7.8.1 General

By virtue of the Road Traffic Regulation Act 1984, ss 81(1) and 89, it is an offence for anyone to drive a motor vehicle on a restricted road at a speed in excess of 30 mph. The Scotland Act 2016 now allows Scottish Ministers to increase or reduce this figure. A member's bill proposing a reduction to a 20 mph limit was introduced on 21 September 2018.

'A restricted road' is defined in s 82 of the Act[4] in Scotland where "there is provided on it a system of carriageway lighting furnished by means of lamps placed not more than 185 metres apart and the road is of a classification or type specified for the purposes of this subsection in regulations made by the Scottish Ministers".

---

1   As amended by RTA 1991, Sch 2 para 31 and impacted by the provisions of the s 45 of the Criminal Proceedings etc (Reform) (Scotland) Act 2007.
2   RTA 1991, s 83 and Sch 8.
3   RTOA 1988, Sch 2, Pt II.
4   As amended by the New Roads and Street Works Act 1991, s 168(1) and Sch 8 para 59 and the Scotland Act 2016.

Speed limits on roads other than restricted roads are provided for in s 84 of the Act, and the responsibility for erecting the necessary speed restriction signs are dealt with under s 85. The Scotland Act 2016 now allows Scottish Ministers to perform this function or give directions as the national authority. This allows for the imposition of variable speed limits. The detailed descriptions of the signs themselves are found in the Traffic Signs Regulations and General Directions 2016.[1]

Failure by the relevant authority to observe these directions in any material respect may preclude a driver being found guilty of a speeding offence. See *Smith v Rankine*.[2] However, as has been noted in the English case of *Peake v DPP*[3] under reference to *Smith v Rankin* and like English authorities, statutory interpretation has moved on and the purpose of the legislation – to ensure that drivers drive at safe speeds – will carry more weight than purported deficiencies in signage.

A similar approach has been taken in Scotland: if the requirement to follow a direction is met, complaints about inadequate guidance, for example that repeaters were not placed precisely the same distance apart, will not succeed.[4] In the same vein, it should be noted that The Traffic Signs Manual produced by the Department of Transport is advisory only, albeit some of its terms may reflect the mandatory terms of the Directions.[5]

In the ordinary course, it would be prudent for officers to speak to the limits in place.

Further speed limits may be imposed by the Scottish Ministers on a temporary basis, and failure to observe these limits is also an offence.[6] Regulations made under this section, and at present continued indefinitely, are the 70 miles per hour, 60 miles per hour, and 50 miles per hour (Temporary Speed Limit) (Continuation) Order 1978.[7]

Temporary prohibitions or restrictions can be imposed, *inter alia*, in respect of road works, cleaning works, 'relevant events' (any sporting event, social event or entertainment which is held on a road) or any danger to the public on the road in terms of ss 14–16E of the Road Traffic Regulation Act 1984, as amended by the Road Traffic (Temporary

---

1   Traffic Signs Regulations and General Directions 2016 (SI 2016/362) as amended by the Traffic Signs Amendment (Scotland) Regulations and General Directions 2018 (SSI 2018/161).
2   *Smith v Rankin* 1977 SLT (Notes) 12.
3   [2010] EHWC 286 (Admin) 2011 RTR 3
4   *Wilson v Watson* [2012] HCJAC 148 XJ174/12, 2013 SCCR 5.
5   *Wilson v Watson* [2012] HCJAC 148 XJ174/12, 2013 SCCR 5 at para [7].
6   RTRA 1984, s 88.
7   Temporary Speed Limit (Continuation) Order 1978 (SI 1978/1548).

Restrictions) Act 1991, the Infrastructure Act 2015 and the Scotland Act 2016. These are powers transferred to the Scottish Ministers by the Scotland Act 1998 (Transfer of Functions to the Scottish Ministers etc) Order (SI 1999/1750).

Finally, it is an offence for any person to drive a motor vehicle of any class on a road at a speed greater than the maximum speed specified for the vehicle of that class.[1] The various speeds specified for various classes of vehicle are set out in Sch 6 to the Road Traffic Regulation Act 1984. Power to vary Sch 6 now lies with the Scottish Ministers.[2]

Fire brigade, ambulance and police vehicles being used for those purposes, are exempt from speed limits if their observance would hinder those purposes.[3] However, the ordinary rules of driving other than that still apply to emergency vehicles, and drivers of such vehicles can be found guilty of any other offence under the Road Traffic Acts, including dangerous and careless driving, in exactly the same way as ordinary drivers, although the fact that they are driving in emergency circumstances may afford significant mitigation in any sentence imposed.

Limited specification of the locus involved in a speeding charge is compliant with Art 6(3)(a) of the European Convention on Human Rights so long as the material facts are alleged – see *Aitken v Spencer* 2005 SCCR 721 where the libel referred simply to the A9 Perth to Inverness road near Dalwhinnie.

In *Strawbridge & Others v Murphy*,[4] a libel 'on A725 between junctions for the M74, and the A721' was sufficiently clear. In reviewing a number of earlier cases, the court observed, at para [10], that 'the sufficiency of specification must be considered in context on a case by case basis', and that 'the need to use a map certainly cannot … be fatal as to the specification of a charge'.

---

1   RTRA 1984, s 86 as amended by, *inter alia*, the Scotland Act 2016.
2   Scotland Act 2012 (c 11) Pt 2, s 21(10) (3 July 2012).
3   RTRA 1984, s 87. This section is to be substituted in due course by the new form contained within s 19 of the Road Safety Act 2006. The new version, as well as providing the current exemptions, allows for regulations setting out further exemptions as required. It also provides that exemption applies only to drivers who have passed or are talking part in the relevant high speed driving course which will stem from further regulations. This is distinct from the current requirement of simply being trained.
4   2014 SCCR 286.

7.8.2 Evidence

Overview

Speeding cases generate perhaps the highest proportion of road traffic appeals, no doubt because of the number of such cases, but also because of the growth of firms focusing on such cases and the resultant testing of a myriad of issues. It has to be said that many of these points are unduly technical and as a result unlikely to find favour. As the court in *Robbie the Pict v PF Dumfries* observed:

> '… this case has occupied days of evidence and submissions at District and Appellate Court levels. Virtually all of this time, and consequent public expense, has been taken up with the appellant's pursuit of ill-founded technical arguments in respect of an offence which ultimately attracted a modest fine and the minimum number of penalty points. Such misuse of the legal process is not acceptable.'[1]

Another example might be over reliance on failure to follow ACPO Code of Practice on the use of equipment without expert evidence and in different circumstances envisaged in the code, remembering also that they are only guidelines and are not mandatory or statutory.[2]

The more practical and purposive approach taken to the road traffic legislation should also be borne in mind.

McPherson v McConnell[3] is an obvious example of that approach. A plea to the competency of a speeding charge under a temporary speed restriction order was taken on the basis that there had not been compliance with mandatory provisions ('shall') in relation to giving notice of the orders to the police and fire services. The court held that the provisions were directory only and were not prerequisites of the making of the order. There had in any event been substantial compliance, remembering that the speed restrictions were signed for the public on the road itself.

Reference, in this regard, should also be made to the House of Lords case of *R v Soneji*,[4] which gives useful guidance for alleged failures to comply with provisions apparently prescribing an action.

---

1   *Robbie the Pict v PF Dumfries* [2009] HCJAC 49 XJ100/08, para 33.
2   *Hunter v McClintock* 2011 SCCR 1, at para [20].
3   2011 SCCR 32.
4   [2005] UKHL 49, [2005] 3 WLR 303.

Identification

Identification of a driver may be achieved from a number of sources: eyewitness evidence, or s 172 compliance[1] alone or along with inference from facts and circumstances allied with registered keeper status.[2] Reference is made to para 1.11.1 above.

Section 20: Road Traffic Offenders Act 1988

In the prosecution of any person for a speeding offence, s 20(1) of the Road Traffic Offenders Act 1988, as amended, provides that evidence of the measurement of speed, produced by a prescribed device, is sufficient to establish that the offence has been committed. In particular, the section allows for the provision of a record produced by a prescribed device, and a certificate of the circumstances in which the record was produced duly signed.[3] The production of the certificate does not exclude other competent evidence.[4]

To be admissible, a copy of the record or certificate must be served on the person charged with the offence not less than seven days before the hearing or trial. That person may in turn serve a notice on the prosecutor requiring the attendance at the hearing or trial of the person who signed the document, not less than three days before the hearing or trial or within such further time as the court may in special circumstances allow.[5]

Despite the fact that such documents should be requested and produced as a matter of routine in advance of an intermediate diet in every case, this still seems to be something that the Crown are unable to consistently achieve, despite it being the subject of criticism from the bench for years.

Any device used must be approved by the Secretary of State; this is done by the passing of an Approval Order. In its original form s 20 of the Road Traffic Offenders Act 1988 was specifically concerned with the measurement of speed by radar. The amendment provided by s 23 of the Road Traffic Act 1991 extended the ambit of the devices covered by the section to other approved equipment, and in addition traffic light and bus lane offences, and using or keeping an unlicenced vehicle on a public

---

1   See 7.8.3 below.
2   See *Elpinstone v Richardson* 2012 SCCR 428 and *McCormick v Harrower* 2011 SCCR 710.
3   See s 20(1).
4   *Straker v Orr* 1994 SCCR 251.
5   See s 20(6) and (7).

road[1] are also now included under this section. There are now various types of device approved by the Secretary of State available in Scotland for the detection of offences, including radar speed measuring devices, photographic or other image recording devices, and devices activated by sensors, cables or light beams. Type of device as opposed to a specific model is what is important.[2]

As the court said 'In terms of subsection 20(9) of the 1988, a prescribed device must be a "device of a description specified in an order made by the Secretary of State". Subsection 20(10) provides that any order must be in the form of a statutory instrument. Thus, there requires to be a statutory instrument which describes a type of device into which the device actually used must fall ... Sub-section 20(4) states that the device must be of a 'type approved by the Secretary of State'. But there is no requirement there, or in the section as a whole, that the approval be contained in a statutory instrument. Approval can be, and is, achieved by the issue of a Notice of Approval signed by, or on behalf of, the Secretary of State.[3]

There has to be some way by which the court can be satisfied that the relevant order, and therefore the particular device in question, has been approved by the Secretary of State. In *Valentine v MacPhail*[4] it was held that the Camic device was sufficiently notorious for it to be regarded as within judicial knowledge that the device had been approved. In *Mackie v Scott*[5] police officers said in evidence that they had been trained in the operation of the speed detection device which they had used, and it was therefore held that the court could infer that the device was approved.

That approach was followed in *Williams v Nisbet*[6] where there was also some documentary evidence of an intention to approve the Unipar device. Again, however, prosecutors should take note that the Court remained 'somewhat baffled as to why the approval order was not simply produced' as that could be done easily including from the Internet.

---

1   Added by the Road Traffic Offenders (Additional Offences and Prescribed Devices) Order 2001 (2001/1814), art 3.
2   *Wylie v Robbie the Pict (No 2)* 2007 SCCR 114, at para 11 and confirmed in *Robbie the Pict v PF Dumfries* [2009] HCJAC 49, 2010 JC 11 and *Robbie the Pict v DPP* [2009] EWHC 1176.
3   *Robbie the Pict v PF Dumfries* [2009] HCJAC 49, 2010 JC 11 at para 17.
4   *Valentine v MacPhail* 1986 JC 131, 1986 SLT 321.
5   *Mackie v Scott* 1992 SCCR 614.
6   [2012] HCJAC 132 (Decision of 25 September 2012).

In *Pickland v Carmichael*,[1] no such evidence was led, and therefore no basis existed to allow the court to draw the necessary conclusions. The orders currently in force are given at 7.8.3 below.

Other evidential considerations

Section 280 of the Criminal Procedure (Scotland) Act 1995[2] allows certificate evidence to vouch the accuracy of speedometers fitted to police traffic patrol cars and other apparatus for measuring speed, time and distance. Such certificates may be covered by the rule that certificates must state that the appropriate examination has been carried out by those who have signed the certificate.[3]

Service by the Crown of the certificate or report must be achieved not less than 14 days before the relevant court date, the trial for summary proceedings most usually; and challenges must be made within seven days of service, or later if the court allows because of special circumstances.[4]

Where there is a gap in time between the date of the certificate and the date of the offence, the inference that it remains accurate is a matter for the court's assessment.[5]

In *Westwater v Scott*[6] it was held that a driver was not prejudiced and could properly be convicted when an inexperienced police officer failed to keep the offending speed on the visual display of the Muniquip gun for inspection.

In *Morrison v McCowan*[7] the distance covered in a speeding charge was held to be calculated with sufficient accuracy by a measuring device and an Ordnance Survey map. Convictions for speeding can theoretically be secured by hand-held stop watches and other observations. In *Morrison v McCowan*[8] a speeding offence was proved by the time taken for a particular journey as measured on a map; see also the five-bench decision

---

1 *Pickland v Carmichael* 1995 SLT 675, 1995 SCCR 76.
2 Under reference to Criminal Procedure (Scotland) Act 1995, Sch 9.
3 *Normand v Wotherspoon* 1993 JC 248, 1994 SLT 487, 1993 SCCR 912; *Donnelly v Schrikel* 1995 SLT 537.
4 See s 280(6).
5 *Cameron v Higson* 2001 SCCR 344.
6 *Westwater v Scott* 1980 SLT (Sh Ct) 63 (and see also *Scott v MacPhail* 1992 SLT 907, 1991 SCCR 760).
7 *Morrison v McCowan* 1939 SLT 422.
8 *Morrison v McCowan* 1939 JC 45, 1939 SLT 422.

in *Gillespie v Macmillan;*[1] *Houston v Leslie;*[2] and *Farrell v Simpson.*[3] These are all now somewhat elderly authorities, and it is extremely unlikely that such procedures are in current use.

However, they now have a new lease of life given the introduction of average speed cameras which perform a very similar task. This has been emphasised in *PF Perth v Martin,*[4] a successful crown appeal after a no case to answer submission was upheld at Perth Justice of the Peace Court.

Under reference to *Scott v Jameson*[5] the court observed that:

'four important or fundamental facts are identified to establish a charge of speeding over a set distance. These are: (1) the point of time the car entered the stretch of road; (2) the time of exit; (3) the length of carriageway and (4) the identity of the car. The third fact is the issue in this appeal. In Scott v Jameson the Lord Justice General was of the opinion that "each of these facts, important as each is, can be proved by one witness, if the tribunal trying the case considers that the evidence in quality is reliable". This case is a 21st century version of *Scott v Jameson*. The fundamental or essential facts which require to be proved are no different. In terms of *Scott v Jameson* which was affirmed by a full bench in *Gillespie v Macmillan* 1957 JC 31 there is no need to corroborate these four fundamental facts.'

As *Scott v Jameson* makes clear, two witnesses gave evidence, but each spoke only to a single fact. As Lord Guthrie noted,[6] 'if several facts require to be proved and these form a consecutive chain, leading to one conclusion, then it appears to me that each may be proved by one witness.'

In *Hogg v MacNeill,*[7] where calibration of speed measuring equipment in a police car used two marks on a road said to be half a mile apart, evidence of measurement of the distance was held to be essential. That case was particular to its facts and in the associated case of *Pervez v Clark,*[8] the same bench held that corroboration of distance measurement was not required.

In *McLean v McLeod,*[9] however, where proof of a specific speed was not required for conviction for dangerous driving, the view was expressed that corroborated evidence of accuracy of a device would be required

1   *Gillespie v Macmillan* 1957 JC 31, 1957 SLT 283.
2   *Houston v Leslie* 1958 JC 8, 1958 SLT 109.
3   *Farrell v Simpson* 1959 SLT (Sh Ct) 23.
4   [2018] SAC (Crim) Decision of 3 July 2018.
5   1914 SC(J) 187, a decision followed in *Gillespie v Macmillan*, supra
6   At page 190.
7   *Hogg v MacNeill* 2001 SCCR 134.
8   *Pervez v Clark* 2001 SCCR 138.
9   *McLean v McLeod* 2002 SCCR 127.

when precise speed was necessary to prove commission of the offence under reference to the device.

In *Cox v McGowan*,[1] the Crown's sufficiency was attacked on the basis that testing of the accuracy of a Unipar SL 700 laser speed detection device involved reliance on a measured distance spoken to by only one officer. In refusing the appeal, the court adopted the approach referred to above in *Gillespie v Macmillan* and found that a variety of adminicles were of assistance.

These included, the experience of the two witnesses involved, by reference to the machine's calibration date, the accuracy of the machine on other respects, and the fact that the machine undertakes checks itself and will not produce a reading if not working properly.[2]

The Court agreed with the approach taken to specific speed in *McLean v McLeod* but with the caveat 'that does not mean that there has to be corroboration of every component part of the evidence. It is sufficient if the concurrence of testimony establishes the accuracy of the device, a fact which may be established in many different ways'.

The approach taken in *Cox* was endorsed in *Egan v PF Irvine*.[3] However, that defence appeal succeeded because of the paucity of evidence led on the subject. Neither police witness gave evidence of the Unipar 700's calibration status, nor evidence of its accuracy and, inevitably perhaps, no certificate had been lodged by the Crown. In such circumstances 'there was no testimony, let alone concurrence of testimony' to establish the device's accuracy.

The reading produced by a device does not have to be corroborated, for example, by the opinion of the police officers as to the speed of the vehicle, but other matters such as the identity of the driver do require to be established by corroborative evidence.[4]

7.8.3 Orders and identification in speeding and traffic light offences

A variety of devices have been approved over the years. The Road Traffic Offenders (Prescribed Devices) Order 1992[5] approves devices designed or adapted for measuring the speed of a motor vehicle by radar. The Road

1   [2011] HCJAC 14, 2011 SCCR 265.
2   See paragraph [9].
3   [2012] HCJAC XJ846/12 (Decision of 4 December 2012).
4   *Scott v MacPhail* 1992 SLT 907, 1991 SCCR 760; see also *Barbour v Normand* 1992 SCCR 331.
5   Road Traffic Offenders (Prescribed Devices) Order 1992 (SI 1992/1209).

Traffic Offenders (Prescribed Devices) (No 2) Order 1992[1] approves a device designed or adapted for recording by photographs or other image recording means the position of motor vehicles in relation to traffic lights. The Road Traffic Offenders (Prescribed Devices) Order 1993[2] (speed measuring devices triggered by sensors, cables or light beams), Road Traffic Offenders (Additional Offences and Prescribed Devices) Order 1997[3] (cameras to detect other vehicles on bus lanes) and the Road Traffic Offenders (Prescribed Devices) Order 1999[4] (image catching devices) have also been made. The Road Traffic Offenders (Prescribed Devices) Order 2008[5] relates to time and distance measurement of speed under reference to odometer pulses.

This certificate evidence referred to at 7.8.2 above demonstrates only that an offence has been committed; the prosecution has also to prove who committed the offence (see 7.8.2 above). Because of the nature of the various radar devices previously available, police officers were usually able to stop, and thus identify, the accused at the time the offence was committed. Such devices will continue to be used in this way. However, it is not proposed that a photographic device will be used in such a way that will involve the driver being stopped at the time of the offence. To surmount the consequent problem of identification, the Road Traffic Act 1991, Sch 4 para 85 attempted to provide a further and particularly Scottish power to s 12 of the Road Traffic Offenders Act 1988, which had previously only applied to England and Wales. Put briefly, a written statement, purporting to be signed by the accused in response to a requirement under s 172(2) (as amended) of the Road Traffic Act 1988, admitting that he was the driver at the material time, will be sufficient evidence of identification. Section 172 is described at 7.5.8 above.

It is envisaged that the police will require the information as to who was driving at the material time in the first instance from the registered keeper. If the keeper names another person as the driver, that person can also be made the subject of a requirement under s 172. This will mean that the statutory procedure allows devices such as cameras to record the offences and an admission under s 172 to identify the accused. The prosecutions based on these procedures are to be carried out by the fixed penalty procedures (see 8.13 below).

---

1   Road Traffic Offenders (Prescribed Devices) (No 2) Order 1992 (SI 1992/2843).
2   Road Traffic Offenders (Prescribed Devices) Order 1993 (SI 1993/1698).
3   Road Traffic Offenders (Additional Offences and Prescribed Devices) Order 1997 (SI 1997/384).
4   Road Traffic Offenders (Prescribed Devices) Order 1999 (SI 1999/162).
5   Road Traffic Offenders (Prescribed Devices) Order 2008 (SI 2008/1332).

In practice, once police officers have retrieved a piece of film showing the offending driving from their cameras, the registered keeper will be asked by letter if he was the driver at the material time. If he replies with a signed statement that he was, the evidential ingredients of the offence are complete. If the registered keeper denies that he was the driver, he must indicate if he knows who was driving. If he does so, the police will then make the conditional offer of a fixed penalty to the named driver. If anyone fails to identify the driver at the material time and cannot rely on the defences provided (see 7.5.8 above) he is liable to a fine, discretionary disqualification and endorsement of his licence with six penalty points.

7.9 PARKING

7.9.1 General

The local roads authority[1] has the power to provide off-street parking, and parking on roads without payment, in terms of s 32ff of the Road Traffic Regulation Act 1984. Parking may also be authorised on the road for payment of a charge, and by the provision of parking meters.[2] Section 52 deals with offences relating to interference with parking devices and the incorrect display of tickets. Excess parking charges are the responsibility of the owner of the vehicle.[3] The power to provide parking places extends to the provision, on roads, or elsewhere, of stands and racks for bicycles.[4] The Secretary of State has power to make regulations in respect of the removal of vehicles illegally, obstructively or dangerously parked, or abandoned, or broken down.[5] A police officer has the power in general terms to fix an immobilisation device to a vehicle illegally parked;[6] as do parking attendants in certain areas (see 7.9.3 below).

The appointment and powers of traffic wardens (who are police staff appointed under s 26 of the Police and Fire Reform (Scotland) Act 2012) is set out in ss 95 and 96 of the RTRA 1984. Their powers, as well as carrying out functions open to local authority parking attendants, include provisions under ss 99 and 100 of the RTRA 1984 and ss 35–37, 163–165, and 169 of the Road Traffic Act 1988.

---

1 See the Roads (Scotland) Act 1984, s 151.
2 RTRA 1984, ss 45–49.
3 RTRA 1984, s 107; but see also ss 108–111.
4 RTRA 1984, s 63 as amended by the Transport (Scotland) Act 2001 (asp 2).
5 RTRA 1984, ss 99, 101, 102 and 104; see also Refuse Disposal (Amenity) Act 1978, s 2.
6 RTRA 1984, ss 104–106.

The power to exempt vehicles with Disabled Persons badges from parking restrictions is found in the Disabled Persons (Badges for Motor Vehicles) (Scotland) Regulations 2000, as amended,[1] (which also allow English and Welsh badges issued under s 21 of the Chronically Sick and Disabled Persons Act 1970 to be used in Scotland. See also s 21 of the 1970 Act, as amended by the Transport (Scotland) Act 2001 (asp 2)).

The local roads authority may also make such orders as it considers expedient for the regulation of traffic.[2] However, once such an order is made, it only becomes effective when the authority has erected the appropriate signs.[3] Such signs (eg 'No Waiting' signs) may be made subject to exemptions (eg for loading).

7.9.2 Statutory provisions, including obstruction

Section 19 of the Road Traffic Act 1988 provides specifically that a heavy commercial vehicle[4] (see 1.6.4 above) cannot be parked wholly or partly on the verge of a road, on any land situated between two carriageways, or on a footway. Exemption is provided in cases where the driver proves that the parking was done with the permission of a uniformed police officer, or took place in an emergency, or that it was engaged in loading or unloading in circumstances described in the section.

Section 22 (as amended) makes it an offence for a person in charge of a vehicle or a trailer to leave it in such a position or in such a condition or in such circumstances as to involve a danger of injury to others using the road. The word 'vehicle' is not qualified in any way in the section (eg by the word 'motor') and no exemptions or defences are indicated.

---

1   Disabled Persons (Badges for Motor Vehicles) (Scotland) Regulations 2000 (SSI 2000/59) and Disabled Persons (Badges for Motor Vehicles) (Scotland) Amendment Regulations 2000 (SSI 2000/170). See also the Local Authorities' Traffic Orders (Exemption for Disabled Persons) (Scotland) Regulations 2002 (SSI 2002/450); the Local Authorities' Traffic Orders (Exemption for Disabled Persons) (Scotland) Amendment Regulations 2002 (SSI 2002/547); and the Disabled Persons (Badges for Motor Vehicles) (Scotland) Regulations 2000 (SSI 2000/59), as amended by SSIs 2000/170, 2002/451, 2007/162, 2011/89, 2011/410, 2014/145, 2015/9,2016/72, 2017/118 and 2018/44.
2   RTRA 1984, s 1ff.
3   Local Authorities Traffic Orders (Procedure) (Scotland) Regulations 1999 (SI 1999/614) as amended by Local Authorities Traffic Orders (Procedure) (Scotland) Amendment Regulations 2002, 2005, and 2008 (SSIs 2002/31, 2005/338 and 2008/3); *MacLeod v Hamilton* 1965 SLT 305; *Macmillan v Gibson* 1966 SLT (Sh Ct) 84.
4   Which is described in RTA 1988, s 20.

Regulation 101 of the Road Vehicles (Construction and Use) Regulations 1986 imposes general restrictions, subject to certain exceptions, on parking on roads during the hours of darkness.

Regulation 103 of the Road Vehicles (Construction and Use) Regulations 1986 provides that no person in charge of a motor vehicle or trailer shall cause or permit the vehicle to stand on a road so as to cause any unnecessary obstruction of the road. This will include prevention of access onto the road by obstruction of a driveway.

7.9.3 Immobilisation and removal

The immobilisation, removal, and disposal of vehicles illegally parked is dealt with in ss 99–106 of the Road Traffic Regulation Act 1984 and ss 69–72 of the Road Traffic Act 1991. As well as police officers, parking attendants in the local government areas of Glasgow, Edinburgh, Aberdeen, Dundee, Perth and Kinross and South Lanarkshire have powers, when in uniform, under s 99 of the 1984 Act and under s 69 of the 1991 Act.[1] Further various local government areas in Scotland, namely Edinburgh, Glasgow, Aberdeen and Perth and Kinross have been designated as permitted parking areas and special parking area with the effect that ss 66, 69–74, 79 and 82, as well as Sch 6, of the 1991 Act apply to them.[2] Parking penalties in these areas are now recovered as a civil debt.

Private clamping may amount to theft but not to extortion.[3]

7.10 PEDESTRIAN CROSSINGS

The local roads authority has the power to establish, alter or remove pedestrian crossings on any roads within its area.[4] Any pedestrian crossings on trunk roads are the responsibility of the national authority, now the Scottish Ministers.[5] The purpose of pedestrian crossings is to afford precedence in certain circumstances to pedestrians using a road

---

1 See, for example, Parking Attendants (Wearing of Uniforms) (City of Glasgow Parking Area) Regulations 1999 (SSI 1999/62).
2 See The Road Traffic (Permitted Parking Area and Special Parking Area) Designation Orders as amended for the relevant areas: Edinburgh SI 1998/1539, Glasgow 1999 SSI 1999/59, Perth and Kinross SSI 2002/398 and Aberdeen City SSI 2003/70.
3 *Black v Carmichael* 1992 SLT 897, 1992 SCCR 709.
4 RTRA 1984, s 23(1), as amended by Transport (Scotland) Act 2005 (asp 12) and the Infrastructure Act 2015.
5 RTRA 1984, s 24 as amended.

over other road users. The power to make regulations in respect of such crossings is contained in s 25 of the Road Traffic Regulation Act 1984.

The current regulations under this section are the Traffic Signs Regulations and General Directions 2016,[1] which provide in detail for the physical characteristics and markings for such crossings, including road markings, studs and globes, and in particular provides an absolute right of precedence in the circumstances therein described to pedestrians within the limits of such crossings. The regulations also provide for prohibitions against the waiting of vehicles and pedestrians on a crossing and against vehicles overtaking within the area of a crossing. Transitional provisions under Reg 14(5) mean that the Zebra, Pelican and Puffin Crossing Regulations 1997 remain in force for pelican crossings.

Cases involving these kinds of crossings as reported are *McKerrell v Robertson*[2] and *Wishart v McDonald*.[3]

7.11 SCHOOL CROSSINGS AND PLAYGROUNDS

In terms of s 26 of the Road Traffic Regulation Act 1984, as amended by the Transport (Scotland) Act 2001 (asp 2), local authorities are empowered to make arrangements for the patrolling of school crossings. A properly appointed school crossing patrol is entitled to require vehicles to stop at places where children are crossing a road on or from their way to school. It is an offence for any person driving a vehicle to fail to comply with such a requirement.[4] It can be punished by discretionary disqualification or obligatory endorsement of three penalty points, and a fine up to level three.

Sections 29 and 31 of the Road Traffic Regulation Act 1984 allow a local roads authority to make orders prohibiting the use of traffic on roads which are to be used as playgrounds. Punishment is discretionary disqualification or obligatory endorsement of two penalty points, and a fine up to level three.

---

1   Traffic Signs Regulations and General Directions 2016 (SI 2016/362) as amended by the Traffic Signs Amendment (Scotland) Regulations and General Directions 2018 (SSI 2018/161).
2   *McKerrell v Robertson* 1956 JC 50, 1956 SLT 290.
3   *Wishart v McDonald* 1962 SLT (Sh Ct) 29, (1962) 78 Sh Ct Rep 3.
4   RTRA 1984, s 28.

7.12 CONSTRUCTION AND USE (S 41)

7.12.1 General

There are a very large number of provisions, normally introduced by statutory instrument, which regulate the construction, maintenance, use, weight and equipment of motor vehicles and trailers on the roads. A considerable number of these statutory provisions currently reflect the terms of EEC and EC directives and regulations. A detailed examination of these regulations is outwith the scope of this book; many of the regulations specify what the statutory requirements are in very considerable detail. It is therefore proposed to deal with this subject in broad outline. Section 41 of the Road Traffic Act 1988,[1] and in particular sub-ss (2)–(4), indicates the general headings under which the various regulations are issued. Section 41(1)–(4) reads as follows:

'(1) The national authority may make regulations generally as to the use of motor vehicles and trailers on roads, their construction and equipment and the conditions under which they may be so used.

Subsections (2) to (4) below do not affect the generality of this sub-section.

(2) In particular, the regulations may make provision with respect to any of the following matters –

(a)   the width, height and length of motor vehicles and trailers and the load carried by them, the diameter of wheels, and the width, nature and condition of tyres, of motor vehicles and trailers,

(b)   the emission or consumption of smoke, fumes or vapour and the emission of sparks, ashes and grit,

(c)   noise,

(d)   the maximum weight unladen of heavy locomotives and heavy motor cars, and the maximum weight laden of motor vehicles and trailers, and the maximum weight to be transmitted to the road or any specified area of the road by a motor vehicle or trailer of any class or by any part or parts of such a vehicle or trailer in contact with the road, and the conditions under which the weights may be required to be tested,

---

1   As amended by, *inter alia*, the RTA 1991, Sch 4 para 50 and the Scotland Act 2016 introducing the potential for regulations, in relation to devolved matters, by the Scottish Ministers. It should also be noted that amendments introduced by the Road Safety Act 2006 remain pending. These amendments will add ss 41(2)(ba), (m) and (2A).

(e)   the particulars to be marked on motor vehicles and trailers (by means of the fixing of plates or otherwise) and the circumstances in which they are to be marked,

(f)   the towing of or drawing of vehicles by motor vehicles,

(g)   the number and nature of brakes, and for securing that brakes, silencers and steering gear are efficient and kept in proper working order,

(h)   lighting equipment and reflectors,

(j)   the testing and inspection, by persons authorised by or under the regulations, of the brakes, silencers, steering gear, tyres, lighting equipment and reflectors of motor vehicles and trailers on any premises where they are (if the owner of the premises consents),

(jj)   speed limiters,

(k)   the appliances to be fitted for –

    (i)   signalling the approach of a motor vehicle, or

    (ii)   enabling the driver of a motor vehicle to become aware of the approach of another vehicle from the rear, or

    (iii)   intimating any intended change of speed or direction of a motor vehicle,

and the use of any such appliance, and for securing that any such appliance is efficient and kept in proper working order,

(l)   for prohibiting the use of appliances fitted to motor vehicles for signalling their approach, being appliances for signalling by sound, at any times, or on or in any roads or localities, specified in the regulations.

(2A) In subsection (1) "national authority" — (a) in relation to a function so far as exercisable within devolved competence, within the meaning of the Scotland Act 1998, means the Scottish Ministers; (b) otherwise, means the Secretary of State.

(2B) Before making any regulations under this section in relation to the parking of vehicles on roads in Scotland, the Secretary of State must consult the Scottish Ministers.

(3) The Secretary of State may, as respects goods vehicles, make regulations under this section –

(a)   prescribing other descriptions of weight which are not to be exceeded in the case of such vehicles,

(d)   providing that weights of any description or other particulars which are to be marked on particular goods vehicles may be determined in accordance with regulations under s 49 of this Act.

(4) Regulations under this section with respect to lighting equipment and reflectors –

(a)   may require that lamps be kept lit at such times and in such circumstances as may be specified in the regulations, and

(b)   may extend, in like manner as to motor vehicles and trailers, to vehicles of any description used on roads, whether or not they are mechanically propelled.

(4A) Regulations under this section with respect of speed limiters may include provision –

(a)   as to the checking and sealing of speed limiters by persons authorised in accordance with the regulations and the making of changes by them,

(b)   imposing or providing for the imposition of conditions to be complied with by authorised persons,

(c)   as to the withdrawal of authorisation.'

7.12.2 Construction and use offences

The offences under the regulations are created by ss 40A, 41A, 41B, and 41D and 42 of the Road Traffic Act 1988, all as introduced by s 8 of the Road Traffic Act 1991 and the Road Safety Act 2006. These sections reflect the broad groupings under which construction and use topics are considered in the legislation, and this arrangement is reflected in other consequential adjustments introduced by the 1991 Act.

It should be noted that s 41C is still not yet in force but exists in s 18 of the Road Safety Act 2006. In due course it will be introduced, along with appropriate regulations, as a measure to prohibit speed assessment equipment detection devices. In other words, equipment designed to warn of or interfere with speed detection efforts although this is not understood to include information as to fixed speed camera sites. Endorsement of 3–6 points (3 for fixed penalty), discretionary disqualification, and fines up to level 3 or 4 subject to the road type, are anticipated.

Section 40A creates an offence where a vehicle is used in a dangerous condition, for example where its condition, purpose of use, number of passengers, or the weight, position or distribution of its load, or the way in which the load is secured, involves a risk of injury to any person. Section 41A creates an offence where there is a contravention of the regulations involving brakes, steering, gear or tyres. Section 41B creates an offence where there is a breach of the requirements as to weight in respect of both goods and passenger vehicles. Section 41B indicates the defences which may be available in charges of overloading or excess weight, and these are discussed at 7.12.7. Section 42 covers other construction and use contraventions.

The penalties for such offences are set out in Sch 2, Pt 1 to the Road Traffic Offenders Act 1988, as amended by the Road Traffic Act 1991, Sch 2 para 17. Concerns as to public safety have led to a firmer approach to contraventions of s 40A. Since s 25 of the Road Safety Act 2006 came into force on 24 September 2007, Sch 2 of the RTOA 1988 provides for obligatory disqualification if the offence is committed within three years of a previous conviction under s 40A.

Section 43 provides for temporary exemption from the regulations, and s 44[1] for authorisation of use on roads of special vehicles which do not comply with the regulations.

Section 48 of the Road Traffic Offenders Act 1988[2] provides a statutory exemption from disqualification and endorsement following conviction of these offences if the accused shows that he did not know, nor had he reasonable cause to suspect, that the facts of the case were such that the offence would be committed. Amendments under the Road Safety Act 2006 remain pending.

A case illustrating some of the considerations relevant to such a defence is *Forrest v Annan*.[3]

In *Morrison v Mackenzie*,[4] a case involving bald tyres, the appeal court held that where no prejudice existed, it was unreasonable to expect the tyres to be produced, and oral evidence of their condition was accepted. Obvious defects can be spoken of in evidence by persons other than authorised examiners.[5]

7.12.3 Statutory instruments

The principal secondary legislation dealing with ss 40–42 offences is the Road Vehicles (Construction and Use) Regulations 1986.[6] These regulations apply to both wheeled vehicles and track-laying vehicles. The definition section of these regulations (reg 3) is particularly comprehensive. Also of importance are the Road Vehicles Lighting Regulations 1989[7] (see 7.12.6 below). In addition, there are a huge number of regulations dealing with a variety of subjects and all of these are subject to a continuous stream of amendments. In practical terms, the only method of keeping up to

1   As amended by RTA 1991, Sch 2 para 51.
2   As amended by RTA 1991, Sch 4 para 101.
3   *Forrest v Annan* 1992 SLT 510, 1990 SCCR 619.
4   *Morrison v Mackenzie* 1990 JC 185.
5   *Mowbray v Valentine* 1992 SLT 416, 1991 SCCR 494.
6   Road Vehicles (Construction and Use) Regulations 1986 (SI 1986/1078).
7   Road Vehicles Lighting Regulations 1989 (SI 1989/1796).

date with the details of this secondary legislation is by recourse to one of the specialist road traffic 'encyclopaedias' which are issued regularly on a loose-leaf system, and which seek to present the current state of all aspects of road traffic legislation.

7.12.4 Type approval schemes

Certain of the construction and use requirements have, however, been superseded by type approval schemes. It is part of the European Community's overall plan to harmonise road traffic law, and eventually it is hoped that a universal and comprehensive series of schemes covering the manufacture of vehicles and parts will be introduced. In terms of such schemes, the manufacturer of a vehicle or of a vehicle part produces to the Secretary of State a type vehicle or part for inspection. If approval is given, the manufacturer is provided with a type approval certificate and is then enabled to produce vehicles or parts, of identical construction, as long as he issues certificates indicating that these further vehicles or parts conform exactly with the approval certificate. These are known as certificates of conformity. This scheme has been introduced to avoid the necessity of all vehicles and parts being individually inspected at the instance of the government. At present, some of these provisions are optional and some, dealing mainly with certain kinds of passenger vehicles, are obligatory. Reference to these schemes is made in ss 54–65A of the Road Traffic Act 1988, as amended; the principal regulations are the Motor Vehicles (Type Approval) (Great Britain) Regulations 1984,[1] although there are a number of other relevant statutory instruments.[2] It is an offence to use, or cause or permit to be used, a vehicle on a road subject in whole or in part to type approval without appropriate compliance under s 63 of the Road Traffic Act 1988. Fines up to level 4 may be imposed.

7.12.5 Maximum lengths

The Road Vehicles (Construction and Use) Regulations 1986, reg 7 provides that, subject to certain exceptions, the overall length of certain vehicles or combination of vehicles, including articulated vehicles and trailers must not exceed prescribed overall maximum lengths. Regulation 8 gives certain prescribed overall width dimensions which must not be exceeded principally in commercial vehicles. Regulation 9 provides for certain maximum heights in the case of buses (4.57 metres).

---

1   Motor Vehicles (Type Approval) (Great Britain) Regulations 1984 (SI 1984/981).
2   For example Road Vehicles (Approval) Regulations 2009 (SI 2009/717).

Regulation 10 provides further requirements in respect of the height of vehicles and, in particular, the indications required in respect of special vehicles and overall travelling height. Regulations 10A–10C[1] require warning devices to be fitted where certain high level equipment is fitted to a vehicle. The maximum overhang permitted and the exceptions to the general provisions are provided in reg 11. Regulation 12 provides details of the minimum ground clearance in respect of various vehicles. Regulations 13, 13A, 13B, and 14 apply to the turning circles, and connecting sections and direction–holding of articulated buses first used on or after 1 April 1982.

Detailed definitions of overall length, overall width, and overhang, together with definition of the various classes of vehicle are provided in the definition section (reg 3). Two cases in which these matters have been considered are *Guest Scottish Carriers Ltd v Trend*[2] and *Hawkins v Russett*.[3]

All the foregoing regulations have been amended in detail since 1986, by various Road Vehicle (Construction and Use) (Amendment) Regulations.

7.12.6 Weight

The regulations governing the weight of various vehicles are of particular importance. As has been indicated above, in terms of s 41 (as amended) of the Road Traffic Act 1988, the Secretary of State has the power to make regulations in respect of the maximum laden and unladen weight of vehicles, and the maximum weight to be transmitted to the road by any vehicle, the conditions under which such weights may be required to be tested, and the particulars to be marked on vehicles and trailers.

The Road Traffic Act 1988, s 190 provides the method of calculating the unladen weight of vehicles and trailers; for cases on this section, see *McCowan v Stewart*[4] and *Blaikie v Morrison*.[5] Regulation 23 of the 1986 Regulations provides that certain multi-wheel vehicles must have a compensating arrangement to ensure that under the most adverse conditions every wheel will remain in contact with the road and will not be subject to abnormal variations of load.

---

1   As amended by the Road Vehicles (Construction and Use) (Amendment) Regulations 1997 (SI 1997/530) and Police and Fire Reform (Scotland) Act 2012 (Consequential Modifications and Savings) Order 2013 (SSI 2013/119).
2   *Guest Scottish Carriers Ltd v Trend* [1967] 3 All ER 52.
3   *Hawkins v Russett* [1983] RTR 406.
4   *McCowan v Stewart* 1936 JC 36, 1936 SLT 370.
5   *Blaikie v Morrison* 1957 JC 46, 1957 SLT 290.

There are detailed and technical provisions in respect of the maximum permitted laden weights of various kinds of vehicles. These are of particular significance to heavy commercial vehicles. The restrictions apply not only to the total laden weights, but also, as a separate matter, to the weight transmitted to the road by one or more wheels and axles. It is therefore possible for a vehicle to commit an overloading offence in respect of the maximum permitted wheel or axle weight even where the total permitted laden weight is not exceeded. The provisions are set out in tabulated form in regs 75–80 of the Road Vehicles (Construction and Use) Regulations 1986, as amended, and are to be read with the definition section (reg 3). In any prosecution of a vehicle or trailer for overloading, the prosecution must adduce evidence that the weighbridge is accurate.[1] Section 17(1) of the Road Traffic Offenders Act 1988 affords a presumption that the plated weight is the weight of the vehicle and s 17(4) provides that in any proceedings in Scotland for a traffic offence where the weight of the vehicle is an issue, a certificate pertaining to be signed by an inspector of weights and measures certifying that the weighbridge or other machine is accurate in sufficient evidence of that fact. Regulations 81–82 and 83–90 provide restrictions on the use of vehicles carrying wide or long loads or appliances, and on the number of trailers to be drawn by particular vehicles, the distance between motor vehicles and trailers, provisions in respect of unbraked trailers, the use of bridging plates between motor vehicles and trailers, requirements on leaving trailers at rest, and on passengers in trailers. Regulation 83 in particular provides for the number of trailers that may be drawn by various classes of vehicle.

Many of the foregoing regulations have been amended in detail since 1986.

7.12.7 Weight offences: defences

In prosecutions in respect of offences under s 41B of the Road Traffic Act 1988[2] where it is alleged that any of the weight regulations described in the preceding paragraph have been contravened, s 41B(2) provides two statutory defences. Firstly, it is a defence if the vehicle is being used on the road at a time when it was proceeding to a weighbridge which was the nearest available one to the place where the loading of the vehicle was completed for the purpose of being weighed or was proceeding from a weighbridge after being weighed to the nearest point at which it was reasonably practicable to reduce the weight to the relevant limit without

---

1   *Grierson v Clark* 1958 JC 22, 1958 SLT 112.
2   As amended by the RTA 1991, s 8.

causing an obstruction on any road. However, this defence is to be strictly applied; courts have in practice been reluctant to sustain such a defence if the vehicle has diverted in any way from what, in the circumstances, can be reasonably described as a direct route between the loading point and the weighbridge. Further, it would not appear to be a sustainable defence to argue that there was no such weighbridge available or open.

Secondly, in cases where the limit of weight has not been exceeded by more than five per cent (and only in such cases), it is a defence to prove that the limit was not exceeded at the time the loading of the vehicle was originally completed, and since that time no person has made any addition to the load. This second statutory defence is designed to cater for the situation where a load can be shown to have increased in weight since the start of its journey. This can happen, for example, where a load such as timber increases in weight through the absorption of snow or rain water. Alternatively, the defence may be relevant where the load can be shown to have shifted during the journey, and the driver is charged with excess weight on a single axle. Again, however, the courts have tended to impose a strict construction on such defences. Apart from the two defences allowed by statute, overloading of any sort is an absolute offence. In particular, any consequence or effect brought about by the circumstances or condition of a particular road is irrelevant in computing the laden weight on a particular vehicle.

The burden of proof is on the defence and the standard used is balance of probabilities

If it appears to an authorised police officer or other authorised official that a vehicle is overloaded, the further use of that vehicle on the road may be prohibited. Alternatively, the vehicle may be used subject to such directions as the authorised official thinks fit.[1]

7.12.8 Plated weights and other plated particulars

The Secretary of State is empowered to make regulations providing for the marking of certain particulars, including weight, applicable to certain classes of goods vehicles.[2] The terms used are 'plated particulars' and 'plated weight', and these are defined in s 41(7) of the Road Traffic Act 1988. These details must be shown on a plate which is securely attached to the vehicle in a conspicuous and readily accessible position.[3] This latter regulation also contains a table which gives general descriptions of various

---

1   See, generally, RTA 1988, ss 70–72, as amended by RTA 1991, ss 9–15.
2   RTA 1988, s 41(2) and (3) (as amended by RTA 1991, Sch 4 para 50).
3   Road Vehicles (Construction and Use) Regulations 1986, reg 66.

classes of vehicles, including trailers, to which the legislation applies, and also lists the kinds of vehicles exempted from the requirements. Schedule 8 to the Regulations provides in detail what particulars must be shown on the plate. Part III of Sch 8 to the regulations makes general provisions in respect of power to weight ratios and also determines the relevant weights to be shown on plates in accordance with reg 66. The plated weight of any particular vehicle therefore is the weight which must be stamped on the plate of the particular vehicle in terms of regulation 66 and Sch 8. It should be noted that the plated weight (or, where appropriate, the train weight) is not necessarily the same as the design weight. In terms of the Road Traffic Act 1988, s 41(6), the Secretary of State has to make sure that the plated weight or train weight of any vehicle is fixed having regard to the design weight of that vehicle, and does not exceed that weight. Further, every vehicle to which the Testing and Plating Regulations apply must have a Ministry Plate.[1]

Speed limiters must be fitted to certain passenger and commercial vehicles and must show plates which indicate that such devices are fitted.[2]

Plates which must be attached to motor cycles are covered in reg 69 and Sch 9.

The phrases 'design weight' and 'train weight' are defined in reg 3.

Tests relating to the satisfactory condition of certain classes of goods vehicles and the determination of plated weights are dealt with in ss 49–53 of the Road Traffic Act 1988.[3] Section 53 now applies to all vehicles rather than just goods vehicles.[4] Provisions dealing with the testing of vehicles on the road by vehicle examiners or police officers, and of their maintenance and loading, together with considerations relevant to the prohibition of unfit or overloaded vehicles, are found in the Road Traffic Act 1988, ss 67–73, as amended by the Road Traffic Act 1991, ss 9–15.

As indicated at 7.12.6 above, the maximum permitted laden weights of various classes of vehicles are furnished in detail in regs 75–80, which should be consulted in detail in respect of any particular case. Reference

1   Road Vehicles (Construction and Use) Regulations 1986, reg 70, as amended by the Road Vehicles (Construction and Use) (Amendment) (No 7) Regulations 1998 (SI 1998/3112) and Schs 10 and 10A, and Road Vehicles (Construction and Use) (Amendment) Regulations 2017/851.

2   Road Vehicles (Construction and Use) Regulations 1986, reg 36A, 36B and 70, (all of which have been further amended).

3   As amended by the RTA 1991, Sch 4 paras 54 and 55). Amendments to s 49 and a new s 49A introduced by the Road Safety Act 2006 remain pending.

4   Goods Vehicles (Plating and Testing) (Miscellaneous Amendments) Regulations 2017/849.

should also be made to Sch 11 which gives measurements in respect of these regulations.

7.12.9 Brakes

The detailed technical regulations concerning brakes are extensive and complex. The principal provisions in respect of brakes are contained in regs 15 and 16 of the Road Vehicles (Construction and Use) Regulations 1986, as amended. These regulations refer in turn to Community Directive 79/489, which amends Council Directive 71/320 on the approximation of braking devices, and Community Directive 85/647.

Regulation 17, however, provides that every motor vehicle which is equipped with a braking system which embodies a vacuum or pressure reservoir is to be equipped with a device readily visible to the driver which is capable of indicating any pending failure of, or deficiency in, the vacuum or pressure system. The section contains certain limited exceptions to this requirement. In *Hamilton v MacKenzie*[1] it was held that there had been a breach of this requirement when the warning device, although installed, was found to be not working properly.

Regulation 17A concerns couplings on trailer pneumatic braking systems.

Regulation 18 provides that every part of every braking system and the means of operating thereof must be maintained in good and sufficient working order and be properly adjusted.

In general terms most vehicles require to have bridging systems, namely a service braking system (which is the principal means by which a vehicle is brought to a halt) and a secondary or parking brake system. Both brake systems require to be maintained to certain levels of efficiency, which are expressed in terms of a percentage of a total braking efficiency of which the brakes should be capable. The phrase 'braking efficiency' and other relevant phrases are defined in the definition reg 3. Regulation 18 contains tables which describes the efficiencies of the respective braking systems which are required for various kinds of vehicle. Section 41A provides an absolute offence and, for example, both a driver and his employers may be found guilty of using a vehicle with inadequately maintained brakes.[2] As the regulation contains an absolute offence, it is therefore not a defence to a charge under these regulations that a regular system of inspection was enforced by the owners of the vehicle.[3]

1   *Hamilton v MacKenzie* 1968 SLT 166, 1968 SLT (Notes) 36.
2   *James & Son Ltd v Smee; Green v Burnett* [1955] 1 QB 78.
3   *Hawkins v Holmes* [1974] RTR 436.

In *Watson v Muir*[1] it was held that although it was desirable that the owner or user of any vehicle should be present while the braking system of any vehicle was being tested, such attendance was not essential and evidence of any such examination conducted in the absence of the owner or user was admissible in evidence.

The foregoing regulations have been severally amended in detail since 1986.

7.12.10 Wheels and tyres

Tyres are also subject to detailed provisions and requirements in terms of reg 24 of the Road Vehicles (Construction and Use) Regulations 1986, which gives a full description of the classes of vehicles and the types of tyres which must be used. The phrases 'pneumatic tyre', 're-cut pneumatic tyre', 'retreaded tyre' and 'resilient tyre' are all defined in the definition section (reg 3). Regulation 25[2] makes provision for tyre loads and speed ratings in such a way as to ensure that the tyres are able to bear the maximum axle weight. The prohibition against the mixing of different kinds of pneumatic tyres on the same vehicle is provided in reg 26. The regulation contains the necessary additional definitions of the different kinds of tyre involved.

Regulation 27 provides for the condition and maintenance of tyres and in particular contains the detailed provisions which can form the basis of a prosecution for driving with a worn or defective tyre. It reads in part as follows:

'27.— Condition and maintenance of tyres

(1) Save as provided in paragraphs (2), (3) and (4), a wheeled motor vehicle or trailer a wheel of which is fitted with a pneumatic tyre shall not be used on a road, if –

(a)   the tyre is unsuitable having regard to the use to which the motor vehicle or trailer is being put or to the types of tyres fitted to its other wheels;

(b)   the tyre is not so inflated as to make it fit for the use to which the motor vehicle or trailer is being put;

1   *Watson v Muir* 1938 JC 181, 1939 SLT 14.
2   As introduced by SI 1990/1981 and amended most recently by the Road Vehicles (Construction and Use) (Amendment) Regulations 2015/142. Regulation 25A, in relation to tyre noise, has been introduced by the Road Vehicles (Construction and Use) (Amendment) Regulations 2010 (SI 2010/312).

(c)   the tyre has a cut in excess of 25 mm or 10% of the section width of the tyre, whichever is the greater, measured in any direction on the outside of the tyre and deep enough to reach the ply or cord;

(d)   the tyre has any lump, bulge or tear caused by separation or partial failure of its structure;

(e)   the tyre has any of the ply or cord exposed;

(f)   the base of any groove which showed in the original tread pattern of the tyre is not clearly visible;

(g)   either –

   (i)   the grooves of the tread pattern of the tyre do not have a depth of at least 1 mm throughout a continuous band measuring at least three-quarters of the breadth of the tread and round the entire outer circumference of the tyre; or

   (ii)   if the grooves of the original tread pattern of the tyre did not extend beyond three-quarters of the breadth of the tread, any groove which showed in the original tread pattern does not have a depth of at least 1 mm; or

(h)   the tyre is not maintained in such condition as to be fit for the use to which the vehicle or trailer is being put or has a defect which might in any way cause damage to the surface of the road or damage to persons on or in the vehicle or to other persons using the road.

(2) Paragraph (1) does not prohibit the use on a road of a motor vehicle or trailer by reason only of the fact that a wheel of the vehicle or trailer is fitted with a tyre which is deflated or not fully inflated and which has any of the defects described in sub-paragraph (c), (d) or (e) of paragraph (1), if the tyre and the wheel to which it is fitted are so constructed as to make the tyre in that condition fit for the use to which the motor vehicle or trailer is being put and the outer sides of the wall of the tyre are so marked as to enable the tyre to be identified as having been constructed to comply with the requirements of this paragraph.

(3) Paragraph (1)(a) does not prohibit the use on a road of a passenger vehicle (not being a bus) by reason only of the fact that a wheel of the vehicle is fitted with a temporary use spare tyre, unless the vehicle is driven at a speed exceeding 50 mph.'

Further exceptions are provided in the regulation as are definitions of 'breadth of tread', 'original tread pattern' and 'tread pattern.

It is an offence to use or cause or permit to be used a vehicle on the road with such defects. The customary definitions apply and in particular it is plain that using includes parking the vehicle on a public road and is not confined to the vehicle being in motion.

Further, if the vehicle in question is the subject of a hire agreement, then the person who is 'using' the vehicle at the material time is the hirer and not the hire firm; see *Farrell v Moggach;*[1] *Mackay Brothers & Co v Gibb.*[2]

These regulations have also been amended in detail since 1986.

7.12.11 Vision and glass

The regulations also provide that each motor vehicle is to be designed and constructed so that the driver has at all times a full view of the road ahead.[3] All glass or other transparent material fitted to a motor vehicle is to be maintained in such a condition that it does not obscure vision of the driver while the vehicle is being driven on a road.[4] There is also provision as to the kind of glass which must be fitted to certain vehicles in certain circumstances and, in particular, regs 31 and 32 make provision for the fitting of safety glass.

Regulation 33 provides comprehensive details on the provision of mirrors to vehicles, and reg 34 provides for windscreen wipers and washers. All have been amended.

7.12.12 Instruments and equipment

Regulation 35 provides that every vehicle shall be fitted with a speedometer capable of indicating speed in both miles per hour and kilometres per hour and reg 36, as amended, provides that speedometers should be properly maintained at all material times. Further, reg 37, as amended, provides that every vehicle subject to the included exceptions shall be fitted with a horn which is not a reversing alarm or a two-tone horn. Apart from such instruments designed to inform members of the public that goods are on a vehicle for sale, it is a specific condition that the sound omitted by any horn other than a reversing alarm or two-tone horn shall be continuous, uniform and not strident. Exceptions are granted to motor vehicles used for fire brigade, ambulance or police purposes and other vehicles in the public or social service. Exceptions also apply to alarms to prevent theft or attempted theft of the vehicle or its contents but these must be fitted with a device to stop the horn or siren emitting noise for a continuous period of more than five minutes. Regulation 39 covers the construction and maintenance of petrol tanks.

1   *Farrell v Moggach* 1976 SLT (Sh Ct) 8.
2   *Mackay Brothers & Co v Gibb* 1969 JC 26, 1969 SLT 216.
3   Road Vehicles (Construction and Use) Regulations 1986, reg 30.
4   Road Vehicles (Construction and Use) Regulations 1986, reg 30(3).

Regulation 36A, as amended,[1] provides that every coach first used on or after 1 April 1974 and up to 1 January 1988 must have a speed limiter, set to restrict the speed of the vehicles to 112.65 kph (70 mph) and that buses, subject to a variety of definitions as to date (from 1 January 1988 onwards) and weight, must have a speed limiter restricting the speed to 100 kph (62.5 mph).

Regulation 36B, as amended by the Road Vehicles (Construction and Use) (Amendment) (No 5) Regulations 2005 (SI 2005/3170), reg 3(5) provides for goods vehicles, again subject to date of first use and weight, and requires speed limiters set to either 60 mph for some vehicles or 90 kph (56 mph).

7.12.13 Protective systems

Seatbelt anchorage points and seatbelts are the subject of the Road Vehicles (Construction and Use) Regulations 1986, regs 46–47, and their maintenance is governed by reg 48; the requirements in respect of their use are described at 7.3 above. Requirements for fitting minibuses and coaches with additional seats is provided by reg 48A, which was introduced by the Road Vehicles (Construction and Use) (Amendment No 2) Regulations 1996.[2] Certain vehicles must have rear under-run protection and side-guards; see regs 49–52. Single-decked coaches must comply with certain requirements in respect of their superstructure;[3] and double-decked coaches must have two staircases or the means on the top deck to break the windows in an emergency.[4] Alternative means of compliance exist as set out in reg 56C.[5]

Every vehicle propelled by an external combustion engine must be fitted with an exhaust system including a silencer and the exhaust gases from the engine are not allowed to escape into the atmosphere without

---

1   Introduced by the Road Vehicles (Construction and Use) (Amendment) (No 3) Regulations 1993 (SI 1993/3048) and subject to further amendments.
2   Road Vehicles (Construction and Use) (Amendment No 2) Regulations 1996 (SI 1996/163).
3   Road Vehicles (Construction and Use) Regulations 1986, reg 53A, introduced by SI 1987/1133, and amended by SI 1989/2630.
4   Road Vehicles (Construction and Use) Regulations 1986, reg 53B, introduced by Road Vehicles (Construction and Use) (Amendment) (No 3) Regulations (SI 2005/2987), reg 3.
5   Road Vehicles (Construction and Use) Regulations 1986, reg 56C introduced by Road Vehicles (Construction and Use) (Amendment) (No 3) Regulations (SI 2005/2987), reg 4 and amended by the Road Vehicles (Construction and Use) (Amendment) Regulations 2009 (SI 2009/142), reg 7(2).

first passing through the silencer.[1] All exhaust systems and silencers must be properly maintained and certain noise limits are applied to various vehicles.[2] Regulation 61 and 61A, which have been extensively amended over the years, provides comprehensive provision in respect of the emission of smoke vapour, gases and oily substances from vehicles. Regulation 60 requires that all vehicles should comply with the EEC or EC regulations on radio interference suppression.

Again, these regulations have been subject to amendment in detail since 1986.

7.12.14 Control of noise and emissions

In terms of reg 97 of the Road Vehicles (Construction and Use) Regulations 1986, no motor vehicle is to be used on a road in such a manner as to cause excessive noises which could have been avoided by the exercise of reasonable care on the part of the driver.

There is further a general duty in terms of reg 98, as amended by the amendment regulations[3] to stop the engine when a vehicle is stationary apart from the necessities of traffic for the purpose of preventing noise or exhaust emissions.

The use of audible warning instruments is regulated in detail by reg 99.

7.12.15 Avoidance of danger

The Road Vehicles (Construction and Use) Regulations 1986 make a number of provisions in respect of the safe use of vehicles. Regulation 100(1) requires that every motor vehicle and trailer drawn thereby and all parts and accessories of such vehicles and trailers shall at all times be in such condition, and the number of any passengers carried by such vehicles or trailers shall be such, that the weight, distribution and adjustment of the load of such a vehicle or trailer shall at all times provide that no danger is caused or is likely to be caused to any person in or on the vehicle or trailer or on the road.

It should be noted that this is different from the restrictions on overloading. Regulation 100(2) requires that the load carried by a vehicle or trailer shall at all times be so secured and be in such a position that neither danger nor nuisance is likely to be caused to any person or

---

1   Road Vehicles (Construction and Use) Regulations 1986, reg 54.
2   See Road Vehicles (Construction and Use) Regulations 1986, reg 55–59, as amended by amendment regulations SI 1994/14 and SIs 1996/16 and 2329.
3   SI 1998/1.

property by reason of the load or any part of it falling or being blown from the vehicle or by reason of any other movement of the load or part thereof in relation to the vehicle.[1] Regulation 100(3) provides that no motor vehicle or trailer shall be used for any purpose for which it is so unsuitable as to cause or be likely to cause danger or nuisance to any person in or on the vehicle or trailer or on a road. These provisions are designed to secure the proper conduct of a vehicle on the road and in particular to avoid items falling from a vehicle onto the road. However, it should be noted that it is not necessary for part of the load actually to fall on a road or off a lorry, for an offence to be committed under this section. In particular, in terms of reg 100(2), it is possible for an accused person to be convicted in circumstances where he was not aware of the defects in the load which caused the contravention of the subsection.[2] Regulation 100(1) therefore requires that the condition of the vehicle shall be at all times safe; that the number of passengers carried by a vehicle is, at all times, not excessive; and that weight distribution and packing of the load is at all times safe. Regulation 100(2) contains an offence of unlawful loading in circumstances where the load has been secured but there is still danger or nuisance or both to the public. Regulation 100(3) is restricted to offences related to the use of a vehicle for a purpose for which it is unsuitable.

Regulation 101 makes specific provision for the parking of motor vehicles in darkness.

Regulation 103 prohibits any person in charge of a motor vehicle or trailer to cause or permit the vehicle to stand on a road so as to cause any unnecessary obstruction. Accordingly, where the accused parked his car in a bus bay for five minutes but the prosecution did not establish that any bus was in fact obstructed, then an offence was not committed under this regulation.[3] The Crown must also show that the obstruction was unnecessary.[4]

Regulation 104 makes it an offence to drive or cause or permit any other person to drive a motor vehicle on a road if proper control of the vehicle and a full view of the road and traffic ahead is not available to the driver.

Regulation 105 makes it an offence to open a door of a vehicle on a road so as to injure or endanger any person; this regulation is sometimes

---

1   See, eg *Wells v Guild* 1988 SCCR 438.
2   *MacNeill v Wilson* 1981 SLT (Notes) 109, 1981 SCCR 80; see also *Wells v Guild* 1988 SCCR 438.
3   *Brown v Cardle* 1983 SLT 218, 1982 SCCR 495.
4   *McDonald v Annan* 1979 CO Circulars A/22.

used as the foundation of prosecutions particularly where a person in a parked vehicle has opened a door so that it comes into contact with a passing vehicle.

Regulation 106 requires that no person shall drive or cause or permit a motor vehicle to be driven backwards on a road further than is necessary.

Regulation 107 makes it an offence to leave a vehicle unattended with the engine running and the parking brake not properly set.

In addition to these provisions in the construction and use regulations, s 40A of the Road Traffic Act 1988[1] makes it an offence to use a vehicle on a road when its condition, the purpose for which it is used, the number of passengers or the manner in which they are carried, or the nature of the load is such that it involves a danger of injury to any person. Offences are charged summarily, and the penalties are found in the Road Traffic Offenders Act 1988, Sch 2.

7.12.16 Lighting

There are again numerous and complex provisions dealing with the lighting requirements of vehicles. These are contained not in the Road Vehicles (Construction and Use) Regulations 1986 but in the Road Vehicles Lighting Regulations 1989, as amended.[2] In general terms, it is an offence to use, or to cause or to permit to be used on a road, any specified vehicle unless that vehicle is equipped with the prescribed lamps, reflectors, rear markings and devices. Regulation 3 contains a comprehensive list of relevant definitions.

Regulation 11 gives detailed provision for the colour of lights to be shown by lamps and reflectors, and reg 12 qualifies the movement of such items. Regulation 13 provides that lamps must show a steady light except in the case of a direction indicator, warning beacons or special warning lamps and the like. Regulation 16 provides that no vehicle, other than an emergency vehicle or a vehicle used for special forces purposes,[3] shall be fitted with a blue warning beacon or special warning lamp, or a device which resembles either of these. This, like other similar prohibitions, is an absolute offence.[4]

Regulation 17 requires slow-moving vehicles such as agricultural tractors and trailers to carry warning beacons. The regulations and relative

---

1   Introduced by the RTA 1991, s 8.
2   Road Vehicles Lighting Regulations 1989 (SI 1989/1796).
3   Words inserted by the Road Traffic Exemptions (Special Forces) (Variation and Amendment) Regulations 2011 (SI 2011/935).
4   *Brown v McGlennan* 1995 SCCR 724.

schedules provide in considerable detail the specification of obligatory or optional lamps and other equipment of all kinds and in all circumstances. It is an offence not to have obligatory lamps, reflectors, rear markings or devices even where they are not at the material time required. Regulation 17A[1] requires buses carrying children to fit certain prescribed signs.

In *Johnston v Cruickshank*,[2] it was held that where a tractor unit draws a trailer, the motor vehicle for the purposes of these regulations is the driving unit and not the whole vehicle.

Certain exemptions are granted to these general requirements by virtue of regs 4–9. Regulation 18, by reference to Sch 1, makes detailed provision for obligatory lamps, reflectors, rear markings and devices. Regulations 19 and 20 specify certain restrictions on the obscuration of lamps and reflectors and the regulation of optional lamps and reflectors.

In terms of regs 21 and 22 provision is made for the lighting of projecting trailers and vehicles carrying overhanging or projecting loads or equipment and additional side marker lamps.

All such lamps and reflectors, rear markings and devices must be properly maintained and kept clean and in good working order.[3] There are requirements about the use of headlamps and front fog lamps in certain situations, such as during the hours of darkness and in reduced visibility.[4] In general, a vehicle must be used with dipped beam headlamps during the hours of darkness, except on a restricted road for the purposes of s 81 of the Road Traffic Regulation Act 1984 by virtue of a system of street lighting when it is lit; and in seriously reduced visibility. There are also specific restrictions on the use of headlamps and front and rear fog lamps, reversing lamps, hazard warning signal devices and warning beacons and work lamps provided in reg 27.

7.12.17 Mobile telephones

The Road Vehicles (Construction and Use) (Amendment) (No 4) Regulations (SI 2003/2695), reg 2 introduced a new reg 110 concerning mobile telephones given their increased use and the associated safety implications as first seen in the careless driving charges referred to at 2.10.4 above. The offence is now punishable under s 41D(b) of the Road Traffic Act 1988, as introduced by s 26 of the Road Safety Act 2006, and has a maximum penalty of a level 3 fine or, in the case of a goods vehicle

1   Introduced by SI 1994/2280, reg 6.
2   *Johnston v Cruickshank* 1963 JC 5, 1962 SLT 409.
3   Road Vehicles Lighting Regulations 1989, reg 23.
4   Road Vehicles Lighting Regulations 1989, reg 25.

or a vehicle adapted to carry more than eight passengers, a level 4 fine. Additionally, and reflecting further concerns as to safety, the 2006 Act has introduced obligatory endorsement of six penalty points[1] and also allows for discretionary disqualification.

Regulation 110 provides that:

'(1) No person shall drive a motor vehicle on a road if he is using –

(a)   a hand-held mobile telephone; or

(b)   a hand-held device of a kind specified in paragraph (4).

(2) No person shall cause or permit any other person to drive a motor vehicle on a road while that other person is using –

(a)   a hand-held mobile telephone; or

(b)   a hand-held device of a kind specified in paragraph (4).

(3) No person shall supervise a holder of a provisional licence if the person supervising is using –

(a)   a hand-held mobile telephone; or

(b)   a hand-held device of a kind specified in paragraph (4), at a time when the provisional licence holder is driving a motor vehicle on a road.

(4) A device referred to in paragraphs (1)(b), (2)(b) and (3)(b) is a device, other than a two-way radio, which performs an interactive communication function by transmitting and receiving data.

(5) A person does not contravene a provision of this regulation if, at the time of the alleged contravention –

(a)   he is using the telephone or other device to call the police, fire, ambulance or other emergency service on 112 or 999;

(b)   he is acting in response to a genuine emergency; and

(c)   it is unsafe or impracticable for him to cease driving in order to make the call (or, in the case of an alleged contravention of paragraph (3) (b), for the provisional licence holder to cease driving while the call was being made).

(5A) A person does not contravene a provision of this regulation if, at the time of the alleged contravention—

(a)   that person is using the mobile telephone or other device only to perform a remote controlled parking function of the motor vehicle; and

---

1   Road Traffic Offenders Act 1988 (Penalty Points) (Amendment) Order SI 2017/104.

(b) that mobile telephone or other device only enables the motor vehicle to move where the following conditions are satisfied—

    (i)   there is continuous activation of the remote control application of the telephone or device by the driver;

    (ii) the signal between the motor vehicle and the telephone or the motor vehicle and the device, as appropriate, is maintained; and

    (iii) the distance between the motor vehicle and the telephone or the motor vehicle and the device, as appropriate, is not more than 6 metres.[1]

"Hand held" means if the telephone or device is, or must be, held at some point during the course of making or receiving a call, or performing any other interactive communication function which includes sending or receiving oral or written messages, sending or receiving facsimile documents, still or moving images and providing access to the internet

"Two-way radio" means any wireless telegraphy (as defined in section 19(1) of the Wireless Telegraphy Act 1949) apparatus which is designed or adapted for the purpose of transmitting and receiving spoken messages and operating on any frequency other than 880 MHz to 915 MHz, 925 MHz to 960MHz, 1710 MHz to 1785 MHz, 1805 MHz to 1880 MHz, 1900 MHz to 1980 MHz or 2110 MHz to 2170 MHz.'

'Using' has been considered in a number of cases.

In *PF Cupar v Edward Brocklebank*,[2] the Crown was unsuccessful in seeking to overturn an acquittal where Mr Brocklebank was driving whilst holding a mobile phone. There was, however, no evidence of him speaking into it, though his head was tilted to one side and down.

By contrast, in *Halliday v PF Paisley*,[3] the Appeal Court found use against a background of the appellant being found asleep at the wheel of his vehicle at a junction, with a mobile phone displaying a text on the screen. When woken, he replied 'I was just texting'.

The issue has been considered more recently in *Smith v Orr*,[4] a case where the police evidence amounted to seeing a driver holding a phone and operating it with his thumb, which was argued to be insufficient. A

---

1   Added by Road Vehicles (Construction and Use) (Amendment) Regulations SI 2018/592.

2   Appeal Court decision of 3 October 2008. No written opinion issued. The stated case itself was referred to in *Smith v Orr*, but was not found 'to be of assistance'.

3   XJ5/09 (Decision of 15 May 2009).

4   2018 SCCR 68.

robust and pragmatic approach was taken to what was required for proof. As the court said:

> '[9] … as was submitted by the advocate depute, the evidence of the police constables would have been no more even if they had in some way examined the mobile phone which they said was being held by the appellant. They were not experts on mobile phone devices and their functions. Such an examination would have added nothing to their evidence. The regulation does not require expert evidence to be led in order to prove that the device falls within the statutory definition.

> [10]…, a hand held mobile phone is an everyday appliance which is in common use. It is an object familiar to the public and police officers alike. A court will be entitled to accept, without the need for further evidence, that a witness can recognise a hand held mobile phone, within the meaning of regulation 110, upon seeing it, and that a mobile phone is capable for the purposes of regulation 110(6)(c) of carrying out an "interactive communication function.'

The decision also echoed earlier ones which found that production of the phone at court is not essential unless its absence is prejudicial.[1]

7.12.18 Cycles

Section 81(1) of the Road Traffic Act 1988 provides for the making of regulations 'as to the use on roads of cycles, their construction and equipment and the conditions under which they may be so used'. Section 81(2) that without prejudice to the generality of s 81(1), regulations may provide for the number, nature and efficiency of brakes and their maintenance in proper working order, appliances to be fitted for signalling approach and their maintenance in proper working order, and testing and inspection of any equipment prescribed under this section and of lighting equipment and reflectors.

The Pedal Cycles (Construction and Use) Regulations 1983[2] focus on the need for working brakes for on pedal and electrically assisted pedal cycles. Constables in uniform are entitled to examine and inspect pedal cycles either on the road or elsewhere within 48 hours of an accident.[3]

---

1   *PF Glasgow v McClumpha* XJ1043/09 (Decision of 30 March 2010). The phone was returned to the respondent at the scene. Had investigation of the phone been required by the respondent, that had been open to her. *McKellar v Normand* 1992 SCCR 393 followed.
2   SI 1983/1176, as amended by SI 2015/474.
3   See reg 11.

Breach of these regulations may be prosecuted on summary complaint up to a level 3 fine under s 91 of the Road Traffic Offenders Act 1988.

Regulation 18 and Sch. 1 of the Road Vehicles Lighting Regulations 1989 provide details of obligatory lamps and reflectors, namely front and rear position lamps and pedal retro reflectors.

7.13 ROADS (SCOTLAND) ACT 1984 OFFENCES

Tried summarily or on indictment, fines at the levels set out in Sch 8 of the Act

The 1984 Act introduces a myriad of offences relating to roads and their surrounds, for example leaving an animal on, or allowing it to stray onto, a road, for which under s 98 a level 3 fine can be imposed. Section 129 in particular provides for a variety of offences affecting roads, footways, footpaths and cycle tracks. The most relevant in an everyday sense might be seen as those contained in s 129(2), (3), (5) and (9). Broadly they concern:

–   placing anything that obstructs or endangers road users (level 2);

–   the loading of vehicles or animals causing endangerment or obstruction of road user (level 3);

–   driving vehicles – including cycles given the exceptions provided – or animals on footways and footpaths (level 2);

–   displaying goods for sale on a footway (level 3).

The section is also of interest given the last vestiges of older styles in the reference to 'furious, reckless or careless riding or driving of horses or other animals' under s 129(7), a level 3 offence. Regard should be had to the interpretation section contained in s 151. The section in full reads as follows:

'129 Miscellaneous summary offences

(1) A person who in or beside any road leaves open and unfenced, or insufficiently covered or insufficiently fenced, an opening into a vault or cellar commits an offence:

Provided that the foregoing provisions of this subsection do not apply in relation to the duty under section 56(5) of this Act first to provide a door or cover.

(2) A person who, without lawful authority or reasonable excuse, places or deposits anything in a road so as to obstruct the passage of, or to endanger, road users commits an offence:

Provided that no person shall, in respect of the same actings, be convicted both under the foregoing provisions of this subsection and under section 59(2), 90, 95, 100(a) or 101 of this Act, or subsection (9) of this section, of an offence.

(3) A person who, in a road, as the case may be drives leads or propels a vehicle or animal commits an offence if any load which is thereby being carried projects beyond the vehicle or animal so as in any way to obstruct or endanger other road users.

(4) Without prejudice to subsection (2) above, a person who, in a road, pitches a tent or encamps commits an offence.

(5) Subject to section 64 of this Act, a person who, in a foot-way, footpath or cycle track, as the case may be drives, rides, leads or propels a vehicle or horse, or any swine or cattle, commits an offence:

Provided that the foregoing provisions of this subsection do not apply –

(a)   where and in so far as the vehicle or animal is being taken across the footway , footpath or cycle track;

(b)   in relation to a pedal cycle which is either not being ridden or is being ridden on a cycle track;

(c)   except on a cycle track where there is no public right of passage on foot, in relation to –

(i)   a perambulator, push-chair or other form of baby carriage; or

(ii)   an invalid carriage whose motive power is provided solely by its rider or some other person, or by an electric motor, or by a combination of these sources; or

(d)   where there is a specific right so to drive, ride, lead or propel.

(6)   A person who parks a motor vehicle ("motor vehicle" having the same meaning as in the Road Traffic Act 1972) wholly or partly on a cycle track commits an offence.

(7) A person who in a road rides or drives furiously, recklessly or carelessly a horse or other animal (whether or not that horse or animal is attached to a cart or carriage) commits an offence.

(8) Without prejudice to subsection (2) above, a person who, over or along a footway, places a shade, awning or other projection less than either or both –

(a)   2.25 metres above the level of the footway;

(b)   50 centimetres inwards from a carriageway,

commits an offence.

(9) A person who displays goods for sale by placing them in, or hanging them over, a footway or footpath commits an offence:

Provided that the foregoing provisions of this subsection do not apply to –

(a)   the offer or exposure for sale of newspapers;

(b)   the display of goods for sale by a street trader trading under and in accordance with a street trader's licence;

(c)   the display of goods for sale in connection with the carrying on of a private market under and in accordance with a market operator's licence; or

(d)   any activity in respect of which a certificate under the Pedlars Act 1871 has been granted, and in the foregoing paragraphs of this proviso "street trader's licence", "private market" and "market operator's licence" shall be construed in accordance with section 97(6) of this Act.

(10)   Where materials, tools, machinery or other equipment –

(a)   have been deposited in any place for use by the roads authority in constructing or maintaining a road; or

(b)   are in a quarry which has been opened by the authority for the purpose of their obtaining such materials for that use,

a person who without reasonable excuse takes away, or displaces, the materials, tools, machinery or equipment commits an offence.'

7.14 TESTING AND INSPECTION

Sections 66A–72A of the Road Traffic Act 1988, as amended by the Road Traffic Act 1991, provides wide-ranging powers for the inspection of vehicles. Under earlier legislation, powers of inspection and testing were given to, among others, certifying officers, public service vehicle examiners, and examiners of goods vehicles. By virtue of s 66A there are now simply vehicle examiners authorised by the Secretary of State, covering all the functions of the former different sorts of examiner.

The powers of inspection include the right to test and inspect not only passenger carrying vehicles (PCVs), which were formerly known as passenger service vehicles (PSVs), and large goods vehicles (LGVs), formerly known as heavy goods vehicles (HGVs), but also private cars. The new s 68 of the Road Traffic Act 1988, allows a vehicle examiner to inspect public passenger vehicles and goods vehicles at any time, to detain the vehicle, to enter premises, to test drive the vehicle, and to require the person in charge to drive the vehicle not more than five miles to a place of inspection. Section 69 gives vehicle examiners powers to prohibit the driving of unfit vehicles (of any description); while s 70 affords the power to prohibit the driving of overloaded vehicles. Offences are provided for by s 71; the removal of prohibitions is covered by s 72; and the provision of testing stations by s 72A.

Section 67 of the Road Traffic Act 1988[1] allows an authorised examiner to test a vehicle on a road to ascertain whether the construction and use requirements, and the requirement that the vehicle should not be in a dangerous condition, are being observed. The examiner may require the driver to comply with his reasonable instructions, and may also drive the vehicle himself. The motorist has the right to ask for deferment of such a test,[2] but can be convicted of an offence revealed by the examination even although he has not had the opportunity to elect for such a deferment.[3] In *Watson v Muir*[4] it was held that although it was desirable that the owner or user of the vehicle should be present at any test, this is not essential. It should be noted that the examiner's powers refer to the driver rather than the owner. Obvious defects can be spoken to in evidence by persons other than authorised examiners.[5]

By virtue of s 75 of the Road Traffic Act 1988[6] it is an offence to sell a vehicle which is in an unroadworthy condition; s 76 of the 1988 Act as amended by the Road Traffic Act 1991, Sch 4 para 58 makes it an offence to fit or supply defective, unsuitable or dangerous vehicle parts. Section 77 of the 1988 Act allows examiners to inspect used vehicles in showrooms. For further discussion on vehicle examiners, see ch 9.

On 31 March 2009, s 5 of the Road Safety Act 2006 came into force (by SI 2008/3164, art 3(b)) and allows vehicle examiners to issue fixed penalties. Schedule 1 of the 2006 Act amended Part III of the Road Traffic Offenders Act 1998 as required. Also introduced is greater scope to recover financial penalties by means of financial deposits and also immobilisation of vehicles. See 7.5.11 above.

The Road Vehicles (Powers to Stop) Regulations 2011 (SI 2011/996) introduced new ss 66B and 66C to the Road Traffic Act 1988, as well as amending s 67 and the Road Traffic Offenders Act 1988. 'Stopping officers' and their powers are introduced by s 66B and associated offences by s 66C. These officers are to be used for checks of commercial vehicles, both domestic and EC, involving licencing and other matters.

---

1   As amended by the RTA 1991, s 10.
2   RTA 1988, s 67(6).
3   *Brown v McIndoe* 1963 SLT 233.
4   *Watson v Muir* 1938 JC 181, 1939 SLT 14.
5   *Mowbray v Valentine* 1992 SLT 416, 1991 SCCR 494.
6   As amended by RTA 1991, s 16.

Chapter 8

Licences, disqualification, endorsement and fixed penalties

8.1 DRIVERS' LICENCES

8.1.1 General and the introduction of the 'driving record'

Section 87 of the Road Traffic Act 1988[1] provides:

'(1) It is an offence for a person to drive on a road a motor vehicle of any class otherwise than in accordance with a licence authorising him to drive a motor vehicle of that class.

(2) It is an offence for a person to cause or permit another person to drive on a road a motor vehicle of any class otherwise than in accordance with a licence authorising that other person to drive a motor vehicle of that class.'

The way in which this section is now phrased emphasises that the offence created is not simply that of driving without a licence of any sort, but can and will occur where a person drives a vehicle of a class not authorised by his licence. This reflects the decision in *Ogilvie v O'Donnell*[2] which held that a licence is only valid when used in accordance with its conditions of issue. The classes of vehicle authorised by a licence are shown on the licence itself. Licences are issued at the instance of the Secretary of State through the DVLA, which is responsible for keeping details of all licences, including disqualifications and endorsements. A universal European Community form of licence is meantime issued which is valid for all member states, and which covers all of the driver's driving entitlements in its authorised classes, including those for commercial and passenger vehicles. HGV licences are now issued separately. Existing old-style licences remain valid until replaced. Duplication of licences is prohibited.[3] Records kept by the Secretary of State in respect of this part of the Act are admissible as copies in evidence, and are sufficient evidence of the facts contained therein.[4]

One significant consequence of the way in which s 87 is now phrased is that all prosecutions based on the failure of the driver to have the appropriate licence (apart from driving while disqualified by order of court which remains an offence under s 103) are now taken under s 87(1). Accordingly, offences involving driving without being the holder of a licence, driving a vehicle otherwise than in accordance with the terms of the licence, driving while disqualified by reason of age, and driving

---

1   As amended by the RTA 1991, s 17.
2   *Ogilvie v O'Donnell* 1983 SCCR 257.
3   RTA 1988, s 102.
4   RTOA 1988, s 13, as amended by the Civil Evidence Act 1995, s 15(1), Sch 1 para 15.

as a provisional licence holder without supervision or L plates, or unauthorised driving with a passenger on a motor cycle are currently prosecuted under s 87.

Certain limited exceptions to the absolute requirement of holding a licence are found in the Road Traffic Act 1988, s 88. Section 88(2A) prevents high-risk offenders – ie those convicted of s 5(1)(a) with a reading of two-and-a-half times the limit or more, s 7, or disqualified twice in ten years for alcohol offences under ss 4 and 5 – from relying on s 88 whilst waiting for their qualifying application to be considered under s 88(1)(b). In other words, medical evidence confirming fitness to drive must be provided and accepted before a licence is issued.

Prescribed classes of driver who are normally resident outside the United Kingdom and who do not hold a European Community licence may drive on licences held by them for a period of one year.[1] Community licence holders are entitled to drive in this country.[2]

Section 49 of the Road Safety Act 2006 allows the Secretary of State to disclose information held by the UK licensing authorities to other countries. This in turn allows resultant sharing of information from other countries – such as details of disqualified drivers.

Any change in the name or address of the licence holder must be intimated to the DVLA forthwith.[3] Relevant considerations in respect of the issue of licences are to be found in the Motor Vehicles (Driving Licences) Regulations 1999 as regularly amended.[4] In particular, the various classes of vehicle which may be authorised on a licence are described in Sch 2 and include categories in respect of heavy goods and passenger carrying vehicles.

In a charge of driving otherwise than in accordance with the conditions of a licence in contravention of s 87(1), once the Crown has shown prima facie that a driver has no licence, the responsibility for proving that he has a licence rests on the accused.[5]

Sections 97 and 98 of the Road Traffic Act 1988 as amended cover the granting and form of licences. It should be noted that s 17 of the Road Traffic Act 1991 deletes ss 97(7) and 98(5) of the 1988 Act; s 100 allows

---

1   Motor Vehicles (Driving Licences) Regulations 1999 (SI 1999/2864), reg 80.
2   RTA 1988, s 99A and subsequent sections introduced by the Driving Licences (Community Driving Licence) Regulations 1996 (SI 1996/1974) and 1998 (SI 1998/1420).
3   RTA 1988, s 99(4).
4   (SI 1999/2864).
5   *Milne v Whaley* 1975 SLT (Notes) 75, *Momoh v McFadyen* 2003 SCCR 679.

an appeal to the sheriff against a refusal to grant a licence, but a further appeal to the sheriff principal is incompetent.[1]

Major change was achieved when the provisions of ss 8–10 and Schs 2 and 3 to the 2006 Act were brought into force. The Great Britain counterpart licence has now been done away with[2] and replaced by the concept of a driving record. It is defined in the new s 97A of the Road Traffic Offenders Act 1988 as meaning 'a record in relation to the person maintained by the Secretary of State and designed to be endorsed with particulars relating to offences committed by the person under the Traffic Acts'. Reference should be made to the detailed provisions but the clearest practical impact relates to the potential to deal with and record offences committed by unlicensed and non-GB licensed drivers. Endorsement of the driving record and the potential to issue fixed penalties to such drivers will be possible.

8.1.2 Definitions and penalties

'*Drives*'. See 1.7.1 above.
'*Road*'. See 1.8.1, 1.8.2 and 1.8.3 above.
'*Motor vehicle*'. See 1.2.1ff above.
'*Causing or permitting*'. See 1.10.3 above.

Penalties for such an offence are found in Sch 2, Pt I of the Road Traffic Offenders Act 1988,[3] and normally involve discretionary disqualification and obligatory endorsement. If disqualification is not ordered, three to six penalty points must be endorsed on the licence.

8.1.3 Test of competence to drive

A driving licence will not be issued unless a test of competence to drive has been passed.[4] Various exceptions are allowed[5] and other alternative provisions are found in s 89A.[6] Section 38 of the Road Safety Act 2006 once in force will provide scope for the Secretary of State to prescribe the period between applying for and passing the test. In addition to the requirements of Pt III of the Road Traffic Act 1988, further provision on categories of entitlement, application for licences, provisional licences, the

1   *Hopkin v Ayr Local Taxation Office* 1964 SLT (Sh Ct) 60.
2   SI 2015/560.
3   As amended by the RTA 1991, Sch 2 para 19.
4   RTA 1988, s 89, as amended, most recently by s 36 of the Road Safety Act 2006.
5   RTA 1988, s 88.
6   Introduced by the Road Traffic Driver Licensing and Information Systems Act 1989, ss 4(1) and 4(4) and amended by s 36 of the Road Safety Act 2006.

nature and conduct of the driving test and special regulations in respect of licences to drive goods and passenger carrying vehicles are found in the Motor Vehicles (Driving Licences) Regulations 1999.[1]

Section 90 allows for a review that the test was properly conducted in accordance with the regulations by way of application to the Sheriff. However, such an appeal is not intended to be a review of the test; to succeed the appellant must demonstrate that the test was not conducted properly, and that there has been, for example, malice or oppression or unfair conduct in the way in which the test was conducted.[2] A further appeal to the Sheriff Principal is incompetent.[3]

8.1.4 Physical fitness

An applicant for a driving licence must furnish a declaration as to whether he is suffering from any relevant or prospective disability which may make his driving a source of danger to the public.[4] Certain prescribed disabilities are given in the Motor Vehicles (Driving Licences) Regulations 1999.[5] These include High Risk Offenders under reg 74 and mentioned at 8.1.1 above. A licence may be revoked if the Secretary of State is at any time satisfied on inquiry that the licence holder is suffering from a relevant or prospective disability.[6] This section may be invoked in practice where a court becomes aware during a road traffic prosecution that the accused may be suffering from such a disability, and intimates this to the Secretary of State in terms of s 22 of the Road Traffic Offenders Act 1988. Section 22 provides that the court must notify the Secretary of State of these disabilities if they become evident, irrespective of the outcome of the prosecution.

If a licence holder becomes aware that he is suffering from a relevant or prospective disability during the currency of his licence, he must likewise intimate this.[7] With an increasingly elderly population

---

1   Motor Vehicles (Driving Licences) Regulations 1999 (SI 1999/2864) as repeatedly amended.
2   *Corrigan v Fox* 1966 SLT (Sh Ct) 79.
3   *Hopkin v Ayr Local Taxation Officer* 1964 SLT (Sh Ct) 60.
4   RTA 1988, s 92 as amended *inter alia* by the RTA 1991 s 18, which also amends s 94, and introduces a new s 94A. Penalties are amended by paras 21–23 of Sch 2 to the 1991 Act.
5   Motor Vehicles (Driving Licences) Regulations (SI 1999/2864), regs 70–75, as amended, most recently by the Motor Vehicles (Driving Licences) (Amendment) Regulations 2017/1208.
6   RTA 1988, s 93.
7   RTA 1988, s 94.

the issue of ongoing fitness may become an ever-growing problem, thinking both in terms of mental health issues such as dementia and physical ailments including vision issues through problems associated with diabetes. Agencies are aware of the problem but no one appears to be taking a lead on the matter, despite it being raised following deaths caused by drivers who were patently unfit to drive. The need to share the unfitness with the individual or the DVLA does not seem to be adequately understood by the medical profession or family members. On a practical level, an individual may not fully understand the need to notify a relevant or prospective disability unless he or she is told about it.

This issue received widespread publicity following the Glasgow bin lorry crash on 22 December 2014. In his determination[1] at the subsequent fatal accident inquiry, the then Sheriff Becket QC observed that Dr Parry, the DVLA's Senior Medical Adviser, acknowledged that there are weaknesses in the current system of self-reporting. The determination also included the following passage:

> 'It may well be that the single most useful outcome of this Inquiry would be to raise awareness of the dangers involved in driving if subject to a medical condition which could cause the driver to lose control of a vehicle. Media outlets reporting on the issuing of this Determination, would be performing a valuable service to the public if they include the following information in their reporting:
>
> > "Guidance, including a list of relevant conditions, can be found on the DVLA website: www.gov.uk/driving-medical-conditions. Drivers can contact DVLA if they are not sure what to do. They can consult their doctor if they are in doubt or if they are in need of advice".'[2]

It should be noted that revocation may follow but not inevitably, and conditional driving may be permitted.

Likewise, any authorised insurer who refuses to provide insurance cover on the basis of unsatisfactory health must notify the Secretary of State of that refusal and the details of the person involved.[3] It is an offence to drive with defective eyesight or to refuse a test to ascertain whether the eyesight is defective.[4]

---

1   Determination of 7 December 2015, [2015] FAI 31, at para [564].
2   At para [562].
3   RTA 1988, s 95 as amended by Financial Services and Markets Act 2000 (Consequential Amendments and Repeals) Order 2001 (SI 2001/3649), Pt 8, art 312.
4   RTA 1988, s 96.

Offences are tried summarily, and generally may lead to discretionary disqualification or three to six obligatory penalty points and a fine up to level 3 on the standard scale for failing to disclose the onset, or deterioration of an existing, condition.

A level 4 fine is available for a false declaration as to fitness.

Imprisonment of up to six months, and up to a level 5 fine, is an option for an offence under s 94A, namely driving after refusal of licence under s 92(3), revocation under s 93 or service of a notice under s 99C or 109B.

An appeal against a refusal by the Secretary of State to grant a licence is available to the Sheriff,[1] but not to the Sheriff Principal.[2] In *McFarlane v Secretary of State for Scotland*[3] the principal consideration was whether the appellant was suffering from a relevant disability likely to cause the driving of a vehicle to be a source of danger to the public.

8.1.5 Duration and form of licences

The earliest ages at which persons may hold licences are specified in s 101 of the Road Traffic Act 1988 (as amended) (see 8.2.1 below). Thereafter, full driving licences are issued and in normal course remain valid until the holder's 70th birthday, after which they have to be renewed at three-year intervals.[4] Different ages and time limits exist for drivers with relevant or prospective disabilities, or those with licences authorising driving of prescribed classes of goods vehicles or passenger-carrying vehicles.[5]

Section 98 requires that the licence should indicate the classes of vehicle that the driver is entitled to drive and any restrictions on the driving of such vehicles. Classes of vehicles are detailed in Sch 2 to the Motor Vehicles (Driving Licences) Regulations 1999;[6] see also regs 4 and 5. Special conditions attaching to the grant of licences authorising the holder to drive large goods vehicles and passenger carrying vehicles are found in Ch 9, Pt IV of the Road Traffic Act 1988, and Pt IV of the above regulations.

Sections 38 Road Safety Act 2006 will introduce new provisions allowing the Secretary of State to specify conditions to be met prior to the

1   RTA 1988, s 100. See, for example, *Carruth v Advocate General* 2006 SLT (Sh Ct) 33.
2   *Hopkin v Ayr Local Taxation Office* 1964 SLT (Sh Ct) 60.
3   *McFarlane v Secretary of State for Scotland* 1988 SCLR (Sh Ct) 623.
4   RTA 1988, s 99.
5   See ss 99(1)(b) and 99A.
6   Motor Vehicles (Driving Licences) Regulations 1999 (SI 1999/2864).

grant of a full licence, for example driving in accordance with an alcohol ignition lock programme.

Section 39 of the same Act introduces a new s 98A which allows for the potential of the Secretary of State ordering the compulsory surrender of old form licences. Failure to comply with any such order will be tried summarily and incur a fine not exceeding level 3.

8.1.6 Provisional licences

Provisional licences are granted for the purpose of enabling the applicant to pass a test of competence to drive.[1] This section, and regs 11, and 15–18 of the Motor Vehicles (Driving Licences) Regulations 1999,[2] provide for the conditions and duration of such licences. In particular these regulations provide that a learner driver can only drive on the road while supervised by a qualified driver who must be over 21 years of age and have held a licence for over three years.[3]

8.1.7 Driving instruction

No instruction in the driving of motor vehicles for payment can be undertaken by any person who is not on the register of approved instructors, and who is not licensed to undertake such instruction. Driving instruction is dealt with in Pt V of the Road Traffic Act 1988. The relevant regulations are the Motor Cars (Driving Instruction) Regulations 2005.[4] The Road Traffic Offenders Act 1988, s 18, provides that a certificate from the Registrar relating to the status of any person on the register is sufficient proof of the facts stated therein.

8.2 DISQUALIFICATION BY REASON OF AGE: OBTAINING LICENCE OR DRIVING WHILE DISQUALIFIED

8.2.1 General

Section 101(1) of the Road Traffic Act 1988[5] provides:

---

1   RTA 1988, s 97(2)–(4), as amended.
2   Motor Vehicles (Driving Licences) Regulations 1999 (SI 1999/2864) as amended.
3   Motor Vehicles (Driving Licences) Regulations 1999 (SI 1999/2864), reg 17.
4   Motor Cars (Driving Instruction) Regulations 2005 (SI 2005/1902).
5   As amended by the Driving Licences (Community Driving Licence) Regulations 1996 (SI 1996/1974).

'A person is disqualified for holding or obtaining a licence to drive a motor vehicle of a class specified in the following Table if he is under the age specified in relation to it in the second column of the Table.'

TABLE

Class of motor vehicle	Age (in years)
1. Invalid carriage	16
2. Moped	16
3. Motor bicycle	17
4. Agricultural or Forestry Tractor	17
5. Small vehicle	17
6. Medium-sized goods vehicle	18
7. Other motor vehicles	21

Section 32 of the Act disqualifies persons under 14 years of age from driving an electrically assisted pedal cycle.

Regard should also be had to the terms of reg 9 of the Motor Vehicles (Driving Licences) Regulations 1999 which provide variations on the ages set out in s 101 for specific vehicles.[1]

8.2.2 Section 103: Obtaining licence or driving while disqualified

Section 103 of the Road Traffic Act 1988[2] provides:

'(1) A person is guilty of an offence if, while disqualified for holding or obtaining a licence, he –

(a)   obtains a licence, or

(b)   drives a motor vehicle on a road.

(2) A licence obtained by a person who is disqualified is of no effect (or, where the disqualification relates only to vehicles of a particular class, is of no effect in relation to vehicles of that class).

(3) A constable in uniform may arrest without warrant any person driving a motor vehicle on a road whom he has reasonable cause to suspect of being disqualified.

(4) Subsections (1) and (3) above do not apply in relation to disqualification by virtue of section 101 of this Act.

---

1   Motor Vehicles (Driving Licences) Regulations 1999 (SI 1999/2864).
2   As amended *inter alia* by the RTA 1991, s 19.

(5) Subsections (1)(b) and (3) above do not apply in relation to disqualification by virtue of section 102 of this Act.

(6) In the application of subsections (1) and (3) above to a person whose disqualification is limited to the driving of motor vehicles of a particular class by virtue of –

(a)   section 102, 117 or 117A of this Act, or

(b)   subsection (9) of section 36 of the Road Traffic Offenders Act 1988 (disqualification until test is passed),

the references to disqualification for holding or obtaining a licence and driving motor vehicles are references to disqualification for holding or obtaining a licence to drive and driving motor vehicles of that class.'

This is an absolute offence and there can be no room for a defence of mistake or ignorance. However, a defence of necessity or duress may be available;[1] reference should also be made to 2.5 above. Duplication of licences is prohibited.[2]

Drivers disqualified in Northern Ireland, the Isle of Man, any of the Channel Islands or Gibraltar are disqualified for holding or obtaining a licence to drive a motor vehicle of any class. A certificate signed by the Secretary of State stating that a person is so disqualified is sufficient evidence for proof. [3]

8.2.3 Definitions and penalties

'Drives'. See 1.7.1 above.
'Road'. See 1.8.1, 1.8.2 and 1.8.3 above.
'Motor vehicle'. See 1.2.1 above.

The penalties for an offence under s 103(1)(b) of the Road Traffic Act 1988 are found in Sch 2, Pt I to the Road Traffic Offenders Act 1988,[4] and normally involve discretionary disqualification and obligatory endorsement.

Given the number of drivers with multiple s 103 convictions, disqualification for life may be seen as a realistic disposal. As was observed in *Laidlaw v Richardson*[5], 'There comes a time when the Court must say enough is enough', remembering that the provisions of s 42 of the Road Traffic Offenders Act (see 8.11.8 below) allow disqualification

---

1   *Moss v Howdle* 1997 JC 123, 1997 SLT 782, 1997 SCR 215.
2   RTA 1988, s 102.
3   RTA 1988, s 102A.
4   As amended by the RTA 1991, Sch 2 para 25.
5   2017 SCCR 359, at para 15.

to be removed after five years, whether it be a determinate period of ten years or a lifelong ban.

If disqualification is not imposed, six penalty points are endorsed on the licence.

Proceedings may be summary or on indictment; the maximum prison sentences under both are 12 months following the provisions of s 45 of the Criminal Proceedings etc (Reform) (Scotland) Act 2007. An offence under s 103(1)(a) has no consequence for the licence.

8.2.4 Section 3ZB: Causing death by driving: unlicensed, or uninsured drivers

On summary complaint 12 months' imprisonment and/or a level 5 fine

On indictment two years' imprisonment and/or a level 5 fine

Disqualification will be obligatory (or obligatory 3–11 points)
Section 21 of the Road Safety Act 2006 introduced a new s 3ZB to the Road Traffic Act 1988 in the following terms:

> 'A person is guilty of an offence under this section if he causes the death of another person by driving a motor vehicle on a road and, at the time when he is driving, the circumstances are such that he is committing an offence under –
>
> (a)   section 87(1) of this Act (driving otherwise than in accordance with a licence), or
>
> (c)   section 143 of this Act (using motor vehicle while uninsured or unsecured against third party risks).'

8.2.5 Section 3ZC: Causing death by driving: disqualified drivers

On summary complaint 12 months' imprisonment and/or a level 5 fine

On indictment ten years' imprisonment and/or a level 5 fine

Disqualification will be obligatory (or obligatory 3–11 points) and until driver passes the appropriate driving test

The Criminal Justice and Courts Act 2015 c 2 Pt 1 s 29(1) (13 April 2015: insertion has effect as SI 2015/778 subject to transitional provision specified in 2015 c 2 s 29(5)) introduced the new s 3ZC, which is in the following terms:

> 'A person is guilty of an offence under this section if he or she—
>
> (a)   causes the death of another person by driving a motor vehicle on a road, and

(b)   at that time, is committing an offence under section 103(1)(b) of this Act (driving while disqualified).'

8.2.6 Section 3ZD: Causing serious injury by driving: disqualified drivers

On summary complaint 12 months' imprisonment and/or a level 5 fine

On indictment four years' imprisonment and/or a level 5 fine

Disqualification will be obligatory (or obligatory three to 11 points) and until driver passes the appropriate driving test

The Criminal Justice and Courts Act 2015 c 2 Pt 1 s 29(1) (13 April 2015: insertion has effect as SI 2015/778 subject to transitional provision specified in 2015 c 2 s 29(5)) introduced the new s 3ZC, which is in the following terms:

'(1) A person is guilty of an offence under this section if he or she—

(a)   causes serious injury to another person by driving a motor vehicle on a road, and

(b)   at that time, is committing an offence under section 103(1)(b) of this Act (driving while disqualified).

(2 In this section "serious injury" means—

(a)   in England and Wales, physical harm which amounts to grievous bodily harm for the purposes of the Offences against the Person Act 1861, and

(b)   in Scotland, severe physical injury.'

These provisions – s 3ZC providing a distinct and higher sentence offence for disqualified driving cases (previously covered by s 3ZA(b) and the newly introduced s 3ZD to echo s 1A in non-fatal cases – are yet further responses to political and press concerns about fatal and serious injury road traffic cases (see 2.16.1 above). They are particularly controversial given the scope for significant sentences in circumstances where the culpability involved may be no greater than the triggering offence, which perhaps emphasises the lost opportunity to increase penalties for offences under ss 87, 103 and 143: the courts have been expressing concerns for years as to the arguably inadequate penalties available for repeat offending under such sections, particularly as regards ss 143 and 103.[1]

---

1   See eg, *Laidlaw v Richardson* 2017 SCCR 359 at para 15.

As was anticipated in the previous edition of this book, guidance has been forthcoming in relation to the difficult issue of causation under s 3ZB cases inevitably given its much earlier introduction, and how such cases, if proved, should be sentenced.

8.2.7 Causation in s 3Z cases

Until the decision of the Supreme Court in *R v Hughes*,[1] delivered on 31 July 2013, causation was achieved under this provision simply if there was 'a factual causal link between the driver being unlawfully on the road and the fatality, the nature and quality of the driving being irrelevant', and despite the 'formidable criticism' of the approach apparently taken by parliament.[2]

That formidable criticism is set out in the decision in *R v Williams*,[3] where the deceased had stepped out in front of the uninsured and unlicensed driver, whom the Crown accepted was, in terms of standard of driving, carelessness, or lack of consideration, without fault.

Nonetheless, the court, in upholding the conviction, said that the test remained that causation had to be more than minute or negligible and that the intention of Parliament was clear, and that was achieved by driving whilst subject to the triggers set out in s 3ZB, no matter that the provision might be seen as 'harsh and punitive'.

Hughes, however, resoundingly overturned the approach in *Williams* and the perceived intention of Parliament. The facts of the case are, if anything, more extraordinary still. The deceased driver was overtired, significantly under the influence of heroin, and on the wrong side of the road. He was also returning to work in a nuclear power station in Scotland when he collided with an uninsured driver, who did his best to avoid the impact. As the court noted, the collision was entirely the fault of the deceased driver.

Against that background, and while only affirming the gravity of non-insured driving generally, the court held that since Parliament had elected to use the words 'causes death by driving', that those words had to be strictly construed given the offence created was a form of homicide, and that had Parliament intended responsibility simply by being uninsured it could have said so unambiguously but had chosen not to, the approach taken in *Williams* was wrong.

---

1   [2013] UKSC 56, [2013] 4 All ER 613, [2013] 1 WLR 2461, [2013] RTR 420, [2014] 1 Cr App Rep 46, (2013) *Times*, 20 August, [2013] All ER (D) 388 (Jul).
2   *Rai v HMA* 2012 SCCR 591, [2011] HCJAC 105, Lord Clarke at para 16.
3   [2010] EWCA Crim 2252, [2010] All ER (D) 19, [2011] WLR 588.

Instead, it followed:

'that in order to give effect to the expression "causes...death...by driving" a defendant charged with the offence under section 3ZB must be shown to have done something other than simply putting his vehicle on the road so that it is there to be struck. It must be proved that there was something which he did or omitted to do by way of driving it which contributed in a more than minimal way to the death. The question therefore remains what can or cannot amount to such act or omission in the manner of driving.'[1]

What that amounts to will, of course, be case specific, but the court made the point that, in finding some additional feature in the driving which is causative, common sense is required, a factor prosecutors should, and no doubt in any event would, keep in mind in assessing the need, in the public interest, for any prosecution.

Ultimately, the correct approach to the provision was summarised as follows:

'[F]rom the use of the expression "causes...death...by driving" that 3ZB requires at least some act or omission in the control of the car, which involves some element of fault, whether amounting to careless/inconsiderate driving or not, and which contributes in some more than minimal way to the death. It is not necessary that such act or omission be the principal cause of the death. In which circumstances the offence under section 3ZB will then add to the other offences of causing death by driving must remain to be worked out as factual scenarios are presented to the courts.'[2]

8.2.8 Sentencing in s 3Z cases

Perhaps reflecting the anxieties of the provision pre *Hughes*, sentences imposed in such Scottish cases as have been reported have tended to be cases where there were even graver charges properly reflecting the degrees of causation involved.[3]

Nonetheless, as was said in *Rai v HMA*, a s 3ZB case, 'Sentencing in respect of this offence may not prove an easy task in any particular case'.[4] There, the Sheriff's conclusion, that the driver should have anticipated the deceased might have been walking on a motorway and that the failure to do so was an aggravation, was criticised and

---

1   At para 28.
2   At para 36.
3   See, for example, *Fleming v HMA* [2012] HCJAC 12A and *Grant v HMA* [2013] HCJAC 11.
4   *Op cit* at para 16.

the sentence, also reflecting previous offending, was reduced from 18 months to 12 months. It is on the facts doubtful that this would have been prosecuted post *Hughes*.

No guidelines yet exist to assist.

8.3 EVIDENCE

In order to obtain a conviction under s 103 of the Road Traffic Act 1988, the prosecution must adduce sufficient evidence that the accused has been disqualified.[1] If the prosecution attempt to prove the disqualification by reference to a schedule of previous convictions in any form, and that schedule reveals that the accused has previous convictions other than that which imposed the period of disqualification, any subsequent conviction under this section will be quashed.[2] However, reference should also be made to *Moffat v Smith*,[3] *Johnston v Allan*,[4] *Kerr v Jessop*,[5] *Harkin v H M Advocate*[6] and *MacLean v Buchanan*.[7] The rule may be less strictly observed in summary cases, and where no real prejudice results.

The statutory provisions which prohibit the disclosure of previous convictions prior to any finding of guilt are found in the Criminal Procedure (Scotland) Act 1995, s 101 (solemn) and s 166 (summary).

In terms of s 19 of the Road Traffic Offenders Act 1988, in any proceedings for an offence under s 103(1)(b) of the Road Traffic Act 1988 (driving while disqualified) a conviction or extract conviction of which a copy has been served on the accused not less than 14 days before his trial, which purports to be signed by the clerk of court, and which shows that the person named in it is disqualified, is to be sufficient evidence of the application of that disqualification to the accused, unless the accused serves notice on the prosecutor, not less than six days before his trial, that he denies that the conviction applies to him. Proof of previous convictions generally is provided for in ss 285, 286, and 286A of the Criminal Procedure (Scotland) Act 1995.

1   *Herron v Nelson* 1976 SLT (Sh Ct) 42; *Andrews v McLeod* 1982 SLT 456, 1982 SCCR 254. See also s 102A of the RTA 1988.
2   *Herron v Nelson* 1976 SLT (Sh ct) 42; *Mitchell v Dean* 1979 SLT (Notes) 12; *Boustead v McLeod* 1979 JC 70, 1979 SLT (Notes) 48; *Robertson v Aitchison* 1981 SLT (Notes) 127, 1981 SCCR 149.
3   *Moffat v Smith* 1983 SCCR 392.
4   *Johnston v Allan* 1984 SLT 261, 1983 SCCR 500.
5   *Kerr v Jessop* 1991 JC 1.
6   *Harkin v H M Advocate* 1996 SLT 1004, 1996 SCCR 5.
7   *MacLean v Buchanan* 1997 SLT 91.

A person who is charged under this section with driving while disqualified by virtue of age is regarded as being in a special capacity in terms of the Criminal Procedure (Scotland) Act 1995, s 255,[1] that is to say, that the fact that he is so disqualified is to be held as admitted unless this is challenged by a preliminary objection before his plea is recorded.[2]

Even where the accused has not disputed the special capacity, the prosecution can lead evidence of a disqualification previous conviction.[3]

8.4 DISQUALIFICATION FOLLOWING OFFENCE

8.4.1 General

Apart from considerations of disability or age described earlier in this chapter, disqualification of a driver by removal of his licence usually occurs as a consequence of penalties imposed for road traffic offences. In general terms, disqualification may follow in three sets of circumstances; firstly, when the legislation provides that disqualification is obligatory following a particular offence;[4] secondly, when the legislation provides that disqualification is discretionary following a particular offence and the court elects to exercise its discretion in favour of disqualification;[5] and thirdly, where the offence committed involves disqualification for repeated offences or the application of what is known as the totting-up procedure.[6] Whether a particular offence carries obligatory or discretionary disqualification is noted in Sch 2, Pt I to the Road Traffic Offenders Act 1988.[7]

However, there are further categories of disqualification.

Section 36 of the Road Traffic Offenders Act 1988 (as amended) provides for disqualification until a test of competence to drive is passed (see 8.11.1 below).

Section 248 of the Criminal Procedure (Scotland) Act 1995 allows disqualification where a vehicle has been used for the purpose of committing an offence (see 8.11.4 below).

Section 248A of the same Act, as amended by s 15(1) of the Crime and Punishment (Scotland) Act 1997, allows disqualification for offences

1   See also *Paton v Lees* 1992 SCCR 212.
2   *Smith v Allan* 1985 SLT 565, 1985 SCCR 190.
3   *Campbell v HM Advocate* 1999 JC 147, 1999 SLT 399.
4   RTOA 1988, s 34(1).
5   RTOA 1988, s 34(2) as amended by the RTA 1991, s 29(2).
6   RTOA 1988, s 35, as amended by RTA 1991, Sch 4 para 95.
7   As amended by RTA 1991, Sch 2.

other than those connected with road traffic (see 8.11.7 below), and s 248B (again, as similarly introduced) allows the court to disqualify fine defaulters from driving (see 8.11.7 below).

New ss 248D and 248E[1] allowing for extensions of periods of disqualification, or consideration of such, where prison sentences are imposed, were brought into force in July 2018[2] (see 8.11.7 below).

Similar provisions also now exist, under ss 35C and 35D of the Road Traffic Offenders Act 1988,[3] in circumstances where disqualification is to be imposed under that Act, by either s 34 or s35, and imprisonment is imposed at the same time, for that or another offence, or where there is an existing sentence of imprisonment still in effect (see 8.11.8 below).

Special provisions concerning newly qualified drivers are dealt with at 8.11.4 below.

Section 26 of the Road Traffic Offenders Act 1988[4] provides for a system of interim disqualification (see 8.4.3 below). Special consideration is also given to short periods of disqualification (see 8.4.2 below).

Where an accused has committed a number of offences which involve disqualification, the correct procedure is for the court to consider what is the appropriate period of disqualification for each offence, and not to take account of the accused's behaviour as a whole in order to increase the cumulative period of disqualification.[5]

The appeal court has often indicated that anyone who is to be disqualified for any reason should normally be given the opportunity to appear and proffer any special reasons why he should not be.

8.4.2 Short periods of disqualification

Section 37(1A) of the Road Traffic Offenders Act 1988[6] provides that where disqualification is imposed by a court for a fixed period shorter than 56 days in respect of an offence involving obligatory endorsement or where interim disqualification is imposed (see 8.4.3 below), the licence is not revoked in terms of s 37(1) of the Road Traffic Act 1988, as is normally the case following disqualification, but simply continues to have effect at the end of the short period of disqualification, including any extension period under s 35C, or interim disqualification. In practice this means that,

---

1 Inserted by the Coroners and Justice Act 2009 (c 25).
2 Added by the Coroners and Justice Act 2009 (16 July 2018: SI 2018/733).
3 Added by the Coroners and Justice Act 2009 (16 July 2018: SI 2018/733).
4 As amended by the RTA 1991, s 25.
5 *McMurrich v Cardle* 1988 SCCR 20.
6 As introduced by the RTA 1991, s 33.

unlike the normal situation following disqualification where the licence is revoked and the motorist has to apply to the DVLA for the issue of a fresh licence, in these cases the licence is in effect suspended and revives at the end of the period of disqualification. Common practice appears to be that the licence remains with the driver on the understanding that he cannot drive until the disqualification period ends. The clerk of court is responsible for updating the driving record by contacting the DVLA with the details of the disqualification.

The purpose of these provisions reflects the desire of the legislature that courts should more frequently disqualify drivers for short periods.

8.4.3 Interim disqualification

Section 26 (particularly sub-ss (3), (4), (5) and (6)) of the Road Traffic Offenders Act 1988[1] allows a court to impose interim disqualification after conviction where sentence has been deferred for reports or for good behaviour, or where the accused has been remitted to the High Court for sentence. Specific provision[2] is made for such interim disqualification to be imposed for periods in excess of six months. In general terms, a court can impose an order for interim disqualification in cases where obligatory or discretionary disqualification is available and sentence is deferred for reports on other inquiries, where sentence is simply deferred for a period, or for good behaviour, or where the accused is remitted for sentence to the High Court. Orders can only be made on one occasion,[3] but can be continued at subsequent hearings.[4] The period of interim disqualification should not have any effect on the period subsequently selected by the court at disposal,[5] but in terms of s 26(12) the final disqualification is deemed to be reduced by the time served under any relevant interim disqualification. This does not apply if the driver has been forbidden to drive under a bail order. Such an order can be appealed by virtue of the Road Traffic Offenders Act 1988, s 38(2) (see 8.11.2 below).

8.4.4 Consequences of disqualification

In every case where disqualification is obligatory or discretionary, and in every case where penalty points are to be imposed, details of the

---

1   As amended by the RTA 1991, s 25, though remarkably reference is still made to the powers to do so under the Criminal Procedure (Scotland) Act 1975.
2   RTA 1988, s 26(5).
3   RTA 1988, s 26 (6).
4   *Edwards v Whelan* 1999 SLT 917, 1998 SCCR 689.
5   *Wilson v Heywood* 1999 SLT 915, 1998 SCCR 686.

convictions, and where appropriate the number of penalty points, must be endorsed on the accused's licence[1] or driving record.[2] However, the court cannot impose disqualification and penalty points for separate offences at the same time.[3]

Following disqualification (either obligatory or discretionary), the court may order the driver to give details of his date of birth and other information;[4] and on conviction of an offence involving obligatory endorsement, the court must order the licence to be produced.[5] The court may take into account any existing endorsements if shown, and from the driving record.[6] Where the licence is not produced, or no licence is in fact held,[7] a document purporting to be information from the Secretary of State's records[8] may likewise be considered. A driver can challenge the accuracy of the record. Reference should also be made to 8.10.4 below.

Where a person fails to comply with a court order to produce his licence to the court in terms of s 27, a police constable may require the production of the licence and seize it.[9]

8.4.5 Duration of disqualification

By virtue of s 37(1) of the Road Traffic Offenders Act 1988, any period of disqualification commences from the moment it is imposed by the court; there is no provision for back-dating or post-dating such an order.

In cases of obligatory or discretionary disqualification not involving the application of the totting-up procedure, a period of disqualification may not be imposed on a consecutive basis.[10] The court is allowed to look at any other period of disqualification being served by the accused, and any other offence which is being considered at the same time for which disqualification is liable to be imposed, in considering the appropriate length of the disqualification order..[11] Also the court may

---

1   RTOA 1988, s 44.
2   RTOA 1988, s 44A.
3   *Ahmed v McLeod* 1999 SLT 762, 1998 SCCR 486.
4   RTOA 1988, s 25.
5   RTOA 1988, s 27, as amended by the RTA 1991, Sch 4 para 91.
6   RTOA 1988, s 31, as amended by Road Safety Act 2006 (c 49), Sch 2 para 6(2) (1 April 2009).
7   See *Hamilton v Ruxton* 2001 SCCR 1.
8   Known as a DVLA print-out.
9   RTA 1988, s 164(5), as amended.
10 *Williamson v McMillan* 1962 SLT 63.
11 *Allan v Crowe* 1994 SCCR 596; *Wishart v Miller* 1998 SCCR 21.

consider a current prison sentence when selecting the length of any ban.[1] However, an excessive approach using such justifications is likely to be overturned by the Court of Appeal. By the nature of the procedure, consecutive disqualification cannot apply in totting-up cases. Any period of disqualification must be for a fixed term; however, in appropriate circumstances a driver may be banned for life.

Where a person is convicted of an offence involving obligatory disqualification, the minimum period of disqualification is 12 months, unless the court considers that special reasons exist for restricting the period of disqualification, or for not imposing disqualification at all.[2]

There are several exceptions to this rule. Firstly, where a driver is convicted of culpable homicide, causing death or serious injury by dangerous driving, causing death or serious injury by disqualified driving, or causing death by careless driving while under the influence of drink or drugs,[3] the minimum period of disqualification is two years.[4]

Further, a minimum period of two years' disqualification is to be imposed in relation to a person on whom more than one disqualification for a fixed period of 56 days or more has been imposed within the three years immediately preceding the commission of the offence.[5] In this latter respect, disqualification imposed as a result of an offence committed by using a vehicle[6] or of taking a vehicle in terms of the Road Traffic Act 1988, s 178 is to be disregarded.[7]

Where a driver is convicted within ten years of a second offence involving (i) s 3A of the Road Traffic Act 1988 (causing death by careless driving when under the influence of drink or drugs), (ii) s 4(1) (driving or attempting to drive while unfit through drink or drugs), (iii) s 5(1)(a) (driving or attempting to drive with excess alcohol), (iv) ss 5A(1)(a) and (2) (driving or attempting to drive with a concentration of specified controlled drug above the specified limit), (v) s 7(6) (failing to provide a specimen where that offence, because it relates to a specimen for analysis rather than for the roadside breathalyser test, involves obligatory disqualification) or (vi) s 7A(6) (failing to allow a specimen to be subjected to laboratory test where that is an offence involving obligatory disqualification), then

---

1   RTOA s 35D and Criminal Procedure (Scotland) Act 1995 s 248E.
2   RTOA 1988, s 34(1).
3   RTA 1988, s 3A.
4   RTOA 1988, s 34(4), as amended.
5   RTOA 1988, s 34(4), as amended.
6   Criminal Procedure (Scotland) Act 1995, s 248.
7   RTOA 1988, s 34(4A), as introduced by RTA 1991, s 29(4).

the second offence carries a minimum period of disqualification of three years.[1]

It is clear that any of these disqualifying offences, if repeated or committed in addition to either of the other disqualifying offences mentioned, causes the three-year minimum period to be introduced; the rule is not restricted to cases where two similar offences under any one of the nominated sections, occur within the prescribed period. However, it should be noted that neither an offence under s 5(1)(b) of the Road Traffic Act 1988 (being in charge of a vehicle with excess alcohol) nor an offence under s 6(6) (failure to cooperate with a preliminary test) is included in the list of offences which trigger the three-year minimum period. The 10-year period mentioned in s 34(3) runs from the date of conviction of the initiating offence to the date of the commission of the second offence.

Finally, under s 34(4B)[2] where a person convicted of an offence under s 40A of the Road Traffic Act 1988 (using vehicle in dangerous condition etc) has within the three years immediately preceding the commission of the offence been convicted of any such offence, a minimum 12-month ban applies

Where conviction follows an offence involving discretionary disqualification, there is no minimum period; the disqualification is for such period as the court thinks fit.[3]

In cases under the totting-up procedure, the minimum period, in the absence of mitigating circumstances, is six months unless there is one or more periods of disqualification within the preceding three years when the minimum periods of disqualification are one and two years respectively.[4]

If disqualification is suspended by virtue of s 41 pending an appeal in terms of s 38, the period of suspension is not included in calculating the period of disqualification.[5] The only ways in which a period of disqualification can be reduced are by the attendance and completion by the accused driver of an approved course[6] (see also 8.11.3 below), or by a petition for restoration of the licence before the end of the period of disqualification (see 8.11.8 and 8.11.9 below), or by a successful appeal (see 8.11.2 below).

1   RTOA 1988, s 34(3) as amended by RTA 1991, s 29(3) and Police Reform Act 2002, s 56(3)(b).
2   Added by the Road Safety Act 2006 (c 49), s 25(2) (24 September 2007).
3   RTOA1988, s 34(2) as amended by RTA 1991, s 29(2).
4   RTOA 1988, s 35 as amended by RTA 1991, Sch 4 para 95.
5   RTOA 1988, s 43.
6   RTOA 1988, ss 34A, 34B and 34C.

8.5 OBLIGATORY DISQUALIFICATION

8.5.1 General

By virtue of s 34 of and Sch 2, Pt I to the Road Traffic Offenders Act 1988,[1] certain offences carry obligatory disqualification. These are contraventions of s 1 of the Road Traffic Act 1988 (causing death by dangerous driving); s 1A (causing serious injury by dangerous driving); s 2 (dangerous driving); s 2B (causing death by careless or inconsiderate driving); s 3ZB and s 3ZC (causing death by driving unlicensed, or disqualified); s 3ZD (causing serious injury by driving disqualified); s 3A (causing death by careless driving when under the influence of drink or drugs); s 4(1) (driving or attempting to drive while unfit through drink or drugs); s 5(1)(a) (driving or attempting to drive with excess alcohol in breath, blood or urine); ss 5A(1)(a) and (2) (driving or attempting to drive with concentration of specified controlled drug above specified limit); s 7 (failing to provide specimen for analysis or laboratory test where the specimen was required to ascertain the ability to drive or the proportion of alcohol at the time the accused was driving or attempting to drive); s 7A (failing to allow a specimen to be subjected to laboratory test where the specimen was required to ascertain the ability to drive or the proportion of alcohol at the time the accused was driving or attempting to drive); s 12 (motor racing and speed trials on public roads); and s 40A (using vehicle in dangerous condition, obligatory if committed within three years of a like conviction).

Culpable homicide by the driver of a motor vehicle also attracts compulsory disqualification.[2] In all of these instances, disqualification can only be avoided if the offending motorist successfully pleads that there are special reasons for him not being disqualified (see 8.5.2ff below).

Disqualification is also obligatory in certain circumstances where the motorist has been guilty of repeated offences within a three-year period (the 'totting-up' procedure: see 8.8 below). Such disqualification may also be avoided on specific grounds provided by statute (see 8.10.5 below).

8.5.2 Special reasons: s 34(1) Road Traffic Offenders Act 1988: general

A court may only refrain from disqualifying a driver for the minimum period as described at 8.4.5 above for the offences referred to at 8.5.1 above, where it is satisfied that special reasons exist for not imposing

1   As amended by the RTA 1991, Sch 2.
2   RTOA 1988, Sch 2, Pt II, as amended by RTA 1991, Sch 2 para 32.

such disqualification, or for reducing the period of disqualification to one shorter than the minimum period specified above.

Special reasons can be defined as mitigating or extenuating circumstances relating to the offence itself, which do not amount to a defence to the charge which results in the obligatory disqualification, but which may justify the court in imposing either no disqualification at all or alternatively a lesser period than the minimum prescribed. A principal consideration in deciding whether such reasons qualify as being special or not is that they must relate to the nature of the offence itself and cannot under any circumstances refer to the personal circumstances of the driver.[1] A further essential condition is that special reasons must as a prime consideration be governed by the overall interests of public safety.[2] Accordingly, special reasons are a question of law and are not purely a matter of discretion for the court. Inevitably, though, each case will turn on its own particular set of facts, and the degree of danger, for example, may be overestimated. The absence of danger by itself does not support special reasons.[3] A combination of factors, which individually may be inadequate, can be capable of amounting to special reasons.[4]

It is important to remember that in all cases of obligatory disqualification, the number of penalty points to be entered on a licence, if for any reason disqualification is not imposed, is within a range of 3 to 11.[5] Parliament has clearly intended that a driver with any relevant points on his licence who escapes disqualification as a result of establishing special reasons should have a further hurdle to clear if he wishes to retain his licence. Should there be any existing points on the licence, the maximum number of points available if disqualification is not imposed (namely 11) will inevitably bring in the totting-up procedure. It may be thought that if special reasons are established, then a low number of penalty points will be imposed, but this is not necessarily the case. Accordingly, in every case where special reasons are established, the successful pleader will then have to address the question of how many penalty points in the range of 3 to 11 the court should cause to be entered on the accused's licence.

In situations not covered by the cases described below, some guidance may, in certain circumstances, be obtained from the cases relating to reasonable excuse for failing to provide a specimen (see 4.13.7 above)

1   *Adair v Munn* 1940 JC 69, 1940 SLT 414.
2   *Adair v Munn* 1940 JC 69, 1940 SLT414; *Fairlie v Hill* 1944 JC 53, 1944 SLT 224; *Carnegie v Clark* 1947 JC 74, 1947 SLT 218.
3   *Hutcheson v Spiers* 2004 SCCR 405.
4   *Tedford v Dyer* 2006 SCCR 285.
5   RTOA 1988, Sch 2, as amended by RTA 1991, Sch 2.

although it must be remembered that the nature of the substantive defence to s 7(6) of the Road Traffic Act 1988 is essentially different from a special reasons submission, which is a plea in mitigation following a finding of guilt.

Different considerations will apply to cases when the accused has been found guilty of driving offences on the one hand, and of failing to provide a specimen on the other. Most of the examples which follow relate to special reasons in relation to driving offences. In *Scott v Hamilton*[1] the appeal court observed that it was difficult to imagine circumstances which would justify a refusal to furnish a specimen when required to do so.

Cases where the evidence falls short of providing a full defence of coercion or duress may provide grounds for establishing special reasons[2] (see also 8.5.4 below).

Special reasons can always be established by uncorroborated evidence.[3] However, the court may question the absence of apparently available confirmatory evidence. The use of joint minutes in appropriate cases should not be overlooked and indeed it should be remembered that there is a positive duty to seek agreement where possible (Criminal Procedure (Scotland) Act 1995, s 257). Likewise, courts should remember to use the plain English meaning of agreed statements of fact rather than distorting them.[4]

8.5.3 Not special reasons

As indicated above, firstly, considerations other than those which apply to the offence itself cannot under any circumstances constitute special reasons. Secondly, the major consideration to be taken into account is the question of danger or risk or potential danger or risk to public safety. The courts have explored various circumstances and concluded that in the following situations, special reasons were not established.

Triviality of offence

The comparative triviality of an offence cannot justify a court considering that special reasons exist for not imposing disqualification, if the legislation provides for obligatory disqualification. For example, if a particular driver has exceeded the statutory alcohol limits in terms of s 5(1)(a) of

---

1   *Scott v Hamilton* 1988 SCCR 262.
2   Eg *McLeod v McDougall* 1989 SLT 151, 1988 SCCR 519.
3   *Watson v Adam* 1996 JC 104, 1996 SLT 459, 1996 SCCR 382.
4   *Hunter v PF Kilmarnock* [2012] HCJAC 42 (Decision of 22 March 2012).

the Road Traffic Act 1988 by a small margin, this cannot justify a claim that special reasons exist for imposing anything less than the statutory minimum period of disqualification.[1]

Personal hardship

As indicated above, special reasons must relate to the quality and nature of the offence and not the circumstances of the offender. Thus in cases involving obligatory disqualification, even exceptional hardship will not justify the court in mitigating or refraining from disqualification. In *Carnegie v Clark*,[2] it was held that where disqualification might result in a medical student being expelled from university, this did not entitle the court not to disqualify the driver.

In *Adair v Munn*[3] and *Muir v McPherson*,[4] it was made clear that loss of livelihood and consequent hardship following therefrom to the driver's family could not amount to special reasons.

Even a disabled driver who requires his licence to remain mobile cannot argue that his condition amounts to special reasons for not disqualifying,[5] although in appropriate cases selection of a reduced disqualification may reflect such background.[6]

Previous character

It has long been established that the fact that a driver has a clean driving record for a long number of years cannot amount to special reasons for not endorsing the licence.[7]

Ability of driver to meet consequences

In a case where the accused was convicted of driving without insurance, the fact that he was financially able to meet any claims made against him arising out of his driving did not justify the court in finding special reasons for not disqualifying.[8]

---

1   *Herron v Sharif* 1974 SLT (Notes) 63.
2   *Carnegie v Clark* 1947 JC 74, 1947 SLT 218.
3   *Adair v Munn* 1940 JC 69, 1940 SLT 414.
4   *Muir v McPherson* 1953 SLT 307.
5   *Copeland v Pollock* 1976 CO Circulars 1428.
6   *Turner v PF Portree* XJ1148/12 (Decision of 21 February 2013). Disqualification of 60 days reduced to 29 days since 30 days or over led to loss of mobility car for five years.
7   *Muir v Sutherland* 1940 JC 66, 1940 SLT 403.
8   *Robertson v McGinn* 1955 JC 57.

Consequences to public interest

The fact that a period of disqualification may have particularly serious consequences for the public interest where the driver has significant public duties to perform, which he cannot do without his licence, again does not amount in normal circumstances to special reasons for refraining from disqualification. In *Murray v Macmillan*,[1] a driver was not disqualified in circumstances which related to his war time duties; but in the subsequent cases of *Fairlie v Hill*,[2] *McFadyean v Burton*[3] and *Robertson v McGinn*,[4] it was made very clear that *Murray* was an exceptional case and not to be followed.

Special reasons unrelated to the offence

In *MacDonald v MacKenzie*,[5] a motorist agreed to give a blood sample from his arm; this was found to be impossible and he declined to give any further samples. The court held that in these circumstances, special reasons did not exist.

In *Smith v Peaston*[6] a vehicle was stopped by police officers purportedly acting under the equivalent of s 163 of the Road Traffic Act 1988. On the subsequent conviction of the driver for a drink-driving offence it was held that an allegation that the police officers had no justification for exercising these powers, even if correct, would not amount to special reasons for not imposing disqualification.

In cases under s 7(6) of the Road Traffic Act 1988 (refusal to provide specimen for analysis), it is well recognised that the special reasons must relate to the refusal, and not to other circumstances which might amount to special reasons in another situation. In *Smith v Nixon*[7] an accused was driving in an emergency to join his mountain rescue team which had been called out in circumstances where the lives of others might be in danger. While it is possible in certain circumstances that such a consideration might amount to special reasons for not disqualifying if the accused had been convicted of a drink-driving offence, it was held that special reasons had not been established in respect of the refusal

1   *Murray v Macmillan* 1942 JC 10.
2   *Fairlie v Hill* 1944 JC 53, 1944 SLT 224.
3   *McFadyean v Burton* 1954 JC 18, 1953 SLT 301.
4   *Robertson v McGinn* 1955 JC 57
5   *MacDonald v MacKenzie* 1975 SLT 190.
6   *Smith v Peaston* 1977 JC 81.
7   *Smith v Nixon* 1985 SLT 192, 1984 SCCR 373.

to provide a specimen. In *McNicol v Peters*[1] it was decided that the fact that the driver had not been drinking did not justify his refusal to give a specimen.

In *Tudhope v O'Kane*[2] a refusal to provide a specimen because the accused was a teetotaller was held, exceptionally, to amount to special reasons. However, it is not a special reason where the accused maintains that he had only taken alcohol after driving had ceased.[3]

Shortness of distance

The fact that a motorist has embarked on only a short journey will not in normal circumstances amount to special reasons.[4] However, the position is not entirely straightforward. In *Mackay v MacPhail*,[5] a driver who had been drinking moved his car a short distance in a car park and came into minor collision with another vehicle; in these circumstances it was held on appeal that special reasons did not exist. On the other hand, where a car was moved only a short distance on the public road, special reasons were held to have been established without apparent reference to the above authorities.[6] In view of the fact that one of the principal considerations is the interest of public safety (see 8.5.4 below,) the fact that a minimal distance was driven may be a relevant consideration in certain circumstances, a view supported in *Hutcheson v Spiers*[7] albeit shortness of distance was viewed as unlikely to be sufficient in itself. In England, the fact that the journey undertaken is of very short duration is a matter which may be taken into account (see 8.5.4 below).

Impairment of ability to drive

A claim, even if established in evidence, that the accused driver's ability to drive was not impaired, for example in terms of s 4(1) of the Road Traffic Act 1988, will not, it is submitted, establish that there are special reasons for not disqualifying in a charge under s 5(1)(a). Nor will the erroneous belief by the accused that he had waited a sufficient time to

---

1   *McNicol v Peters* 1969 SLT 261.
2   *Tudhope v O'Kane* 1986 SCCR 538.
3   *Emms v Lockhart* 1988 SLT 222, 1987 SCCR 622.
4   *Skeen v Irvine* 1980 SCCR Supp 259; *Lamb v Heywood* 1988 SLT 728, 1988 SCCR 42.
5   *Mackay v MacPhail 1989* SCCR 622.
6   *Lowe v Mulligan* 1991 SCCR 551.
7   *Hutcheson v Spiers* 2004 SCCR 405.

allow the level of alcohol in his system to fall below the permitted level.[1] The fact that an alcohol reading is fractionally above the limit will not of itself amount to special reasons, but has been taken account of as part of a number of factors in cumulo justifying special reasons.[2]

Medical condition

In *Scott v Hamilton*[3] a lady motorist pled guilty to failing to provide a specimen for analysis, but claimed that she had been suffering from premenstrual tension and was not amenable to reason. It was held that this was not a special reason for not disqualifying.

8.5.4 Circumstances which may justify special reasons

As indicated above, the case of *Adair v Munn*[4] is authority for the view that special reasons are a question of law and not of discretion, and that prime consideration must be given to the interest of public safety. Further, special reasons must relate to the offence, rather than to the accused. If special reasons are established, the court has the discretion to reduce the normal obligatory period of disqualification, or to refrain from imposing disqualification completely. The onus is generally on the accused to establish special reasons on the balance of probabilities.[5] The courts have held that special reasons may exist in the following circumstances.

Medical emergency

Where a driver is compelled to drive by an unforeseen medical emergency and circumstances where he assured he would not have otherwise driven, special reasons may exist.[6] However, failure to use another reasonably available method of undertaking the journey will exclude the establishment of special reasons.[7] Cases will inevitably be fact specific and a number of factors may come into play which in combination amount to special reasons.[8]

---

1   *Normand v Cameron* 1992 SCCR 390.
2   *Tedford v Dyer* 2006 SCCR 285
3   *Scott v Hamilton* 1988 SCCR 262.
4   *Adair v Munn* 1940 JC 69, 1940 SLT 414.
5   *Skinner v Ayton* 1977 SLT (Sh Ct) 48.
6   *Copeland v Sweeney* 1977 SLT (Sh Ct) 28; *Graham v Annan* 1980 SLT 28; *Watson v Hamilton* 1988 SLT 316, 1988 SCCR 13.
7   *Copeland v Sweeney* 1977 SLT (Sh Ct) 28.
8   *Tedford v Dyer* 2006 SCCR 285.

Other emergencies

In *Ortewell v Allan*[1] a disqualified driver pushed a broken-down car off a busy main road and then got into the driving seat and was pushed or free-wheeled into a car park where it collided with another vehicle. In these circumstances, the appeal court held that there were grounds for restricting the period of disqualification. Where the accused extricated a car from a snow drift when the driver was unable to do so, and then reversed some distance down the road to allow other cars to get by, it was held that the accused need not be disqualified.[2] Necessity or duress may constitute a defence to any driving offence (see 2.5 above). However, where the circumstances do not justify such a defence, they may nonetheless form the basis of a special reasons submission.

Similarly, the drivers of emergency service vehicles are under the same duties of care on the road as other drivers apart from the observance of speed limits,[3] but the situation may indicate that special reasons exist. *Watt v Murphy*[4] is just such an example where a police officer, responding to a distress call, drove through a red light at 10 mph and was involved in a collision. She had activated the blue light but not, inadvertently, the vehicle's siren, and had tendered a plea to dangerous driving. The Sheriff Appeal Court quashed the mandatory 12-month disqualification, noting that the fact the officer was not an accredited emergency driver was not of significance, that the extenuating circumstances were directly related to the offence, and the sentencing Sheriff's comment 'that it was not inexpedient to inflict punishment' on the accused was not 'a useful approach to the issue' of special reasons. The case contains a useful summary of relevant authorities.

In *Connorton v Annan*[5] a driver claimed he was driving under duress. The appeal court rejected this but considered that the circumstances justified reducing a discretionary period of disqualification. See also *Morrison v Valentine*[6] and *McLeod v McDougall.*[7]

A combination of factors, including emergency, may amount to special reasons. In *Ferguson v McPherson*[8] the appellant was found to be

---

1   *Ortewell v Allan* 1984 SCCR 208.
2   *Riddell v MacNeill* 1983 SCCR 26.
3   RTRA 1984, s 87.
4   *Watt v Murphy* 2016 SCCR 314, 2016 SLT (Sh Ct) 247.
5   *Connorton v Annan* 1981 SCCR 307.
6   *Morrison v Valentine* 1991 SLT 413, 1990 SCCR 692.
7   *McLeod v McDougall* 1989 SLT 151, 1988 SCCR 519.
8   2011 SCCR 60.

reasonably fearful in circumstances where she had been thrown out of her brother's house wearing only nightclothes, it was snowing, and she drove over the limit only 25m to a different street, before phoning for assistance.

Laced drinks

Where a driver consumes alcohol unknown to himself because his drink has been interfered with, by the addition of an alcoholic beverage by a third party, special reasons for not disqualifying may exist. However, if the accused shows that his drinks were interfered with without his knowledge in such a way that he totally lost control of his actions he may have a complete substantive defence to any drink-driving charge[1] (see 2.5 above). If for any reason this defence cannot be made out (where, for example, there is insufficient evidence as to the nature of the substance introduced into the drink consumed by the accused, or of its effect) it may still be possible to argue after conviction that special reasons exist for not disqualifying. In *Skinner v Ayton*[2] it was held that special reasons could only be found in these circumstances if the accused establishes in evidence that his drink was in fact laced, that he did not know or have reasonable cause to suspect that this had happened, and that the alcohol level in the accused's blood would not have exceeded the legal limit but for the lacing of the drink. In *Watson v Adam*[3] a motorist drove in circumstances where he realised that he had taken alcoholic instead of non-alcoholic liquor, but wrongly believed he was fit to drive. It was held that this did not amount to special reasons. It is submitted that in presenting an argument that special reasons exist in these circumstances, the same overall approach should be taken as in the case of post-accident drinking defences (see 3.9 and 3.17.1 above). In particular, it is submitted that in establishing that the alcohol level in the accused's blood would not have exceeded the legal limit but for the fact that further alcohol had been introduced unknown to him into his system, evidence (by an analyst or suitably qualified doctor) relating to the effect that such addition of alcohol would have had on his system should normally be adduced where possible. In *McLeod v Napier*[4] the appeal court held that there should be evidence as to the effect of the particular substance introduced into the drink on the human metabolism.

Whether the accused should plead not guilty or rely on special reason submissions in these circumstances is a matter of judgment, although

1   *Ross v HM Advocate* 1991 SLT 546, 1991 SCCR 823.
2   *Skinner v Ayton* 1977 SLT (Sh Ct) 48.
3   *Watson v Adam* 1996 JC 104, 1996 SLT 459, 1996 SCR 382.
4   *McLeod v Napier* 1993 SCCR 303.

there is nothing to stop an accused pleading not guilty, and if that is not successful, going on to argue for special reasons.

Reference should also be made to Appendix E.

Driving when instructed by police

In *Farrell v Moir*[1] a driver was ordered to drive his vehicle by a police officer in order that it should cease being an obstruction to other traffic. In these circumstances, because it was demonstrated that the driver would not otherwise have been driving but for the direction of the police officer, it was held that there were special reasons for not imposing a period of disqualification. A mere request, as opposed to an instruction, is unlikely to be sufficient.[2]

Reasons unconnected with offence

Where a driver refused to give a specimen for analysis on the ground that he was a teetotaller, this was held to amount to a special reason.[3] This is perhaps a somewhat exceptional case.

Public interest

As indicated earlier, in *Murray v McMillan*,[4] it was held that where very special and significant damage might be caused to the public interest by the disqualification of an offender (as in the case of a doctor who had to carry out essential tasks during the time of war), special reasons for not disqualifying were established. However, it has been repeatedly said in other cases[5] that such a situation was entirely remarkable and it is extremely unlikely that it would be followed in any circumstances.

General directions in English cases

In England, the Court of Appeal in the case of *Chatters v Burke*[6] laid down a number of considerations which should be looked at in coming to the conclusion that special reasons exist. These matters are as follows: firstly, how far the vehicle was driven; secondly, in what manner it was driven;

---

1   *Farrell v Moir* 1974 SLT (Sh Ct) 89.
2   *Hutcheson v Spiers* 2004 SCCR 405.
3   *Tudhope v O'Kane* 1986 SCCR 538.
4   *Murray v McMillan* 1942 JC 10.
5   Eg in *Fairlie v Hill* 1944 JC 53, 1944 SLT 224; *McFadyean v Burton* 1954 JC 18, 1953 SLT 301; *Robertson v McGinn* 1955 JC 57.
6   *Chatters v Burke* [1986] RTR 396, DC.

thirdly, the state of the vehicle; fourthly, whether it was the intention of the driver to go further; fifthly, an assessment of the conditions of the road and traffic travelling at the time; sixthly whether there was a possibility of danger of the driver coming into contact with other road users or pedestrians; and finally, the reasons for the driving of the vehicle. The appeal court made it clear that the sixth of these considerations was by far the most important.

8.6 PROCEDURE IN SPECIAL REASON SUBMISSIONS

8.6.1 General

It is for the accused to raise the question of special reasons at the time of sentence. The court is not entitled to conclude that special reasons exist for not imposing disqualification from the submissions made to him without the matter having been specifically argued by the accused. Reference should be made to *McLeod v Scoular*,[1] *Tudhope v Birbeck*[2] and *McNab v Feeney*.[3] The facts relied on may have become sufficiently clear from the evidence if the matter has gone to trial.

If, however, the accused pleads guilty the appropriate procedure is for the accused or his solicitor to indicate, at the time of pleading guilty, that the plea is qualified by the submission that special reasons exist for not imposing disqualification. It is considered good practice for the defence agent to indicate this intention in advance of the date of sentence to the procurator fiscal in order to allow the fiscal suitable opportunity for considering the nature of the special reasons. If, on hearing the nature of the special reasons at the time of sentence, the procurator fiscal requires further time to examine the reasons so adduced, the court will normally grant a continuation for that purpose. It should be emphasised that if a form of motion is not made at the time of sentence to the effect that special reasons exist for not disqualifying, the accused will not be permitted to raise the question of special reasons thereafter unless the circumstances are exceptional.[4]

It is proper practice for evidence to be led in support of the special reasons that are to be established rather than simply to rely on *ex parte* statements by the accused's solicitor. However, it is open for the prosecutor

---

1   *McLeod v Scoular* 1974 JC 28, 1974 SLT (Notes) 44.
2   *Tudhope v Birbeck* 1979 SLT (Notes) 47.
3   *McNab v Feeney* 1980 SLT (Notes) 52.
4   *Hynd v Clark* 1954 SLT 85, distinguishing *Trotter v Burnett* 1947 JC 151.

to accept *ex parte* statements as correct in appropriate circumstances.[1] The use of a joint minute agreeing evidence is to be commended where possible.[2]

If the Crown does not accept what is said by the accused, then the onus of proof is on the accused and the standard of proof that must be reached is the balance of probabilities.[3]

In particular, in *McLeod v Scoular*,[4] the High Court laid down the rules relating to the onus and standard of proof and the procedure to be followed in cases where special reasons are argued. Firstly, the prosecutor may agree that what is said by the accused is true, in which case the court may deal with the submissions in the absence of evidence. It is, of course, always open to the court to continue the case for further information if required. Secondly, if the accused has been found guilty following a trial, the court may be satisfied from the evidence heard as to whether special reasons have been established or not without further inquiry. Thirdly, where the Crown disputes the statement by the defence, the court should order a further hearing to allow the defence to lead evidence in support of its case and the opportunity of leading evidence to contradict the defence case. This procedure should also be adopted in cases where the procurator fiscal can neither admit nor deny what is said by the accused. The proper procedure in all circumstances where special reasons are to be put forward is that the accused or his solicitor should at the time of tendering the plea of guilty when sentence is to be imposed intimate that special reasons are to be advanced and give a general outline of the facts on which these reasons are to be based. Thereafter, the procurator fiscal should be asked whether he is in a position to accept what is said or whether he either denies the accused's version of events or is in a position neither to confirm nor deny that version. If the procurator fiscal is in a position to confirm the submissions made by the defence, the matter can then be dealt with. However, in all other circumstances, it is submitted that the proper course is to defer sentence for the purpose of fixing a hearing on the special reasons.

1   *McLeod v Scoular* 1974 JC 28, 1974 SLT (Notes) 74 *McLeod v Scoular* 1974 JC 28, 1974 SLT (Notes) 74.
2   See 8.5 2 above under reference to *Hunter v PF Kilmarnock* [2012] HCJAC 42.
3   *Farrell v Moir* 1974 SLT (Sh Ct) 89; *Skinner v Ayton* 1977 SLT (Sh Ct) 48; see also *Irvine v Pollock* 1952 JC 51, 1952 SLT 185 and *MacFadyean v Burton* 1954 JC 18, 1953 SLT 301; *Farrell v Moir* 1974 SLT (Sh Ct) 89; *Skinner v Ayton* 1977 SLT (Sh Ct) 48; see also *Irvine v Pollock* 1952 JC 51, 1952 SLT 185 and *MacFadyean v Burton* 1954 JC 18, 1953 SLT 301.
4   *McLeod v Scoular* 1974 JC 28, 1974 SLT (Notes) 44.

If the accused does not appear personally and is not represented by a solicitor, but pleads guilty by letter, the responsibility still remains on the accused to raise the question of special reasons. If he does not do so in the course of his letter, then the mandatory period of disqualification or endorsement, as appropriate, must be imposed. However, the appeal court has made it clear that where an accused pleads guilty by letter, the court should normally continue the matter to allow for the personal appearance of the accused. If therefore the accused states in his letter that special reasons do or might exist for not imposing disqualification, then in general terms the same procedure should be followed as in the preceding paragraph. In other words, if the procurator fiscal is in a position to agree expressly with what is said in the letter for the purposes of considering special reasons, it may be possible for the court to dispose of the case on that basis. However, in all other circumstances, a continuation should be granted in order to allow a hearing to be fixed on the question of special reasons and the accused given an opportunity to attend. Further details about the procedure to be adopted in this situation were given in the case of *Keane v Perrie*.[1]

Where an accused is abroad, and cannot attend court, his case may be dealt with in his absence, even if obligatory disqualification is involved.[2]

The appeal court is normally reluctant to listen to reasons not raised in the lower court.[3]

8.7 DISCRETIONARY DISQUALIFICATION: STATUTORY OFFENCES

Discretionary disqualification is available in a significant number of offences, which are detailed in the tables forming Pts I and II of Sch 2 to the Road Traffic Offenders Act 1988.[4] Discretionary disqualification is always a matter for the court.[5] The court must take into account all facts and circumstances which are relevant in reaching its decision. However, the accused should always be given an opportunity of leading before the

---

1   *Keane v Perrie* 1983 SLT 63, 1982 SCCR 377.
2   *Imrie v McGlennan* 1990 SCCR 218.
3   *Stewart v Carnegie* 1988 SCCR 431.
4   As amended by the RTA 1991, Sch 2.
5   RTOA 1988, s 34(2), as amended by RTA 1991, s 29(2).

court any reasons why he should not be disqualified in such cases.[1] The reason for disqualifying must properly relate to the offence.[2]

See also 8.11.5–8.11.8 below.

8.8 DISQUALIFICATION FOR REPEATED OFFENCES

In addition to offences which carry obligatory or discretionary disqualification, disqualification will also follow in certain circumstances where a driver has been guilty of repeated offences within a three-year period, by virtue of s 35 of the Road Traffic Offenders Act 1988. Generally, in addition to other penalties, a number of offences under the legislation carry penalty points which on conviction are endorsed on the licence or driving record by the court or the DVLA. In the event of a motorist acquiring 12 or more such points within a three-year period, the court must order disqualification for specified minimum periods, unless there are grounds for not doing so. The three-year period is computed *de die in diem* and the day of the later or last offence is not included in the reckoning; so that an offence committed on 25 July 2013 falls one day outwith the three-year period following an offence committed on 25 July 2010.[3]

In respect of some offences, a set number of penalty points must be endorsed on the driver's licence; in respect of others, the court must select a number of penalty points from a range provided. The offences to which penalty points relate are found in the Road Traffic Regulation Act 1984 and the Road Traffic Act 1988. The penalty points themselves are detailed against the appropriate offences in Sch 2, Pts I and II of the Road Traffic Offenders Act 1988. However, disqualification under the totting-up procedure cannot be imposed consecutively on other periods of disqualification given at the same time.[4]

The general purpose of what has become known as the totting-up procedure is to penalise, by disqualification, drivers who repeatedly commit relatively minor offences, as opposed to the imposition of obligatory disqualification for the more serious offences. However, the use of penalty points to accelerate the penalty of disqualification has been employed in two ways by the Road Traffic Act 1991. Firstly, as

---

1   *MacDonald v McGillivray* 1986 SCCR 28; but see also *Imrie v McGlennan* 1990 SCCR 218.
2   *Henderson v McNaughtan* 1992 SCCR 767. *Henderson v McNaughtan* 1992 SCCR 767.
3   *Keenan v Carmichael* 1992 SLT 814, 1991 SCCR 680.
4   *Middleton v Tudhope* 1986 JC 101, 1986 SCCR 241.

indicated at 8.5.2 above, the introduction of a range of penalty points of between 3 and 11 in all cases of obligatory disqualification, where such disqualification is in the event not imposed (as, for example, where special reasons are established), is intended to restrict the opportunity for the motorist to escape disqualification, by making totting-up more readily available. Secondly, in terms of the amendments to the totting-up legislation introduced by the Road Traffic Act 1991, the court may in certain circumstances aggregate penalty points where more than one offence has been committed on the same occasion (see 8.10.2 below).

8.9 NOTICE OF PENALTIES

Following the passing of the Criminal Procedure (Scotland) Act 1995 the Crown no longer has to serve a notice of penalties on the accused.

8.10 TOTTING-UP AND PENALTY POINTS: STATUTORY PROVISIONS

8.10.1 General operation

For the practitioner, the principal subsections of s 28 of the Road Traffic Offenders Act 1988[1] are as follows:

'(1) Where a person is convicted of an offence involving obligatory endorsement, then, subject to the following provisions of this section, the number of penalty points to be attributed to the offence is –

(a)   the number shown in relation to the offence in the last column of Part I or Part II of Schedule 2 to this Act, or

(b)   where a range of numbers is shown, a number within that range.

(2) Where a person is convicted of an offence committed by aiding, abetting, counselling or procuring, or inciting to the commission of, an offence involving obligatory disqualification, then, subject to the following provisions of this section, the number of penalty points to be attributed to the offence is ten.

    …

(4) Where a person is convicted (whether on the same occasion or not) of two or more offences committed on the same occasion and involving obligatory endorsement, the total number of penalty points to be attributed to them is the number or highest number that would be attributed on

---

1   As amended by the RTA 1991, s 27.

a conviction of one of them (so that if the convictions are on different occasions the number of penalty points to be attributed to the offences on the later occasion or occasions shall be restricted accordingly).

(5) In a case where (apart from this subsection) subsection (4) above would apply to two or more offences, the court may if it thinks fit determine that that subsection shall not apply to the offences (or, where three or more offences are concerned, to any one or more of them).

(6) Where a court makes a determination it shall state its reasons in open court and, if it is a magistrates' court, or in Scotland a court of summary jurisdiction, shall cause them to be entered in the register (in Scotland, record) of its proceedings.'

Where Sch 2 to the Road Traffic Offenders Act 1988[1] provides a fixed number of penalty points, the court has no option on conviction but to impose that number of points on the licence. Where a range of penalty points is available, the procedure that the court must adopt is to consider what number of points within the specified range is appropriate to the particular offence, having regard to all the circumstances of the offence and the offender.[2]

In normal circumstances, in the event of the accused person being convicted of two or more offences which carry penalty points and which were committed on the same occasion, the proper procedure for the court is to consider the appropriate number of points to be imposed in respect of each offence, and order that the higher or highest of these numbers is to be the number of penalty points to be endorsed on the licence. Subsection (4) does not require that the court must impose the highest possible number of points available for any of the relevant charges. For example, an accused may face a charge under s 3 of the Road Traffic Act 1988 (careless driving) which carries 3 to 9 points, and a further charge under s 143 (driving without insurance) which carries 6 to 8 points. If the court considers that the appropriate number of points for the careless driving charge is 7, and for the insurance charge is 6, then 7 penalty points will be endorsed on the careless driving charge. If the court considers that the careless driving charge should carry 6 points, and the insurance charge 8, then the latter number of points will be endorsed against the insurance offence.

Subsection (4) applies to offences committed 'on the same occasion'. What is meant by this phrase is that the offences must be committed during the same incident of driving, or during a series of closely related

---

1   As amended by Road Safety Act 2006 (c 49) from April 2009.
2   *Briggs v Guild* 1987 SCCR 141.

incidents, and further that the offences themselves must be related. Thus, illegal parking and a subsequent refusal to take a breath test were held in the circumstances to be unrelated and thus not committed on the same occasion and two sets of penalties were imposed.[1]

Maclean v Murphy[2] considered the matter in relation to a careless driving and an associated failure to report charge. The court, having considered earlier cases, including the English case of *Johnson v Finbow*,[3] disagreed with the Sheriff's assessment and found that that the offences did arise on the same occasion, but chose not to aggregate (see 8.10.2 below). It was concluded however, 'that whether or not two or more offences are committed on the same occasion, or arise out of precisely the same incident, will be a question of fact or degree'.[4]

Whether *Maclean v Murphy* was correctly decided was to have been argued in another appeal in 2017. Written submissions were requested by the sift judges on the point, but the appeal, which focused on consecutive sentences of imprisonment for failing to stop and failing to report, was abandoned.

What is not yet clear is whether a series of offences committed over an extended period of driving, such as overtaking a number of vehicles on the inside on a motorway (which is normally regarded as careless driving) would result in a number of charges which were committed 'on the same occasion'.

It will also be noted that, so long as the offences charged were committed on the same occasion, the rule contained in sub-s (4) applies even when the charges are split up and brought against the accused on different occasions. It would seem that if a charge brought on a later occasion has a higher pointage, the court may have to instruct that the higher points are endorsed on the licence, and the lesser ones removed. It is not thought that this should prove to be a course to which the DVLA would object. The situation is not likely to arise where a motorist is charged with two offences, one of which is taken under the fixed penalty procedure, and one which is prosecuted (under a different time scale) by summary complaint.[5]

---

1   *Cameron v Brown* 1997 SLT 914, 1996 SCCR 675; see also *Robertson v McNaughtan* 1993 SLT 1143, 1993 SCCR 526; *McDonald v Hingston* 1994 SCCR 268; and *McKeever v Walkinshaw* 1996 SCCR 189.
2   2015 SCCR 369.
3   [1983] 1 WLR 879, (1983) 5 Cr App R (S) 95, [1983] RTR 356.
4   Supra, at para [21].
5   See *Green v O'Donnell* 1997 SCCR 315, overturning *Reith v Thomson* 1994 SCCR 577.

8.10.2 Aggregation

Section 28(5) of the Road Traffic Offenders Act 1988, introduced by s 27 of the Road Traffic Act 1991, however, provides an important exception to the foregoing general rule. In effect, s 28(5) allows a court, if it sees fit, not to bind itself to the restrictions imposed by s 28(4). The apparent purpose of s 28(5) is to let the court choose, where it is dealing with two or more offences, to impose penalty points on more than one, or indeed all, of such offences, and thus in effect aggregate points on all the charges, so that totting-up disqualification may become instantly available. It would seem from the way in which s 28(4) and (5) is framed that aggregation of penalty points is meant to be an exceptional procedure, but the Act does not specifically say so, nor does it give any indication of the circumstances under which aggregation should be used.

It is submitted that the court should only use the powers of aggregation in exceptional circumstances. This view was endorsed in the unreported case of *Dawson v PF Perth* (Decision of the Court of Appeal, dated 7 April 2004). For example, it would be wrong to aggregate penalty points to punish what the court considered to be a particularly serious offence of its sort. A motorist charged with no insurance and two unrelated construction and use offences may have caused considerable damage and loss; however, as the other offences are unconnected, the legislation appears not to contemplate that the serious nature of the insurance charge should justify aggregating its penalty points with those of the other offences to achieve instant disqualification. It appears that aggregation should only occur when the particular combination of offences demonstrates, by virtue of that combination alone, that a serious danger to road safety is thereby created. Should the court choose to make such a determination in terms of s 28(5), the reasons must be stated in open court and marked on the complaint.[1]

Cases where aggregation has been considered are *Robertson v McNaughtan*[2] and *McDonald v Hingston*.[3] In *Maclean v Murphy*,[4] which considered careless driving and failure to report, the view was expressed that it might be appropriate to aggregate where a decision not to report was taken to avoid detection of other offences.

1   RTOA 1988, s 28(6).
2   *Robertson v McNaughtan* 1993 SLT 1143, 1993 SCCR 526.
3   *McDonald v Hingston* 1994 SCCR 268.
4   2015 SCCR 369

8.10.3 Statutory provisions (s 29): penalty points to be taken into account

Section 29 of the Road Traffic Offenders Act 1988[1] provides:

'(1) Where a person is convicted of an offence involving obligatory endorsement, the penalty points to be taken into account on that occasion are (subject to subsection (2) below) –

(a)   any that are to be attributed to the offence or offences of which he is convicted, disregarding any offence in respect of which an order under section 34 of this Act is made, and

(b)   any that were on a previous occasion ordered to be endorsed on his driving record, unless the offender has since that occasion and before the conviction been disqualified under section 35 of this Act.

(2) If any of the offences was committed more than three years before another, the penalty points in respect of that offence shall not be added to those in respect of the other.

The critical starting date in the calculation of the number of penalty points on a licence is the date of the commission of the offences, rather than the date of the conviction. Any penalty points imposed on a licence outwith the three-year period from the date of commission of the starting offence to the date of commission (not the date of conviction) of the offence or offences currently under consideration fall to be disregarded.

However, this means that any penalty points endorsed on a licence for a conviction which predates the conviction now being considered, but where that offence postdates the date of the commission of the offence now under consideration, have also to be taken into account if they fall within the three-year period.

In other words, penalty points for any offences committed after, but dealt with before, the current offence are included in the calculation. The section also makes it clear that any period of disqualification imposed under s 34 of the Act (for offences involving obligatory or discretionary disqualification), does not have the effect of cancelling out all penalty points within the three-year period prior to the disqualification. This amended provision reverses the previous position in respect of any order of obligatory or discretionary disqualification. However, an order of totting-up disqualification continues to have the effect of wiping out previous penalty points.

The three-year period is computed *de die in diem* and the day of the later or last offence is not included in the reckoning.[2]

---

1   As amended by RTA 1991, s 28 and Road Safety Act 2006 (c 49), Sch 2 para 4.
2   *Keenan v Carmichael* 1992 SLT 814, 1991 SCCR 680.

8.10.4 Statutory provisions: production of licence

In terms of s 27 of the Road Traffic Offenders Act 1988, where a person who is the holder of a licence is convicted of an offence involving obligatory or discretionary disqualification the court must require the licence to be produced to it before it can make any order involving such endorsement. Conversely, s 7 of the Road Traffic Offenders Act 1988 imposes a duty on every accused prosecuted for an offence involving obligatory disqualification to produce his licence for the hearing.

Section 31 then provides:

'(1) Where a person is convicted of an offence involving obligatory or discretionary disqualification and his licence is produced to the court –

(a)   any existing endorsement on his driving record is prima facie evidence of the matters endorsed, and

(b)   the court may, in determining what order to make in pursuance of the conviction, take those matters into consideration.

(2) This section has effect notwithstanding anything in s 166 (1) to (6) of the Criminal Procedure (Scotland) Act 1995 (requirements as to notices of penalties and previous convictions).'

This section is self-explanatory[1] but must be read along with the terms of s 29, which for totting-up purposes, restricts consideration of such previous endorsements to the preceding three years.

Where the licence is not available for production to the court (for whatever reason, for example where it is lost or destroyed, has been sent to the DVLA for alteration, or there is no licence to produce)[2] then it is open to the court to consider a DVLA print-out, if the accused agrees that the particulars therein are accurate and relate to himself.[3]

In terms of s 201 of the Criminal Procedure (Scotland) Act 1995 a deferment of sentence or *inter alia* the production of a DVLA print-out cannot, subject to s 21(9) of the Criminal Justice (Scotland) Act 2003 (asp 7), exceed four weeks, or eight weeks on cause shown.[4]

---

1   Taking account of relevant endorsations has been confirmed in *Westwater v Nicholson* 1975 SLT 1018 and *Urquhart v Lees* 2000 SLT 1109.
2   *Hamilton v Ruxton* 2001 SCCR 1.
3   See also *McCallum v Scott* 1987 SLT 491.
4   *Wilson v Donald* 1993 SLT 31, *Holburn v Lees* 1993 SCCR 426; *Burns v Wilson* 1993 SCCR 418; *McCulloch v Scott* 1993 SLT 901; *Douglas v Jamieson* 1993 SLT 816; and *Douglas v Peddie* 1993 SCCR 717, which are all cases under the previous statutory provisions.

The DVLA code used in noting convictions on licences is given in Appendix B.

8.10.5 Statutory provisions (s 35): mitigating circumstances

Section 35 of the Road Traffic Offenders Act 1988[1] provides:

'(1) Where –

(a)   a person is convicted of an offence to which this subsection applies, and

(b)   the penalty points to be taken into account on that occasion number twelve or more,

the court must order him to be disqualified for not less than the minimum period unless the court is satisfied, having regard to all the circumstances, that there are grounds for mitigating the normal consequences of the conviction and thinks fit to order him to be disqualified for a shorter period or not to order him to be disqualified.

(1A) Subsection (1) above applies to –

(a)   any offence involving discretionary disqualification and obligatory endorsement, and

(b)   an offence involving obligatory disqualification in respect of which no order is made under s 34 of this Act.

(2) The minimum period referred to in subsection (1) above is –

(a)   six months if no previous disqualification imposed on the offender is to be taken into account, and

(b)   one year if one, and two years if more than one, such disqualification is to be taken into account;

and a previous disqualification imposed on an offender is to be taken into account if it was for a fixed period of 56 days or more and was imposed within the three years immediately preceding the commission of the latest offence in respect of which penalty points are taken into account under s 29 of this Act.

(3) Where an offender is convicted on the same occasion of more than one offence to which subsection (1) above applies –

(a)   not more than one disqualification shall be imposed on him under subsection (1) above,

(b)   in determining the period of the disqualification the court must take into account all the offences, and

1   As amended by RTA 1991, Sch 4 para 95.

(c)   for the purposes of any appeal any disqualification imposed under subsection (1) above shall be treated as an order made on the conviction of each of the offences.

(4) No account is to be taken under subsection (1) above of any of the following circumstances –

(a)   any circumstances that are alleged to make the offence or any of the offences not a serious one,

(b)   hardship, other than exceptional hardship, or

(c)   any circumstances which, within the three years immediately preceding the conviction, have been taken into account under that subsection in ordering the offender to be disqualified for a shorter period or not ordering him to be disqualified.

(5) References in this section to disqualification do not include a disqualification imposed under section 26 of this Act or section 147 of the Powers of Criminal Courts Act 2000 or sections 223A or 436A of the Criminal Procedure (Scotland) Act 1975 (offences committed by using vehicles) or a disqualification imposed in respect of an offence of stealing a motor vehicle, an offence under sections 12 or 25 of the Theft Act 1968, an offence under section 178 of the Road Traffic Act 1988, or an attempt to commit such an offence.

(5A) The preceding provisions of this section shall apply in relation to a conviction of an offence committed by aiding, abetting, counselling, procuring or inciting to the commission of an offence involving obligatory disqualification as if the offence were an offence involving discretionary disqualification.

(6) In relation to Scotland, references in this section to the court include the justice of the peace court.[1]

(7) This section is subject to section 48 of this Act.'

It is clear from the terms of s 35(1) that it does not matter on how many occasions during the three-year period that endorsement has taken place. Once 12 penalty points have been accumulated on a driver's licence within that period, then the totting-up procedure automatically comes into effect. It is therefore possible that the procedure will operate following a second endorsement. Immediately 12 points are accumulated on a licence then the court has no option but to impose the minimum period of disqualification as described in sub-s (2), unless there are mitigating circumstances. Indeed, a motorist may be disqualified under

---

1   As amended by the Criminal Proceedings etc (Reform) (Scotland) Act 2007 (asp 6) Sch 1 para 7(d)).

the totting-up provisions on his first court appearance if the court chooses to use its powers of aggregation, although if this is to happen, reasons for doing so should be stated in open court and it has been emphasised that aggregation is an exceptional procedure (see *Dawson v PF Perth*, unreported decision of the Court of Appeal, 7 April 2004 and see also 8.10.2 above).

Section 35(1) provides the basic requirement that a court must impose disqualification if the totting-up procedure applies, unless mitigating circumstances exist. Subsection (1A)(a) suggests that where discretionary disqualification is available, the totting-up procedure should nonetheless be adopted, although it is submitted that in such circumstances the court can always impose a period of disqualification in excess of the minimum of six months. Subsection (1A)(b) emphasises that totting-up may apply if penalty points are imposed on the licence in an offence involving obligatory disqualification where special reasons have been established.

Section 35(2) provides certain minimum periods of disqualification; six months in the ordinary case, and one year and two years where one or two previous disqualifications respectively have to be considered. A previous disqualification is to be considered if it was within the three-year period preceding the commission (not the conviction) of the latest offence for which penalty points are to be taken into account, so long as the previous disqualification was for more than 56 days.

Section 35(3) deals with the situation where more than one offence involving obligatory or discretionary disqualification is dealt with on the same occasion. It may be that the offences were committed on different dates; the important consideration in this subsection is that such offences are dealt with on the same occasion. The subsection provides that only one period of disqualification under the totting-up procedure is to be imposed in such circumstances. However, the court is entitled to take into account all the offences in determining the length of that period of disqualification. It will also be noted that while s 35(2) provides certain minimum periods of disqualification in certain circumstances, no upper ceiling is given.

Section 35(4) imposes significant qualification on what may be adduced as mitigating circumstances in an effort to avoid disqualification under s 35(1). However, it is clear that the standard required to establish mitigating circumstances is not so exacting or high as that which applies in the establishment of special reasons for avoiding obligatory disqualification. In particular, the circumstances which can be considered in determining whether or not mitigating circumstances exist are not confined to the nature of the offence as in the case of special reasons. Both the circumstances of the offence and of the offender may be relevantly considered. Accordingly, the court can take into account such matters as the fact that the accused has a previously unblemished personal character.

Although in general terms the discretion open to the court in considering mitigating circumstances is far wider than is the case in special reasons, s 35(4)(a) emphasises that the triviality of the particular offence for which the accused has been convicted is not a mitigating circumstance.[1] Nor is the court entitled to take into account that there is a significant period between the current offence and the earlier offences which contributed to the accumulation of 12 penalty points.[2] However, as a matter to be weighed in the balance, it is possible for the accused to submit that consideration should be given to the relative triviality of the other offences which go to make up the 12 points. It should also be borne in mind that in these circumstances there may be special reasons for not endorsing the licence in the first place, which obviously does away with the need to consider mitigating circumstances.[3]

Reference to public safety is irrelevant as a basis for refusing mitigating circumstances.[4]

In terms of s 35(1), the court is entitled to have regard to all the circumstances of the offence (under reference to what is referred to in s 35(4)); accordingly, when an accused genuinely believed that he was covered by insurance when in fact he was not, the court was entitled not to disqualify under the totting-up procedure.[5]

Section 35(4)(b) makes it clear that any hardship caused by the disqualification must be exceptional to qualify as mitigating circumstances.

Each case must be considered on its own merits and care must be taken not to attribute the status of a rule to statements made in other cases.[6]

However, they do give an indication of what may amount to exceptional hardship. For example a series of authorities, culminating in *Allan v Barclay*,[7] held that the fact that the accused is likely to lose his

---

1   However, see *North v Tudhope* 1985 SCCR 161 at 163 where it was said that the nature of the offence could be taken into account once special hardship had been established.

2   See *Smith v Baker* 1979 SLT (Notes) 19; *Macnab v Smith* 1977 CO Circulars A/30.

3   *Scott v Ross* 1994 SLT 945, 1994 SCCR 538; *Gordon v Russell* 1999 SLT 897.

4   *Watson v PF Dundee* [2016] SAC(CRIM) Decision of 20 April 2016 SAC/2016/00008.

5   *Howdle v Davidson* 1994 SCCR 751, *McPake v Lees* 1998 SCCR 184, *Griffiths v Brierley* 2006 SCCR 197, 2006 SLT 531.

6   *Carmichael v Shevlin* 1992 SLT 113, 1992 SCCR 247.

7   *Allan v Barclay* 1986 SCCR 111.

employment is not in itself exceptional hardship, but that if the ensuing hardship is extended to others it may in suitable circumstances be described as exceptional. The appeal court has further examined what is exceptional hardship in a number of subsequent cases. Exceptional hardship need not always involve hardship to others. Also, loss of employment or difficult financial consequences are not the only grounds for establishing exceptional hardship. A driver who had to drive a sick child regularly to hospital, a previous child having died,[1] and a single parent who had to drive disabled children[2] both established that they would experience exceptional hardship. Other cases referred to are *Railton v Houston;*[3] *Miller v Ingram;*[4] *Robinson v Aitkenson;*[5] *McFadyen v Tudhope;*[6] *Briggs v Guild;*[7] *Gray v Jessop;*[8] *Mowbray v Guild;*[9] *Bibby v McDougall;*[10] *Clumpas v Ingram;*[11] *McLaughlin v Docherty;*[12] *Marshall v McDougall;*[13] *Ewan v Orr;*[14] *Howdle v Davidson;*[15] *Brennan v McKay;*[16] *Findlay v Walkingshaw;*[17] and *McPake v Lees.*[18] In a number of unreported decisions exceptional hardship was established where disqualification would mean future employment would be unlikely given the appellant's age: see *Piacentini v PF KIlmarnock*[19] (60 year old professional driver) and *Shambrook v PF Duns*[20] (66 year old and additional impact on wife and current employer).

As stated, though, the foregoing cases only provide guidelines; there are no hard and fast rules as to what circumstances will or will not

1   *Edmonds v Buchanan* 1993 SCCR 1048.
2   *Colgan v McDonald* 1999 SCCR 901.
3   *Railton v Houston* 1986 SCCR 428.
4   *Miller v Ingram* 1986 SCCR 437.
5   *Robinson v Aitkenson* 1986 SCCR 511.
6   *McFadyen v Tudhope* 1986 SCCR 712.
7   *Briggs v Guild* 1987 SCCR 141.
8   *Gray v Jessop* 1988 SCCR 71.
9   *Mowbray v Guild* 1989 SCCR 535.
10   *Bibby v McDougall* 1990 SCCR 121.
11   *Clumpas v Ingram* 1991 SCCR 223.
12   *McLaughlin v Docherty* 1991 SCCR 227.
13   *Marshall v McDougall* 1991 SCCR 231.
14   *Ewan v Orr* 1993 SCCR 1015.
15   *Howdle v Davidson* 1994 SCCR 751.
16   *Brennan v McKay* 1997 SLT 603.
17   *Findlay v Walkingshaw* 1998 SCCR 181.
18   *McPake v Lees* 1998 SCCR 184.
19   *Piacentini v PF KIlmarnock* (Decision of the Court of Appeal 22 February 2001).
20   *Shambrook v PF Duns* unreported decision of the Court of Appeal dated 25 January 2005.

justify exceptional hardship. Success in such applications often reflects in significant measure the care and skill exercised in their presentation, as well as on the particular circumstances. This may involve leading witnesses and documentary evidence but can also be achieved in part or in whole by agreed evidence with the Crown. Failure to do so may be fatal. [1]

It should be noted, however, that acceptance of undisputed evidence as to effect on an accused and other members of his family may lead to exceptional hardship inevitably being made out.[2] To do otherwise may be irreconcilable with unchallenged evidence and lead to a successful appeal, as in *Waine v Harvey*.[3]

Likewise, the court should not use too high[4] a test. In *LW v PF Glasgow*,[5] the Appeal Court, in finding that exceptional circumstances had been made out, observed that it was not for the appellant to prove, for example, that whilst disqualified she would definitely be unable to find work, but rather there was a real risk of this, as well as other factors such as impact on a child's schooling and loss of family home.

The correct procedure for the court to adopt is firstly to decide what is the appropriate number of penalty points which should be applied to the offence, and thereafter go on to see whether totting-up applies.[6] The court should not proceed by determining the number of penalty points needed to bring the totting-up procedure into operation as the first consideration.

Section 35(4)(c) provides that an accused person can argue that a particular set of mitigating circumstances exists and so avoid totting-up disqualification only once within any three-year period. If an accused successfully argues that he should not be disqualified for given reasons under the totting-up procedure, then he is disallowed from presenting similar arguments for a similar purpose in any court in the United Kingdom within three years of the conviction following which he avoided disqualification. It would seem to be open for an accused to argue that exceptional hardship or other mitigating circumstances exist for quite separate reasons on a second occasion.

---

1   *Watson v PF Dundee* [2016] SAC(CRIM) Supra
2   *Findlay v PF Aberdeen* unreported decision of the Court of Appeal dated 26 April 2004.
3   2016 SLT (Sh Ct) 169.
4   Though the test is a high one – *Glass v PF Ayr* [2016] SAC(CRIM) Decision of 16 November 2016 SAC/2016/00588.
5   [2012] HCJAC 30 (Decision of 23 February 2012).
6   *Briggs v Guild* 1987 SCCR 141.

Section 35(5) still has not been updated to change the reference to the Criminal Procedure (Scotland) Act 1975, s 223A or 436A to the Criminal Procedure (Scotland) Act 1995, s 248. The rest of the subsection is self-explanatory.

8.10.6 Procedure in mitigating circumstances submissions

The procedure in dealing with pleas of guilty to offences which do not involve obligatory or discretionary disqualification but which do involve disqualification under the totting-up procedure is broadly the same as in the case of letter pleas and special reasons cases (see 8.6.1 above). It should be emphasised that if the accused is to be disqualified, then it is proper practice for him to be given every opportunity to put forward reasons why he should not be disqualified. The Appeal Court has made it clear that it regards it as a 'sensible practice' for the accused to be required to appear personally if disqualification is a possibility.[1]

It is understood that in some courts, where disposal by way of points as opposed to discretionary disqualification has been achieved but unsuccessful mitigating circumstances submission follow, some agents then urge the court to impose a short period of discretionary disqualification instead of the six-month totting up ban. Apart from being illogical this is questionable conduct and should be challenged.

Likewise, as pointed out forcefully in *Hamand v Harvie*,[2] it is 'illegitimate' of a court having found exceptional hardship to be made out, to then impose discretionary disqualification.

8.10.7 Procedural consequences

If a period of disqualification (either obligatory or under the totting-up procedure) is avoided because of special reasons or mitigating circumstances, the court must give the reasons for its decision in open court, and cause these reasons to be entered on the record of proceedings.[3] If the court does not order disqualification, the appropriate number of penalty points must be endorsed on the licence.[4] Where endorsement is ordered the court may, and where disqualification for more than 56 days is ordered it must, send the licence to the DVLA.[5]

---

1   *Stephens v Gibb* 1984 SCCR 195 and *MacDonald v McGillivray* 1986 SCCR 28.
2   2016 SCCR 379.
3   RTOA 1988, s 47(1).
4   RTOA 1988, s 44.
5   RTOA 1988, s 47(2), as amended by the RTA 1991, Sch 4 para 100.

Following the expiry of a period of disqualification, a person may not drive until he has applied for and received the return of his licence.[1]

8.10.8 Courses for offenders

Section 34 of the Road Safety Act 2006, once in force, will introduce new ss 30A, 30B, 30C and 30D to the Road Traffic Offenders Act 1988.

Regard should be had to the terms of the new legislation but, in broad terms, the purpose of these new provisions is to allow retraining course for drivers convicted of specified offences where disqualification is not imposed but at least seven but no more than 11 penalty points are to be taken into account on the occasion of the conviction.

The offences envisaged by s 30A are contraventions of ss 3 (careless driving), 36 (failing to comply with traffic signs), and 89 (speeding) of the Road Traffic Act 1988, and s 17 of the Road Traffic Regulation Act 1984 (regulation of special roads). There is scope for extension to include further offences in the future.

If the course is accepted by the driver – and he will have to pay for it – and there is successful completion within ten months of the date of the order, the effect will be that after 12 months from the date of the order points will cease to be considered for the purposes of s 29 of the RTOA. The number of points involved will be three or fewer if fewer points were imposed for the offence. Obviously this impacts on the risk of totting up disqualification under s 35.

The courses will have to be approved and there are to be similar provisions as currently exist under the ss 34A–34C courses for drink drive offences in terms of availability and consent.

The scheme is not to be used where an offender has in the three years prior to the date of the commission of the offence committed a specified offence and completed either a s 30A course or one of the new s 34A courses (see 8.11.3 below), or where the offence was committed during the probationary period of the Road Traffic (New Drivers) Act 1995.

8.11 ADDITIONAL AND FURTHER CONSEQUENCES OF DISQUALIFICATION

8.11.1 Disqualification until test is passed

Section 36 of the Road Traffic Offenders Act 1988 provides:

---

1   *Stewart v Paterson* 1959 SLT (Sh Ct) 66.

'(1) Where this subsection applies to a person the court must order him to be disqualified until he passes the appropriate driving test.

(2) Subsection (1) above applies to a person who is disqualified under section 34 of this Act on conviction of –

(a)   manslaughter, or in Scotland culpable homicide, by the driver of a motor vehicle,

(b)   an offence under section 1 of the Road Traffic Act 1988 (causing death by dangerous driving),

(c)   an offence under section 1A of that Act (causing serious injury by dangerous driving),

(d)   an offence under section 2 of that Act (dangerous driving),

(e)   an offence under section 3ZC of that Act (causing death by driving: disqualified drivers),

(f)   an offence under section 3ZD of that Act (causing serious injury by driving: disqualified drivers).

(3) Subsection (1) above also applies –

(a)   to a person who is disqualified under section 34 or 35 of this Act in such circumstances or for such period as the Secretary of State may by order prescribe, or

(b)   to such other persons convicted of such offences involving obligatory endorsement as may be so prescribed.

(4) Where a person to whom subsection (1) above does not apply is convicted of an offence involving obligatory endorsement, the court may order him to be disqualified until he passes the appropriate driving test (whether or not he has previously passed any test).

(5) In this section –

"appropriate driving test" means –

(a)   an extended driving test, where a person is convicted of an offence involving obligatory disqualification or is disqualified under section 35 of this Act,

(b)   a test of competence to drive, other than an extended driving test, in any other case,

"extended driving test" means a test of competence to drive prescribed for the purposes of this section, and

"test of competence to drive" means a test prescribed by virtue of section 89(3) of the Road Traffic Act 1988.

(6) In determining whether to make an order under subsection (4) above, the court shall have regard to the safety of road users.

(7) Where a person is disqualified until he passes the extended driving test –

(a)   any earlier order under this section shall cease to have effect, and

(b)   a court shall not make a further order under this section while he is so disqualified.

(8) Subject to subsection (9) below, a disqualification by virtue of an order under this section shall be deemed to have expired on production to the Secretary of State of evidence, in such form as may be prescribed by regulations under section 105 of the Road Traffic Act 1988, that the person disqualified has passed the test in question since the order was made.

(9) A disqualification shall be deemed to have expired only in relation to vehicles of such classes as may be prescribed in relation to the test passed by regulations under that section.

(10) *Repealed*

(10A) Where a person's driving record is endorsed with particulars of a disqualification under this section, it shall also be endorsed with the particulars of any test of competence to drive that he has passed since the order of disqualification was made.

(11) For the purposes of an order under this section, a person shall be treated as having passed a test of competence to drive other than an extended driving test if he passes a corresponding test conducted –

(a)   under the law of Northern Ireland, the Isle of Man, any of the Channel Islands, another EEA State, Gibraltar or a designated country or territory, or

(b)   for the purposes of obtaining a British Forces licence (as defined by section 88(8) of that Act);

and accordingly subsections (8) to (10) above shall apply in relation to such a test as they apply in relation to a test prescribed by virtue of section 89(3) of that Act.

(11A) For the purpose of subsection (11) above, "designated country or territory" means a country or territory designated by order under section 108(2) of the Road Traffic Act 1988 but a test conducted under the law of such a country or territory shall not be regarded as a corresponding test unless a person passing such a test would be entitled to an exchangeable licence as defined in section 108(1) of that Act.

(12) This section is subject to section 48 of this Act.

(13) The power to make an order under subsection (3) above shall be exercisable by statutory instrument; and no such order shall be made unless a draft of it has been laid before and approved by resolution of each House of Parliament.

(14) The Secretary of State shall not make an order under subsection (3) above after the end of 2001 if he has not previously made such an order.'

In terms of s 36 as originally enacted under the Road Traffic Offenders Act 1988, the court had the discretionary power to order a driver to be disqualified until he passed a driving test on the expiry of the period of disqualification in any case where obligatory or discretionary disqualification was competent. The courts held that this discretionary requirement should not be exercised to provide an additional punishment to the sentences imposed on a driver in a particular case. Such an order could only be imposed where the circumstances of the offence, or the driver's previous convictions for road traffic offences, indicated that it was in the public interest that the driver's ability and skill should be checked before he was allowed to resume driving following his period of disqualification.[1] In particular, a token period of disqualification should not be imposed where the purpose of so doing was simply to make the driver resit a driving test;[2] nor should such a requirement be made automatically in cases where a long period of disqualification was imposed.[3] These considerations will continue to apply to those cases where statute does not require a driving test be re-taken, but the court is considering its discretionary power in this respect in terms of s 36(4).

Under the provisions of s 36, as now amended *inter alia* by s 32 of the Road Traffic Act 1991, the test of when this requirement should be imposed is significantly altered. The requirement to resit an appropriate driving test is now obligatory where an accused is disqualified for an offence of culpable homicide, or s 1, s 1A, s 2, s 3ZC and s 3ZD of the Road Traffic Act 1988.[4] The section also provides that this obligatory requirement may be extended by the Secretary of State if he decides to make the appropriate order covering (1) cases involving obligatory, discretionary or totting-up disqualification[5] or (2) cases simply involving obligatory endorsement.[6] The Secretary of State has made an order under s 36(3) in respect of contraventions of s 3A of the Road Traffic Act 1988 (committed on or after 31 January 2002 – see SI 2001/4051). In the absence of further orders, a driver with a totting-up disqualification regains his licence in the normal way. As will be noted, s 36(14) contains a sunset provision, which restricts the Secretary of State's power to make such an order to the end of 2001.

1   See *Sweeney v Cardle* 1982 SLT 312, 1982 SCCR 10.
2   *McLean v Annan* 1986 SCCR 52.
3   *Sweeney v Cardle* 1982 SLT 312, 1982 SCCR 10.
4   RTOA 1988, s 36(1).
5   RTOA 1988, s 36(3)(a).
6   RTOA 1988, s 36(3)(b).

The appropriate driving test is therefore to be an extended driving test in cases of obligatory disqualification and will be when the relevant order is made in cases of totting-up disqualification.[1] The ordinary driving test is to be passed in all other cases (in other words, where disqualification is discretionary). The extended test is about twice the length of the ordinary test. The motorist can only take the test once his period of disqualification has expired. Section 37(3) allows a driver to obtain a provisional licence in order to pass his test.[2] The provisions in respect of driving tests are found in the Motor Vehicles (Driving Licences) Regulations 1999.[3]

Accordingly, the current position is that the extended driving test must be taken at the end of a period of disqualification following conviction on a charge of culpable homicide; s 1, s 1A, s 2, s 3ZC and s 3ZD.[4] The Secretary of State had the power to extend this requirement to disqualifications *inter alia* under the totting-up procedure in terms of s 36(5) but has not done so. The court continues to have the discretionary power to require a driver in other circumstances to resit a driving test.[5] However, the test in this respect was significantly changed by s 36(6) of the Act; in determining whether to make such an order the court shall simply have regard to the safety of road users. This change is thought to reflect the desire of the legislature to make the requirement to resit the test of competence to drive more widely used by the courts. This test will remain for all cases of discretionary disqualification irrespective of what future alterations are made to the system of obligatory disqualification.

Section 37 of the Road Safety Act 2006 will amend s 36 of the RTOA once in force. The most significant amendments relates to the terms of s 36(3) which will focus on orders specified by the Secretary of State and the definition of appropriate driving test in s 36(5) which will become:

'"appropriate driving test" means—

(a)   in such circumstances as the Secretary of State may prescribe, an extended driving test, and

(b)   otherwise, a test of competence to drive which is not an extended driving test,'

and, in the definition of 'extended driving test', after 'section' insert 'by regulations made by the Secretary of State'.

---

1   RTOA 1988, s 36(5)(a).
2   See also *Stewart v Paterson* 1959 SLT (Sh Ct) 66.
3   Motor Vehicles (Driving Licences) Regulations 1999 (SI 1999/2864).
4   RTOA 1988, s 36(3).
5   RTOA 1988, s 36(4).

In terms of the new s 36(13A), orders specified by the Secretary of State under the amended s 36(3) must follow consultations with representative bodies, but only those he sees fit to consult.

8.11.2 Appeal against disqualification and requirement to resit test

Section 38(2) of the Road Traffic Offenders Act 1988 provides: 'A person disqualified by an order of a court in Scotland may appeal against the order in the same manner as against sentence.'

The form of such an appeal is therefore the same as in an appeal against sentence. The appellant may apply for an interim suspension of the disqualification to the court which made the order[1] or, which failing, to the Sheriff Appeal Court or the High Court of Justiciary.[2] Suspension is also available where a person makes an application under s 34B (see 8.11.3 below) for a drink-driving course, pending the outcome of the determination.[3] In the latter case, the application may be to a single judge. Any period of interim suspension is not included in the period of disqualification.[4] Because the requirement to resit a test is formally part of an order of disqualification, any appeal against the imposition of the requirement is taken under this section. There appears to be no grounds for appealing against the mandatory requirements to resit and pass a driving test[5] but discretionary orders are available under other sections of the Act and can be appealed.

The question of ordering the accused to be disqualified until a driving test was passed was considered in *Smith v Wilson*;[6] *Neill v Annan*;[7] and *Fraser v Lockhart*.[8] In *Harper v Lockhart*[9] the fact that a driver was 81 years old was held not to be a reason by itself for imposing a period of disqualification with a condition that a driving test be thereafter passed.

---

1 RTOA 1988, s 39(2).
2 RTOA 1988, s 41 as amended. *Mackay v Murphy* 2016 SCCR 83 makes plain that there is no right of appeal under s194ZB of the Criminal Procedure (Scotland) Act 1995 where leave to appeal has been refused by the Sheriff Appeal Court. That being so there is no basis to seek interim suspension to the High. Court.
3 RTOA 1988, s 41A, as introduced by RTA 1991, s 48 and Sch 4 para 97.
4 RTOA 1988, s 43.
5 Eg under RTA 1988, ss 1 and 2.
6 *Smith v Wilson* 1989 SCCR 395.
7 *Neill v Annan* 1990 SCCR 454.
8 *Fraser v Lockhart* 1992 SCCR 275.
9 *Harper v Lockhart* 1992 SCCR 429.

8.11.3 Courses for offenders

Sections 34A, 34B, 34BA and 34C of the Road Traffic Offenders Act 1988, as substituted by the Road Safety Act 2006 s 35, make provision for a scheme whereby a driver convicted of a variety of offences may have his period of disqualification reduced if he satisfactorily completes an approved course prescribed by the Secretary of State. In terms of s 34A(1), the disqualification period (under s 34 of the RTOA) must not be less than 12 months, disregarding any extension period under s 35A or s 35C.

These provisions replace the previous ss 34A–34C which only concerned drink driving cases. The current provisions are not fully in force and still only apply to 'a relevant drink offence'.[1]

As set out in s 34A(2), that means offences under ss 3A, 4, 5(1), 7(6) and s 7A(6) (in the course of an investigation into one of the earlier offences) of the Road Traffic Act 1988.

In due course the other 'specified' offences mentioned in s 34A(3) will apply too. Currently, these are to be s 3 (careless, and inconsiderate, driving), s 36 (failing to comply with traffic signs) of the Road Traffic Act 1988, s 17(4) (use of special road contrary to scheme or regulations) and s 89(1) (exceeding speed limit) of the Road Traffic Regulation Act 1984. Further specified offences may be added by regulations of the Secretary of State under s 34A(3). offences.

The effect of participation and limitations on who may take part are set out in s 34A(7)–(9):

'(7) The reduction made in a period of disqualification by an order under this section is a period specified in the order of –

(a)   not less than three months, and

(b)   not more than one quarter of the unreduced period,

(and, accordingly, where the unreduced period is twelve months, the reduced period is nine months).

(8) A court shall not make an order under this section in the case of an offender convicted of a specified offence if –

(a)   the offender has, during the period of three years ending with the date on which the offence was committed, committed a specified offence and successfully completed an approved course pursuant to an order made under this section or section 30A of this Act on conviction of that offence, or

(b)   the specified offence was committed during his probationary period (of the Road Traffic (New Drivers) Act 1995).

---

1   SI 2012/2938, art 2(1)(a).

(9) A court shall not make an order under this section in the case of an offender unless –

(a)   the court is satisfied that a place on the course specified in the order will be available for the offender,

(b)   the offender appears to the court to be of or over the age of 17,

(c)   the court has informed the offender (orally or in writing and in ordinary language) of the effect of the order and of the amount of the fees which he is required to pay for the course and when he must pay them, and

(d)   the offender has agreed that the order should be made.'

The opportunity to take such a course only arises when the court at the time of imposing the disqualification also makes an order that the period of disqualification may be reduced if the offender satisfactorily completes the course. The reduction will only apply in cases of 12 months' disqualification or more, and will amount to a period between three months and one quarter of the total period of disqualification. This scheme is now introduced throughout Scotland but is not always available.

There is no clear indication given in the legislation as to which drivers should benefit from the provisions. From cases before the Appeal Court under the previous scheme it was apparent that some Sheriffs felt it apt to apply the provisions only in borderline drink drive cases. Others, however, only gave effect in cases where there was a clear alcohol problem. Either way, in a number of cases, the Appeal Court has thought it appropriate to interfere in appeals attacking the length of disqualification and failure to apply the scheme.

Section 15 of the Road Safety Act 2006 has also introduced the potential for the alcohol ignition interlock programme which will allow offenders to reduce the period of disqualification on successful completion. New ss 34D–34G and 41B of the Road Traffic Offenders Act 1988 are anticipated and, once in force, will focus on drivers who have been convicted for a second time in ten years of a relevant offence – namely ss 3A, 4, 5, 7(6) and 7A(6) – and where the unreduced disqualification is not less than two years. The programme can only operate where an order under s 34A is not made.

The reduction will be not less than 12 months and not more than one-half of the unreduced period. As well as education an integral part of the programme will be the fitting of a device yet to be given type approval – the alcohol ignition interlock – which will prevent the vehicle being driven unless a breath specimen is within limits currently anticipated at 9 microgrammes of alcohol in 100 millilitres of breath. Interference with the device will trigger a fresh offence and non-compliance will lead to the imposition of the full unreduced disqualification.

Section 16 of the Road Safety Act 2006 makes clear that initially at least the programme will be on an experimental basis and restricted to designated court areas. In that period it will not apply to s 3A offences. However, both sections remain pending.

8.11.4 Disqualification of newly qualified drivers

The Road Traffic (New Drivers) Act 1995, as amended, makes provision in respect of offences committed by drivers who thereby acquire six or more penalty points within a period of two years of passing their driving test. The court must in these circumstances send a notice of the relevant information to the Secretary of State;[1] the Secretary of State then serves a notice on the driver revoking his licence.[2] The driver then reverts to the status of a learner. Provisions to prevent further consequences of the disqualification to the driver are found in s 7, and the licence is restored by virtue of s 5 in the event of a successful appeal.

In dealing with cases under this legislation it would be wrong to select a given number of points to trigger or avoid the application of the Act.[3]

8.11.5 Disqualification where vehicle used to commit offence

Section 248 of the Criminal Procedure (Scotland) Act 1995[4] provides:

'(1) Where a person is convicted of an offence (other than one triable only summarily) and the court which passes sentence is satisfied that a motor vehicle was used for the purpose of committing, or facilitating the commission of that offence, the court may order him to be disqualified for such period as the court thinks fit from holding or obtaining a licence to drive a motor vehicle granted under Part III of the Road Traffic Act 1988.

(2) A court which makes an order under subsection (1) above disqualifying a person from holding or obtaining a licence under Part III of the Road Traffic Act 1988 shall require him to produce –

(a)   any such licence;

(b)   any Community licence (within the meaning of that Part); and

---

1   Road Traffic (New Drivers) Act 1995, s 2.
2   RT(ND)A 1995, s 3.
3   *Lappin v O'Donnell* 2001 SCCR 219, *McKenzie v PF Aberdeen* [2017] SAC (Crim) 18.
4   As amended by the Driving Licences (Community Driving Licence) Regulations 1996 (SI 1996/1974), Sch 4 para 6(3).

(c)   any counterpart of a licence mentioned in paragraph (a) or (b) above, held by him.

(3) Any reference in this section to facilitating the commission of an offence shall include a reference to the taking of any steps after it has been committed for the purpose of disposing of any property to which it relates or of avoiding apprehension or detection.

(4) In relation to licences, other than Community licences which came into force before 1st June 1990, the reference in subsection (2) above to the counterpart of a licence shall be disregarded.'

The power to disqualify under this section may only be exercised in cases other than those which can only be tried on summary complaint. Disqualification may be imposed on any person involved in the offence, even if that person was not driving, or even in, the vehicle at any time.

This form of disqualification is unusual in that it is not associated with endorsement of the licence or the alternative imposition of penalty points, but exists, and is to be imposed, as a separate and individual penalty.

8.11.6 Forfeiture of vehicle following offence

Section 33A of the Road Traffic Offenders Act 1988, as introduced by s 5 of and Sch 4 para 71(6) to the Criminal Procedure (Consequential Provisions) (Scotland) Act 1995, provides:

'(1) Where a person commits an offence to which this subsection applies by –

(a)   driving, attempting to drive or being in charge of a vehicle, or

(b)   failing to comply with a requirement made under section 7 of the Road Traffic Act 1988 (failure to provide a specimen for analysis or laboratory test) in the course of an investigation into whether the offender had committed an offence while driving, attempting to drive or being in charge of a vehicle, or

(c)   failing, as the driver of a vehicle, to comply with subsections (2) and (3) of section 170 of the Road Traffic Act 1988 (duty to stop and give information or report an accident),

the court may, on an application under this subsection, make an order forfeiting the vehicle concerned, and any vehicle forfeited under this subsection shall be disposed of as the court may direct.

(2) Subsection (1) above applies –

(a)   to an offence under the Road Traffic Act 1988 which is punishable with imprisonment; and

(b)   to an offence of culpable homicide.

(3) An application under subsection (1) above shall be at the instance of the prosecutor made when he moves for sentence (or, if the person has been remitted for sentence under section 195 of the Criminal Procedure (Scotland) Act 1995 made before sentence is pronounced.

(4) Where –

(a)   the court is satisfied, on an application under this subsection by the prosecutor –

    (i)   that proceedings have been, or are likely to be, instituted against a person in Scotland for an offence to which subsection (1) above applies allegedly committed in the manner specified in paragraph (a), (b) or (c) of that subsection; and

    (ii)   that there is reasonable cause to believe that a vehicle specified in the application is to be found in a place or in premises to specified; and

(b)   it appears to the court that there are reasonable grounds for thinking that in the event of the person being convicted of the offence an order under subsection (1) above might be made in relation to the vehicle, the court may grant a warrant authorising a person named therein to enter and search the place or premises and seize the vehicle.

(5) Where the court has made an order subsection (1) above for the forfeiture of a vehicle, the court or any justice may, if satisfied on evidence on oath –

(a)   that there is reasonable cause to believe that the vehicle is to be found in any place or premises; and

(b)   that admission to the place or premises has been refused or that a refusal of such admission is apprehended, issue a warrant of search which may be executed according to law.

(6) In relation to summary proceedings, the reference in subsection (5) above to a justice includes a reference to the sheriff and to a magistrate.

(7) Part II of the Proceeds of Crime (Scotland) Act 1995 shall not apply in respect of a vehicle in relation to which this section applies.

(8) This section extends to Scotland only.'

This section therefore allows the court to forfeit vehicles where a road traffic offence punishable by imprisonment has been committed, and also in cases of culpable homicide. Applications may be made before proceedings commence where powers of search and seizure are sought prior to sentence.

It is for the Crown to make the motion at the time of moving for sentence, or in cases remitted to the High Court, before sentence is passed.

However, the concession by the Crown in *Shaw v Conley*[1] that s 33A only applies in solemn cases is unlikely to be supported. Arguably, it is inconsistent with the references to justices and magistrates in subsections (5) and (6). More pointedly it does not fit with the forfeitures consistently sought post the Association of Chief Police Officers in Scotland 2009 festive drink drive campaign in 2009 and subsequent drives. Currently, forfeiture is sought not only in repeat drink and drug driving cases, but also those involving high level (three times the limit and over) first offenders and those who fail to provide specimens under s 7 of the Road Traffic Act.

Forfeiture should not be regarded as automatic.[2]

It can be used to tailor a sentence that achieves public protection.[3] As was said in *Li v Dunn*,[4] 'each case requires to be considered on its own facts and circumstances with public protection, the overall penalty imposed on an offender and the financial means of the offender all being factors which may be relevant, either together or in isolation, when considering the making of a forfeiture order in relation to a motor vehicle'.

Forfeiture is possible even where the vehicle has been disposed of, although the original owner may still have a right of relief.[5] Where the total financial penalty is obviously excessive in light of means forfeiture should not be used.[6] Likewise, fining at a level equivalent to the value of a vehicle may well be excessive.[7] Nonetheless, where means are not in issue, a significant fine and forfeiture is likely to be within discretion.[8] The power to forfeit is arbitrary.[9]

Forfeiture has been ordered where a wife did not do enough to stop her disqualified husband from driving her car,[10] and where a very drunk

---

1   1998 SLT 17.
2   *Carron v Russell* 1994 SCCR 681; *Donald, Petitioner* 1996 JC 22, 1996 SLT 505, 1996 SCCR 321.
3   *McLean v PF Stranraer* XJ1142/10 (Decision of 14 December 2010).
4   2016 SCCR 272, at para 13.
5   *Lloyds and Scottish Finance v HM Advocate* 1974 JC 24, 1974 SLT 3; *Woods, Petitioner* 1993 SCCR 105.
6   *Wilson v Hamilton* 1996 SCCR 193; *Quinn v PF Glasgow* XJ652/10 (Decision of 25 August 2010) where a fine of £400, was imposed. Car worth £4,200 and outstanding finance payments totalling over £8,000. Order for forfeiture quashed.
7   *Wilson v Hamilton* 1996 SCCR 193.
8   *Li v Dunn*, supra.
9   *Purdie v MacDonald* 1997 SLT 483.
10 *Donald, Petitioner* 1996 JC 22, 1996 SCCR 68.

driver drove dangerously after being warned by the police not to take to the road.[1]

Suspended forfeiture orders are available to the court on conviction in respect of any property including vehicles.[2] The property must, at the time of the accused's apprehension, be in his ownership or possession or under his control and must have been used to commit the offence. Before conviction the property may be seized on warrant.[3] Search warrants in respect of forfeiture are empowered by s 254 of the Criminal Procedure (Scotland) Act 1995.

8.11.7 Disqualification of general offenders and fine defaulters: ss 248A–248D Criminal Procedure (Scotland) Act 1995

Section 248A of the Criminal Procedure (Scotland) Act 1995, introduced by s 15 of the Crime and Punishment (Scotland) Act 1997[4] allows the court to disqualify an offender even where a vehicle is not involved in the offence. This can be in addition to, or instead of, any other penalty, save in offences with sentences fixed by law.

Section 248B applies the same power to fine defaulters in cases where the court has power to impose a period of imprisonment in default of payment of a fine, or any part or instalment of a fine.

The court may, instead of imposing imprisonment, order that where the offender is in default, he shall be disqualified from holding a licence to drive a motor vehicle granted under Part III of the Road Traffic Act 1988 for such period not exceeding 12 months as the court thinks fit. If the fine is paid or part paid the disqualification will cease or be reduced.

It appears from the terms of these sections that persons so disqualified need not have been driving, or indeed in, the vehicle at the material time.

No guidelines are available as to how these powers should be used or how the orders should be recorded. The Secretary of State may by order prescribe which courts or classes of courts may make orders under ss 248A and 248B, as set out in s 248C. It is to be assumed that the normal powers of appeal will be available. The experience of the operation of these provisions in pilot courts suggests that the use of these powers may not be widespread, but restricted to particularly deserving cases. An example of the use of such powers is found in *Patterson v Gilchrist*.[5]

---

1 *Craigie v Heywood* 1996 SCCR 654.
2 Proceeds of Crime (Scotland) Act 1995, s 21(2).
3 *Shaw v Conley, supra.*
4 Which came into effect by virtue of SI 1997/2323.
5 *Patterson v Gilchrist* 1999 SCCR 419.

Sections 248D and 248E came into effect in July 2018.[1]

Both, to quote the language of s 248E(3), are concerned with 'the diminished effect of disqualification as a distinct punishment if the person who is disqualified is also detained in pursuance of a sentence of imprisonment'.

S 248D allows for the appropriate extension' of a disqualification imposed under s 248 or 248A and where the court also imposes a sentence of imprisonment (which includes an order for detention in residential accommodation under s 44 and a sentence of detention under s 205, 207 or 208 of the 1995 Act[2]).

The appropriate extension is set out s 248D(4) as follows:

'(a) in the case of a life prisoner, a period equal to the punishment part of the life sentence;

(b) in the case of a custody and community prisoner, a period equal to half the custody part of the sentence of imprisonment;

(c) in the case of a person serving an extended sentence, a period equal to half the confinement term;

(d) in any other case, a period equal to half the sentence of imprisonment imposed.'

Section 248E is concerned with disqualifications under s 248 or s 248A where either a sentence of imprisonment for another case is imposed at the same time, or there is an existing sentence of imprisonment being served at the time of sentence (sentence of imprisonment is defined as in s 248D). In both scenarios the court must have regard to 'the diminished effect of disqualification as a distinct punishment if the person who is disqualified is also detained in pursuance of a sentence of imprisonment'.

8.11.8 Extension of disqualification due to sentences of imprisonment: ss 35C and 35D of the Road Traffic Offenders Act 1988

The approach in ss 248D and 248E, above, is mirrored for disqualifications under ss 34 and 35 of the Road Traffic Offenders Act 1988.

Section 35C triggers where a court imposes a sentence of imprisonment, and orders the person to be disqualified under s 34 or 35. The 'appropriate extension' and the meaning of 'imprisonment' are the same as under s 248D mentioned in 8.11.7 above.

1   Inserted by the Coroners and Justice Act 2009 (c 25).
2   See s 248D(10).

Section 35D is concerned with disqualifications where either a sentence of imprisonment for another case is imposed at the same time, or an existing sentence of imprisonment is being served at the time of sentence. As under s 248E, supra, the court must have regard to 'the diminished effect of disqualification as a distinct punishment if the person who is disqualified is also detained in pursuance of a sentence of imprisonment'.

8.11.9 Removal of disqualification

Section 42 of the Road Traffic Offenders Act 1988[1] provides:

'(1) Subject to the provisions of this section, a person who by an order of a court is disqualified may apply to the court by which the order was made to remove the disqualification.

(2) On any such application the court may, as it thinks proper having regard to –

(a)   the character of the person disqualified and his conduct subsequent to the order

(b)   the nature of the offence, and

(c)   any other circumstance of the case,

either by order remove the disqualification as from such date as may be specified in the order or refuse the application.

(3) No application shall be made under subsection (1) above for the removal of the disqualification before the expiration of whichever is relevant of the following periods from the date of the order by which the disqualification was imposed, that is –(a) two years, if the disqualification is for less than four years, (disregarding any extension period)

(b)   one half of the period of disqualification, (disregarding any extension period) if the disqualification is (disregarding any extension period) for less than ten years but not less than four years,

(c)   five years in any other case;

and in determining the expiration of the period after which under this subsection a person may apply for the removal of a disqualification, any time after the conviction during which the disqualification was suspended or he was not disqualified shall be disregarded.

(3A) In subsection (3) "the relevant date" means—

(a)   the date of the order imposing the disqualification in question, or

---

1   As amended by the RTA 1991, s 48 and Sch 4 para 98, the Road Safety Act 2006 (c 49), and the Coroners and Justice Act 2009.

(b)   if the period of the disqualification is extended by an extension period, the date in paragraph (a) postponed by a period equal to that extension period.

(3B) "Extension period" means an extension period added pursuant to—

(a)   section 35A or 35C,

(b)   section 248D of the Criminal Procedure (Scotland) Act 1995, or

(c)   section 147A of the Powers of Criminal Courts (Sentenc ing) Act 2000.

(4) Where an application under subsection (1) above is refused, a further application under that subsection shall not be entertained if made within three months after the date of the refusal.

(5) If under this section a court orders a disqualification to be removed, the court –

(a)   must send notice of the order to the Secretary of State,[1]

(b)   may in any case order the applicant to pay the whole or any part of the costs of the application.

(5A) [2]

(5AA) If the disqualification was imposed in respect of an offence involving obligatory endorsement, the Secretary of State must, on receiving notice of an order under subsection (5)(a)(ii) above, make any necessary adjustments to the endorsements on the person's driving record to reflect the order.

(5B) A notice under subsection (5)(a) above must be sent in such a manner and to such address, and must contain such particulars, as the Secretary of State may determine.

(6) The preceding provisions of this section shall not apply where the disqualification was imposed by order under section 36(1) of this Act.'

This section is self-explanatory. The relevant date must wait for any extension periods to have had effect. Apart from the restrictions in sub-ss (3) and (4), there is no limit on the number of such applications that may be made during the period of disqualification. It is clear from the terms of the section that the application is to be made to the court where the disqualification was imposed. If an accused person has received periods of disqualification in more than one court, it follows that an

1   Substituted by the Road Safety Act 2006 c 49 Sch 3 para 40(2) (8 June 2015, subject to transitional provisions specified in SI 2015/560 Pt 3).

2   Repealed by the Road Safety Act 2006 c 49 Sch 7 para 1 (8 June 2015: repeal has effect as SI 2015/560, subject to transitional provisions specified in SI 2015/560 Pt 3).

order in one court lifting the disqualification imposed there will not in any way affect the disqualifications imposed in other courts. The section affords no power to reduce the disqualification; an application must be either refused or granted *simpliciter*. An application can be made in cases involving disqualification under s 34 with the requirement to resit an extended test under s 36. It is only the former that is affected by the application if successful.[1]

8.11.10 Removal of disqualification: procedure

Whether the application is made in the Sheriff Court or the High Court of Justiciary, it is presented in the form of a petition. Although there is no specific provision governing the procedures to be observed, it is normal and proper practice for the applicant to serve a copy of the petition on the procurator fiscal or the Crown Agent, depending on whether the application is in the Sheriff Court or the High Court of Justiciary. Service should be made in sufficient time to allow the Crown to instruct its own report (normally from a local police officer) on the merits of the petition. A separate petition is required for each indictment or complaint in respect of which disqualification was imposed. In terms of this section it is suggested that the court should have regard to the character of the person disqualified and his conduct subsequent to the order, the nature of the offence committed which caused the disqualification and any other circumstances of the case.

In presenting the application to the court, it is submitted that the applicant should be prepared to lead evidence in support of his application rather than rely on *ex parte* statements. However, if the circumstances are sufficiently clear, and the police report is favourable, and if in addition, the Crown does not dispute the salient facts put up by the petitioner, there appears to be no bar to such an application proceeding entirely on the basis of statements made by the accused or his solicitor. Such applications should be presented with considerable care. It is normal for such applications to be granted only where the applicant can demonstrate clearly that his behaviour since the commission of the offence is such as to indicate that it is unlikely that he will commit such offences again. In addition, pressing reasons must be adduced to demonstrate why the appellant should have his licence restored. These can include the avoidance of hardship, for example by indicating that the restoration of the licence will allow the applicant to resume employment, or by demonstrating that the lack of a licence causes the applicant serious personal difficulty or hardship to

---

1   *R v Nuttal* [1971] RTR 279.

his family. Any such claims, however, should be properly vouched and supported where appropriate by evidence. It is also normal for such applicants to provide testimonials of good conduct which will satisfy the court that the applicant can safely have his licence restored to him.

There is no appeal from the decision of the court to which the application is made.[1]

The appeal is to the court of original jurisdiction, and not necessarily the same judge.[2]

8.11.11 Compensation orders

On conviction of an offence, the court, subject to the provisions of s 249 of the Criminal Procedure (Scotland) Act 1995, as amended, may make an order requiring the convicted person to pay compensation for any personal injury loss or damage caused, whether directly or indirectly, or alarm or distress caused directly by the acts which constituted the offence.[3]

Road traffic offences may not give rise to many such orders, although the section has been amended to include situations where accidents involved uninsured drivers and no alternative compensation scheme is available.

The section provides:

'(3) Where, in the case of an offence involving dishonest appropriation, or the unlawful taking and using of property or a contravention of section 178(1) of the Road Traffic Act 1988 (taking motor vehicle without authority etc.) the property is recovered, but has been damaged while out of the owner's possession, that damage, however and by whomsoever it was in fact caused, shall be treated for the purposes of subsection (1) above as having been caused by the acts which constituted the offence.

(3A) A compensation order may be made in respect of personal injury, loss or damage (apart from loss suffered by a person's dependents in consequence of a person's death) that was caused directly or indirectly by an accident arising out of the presence of a motor vehicle on a road if—

(a)   it was being used in contravention of section 143(1) of the Road Traffic Act 1988 (c.52), and

(b)   no compensation is payable under arrangements to which the Secretary of State is a party.

---

1   *McLeod v Levitt* 1969 JC 16, 1969 SLT 286.
2   *McIntyre v Henderson* 1911 JC 73.
3   CP(S) Act 1995, s 249(1).

(3B) Where a compensation order is made by virtue of subsection (3) or (3A), the order may include an amount representing the whole or part of any loss of (including reduction in) preferential rates of insurance if the loss is attributable to the accident.

(3C) A compensation order may be made—

(a)   for bereavement in connection with a person's death resulting from the acts which constituted the offence,

(b)   for funeral expenses in connection with such a death,

except where the death was due to an accident arising out of the presence of a motor vehicle on a road.

(4) Unless and to the extent that subsections (3) to (3C) allow a compensation order to be made, no compensation order shall be made in respect of—

(a)   loss suffered in consequence of the death of any person; or

(b)   injury, loss or damage due to an accident arising out of the presence of a motor vehicle on a road.'[1]

Accordingly, it appears that compensation in reality will be restricted to s 178 cases, cases involving damage and injury caused by s 2 offences, or accidents involving non-insured drivers. *Nazir v Normand*[2] is suggestive of a broader approach involving a compensation order for causing and permitting a car to be driven without insurance. However, the question of competency was not apparently considered in that case whereas in *Brough v PF Kirkwall* (unreported decision of 5 February 2004) a compensation order of just under £5000 – which also completely ignored the complainer's means as required by s 249(5) – was suspended. It had been imposed following a plea to careless driving involving destruction of a wall.

The fact that the victim was insured does not matter – see *Ely v Donnelly*.[3]

8.12 ENDORSEMENT OF LICENCES

8.12.1 General

Section 44 of the Road Traffic Offenders Act 1988, as amended, and now headed 'Orders for endorsement' provides:

---

1   Added by Criminal Justice and Licensing (Scotland) Act 2010 asp 13(Scottish Act).
2   *Nazir v Normand* 1994 SCCR 265.
3   *Ely v Donnelly* 1996 SCCR 537.

'(1) Where a person is convicted of an offence involving obligatory endorsement, the court must order there to be endorsed on his driving record particulars of the conviction and also –

(a)   if the court orders him to be disqualified, particulars of the disqualification, or

(b)   if the court does not order him to be disqualified –

    (i)   particulars of the offence, including the date when it was committed, and

    (ii)   the penalty points to be attributed to the offence.

(2) Where the court does not order the person convicted to be disqualified, it need not make an order under subsection (1) above if for special reasons it thinks fit not to do so.

(3) In relation to Scotland, references in this section to the court include the justice of the peace court.

(4) This section is subject to section 48 of this Act.'

Section 44A[1] of the Act provides:

'(1) Where the court orders the endorsement of a person's driving record with any particulars or penalty points it must send notice of the order to the Secretary of State.

(2) On receiving the notice, the Secretary of State must endorse those particulars or penalty points on the person's driving record.

(3) A notice sent by the court to the Secretary of State in pursuance of this section must be sent in such manner and to such address and contain such particulars as the Secretary of State may require.'

Endorsement is not a penalty as such; rather, it is a direction that certain matters must be marked or noted on the driving record. These matters are details of any period of disqualification, or if no disqualification is imposed, details of the offence and the number of penalty points attributed by the court thereto. Details of offences which require endorsement, and the number of penalty points for such offences are found in the Road Traffic Offenders Act 1988, Sch 2, as amended by the Road Traffic Act 1991, Sch 2.

It is not possible to enforce disqualification and penalty points at the same time, irrespective of when the separate offences were committed.[2]

---

1   Added by Road Safety Act 2006 c 49 s 9(3).
2   *Ahmed v McLeod* 1999 SLT 762, 1998 SCCR 486.

Where disqualification for a period of 56[1] days or more is ordered, the court must send the licence with the details of the disqualification to the DVLA; where endorsement is ordered, the court may do likewise.[2] Any endorsements on a driving record are prima facie evidence of the matters so endorsed.[3]

The effect of endorsement and the periods for which various endorsements remain live and the procedure for having spent endorsements removed and a clean licence issued are described in the Road Traffic Offenders Act 1988, s 45A, introduced by the Road Safety Act 2006. It provides as follows:

'(1) An order that any particulars or penalty points are to be endorsed on a person's driving record shall operate as an order that his driving record is to be so endorsed until the end of the period for which the endorsement remains effective.

(2) At the end of the period for which the endorsement remains effective the Secretary of State must remove the endorsement from the person's driving record.

(3) An endorsement ordered on a person's conviction of an offence remains effective (subject to subsections (4) and (5) below)–

(a)   if an order is made for the disqualification of the offender, until four years have elapsed since the conviction, and

(b)   if no such order is made, until either–

(i)   four years have elapsed since the commission of the offence, or

(ii) an order is made for the disqualification of the offender under section 35 of this Act.

(4) Where the offence was under one of the following sections of the Road Traffic Act 1988, the endorsement remains effective until four years have elapsed since the conviction—

(a)   section 1 (causing death by dangerous driving),

(b)   section 1A (causing serious injury by dangerous driving),

(c)   section 2 (dangerous driving),

(d)   section 3ZC (causing death by driving: disqualified drivers), or

(e)   section 3ZD (causing serious injury by driving: disqualified drivers).

1   Unlike shorter periods where the provisions of Section 37(1A) of the Road Traffic Offenders Act 1988 apply.
2   RTOA 1988, s 47(2), as amended by the RTA 1991, the Road Safety Act 2006 and the Coroners and Justice Act 2009.
3   RTOA 1988, s 31, as amended by RTA 1991, and the Road Safety Act 2006.

(5) Where the offence was one–

(a) under section 3A, 4(1), 5(1)(a) or 5A(1)(a) and (2) of that Act (driving offences connected with drink or drugs),

(b) under section 7(6) of that Act (failing to provide specimen) involving obligatory disqualification, or

(c) under section 7A(6) of that Act (failing to allow a specimen to be subjected to laboratory test), the endorsement remains effective until eleven years have elapsed since the conviction.'

8.12.2 Special reasons for not endorsing licence

Section 44(2) of the Road Traffic Offenders Act 1988 allows a court to refrain from endorsing a licence if there are special reasons for doing so. As in the case of special reasons for not disqualifying, a special reason for not endorsing is a matter of law, and not at large for the discretion of the court.[1] Triviality of the offence is not a ground for not endorsing,[2] particularly since the introduction of the penalty points system. In addition, *Stephens v Gibb*,[3] and *Holden v MacPhail*[4] make it clear that endorsement should normally follow on the appropriate conviction. It is for the accused to raise the question of special reasons.[5] A useful general rule of reference is whether the special reasons explain why the offence was committed in circumstances where it would otherwise not have been.

The procedure for putting forward and considering special reasons submissions is described in *McLeod v Scoula*,[6] *McNab v Feeney*[7] and *Keane v Perrie*.[8] The court may not refrain from endorsement unless special reasons are spoken to by or on behalf of the accused at the time. The fiscal is always entitled to be heard. If the court finds that special reasons exist for not endorsing the licence, these reasons must be given in open court and marked on the record (complaint) by the clerk of court.[9]

---

1   *Muir v Sutherland* 1940 JC 66, 1940 SLT 403.
2   *Tudhope v Birbeck* 1979 SLT (Notes) 47, not following *Smith v Henderson* 1950 JC 48, 1950 SLT 182.
3   *Stephens v Gibb* 1984 SCCR 195.
4   *Holden v MacPhail* 1986 SCCR 486.
5   *McLeod v Scoular* 1974 JC 28, 1974 SLT (Notes) 44; *Heywood v O'Connor* 1994 SLT 254, 1993 SCCR 471.
6   *McLeod v Scoular* 1974 JC 28, 1974 SLT (Notes) 44.
7   *McNab v Feeney* 1980 SLT (Notes) 52.
8   *Keane v Perrie* 1983 SLT 63, 1982 SCCR 377.
9   RTOA 1988, s 47(1); see also *MacNab v MacPherson* 1978 JC 21.

The use of joint minutes in appropriate cases should not be overlooked and indeed it should be remembered that there is a positive duty to seek agreement where possible (Criminal Procedure (Scotland) Act 1995, s 257). Likewise, courts should remember to use the plain English meaning of agreed statements of fact rather than distorting them.[1]

In *McDade v Jessop*[2] it was observed that factors which constitute special reasons for not disqualifying might not carry the same weight in relation to endorsement; and the fact that the penalty points available where the accused had failed to provide a specimen were in excess of what would have been imposed if the accused had been driving was not a special reason for not ordering endorsement.

Where a driver was genuinely unaware for legitimate reasons that he was no longer qualified to drive, special reasons existed for not endorsing penalty points.[3] This should be contrasted with the slightly different situation in *Carmichael v Shevlin*[4] where a motorist's belief that he was insured to drive founded mitigating circumstances for not adopting the totting-up procedure. Something which happens after the offence will not normally justify a failure to order endorsement.[5]

In *Heywood v O'Connor*[6] it was held in a case where a driver had no insurance that it was not a special reason for refraining from endorsement that the vehicle was not much used; and in *McDade v Jessop*,[7] the fact that the accused was not driving or intending to drive when he refused to give a specimen was similarly unsuccessful.

If there is credible evidence from a single witness that he believed that he was insured to drive, this may afford grounds for non-endorsement.[8]

The particular facts and circumstances of a given case will of course be determinative, as shown by two relatively recent reports, which echo the approach taken in *Hunter v Brown*.[9]

In *Wilkinson v PF Ayr*, a 'genuine case of forgetfulness by one person, and reasonable reliance by another, over a short period of time' in a no insurance case amounted to special reasons after a husband drove

---

1   *Hunter v Brown* 2012 SLT 665.
2   *McDade v Jessop* 1990 SCCR 156.
3   *Robertson v McNaughtan* 1993 SLT 1143, 1993 SCCR 526; see also *Gordon v Russell* 1999 SLT 897.
4   *Carmichael v Shevlin* 1992 SLT 1113, 1992 SCCR 247.
5   *Morton v Munro* 1998 SCCR 178.
6   *Heywood v O'Connor* 1994 SLT 254, 1993 SCCR 471.
7   *McDade v Jessop* 1990 SLT 800, 1990 SCCR 156.
8   *Marshall v McLeod* 1998 SLT 1199, 1998 SCCR 317.
9   Supra.

uninsured against a background of a decade of regular renewal by a wife, and her failure to renew due to ill health and assumption.[1]

Similarly, in *PF Lerwick v Siegel*, a son's failure to make specific enquiry of the insurance position was not fatal to a successful special reasons plea, since his mother's clear intention to have her son added as a named driver failed because her arrangements to do so were ineffective.[2]

Emergency vehicle drivers may in certain situations escape endorsement.[3] Section 87 of the Road Traffic Regulation Act 1984 exempts fire brigade, ambulance and police vehicles from speed limits if the limit is likely to hinder the use of the vehicle for the purpose for which it is being used at the time. See 7.8.1 above.

8.12.3 Notice of penalties

Since the passing of the Criminal Procedure (Scotland) Act 1995 the prosecution do not need to serve a notice of penalty on any accused.

8.12.4 Connected offences

Where a number of offences occur at the same time, the prosecution of these may be separated, some being processed under the normal procedure of service of a complaint, others by the procedure of fixed penalty. The fixed penalty procedure covers offences to which a fixed number of penalty points applies. If, in dealing with such a case, the court becomes aware that a connected offence is to be, or has been considered by the fixed penalty procedure, the number of penalty points that will apply or has been applied must be deducted from the penalty points to be imposed by the court.[4] Reference should be made to *Green v O'Donnell*[5] and 8.10.1 above.

---

1   [2014] HCJAC HCA/2014-004478-XJ.
2   [2016] SC LER 49.
3   *Husband v Russell* 1997 SCCR 592 and *McAllister v PF Aberdeen* 2017 SLT (Sh Ct) 80, [2017] SAC (Crim) 15, a somewhat perplexing case involving a collision between a car correctly indicating a right turn which took it into an overtaking police car travelling on the wrong side of the road, but with lights and siren operating. Both drivers were convicted of careless driving and both were fined £400 and received four penalty points, notwithstanding the civilian driver's evidence that the siren and lights were not activated was not accepted.
4   RTOA 1988, ss 28–30
5   *Green v O'Donnell* 1997 SCCR 315.

8.12.5 Exemption from disqualification and endorsement: construction and use

Section 48 of the Road Traffic Offenders Act 1988 provides that where a person is convicted of an offence under s 40A or 41A of the Road Traffic Act 1988 (which relate to using a vehicle in a dangerous condition and to contraventions of the construction and use regulations), the court must not order him to be disqualified or order his licence to be endorsed with or without penalty points if he proves that he did not know, and had no reasonable cause to suspect that the use of the vehicle involved a danger of injury to any person (s 40A) or the facts of the case were such that the offence would be committed (s 41A).

It is submitted that the standard of proof required to establish this defence is on the balance of probabilities. A case which usefully illustrates some of the relevant features of such a defence is *Forrest v Annan*.[1]

8.12.6 Offender escaping endorsement by deception

Where a person is convicted of an offence involving a deception which might have had a bearing on disqualification, the court dealing with the deception offence has the same powers of disqualification as the deceived court, and must take into account any orders actually imposed by that court.[2]

8.13 EARLY PLEAS AND OTHER SENTENCING CONSIDERATIONS

8.13.1 Early pleas

Section 196 of the Criminal Procedure (Scotland) Act 1995, as amended, makes plain that a sentencer shall take account of the stage of proceedings at which an indication to plead is given and the circumstances in which the indication was given. Following the guidance issued in *Du Plooy v HMA 2003*[3] this aspect of sentencing has been the subject of many appeals, principally in relation to reduction in the length of jail sentences and monetary penalties.

The fourth edition of this book suggested that, despite the decision in *Stewart v Griffiths*,[4] penalty points might be afforded consideration in the

---

1   *Forrest v Annan* 1992 SLT 510, 1990 SCCR 619.
2   RTOA 1988, s 49.
3   *Du Plooy v HMA* 2003 SCCR 640, 2003 SLT 1237.
4   2005 SCCR 291.

same way that disqualification had been under reference to cases such as *Weir v HMA*[1]and *Rennie v Frame.*[2]

Appeals were taken on the point and, ultimately, as part of a broad review of the principles of discount, resulted in the guidance issued in the five-bench decision in *Gemmell v HMA* and the six associated appeals.[3] As regards road traffic cases, the guidance is found at paras [69]–[72] of the opinion and confirms that discount *can* be applied to both disqualification and points:

'Disqualification from driving and penalty points

[69] These disposals, in my opinion, constitute a sentence and come within the express wording of section 196.

Disqualification from driving

[70] In my opinion, a period of disqualification from driving is a penalty (*cf Adair v Munn*[4]). As such it is a 'sentence ... or other disposal or order'. However, in the case of a disqualification, any discount granted cannot take the period of disqualification below the statutory minimum. The absence of an enabling provision such as is contained in section 196(2) of the 1995 Act indicates that this result was intended by the Parliament, whether it was to protect the public or to punish the offender.

Penalty points

[71] For the same reasons, I consider that sentence discounting applies also to the imposition of penalty points for road traffic offences. The question was considered by a court of two judges in *Stewart v Griffiths.*[5] In an extempore judgment that runs to 18 lines in the law report, the court held that penalty points were not like a financial penalty. They were in the nature of a warning to the accused as to his future driving. For that reason the court refused to reduce the number of penalty points imposed. The relevant authorities on the point were not cited to the court.

[72] In *Tudhope v Eadie*[6] a Full Bench decided that the imposition of penalty points was a penalty in itself (*cf Coogans v MacDonald,*[7] Lord Justice-General Cooper at p 104). The imposition of penalty points is a form of order that falls within the ambit of section 196. The Strasbourg jurisprudence is to

1   *Weir v HMA* 2006 SCCR 206.
2   *Rennie v Frame* 2005 SCCR 608.
3   2012 SCCR 176.
4   1940 JC 69, 1940 SLT 414.
5   2005 SCCR 291.
6   1984 JC 6, 1984 SLT 178.
7   1954 JC 98, 1954 SLT 279.

the same effect (*Malige v France*[1]). In my opinion, *Stewart v Griffiths* was wrongly decided and should be overruled.'

A majority of the court, three to two, found that any element of a sentence referable to public protection should not be taken out of account in considering a discount. In dissenting on this point, along with Lady Paton, Lord Osborne observed at para [133] that Scotland and England now approach the matter differently.

More broadly, however, it was emphasised that discount is very much a matter for discretion, that an accused is not entitled to any particular level of discount, and that only exceptionally would the Court of Appeal interfere with any discount, or none, if cogent reasons had been given by the sentencer (see para [81]).[2]

Harkin v Brown[3] also emphasises that any discount is to be taken from the headline sentence selected, not after deduction of any statutory minimum, that the end result cannot fall below the statutory minimum, and that discount in disqualification may mean restricted allowance for any rehabilitation course.

The number of such appeals appeared to have fallen as a result of the guidance, which had effect almost immediately.[4]

However, the point is still taken regularly in relation to all aspects of sentencing and as a result the Sheriff Appeal Court, as a matter of principle, referred two cases to the Appeal Court for guidance. These were *Wilson v PF Aberdeen*[5] and *Gallagher v PF Glasgow*.[6]

Three questions posed were succinctly answered as follows:

'(1) What is the proper construction of section 196 of the 1995 Act in road traffic cases where the sentencing process involves the imposition of a fine or other penalty and separately the imposition of penalty points?

Section 196 applies to both a fine and other parts of a sentence such as penalty points or disqualification from driving. All are penalties and, in a given case, should be discounted for an early plea of guilty at approximately the same rate. Other than in exceptional cases, such as where statutory minimums apply or a discount is otherwise impracticable,

---

1   Application No 27812/95.
2   See *Saini v Harrower* 2017 SCCR 530 and *McInally v Dunn* 2016 SCCR 243.
3   2012 SCCR 617.
4   See *Willis v HMA* XC590/11, decision issued two days after *Gemmell* and where an otherwise correct one-year disqualification was discounted by 25 per cent to reflect the early plea.
5   [2018] HCJAC 50.
6   [2018] HCJAC 51.

the rate of discount should be uniform across all parts of the sentence. Any differential would require to be fully reasoned in the event of a challenge.

(2) In keeping with the court's discretion on matters of discount, may the court adopt a discriminating approach to discount over separate penalties in road traffic cases?

No. A "discriminating" approach to discount, in so far as this is taken to mean the application of different discount rates for different parts in the one sentence, is not normally legitimate.

(3) May the court take account of public interest considerations such as road safety or public protection when considering whether to discount road traffic penalties, in this case disqualification, and in determining what level of discount to apply to same?

No.'

These answers reflect earlier decisions. For example, *Watt v Dunn* explains that 'consideration of public protection does not justify declining to discount for an early plea' – albeit the Court, having concluded that the Justice had erred, declined to alter the sentence (four points) in the absence of a miscarriage of justice, given the level of speed (96/70mph).[1]

They are, however, a very useful summary which should prevent many unnecessary appeals.

Particularly helpful and pragmatic guidance was issued in *Gallagher* as to how to approach the sentencing process and it is worth quoting in full:

'[19] There are obvious cases in which the rate of discount cannot be the same or where, in respect of one part, cannot apply at all. These include, respectively, situations where applying the same discount would reduce the penalty to below the statutory minimum or where the relevant statute does not permit a discount. Comparative justice only arises where two or more accused are convicted of the same charge. There may be cases where the application of a discount to one accused, who has pled guilty early, will result in an imbalance in relation to another accused who has not. This may occur in cases where one accused is a repeat offender and another is not. This is the effect of any penalty discounting system, whether applicable to specific road traffic offences or otherwise. There may be an element of inconsistency in the imposition of sentences for similar offences, but that again is the general effect of discounting. It is a pragmatic feature designed to improve the efficiency of the justice system. It must be applied in a consistent fashion.

1   2016 SCCR 131.

[20] In relation to the indivisibility of certain numbers of penalty points by particular rates of discount, an element of pragmatism must again be employed. This is seen in what happened in the road traffic cases assessed in *Gemmell v HM Advocate* (supra). The fractions arrived at may require to be rounded up or down to achieve a practical result. This should not be a difficult exercise. In this case, for example, the discount of 0.8 penalty points could easily be rounded up to 1 point.'

The following decisions may also be of note.

In relation to custody, *Kirk v HMA*[1] makes plain that real utilitarian value achieved may still lead to discount notwithstanding multiple preliminary hearings. Lord Turnbull, in giving the opinion of the Court, observed at para 5:

'In the present case it is of course correct that there were three first diet hearings before the plea was tendered and accepted. However, these were short procedural hearings at which no evidence was led and no witnesses were cited to attend... The list of witnesses attached to the indictment included a number of police officers and four doctors, each with different specialities. The plea of guilty avoided any interruption to the ordinary and important duties performed by these witnesses... in addition, of course, the plea of guilty avoided the necessity of the two passengers within the appellant's vehicle giving evidence...The plea of guilty avoided the need for either witness to relive the experience of what, for one at least, turned out to be a lifechanging event.'

At para 6 the court said: 'The circumstances which we have identified are important and contribute towards the extent of the benefit brought by the plea of guilty.'

It is perhaps also worth noting that the starting sentence appealed was four years, two months, with two months then deducted for the plea.

By contrast, *Divers v PF Airdrie* makes the point that late pleas on the date of the trial are likely to attach at most token discount if witnesses are present.[2]

As for points, and with discount generally in mind, *Saini v Harrower* emphasises again that 'to suggest that the strength of the Crown Case was a factor which might be prayed in aid in withholding or restricting discount' would be in error. [3]

---

1   [2016] HCJAC decision of 20 December 2016.
2   [2017] SAC (Crim) 12.
3   2017 SCCR 530 at para. 4. The case is also a useful reminder of the potential to appeal of a decision of the Sheriff Appeal Court on a point of law under s.194ZB of the Criminal Procedure (Scotland) Act 1995.

Finally, while it may seem trite, *Jackson v Murphy*[1] is a useful reminder of s 211(7) of the Criminal Procedure (Scotland) Act 1995, and that the long-held approach, demonstrated by *Paterson v McGlennan*,[2] that fines payable by instalment ought to be capable of payment in about a year should be followed.

8.13.2 Totality

The Sentencing Council in England has produced definitive guidelines in relation to totality.[3] Two elements are identified:

'1. all courts, when sentencing for more than a single offence, should pass a total sentence which reflects all the offending behaviour before it and is just and proportionate. This is so whether the sentences are structured as concurrent or consecutive. Therefore, concurrent sentences will ordinarily be longer than a single sentence for a single offence.

2. it is usually impossible to arrive at a just and proportionate sentence for multiple offending simply by adding together notional single sentences. It is necessary to address the offending behaviour, together with the factors personal to the offender as a whole.'

Clearly, each case will turn on its own facts and circumstances, but road traffic matters regularly throw up tensions given it is common to be dealing with either multiple charges or multiple complaints/indictments.

McMurrich v Cardle[4] is authority that the appropriate approach to disqualification on multiple charges on one complaint is not to approach the matter 'from the point of view of determining whether the conduct as a whole justified a total period of disqualification', but 'to determine what period of disqualification was appropriate for each particular charge'. In *McMurrich*, that had the effect of reducing the overall disqualification by a year from the Sheriff's view of what the total sentence should have been, which he then imposed on one of the two charges open to him.

Nicholson v Lees[5] provides guidance on the approach to be taken in considering whether concurrent or consecutive sentences are appropriate, noting in particular that if the charges appear on separate complaints for technical reasons, they fall to be treated as if they had appeared on one

---

1   2016 SLT (Sh Ct) 55, [2016] SAC (Crim) 1.
2   1991 JC 141, 1991 SLT 832, 1991 SCCR 616.
3   'Offences Taken Into Consideration and Totality', published 6 March 2012.
4   1988 SCCR 20.
5   1996 JC 173; 1996 SLT 706; 1996 SCCR 551.

complaint, so that the sentences in aggregate cannot exceed the limit of the court's sentencing power on one complaint.

However, that does not preclude a severe approach, where a schedule of previous convictions demonstrates a persistent offender. See for example *McKinsley v HMA*.1

8.13.3 Sentencing Guidelines

As noted already (see 2.3.3 above), reference to the English sentencing guidance for death by driving cases is now commonplace.

More widely, as the then Lord Justice Clerk, Lord Carloway, observed in *Sutherland v HMA*:

> 'Definitive guidelines from the Sentencing Council of England and Wales often provide a useful cross check for sentences in Scotland especially where the offences are regulated, as here, by a UK statute and there are identical sentencing maxima. They should not, however, be applied in Scotland in a rigid or mechanistic fashion, given the differences in sentencing purposes, practices and regimes between the two jurisdictions.'[2]

That approach was followed by the Sheriff Appeal Court in *Haider v PF Glasgow*,[3] which chose not to have regard to applicable part of the Magistrates Court Sentencing Guidelines, revised in 2017, as regards disqualified driving, given different sentencing maxima now apply between the two jurisdictions. Presumably, where such distinctions do not apply the guidelines could provide a useful cross check.

8.13.4 Dealing with children

Section 49 of the Criminal Procedure (Scotland) Act 1995 gives courts the ability to remit cases involving children to the Principal Reporter for the disposal of the case by a children's hearing.

The case of *McCulloch v Murray*[4] makes it clear that if that approach is followed, then disposal of the case becomes entirely a matter for the hearing, even in road traffic cases where disposal by the court would otherwise lead to either obligatory or discretionary disqualification or penalty points.

It is worth noting that the court in *McCulloch* was not unsympathetic to the potential, in given cases, of remitting and disqualifying. Despite

---

1   2016 HCJAC, unreported decision of 11 October 2016.
2   [2015] HCJAC 115, 2016 SLT 93, 2016 SCCR 41, at para 20.
3   [2017] SAC (Crim) 9, 2017 SLT (Sh Ct) 137.
4   *McCulloch v Murray* 2005 SCCR 775.

questioning whether the Scottish Executive might not consider amending the 1995 Act accordingly, it has not happened thus far.

8.13.5 Antisocial behaviour

The Antisocial Behaviour etc (Scotland) Act 2004 (asp 8) provides in terms of s 126(2), that where a constable in uniform:

> 'has reasonable grounds for believing that a motor vehicle –
>
> (a)   is being used on any occasion in a manner which –
>
>> (i)   contravenes section 3 or 34 of the Road Traffic Act 1988 (c 52) (careless and inconsiderate driving and prohibition of off-road driving); and
>>
>> (ii)   is causing, or is likely to cause, alarm, distress or annoyance to members of the public; or
>
> (b)   has been used on any occasion in a manner which –
>
>> (i)   contravened either of those sections of that Act; and
>>
>> (ii)   caused, or was likely to cause, such alarm, distress or annoyance',

he has, in terms of s 126(3):

> '(a)   if the motor vehicle is moving, power to order the person driving it to stop the vehicle;
>
> (b)   subject to subsection (4), power to seize and remove the motor vehicle;
>
> (c)   for the purposes of exercising a power falling within paragraph (a) or (b), power to enter any premises (other than a private dwelling house) on which the constable has reasonable grounds for believing the motor vehicle to be;
>
> (d)   power to use reasonable force, if necessary, in the exercise of a power conferred by any of paragraphs (a) to (c).'

Warnings should be given first where practicable and the relevant regulations in relation to the operation of the legislation, the Police (Retention and Disposal of Motor Vehicles) (Scotland) Regulations 2005 (SSI 2005/80), came into force in March 2005. These set out the details of retention and associated fees, and the recovery and disposal of vehicles.

8.13.6 Prostitution

For offences post 10 November 2011, the Prostitution (Public Places) (Scotland) Act 2007 (Disqualification from Driving) Order 2011[1] has given

---

1   SI 2011/2490.

courts discretionary power to disqualify an offender convicted under summary procedure of a contravention of s 1(1) or (3) of the Prostitution (Public Places) (Scotland) Act 2007. The length of disqualification chosen turns on the circumstances of the case.

Article 3 provides:

'(1) Where –

(a)   a person is convicted by a court of a relevant offence; and

(b)   the court is satisfied that, at the time the offence was committed, the person was driving or was otherwise in charge of a motor vehicle, the court may make an order that the person is to be disqualified from holding or obtaining a licence to drive a motor vehicle granted under Part III of the 1988 Act.

(2) For the purposes of paragraph (1), a "relevant offence" is an offence under any of the following provisions of the 2007 Act –

(a)   section 1(1) (soliciting for prostitution); and

(b)   section 1(3) (loitering for prostitution).

(3) A disqualification order –

(a)   may be made in addition to, or instead of, any other disposal available to the court (including a disposal under section 1(5) of the 2007 Act); and

(b)   is to be framed so as to have effect for such period as the court considers appropriate in all the circumstances.'

'Motor vehicle' has the meaning given by s 185(1) of the Road Traffic Act 1988 and the penalty referred to in s 1(5) is a fine up to level 3. Provision for surrendering any licence is set out in art 4, including Northern Ireland and Community licences, and any appeal against disqualification imposed is by way of summary sentence appeal as provided for by art 5.

8.14 FIXED PENALTIES AND CONDITIONAL OFFERS

In order to reduce the volume of road traffic cases going through the courts, a system of fixed penalties has been introduced which allows for the avoidance of prosecution by an offender by payment of a fixed penalty in respect of certain minor traffic offences. It is a feature of the general system that a number of these offences involve endorsement and penalty points being imposed on a driving record without any order of court. Significant change was enacted by way of ss 3 and 4 of the Road Safety Act 2006 which came into force in 2009. Sections 28 and 53 of the Road Traffic Offenders Act are amended to allow for graduated fixed penalties and penalty points. These are set taking account of the nature of the offence, its gravity, where it took place and whether there has been other prescribed offending in a prescribed period.[1] How this will work in detail will be subject to orders prescribed by the Secretary of State.

The many offences in respect of which fixed penalties and conditional offers may be made are listed in Schs 3 and 5 to the Road Traffic Offenders Act 1988. These include driving otherwise than in accordance with a licence (s 87(1)) and without insurance (s 143), parking offences, signage offences, seatbelt offences, and construction and use offences including use of mobile telephones (fixed penalty of £200 and endorsement of six penalty points). In addition, many fixed penalties are available in relation to commercial vehicles.

The levels of fixed penalties are set out in the Fixed Penalty order 2000(SI2000/2792). Since 16 August 2013, careless and inconsiderate driving offences in terms of s 3 of the Road Traffic Act 1988 have been added to the list in Sch 3, although presumably with the intention that this will only apply to lower-level offences. The fixed penalty has been set at £100 and three penalty points.

This reflects the increase in all fixed penalties from the same date. The number of points for each fixed penalty offence can be found in Sch 2 of the Road Traffic Offenders Act.

In England and Wales, s 54 allows fixed penalties to be issued on the spot by police officers, vehicle examiners or traffic wardens, subject to access to either the driving record or sight of the licence, to assess whether totting up might apply. The benefit in saving the need for involvement of prosecutors or courts is obvious. The Scottish government has proposed that the legislation be amended to include Scotland and the UK government supports this. A consultation process was undertaken in the first half of 2018 and it seems likely, given the cost savings if nothing else, that the legislation will in due course take effect north of the border.

Meantime, the conditional offers of fixed penalty under ss 75–77A and fixing notices to vehicles under s 62 remain the only options.

The statutory procedure for the system is found in Pt III of the Road Traffic Offenders Act 1998. Conditional offers may be made by a police officer or a vehicle examiner. Practice can vary, but often the police issue a conditional offer of a fixed penalty which if accepted avoids the formal process of prosecution. If the offence is speeding or otherwise involves penalty points, the driver must submit his licence to the relevant clerk of court in order for the driving record to be checked and thereafter

---

1   RTOA s53(2).

endorsed. The fixed penalty must be paid within 28 days.[1] If the licence holder is subject to disqualification the conditional offer procedure is not available. If the conditional offer is not accepted, the fiscal normally thereupon proceeds a prosecution, although he can also issue a further conditional offer.

Put briefly, where it appears that certain sorts of offences have been committed, the fiscal may make a conditional offer to the alleged offender to the effect that on payment of a fixed penalty any liability to conviction will be discharged. Where the offence involves obligatory endorsement, the alleged offender must deliver his licence to the relevant clerk of court, who then transmits details to be added to the individual's driving record. The fixed penalty must be paid within 28 days.[2] If the licence holder may be subject to disqualification, the conditional offer procedure is not available.[3] If the alleged offender declines the offer, prosecution for the offence will normally follow.

There have been numerous appeals on this subject, stemming from inability to take up the offer because the licence is not available for submission, for whatever reason. In such circumstances the court is not bound in any way by the terms of the offer although the fact it was made is relevant.[4] However where the inability to produce the licence stems from compliance with other obligations, such as amendment of address by the DVLA, it would not be consistent with a fair exercise of discretionary power to penalise beyond the terms of the fixed penalty.[5]

Where an offence does not involve obligatory endorsement, the notice of penalty may be fixed to the offending vehicle, rather than given at the time to the motorist.[6] The subsequent procedure is described in ss 63–65. Briefly, the police then serve a 'notice to owner' in terms of s 63(2). The owner can either pay the fixed penalty, or, if he does not, a prosecution will then be initiated by the service of a complaint. Alternatively, the motorist may deny that he was the driver of the vehicle at the material time, and provide a statutory statement of ownership, together with a signed request by the person purporting to be the driver to request a hearing (or in other words inviting a prosecution). It would seem that if the driver does not sign the statutory statement, the registered keeper will

---

1   RTOA 1988, s 75.
2   RTOA 1988, s 75.
3   RTOA 1988, s 75.
4   *Lappin v O'Donnell* 2001 SCCR 219, and *Watt v Dunn* 2016 SCCR 131.
5   Eg *Bryson v Currie* 2005 SCCR 4, 2005 SLT 253, and *Stockton v Gallacher* 2004 SCCR 400.
6   RTOA 1988, s 62.

become liable for what is known as a registered fine, which amounts to one and a half times the fixed penalty. If the fixed penalty is ignored, it is, after the response period has expired, registered with the clerk of a court of summary jurisdiction (in effect the local Justice of the Peace Court) for the area in which the defaulter appears to reside as a fine amounting to one and a half times the fixed penalty. The clerk of court is then required to notify the defaulter of the registration. At this stage the defaulter can have the registration made invalid if he makes a statutory declaration within 21 days to the effect that either:

(a)   he did not know of the fixed penalty until he received the notice of registration; or

(b)   he was not the owner of the vehicle at the time of the alleged offence and he has a reasonable excuse for failing to comply with the notice; or

(c)   he gave notice requesting a hearing.[1]

It is not clear how a reasonable excuse is to be determined, or in what form the statutory declaration is to proceed. It is, however, to be conclusively presumed that a person on whom the notice of fixed penalty was served was the driver of the vehicle at the material time, unless it is shown that the vehicle was in the possession of some other person without the consent of the accused.[2] Fixed penalty notices under s 62 may be fixed to vehicles by traffic wardens as well as by police officers.[3] Particular provision is made for hired vehicles by s 66.

The intended consequence of the present fixed penalty system is to put the onus on any accused motorist who wishes to dispute any charge to take the necessary statutory action, and failure to do so will mean that either the fixed penalty must be paid or, failing such payment, an increased fine is registered against the motorist, subject to the safeguards described above.

The powers of the district court were restricted in this area in that it could not impose disqualification. That has been removed by the Criminal Proceedings etc (Reform) (Scotland) Act 2007 (Powers of District and JP Courts) Order 2007 which now means that Justice of the Peace Courts are only restricted to 60-day prison sentences and level 4 fines.[4]

---

1   RTOA 1988 s 73.
2   RTOA 1988, ss 64(5) and (6).
3   RTOA 1988, s 86, as amended by RTA 1991, Sch 4 para 106.
4   RTOA 1988, ss 10 and 50 and SI 2007/3480, art 2(1)(c) (10 December 2007).

8.15 INSURANCE

8.15.1 Section 143

Section 143 of the Road Traffic Act 1988 as amended by Motor Vehicles (Compulsory Insurance) Regulations 2000 (SI 2000/726), reg 2 provides:

'(1) Subject to the provisions of this Part of this Act –

(a)   a person must not use a motor vehicle on a road or other public places unless there is in force in relation to the use of the vehicle by that person such a policy of insurance or such a security in respect of third party risks as complies with the requirements of this Part of this Act, and

(b)   a person must not cause or permit any other person to use a motor vehicle on a road or other public place unless there is in force in relation to the use of the vehicle by that other person such a policy of insurance or such a security in respect of third party risks as complies with the requirements of this Part of this Act.

(2) If a person acts in contravention of subsection (1) above he is guilty of an offence.

(3) A person charged with using a motor vehicle in contravention of this section shall not be convicted if he proves –

(a)   that the vehicle did not belong to him and was not in his possession under a contract of hiring or of loan,

(b)   that he was using the vehicle in the course of his employment, and

(c)   that he neither knew nor had reason to believe that there was not in force in relation to the vehicle such a policy of insurance or security as is mentioned in subsection (1) above.

(4) This Part of this Act does not apply to invalid carriages.'

8.15.2 Definitions

'Motor vehicle'. See 1.2.1 above.

'Road'. See 1.8.1 above.

'Public place'. This was added to cover public places such as car parks in England to comply with EEC Directives.

'Policy of insurance'. The requirements in respect of a policy of insurance are provided by s 145 of the Road Traffic Act 1988. A policy of insurance includes a cover note.[1]

'Causing or permitting'. See 1.10.3 above.

---

1   RTA 1988, s 161(1).

8.15.3 Insurance: general

From the terms of s 143 of the Road Traffic Act 1988, it is clear that the principle which underlies the requirement of compulsory insurance is that cover must be provided in respect of the use to which the vehicle is to be put, rather than in respect of the person who is using the vehicle. It therefore follows that anyone charged with a contravention of the section does not necessarily have to be the owner of the vehicle, and that a corporate body may competently be charged with such an offence. Whether insurance cover is effective in respect of any particular use is a matter of fact and law to be understood from the facts and circumstances of each case; the question to be determined is whether the material use is legally covered by the insurance contract.[1] Vehicle development is to be reflected in forthcoming amendments to the 1988 Act – see, for example, proposed s 143(1A) within the Automated and Electric Vehicles Act 2018, which is not yet in force.

The insurance contract normally stipulates the conditions under which insurance cover is to be effective. If these conditions are not observed in any material respect, the contract may be avoided and an offence will result. For example, most contracts of insurance require that the user of any vehicle is properly licensed. Accordingly, if a person drives a vehicle of a class not covered by his licence, he will in normal circumstances automatically also be guilty of an offence under this section.

The extent of the cover provided by an insurance document must be disclosed by the terms of the document. The principal sorts of cover are comprehensive (which covers damage to both the owner's vehicle and vehicles owned by third parties) and third party, fire and theft (which extends to damage caused to vehicles owned by third parties only, as well as loss caused by fire or the theft of the vehicle). The latter form of insurance is the minimum cover allowed (see 8.14.5 below).

No policy of insurance is valid or effective for this part of the Act unless and until a certificate of insurance is delivered by the insurer to the person by whom the policy is effected.[2] Even if all the other requirements of drawing up a policy of insurance have been satisfied, it is an offence for a vehicle to be used on the road before the certificate of insurance is delivered.

Given the use of Internet comparison websites and online insurance generally, provision finally exists for the delivery of the certificate by

---

1   *Agnew v Robertson* 1956 SLT (Sh Ct) 90.
2   RTA 1988, s 147(1).

email or by access to it online. See ss 147(1A)–(1E) and (4A)–(4E) of the 1988 Act.[1]

Once the certificate has been delivered, the fact that the person to whom it has been delivered subsequently becomes bankrupt, or the company to which it is delivered is wound up or goes into receivership does not affect claims by third parties.[2] If a contract of insurance is avoidable, the contract remains valid until it is in fact avoided.[3] A driver may not be covered before he pays the premium, if that is a condition of the policy even after delivery of the policy.[4]

As an offence is constituted under s 143(1) by use of a vehicle on a road or public place without being covered by insurance, prosecutions are not confined to instances where the vehicle is being driven at the material time. The section is also contravened if a vehicle is parked on a public road and is not covered; and this will apply even in cases where the vehicle cannot physically be moved.[5] Similarly, a vehicle being towed is in use and must be insured.[6] The owner is still using the vehicle when he gives it to another person to repair.[7] A motorist was deemed to be the user of his vehicle for insurance purposes as soon as it was returned to him after he had lent it to another.[8]

8.15.4 Onus of proof

It has been held in both Scotland and England that the onus of proof that a particular use is covered by an appropriate policy of insurance rests on the person charged with using the vehicle at the material time, on the principle that whether insurance for such use at the material time was in force or not is a matter which should be within the user's knowledge.[9] It is, of course, open to any accused person in these circumstances to show that he was not using the vehicle at the material time.

---

1   Introduced by the Motor Vehicles (Electronic Communication of Certificates of Insurance) Order 2010 (2010/1117) Pt 1, art 3(5) (30 April 2010).
2   RTA 1988, s 153; see also Third Parties (Rights Against Insurers) Act 1930.
3   *Goodbarne v Buck* [1940] 1 KB 77 but reference should also be made to *Barr v Carmichael* 1993 SLT 1030, 1993 SCCR 366.
4   *McCulloch v Heywood* 1995 SLT 1009, 1995 SCCR 221.
5   *Simpson v McDonald* 1960 SLT (Notes) 83; *Tudhope v Every* 1976 JC 42, 1977 SLT 2.
6   *Robb v McKechnie* 1936 JC 25, 1936 SLT 300.
7   *Dickson v Valentine* 1989 SLT 19, 1988 SCCR 325.
8   *McLaughlin v Friel* 1997 SLT 824.
9   *Philcox v Carberry* [1960] Crim LR 563; *Milne v Whalley* 1975 SLT (Notes) 75.

If a driver allows another to drive his vehicle so long as that other insures the vehicle, he is not deemed to have permitted its use if the other driver does not in fact get insurance.[1]

Section 143(3) of the Road Traffic Act 1988 provides a statutory defence to persons who are driving a vehicle which they do not own and have not hired or leased, who are using the vehicle in the course of their employment, and who neither knew or had reason to believe that no policy of insurance was in force at the material time.

Section 143(1) does not apply to invalid carriages. Further exemptions are granted in s 144, as amended by the Road Traffic Act 1991, s 20; and in terms of s 183, the requirement for insurance does not apply to vehicles and persons who are at the material time in the service of the Crown. These include vehicles owned by a council constituted under s 2 of the Local Government etc (Scotland) Act 1994 in Scotland or the Scottish Fire and Rescue Service.2

However, on the principle that it is the use of the vehicle that is important, there must be insurance cover in respect of any private use of Crown vehicles.[3]

8.15.5 Requirements of insurance policies

To comply with the requirements of the Road Traffic Act 1988, an insurance policy must be issued by an authorised insurer.[4] The term 'authorised insurer' is defined in s 145(5) (which refers back to s 95) and it is a prerequisite of authorisation that the insurance company is a member of the Motor Insurers' Bureau.[5] The policy must insure specified persons or classes of persons in respect of any liability by the policy holder in respect of the death of, or bodily injury to, any person, or damage to property which may be caused by, or arise out of, the use of the vehicle on the road in Great Britain or in the states of the European Union.[6] This is generally known as third party insurance, and is the minimum required; additional or comprehensive insurance is also offered by insurance companies.[7]

---

1   *MacDonald v Howdle* 1995 SLT 779, 1995 SCCR 216.
2   Police and Fire Reform (Scotland) Act 2012 (Consequential Provisions and Modifications) Order 2013/602 Sch 2(1) para.22(3) (1 April 2013).
3   *Salt v McKnight* 1947 JC 99, 1947 SLT 327.
4   RTA 1988, s 145(1).
5   RTA 1988, s 145(5) and (6).
6   RTA 1988, s 145(3) and (4).
7   RTA 1988, s 145(3).

The policy must also insure against any liability for emergency treatment[1] in terms of ss 157–159; however, such payments must be made 'under or in consequence of' the policy.[2] The policy is not required to cover liability for death or bodily injury of any person employed by the insured in respect of that person's employment.[3]

There are restrictions on attempts by insurance companies to qualify the cover provided by a policy,[4] and on private agreements to avoid liability;[5] and special provision in respect of car-sharing agreements.[6]

8.15.6 Evidence, procedure and penalties

Tried summarily, level 5 fine, discretionary disqualification and obligatory endorsement of 6–8 points

If an accused gives credible but uncorroborated evidence that, for example, he believed that he was properly covered by insurance at the material time, theoretically he might be entitled to be acquitted.[7] More realistically, where a driver drove in circumstances where he believed he had permission, this may amount to special reasons for not imposing penalty points.[8]

Should he be convicted, but subsequently produces documents confirming insurance, it is possible that a conviction may be set aside. It may be important that the potential of the documents was raised at the lower court.[9]

If a driver does not have his insurance with him at any material time he may require to produce his documents at a police station of his choice within seven days. Failure to do so is a separate offence.[10]

The appeal court has confirmed that a straightforward first offence of having no insurance may well attract a penalty of disqualification.[11] This

---

1   RTA 1988, s 145(3)(c).
2   *Glasgow Royal Infirmary v Municipal Mutual Insurance* (1953) 69 Sh Ct Rep 297.
3   RTA1988, s 145(4).
4   RTA 1988, s 148.
5   RTA 1988, s 149.
6   RTA 1988, s 150.
7   *Marshall v McLeod* 1998 SLT 1199, 1998 SCCR 317.
8   *Gordon v Russell* 1999 SLT 897 and *Hunter v PF Kilmarnock* [2012] HCJAC 42 which emphasises the scope for use of joint minute in such proceedings. See 8.5.2 above.
9   See *Pazhiyoor v PF Hamilton* [2013] HCJAC 39 XJ1002/12 distinguishing *Pirie v McNaughton* 1991 SCCR 483.
10   RTA 1988, s 165(3).
11   *Docherty v Normand* 1995 SCCR 20.

reflects the significance of the problem of uninsured drivers which is now further reflected in the powers to seize and retain uninsured vehicles (see 7.5.4 above), though not by the addition of the charge as one dealt with by fixed penalty.

8.15.7 Sections 144A–144D

Section 144A: Tried summarily, level 3 fine

In an attempt to combat the problem of uninsured driving, the Road Safety Act 2006 introduced a new offence under s 144A of the Road Traffic Act 1988 of keeping a vehicle which does not meet insurance requirements. Detection of the offence will arise from rapid access to records held by the DVLA and motor insurers as in s 165A procedure. Regulations as to release of such information may be made by the Secretary of State under ss 159A[1] (information from the Motor Insurers' Information Centre) and 160.[2]

Section 144A, offence of keeping vehicle which does not meet insurance requirements, reads:

'(1) If a motor vehicle registered under the Vehicle Excise and Registration Act 1994 does not meet the insurance requirements, the person in whose name the vehicle is registered is guilty of an offence.

(2) For the purposes of this section a vehicle meets the insurance requirements if –

(a)   it is covered by a such a policy of insurance or such a security in respect of third party risks as complies with the requirements of this Part of this Act, and

(b)   either of the following conditions is satisfied.

(3) The first condition is that the policy or security, or the certificate of insurance or security which relates to it, identifies the vehicle by its registration mark as a vehicle which is covered by the policy or security.

(4) The second condition is that the vehicle is covered by the policy or security because –

(a)   the policy or security covers any vehicle, or any vehicle of a particular description, the owner of which is a person named in the policy or security or in the certificate of insurance or security which relates to it, and

(b)   the vehicle is owned by that person.

---

1   Added by the Road Safety Act 2006 (c 49) s 22(2) (4 February 2011).
2   As amended by the Motor Vehicles (Electronic Communication of Certificates of Insurance) Order 2010 (SI 2010/1117) Pt 1, art 5(b)(ii) (30 April 2010) to reflect electronic access.

(5) For the purposes of this section a vehicle is covered by a policy of insurance or security if the policy of insurance or security is in force in relation to the use of the vehicle.'

Exceptions to the section are contained in s 144B and mirror in many respects the existing exemptions to s 143 set out in s 144. Other examples are where the keeper no longer keeps the vehicle, it is not kept on a road or public place, or has been stolen, and where the appropriate notification has been given.

Section 144C allows for fixed penalties to be issued where the Secretary of State has reason to believe that an offence under s 144A has been committed. The fixed penalty is currently set at £100.

Section 144D introduces a new Sch 2A to the RTA 1988. This is a *second* Sch 2A since a drafting error ignored the existing one (about bus seat belts). It allows for the making of regulations which will allow for clamping of vehicles where there is a reasonable suspicion of a breach of s 144A. New offences involving interference with clamps may be made by further regulations made under the terms of s 160 of the RTA 1988. Schedule 2 of the RTOA 1988 is to be amended to reflect penalties for breach of these regulations which will attract varying levels of fines for summary cases subject to the circumstances, but will include custody for up to two years on indictment in cases where false or misleading declarations are made to secure release of a vehicle from immobilisation or to secure possession in a person's custody.

8.15.8 Motor Insurers' Bureau

As indicated in the preceding paragraphs, an authorised insurer must be a member of the Motor Insurers' Bureau. By s 151 of the Road Traffic Act 1988,[1] the insurers are required to satisfy any judgment against persons insured for third party risks. Such risks must of course be *ex facie* of the policy.[2] If such a judgment is not satisfied by the insurers, then the claim must be met by the Motor Insurers' Bureau, in terms of an agreement between the Bureau and the Ministry of Transport. A further agreement extends the obligation to judgments obtained against untraced drivers. The texts of these agreements are published by Her Majesty's Stationery Office. The address of the Bureau is Linford Wood House, 6–12 Capital Drive, Linford Wood, Milton Keynes, MK14 6XT (01908 830001 and www. mib.org.uk). It should be stressed that notice of the commencement of any action against an uninsured driver must be given to the Bureau within 21

1   Subject to the provisions of s 152, as amended.
2   *Robb v McKenzie* 1936 JC 25, 1936 SLT 300.

days, and it is advisable to give such notice in any case where it is thought that the judgment might be unsatisfied.

Notwithstanding the Bureau's obligations, the principal responsibility for meeting any claim rests with the insured,[1] and the Bureau is not accountable for any unsatisfied judgment which proceeds on a liability which the Act does not require to be covered.[2]

8.16 VEHICLES EXCISE AND REGISTRATION

8.16.1 General

These matters are consolidated for the first time in the Vehicle Excise and Registration Act 1994 (universally known as 'VERA').

Section 1, as amended by the Finance Act 2002 (c 23), Sch 5 para 2, provides:

'(1) A duty of excise ("vehicle excise duty") shall be charged in respect of every mechanically propelled vehicle that –

(a)   is registered under this Act (see section 21), or

(b)   is not so registered but is used, or kept, on a public road in the United Kingdom.

(1A) Vehicle excise duty shall also be charged in respect of every thing (whether or not it is a vehicle) that has been, but has ceased to be, a mechanically propelled vehicle and –

(a)   is registered under this Act, or

(b)   is not so registered but is used, or kept, on a public road in the United Kingdom.

(1B) In the following provisions of this Act "vehicle" means –

(a)   a mechanically propelled vehicle, or

(b)   any thing (whether or not it is a vehicle) that has been, but has ceased to be, a mechanically propelled vehicle.

(1C) Vehicle excise duty charged in respect of a vehicle by subsection (1) (a) or (1A)(a) shall be paid on a licence to be taken out –

(a)   by the person in whose name the vehicle is registered under this Act, or

(b)   if that person is not the person keeping the vehicle, by either of those persons.

---

1   *Corfield v Groves* [1950] 1 All ER 488.
2   *Lees v Motor Insurers' Bureau* [1952] 2 All ER 511.

(1D) Vehicle excise duty charged in respect of a vehicle by subsection (1)(b) or (1A)(b) shall be paid on a licence to be taken out by the person keeping the vehicle.

(2) A licence taken out for a vehicle is in this Act referred to as a "vehicle licence".'

An excise duty is therefore charged on every mechanically propelled vehicle registered under the Act or used or kept on the public roads and this duty is paid in respect of a licence which must be taken out by the person in whose name the vehicle is registered under this Act or the keeper of the vehicle.

8.16.2 Definitions

'Public road'. See 1.8.1 and 1.8.2 above. The statutory definition is supplied by s 62(1) of the VERA and has the same meaning as in the Roads (Scotland) Act 1984.[1]

'Mechanically propelled vehicle'. See 1.2.1 above. The Act does not require any duty to be paid in respect of any vehicle which is not mechanically propelled. Section 185(1) of the Road Traffic Act 1988 provides a number of definitions of mechanically propelled vehicles, but this list of definitions is not exhaustive.

'Used or kept'. The section does not qualify the word 'used' in any way. Any kind of use will therefore require the vehicle to be licensed. Further, s 62(2) of the Act provides:

'For the purposes of this Act and any other enactment relating to the keeping of vehicles on public roads, a person keeps a vehicle on a public road if he causes it to be on such a road for any period, however short, when it is not in use there.'

Accordingly, it is clear that, in terms of this Act, Parliament intended that any vehicle which is mechanically propelled and which is on a public road in any circumstances whatsoever, irrespective of the time or the nature of the use involved, must be covered by an excise licence; see also 8.15.5 below.

The duty charged in terms of the Act is described in the Schedules to the Act.

---

1 See *Russell v Annan* 1993 SCCR 234 which is also a reference for whether the court can assume that a road is public when there is no evidence on the matter.

8.16.3 Obtaining a licence

Sections 7–10 of the Act provide for the issue transfer and surrender of licences. Reference should also be made to regs 5, 9 and 9A of the Road Vehicles (Registration and Licensing) Regulations 2002.[1] Emission levels have become a highly relevant factor.

Different classes and weights of vehicle attract different rates of duty, and these are described in the Schedules to the Act. The annual rates of duty, the duration of the licence and the amount of duty are provided for in ss 2–4 of the Act.

8.16.4 Exemptions

There are certain exemptions from excise duty given principally to vehicles such as fire engines, ambulances, police vehicles, vehicles for disabled people, old vehicles (40 years) and vehicle testing operations (Sch 2). However, although the excise duty is not chargeable the licence will still have to be obtained.[2]

8.16.5 Using and keeping a vehicle without a licence

Offences in respect of using or keeping a vehicle on a public road are dealt with in Pt III of the Vehicle Excise and Registration Act 1994, and in particular by ss 29–41 as amended. Section 29(1) contains the principle offence, and s 29(3) provides that the excise penalty is either level 3 in the standard scale or five times the excise duty chargeable in respect of the vehicle, whichever is greater.

Accordingly, it is an offence to use or keep a mechanically propelled vehicle on a public road for any purpose whatsoever when a licence is not in force in respect of that vehicle.[3]

Section 29(3A) provides that a person who has made a statement or declaration that a vehicle will not be used or kept on a public road, but does so, may be liable to a level 4 penalty for a breach of s 29(1).

An offence in terms of s 29(1) can be proved by the evidence of only one witness.[4]

Sch 2A of the 1994 Act as introduced by the Finance Act 2005 now provides that regulations may be made under the Schedule allowing

1   Road Vehicles (Registration and Licensing) Regulations 2002 (SI 2002/2742) as regularly amended.
2   VERA 1994, s 43A, as introduced by the Finance Act 1997, s 18, and Sch 3 para 5.
3   *MacNeill v Dunbar* 1965 SLT (Notes) 79.
4   VERA 1994, s 54.

for the immobilisation, removal and disposal of vehicles where an authorised person has reason to believe that, on or after such date as may be prescribed, an offence under s 29(1) is being committed as regards a vehicle which is stationary on a public road.

Regulations were put in place for England and Wales by the Vehicle Excise Duty (Immobilisation, Removal and Disposal of Vehicles) Regulations 1997 (SI 1997/2439) and these were extended to Scotland by SI 1998/1217. An authorised person is defined in reg 3 and the various offences arising from immobilisation are set out in regs 7 and 8. In terms of disposal these vary from a level 2 fine for interference with an immobilisation device up to two years' imprisonment on indictment for false declaration that a vehicle was exempt in an effort to have the vehicle released.

A broken-down vehicle or one which is not capable of being moved still may require to have a licence. The only qualification which the Act applies to the requirement is that the vehicle must be mechanically propelled. However, in *MacLean v Hall*,[1] a van which had neither an engine nor a gear box and which was being towed along a public road on its way to a scrap yard was held not to be a mechanically propelled vehicle within the meaning of the Act.

8.16.6 Vehicles excise: general provisions

Section 30 of the Road Traffic Act 1988[2] provides that a further liability may attach to the keeper of an unlicensed vehicle in respect of any unpaid excise duty.

This is calculated on a monthly basis. If the amount of unpaid duty is challenged by the keeper of the vehicle (who for example may claim that he has not been the keeper for the whole period of the unpaid duty) then what is called a back duty proof may have to be fixed. In *Peacock v Hamilton*[3] it was held that where a motorist was charged with using a vehicle it was therefore not competent to require her to pay back duty as keeper of the vehicle.

Section 31A (introduced by the Finance Act 2002, Sch 5) provides a new offence which applies to the person in whose name the vehicle is registered if the vehicle is unlicensed. Exceptions are provided in s 31B and penalties set out in s 31C. These repeat the penalties for breach of s 29 but also include the potential for an additional penalty if the conditions

---

1   *MacLean v Hall* 1962 SLT (Sh Ct) 30.
2   As amended by the Finance Act 2008 (c 9), Sch 45 para 3 (21 July 2008).
3   *Peacock v Hamilton* 1996 SLT 777.

set out in s 31C(3) are met. This offence can be proved by the evidence of one witness only.

It is to be noted that the phrase used, as in s 29, is an 'excise penalty of level 3 on the standard scale'. In *Melville v Thomson*[1] it was confirmed by the Court of Appeal that since excise penalty is not defined within the 1994 Act, in Scotland at least, it should be treated as within the definition of a fine under s 307(1) of the Criminal Procedure (Scotland) Act 1995, thereby allowing reduction in the amount of penalty under reference to s 211(7). In the lower court, given the terms of a letter from DVLA to the appellant, and following legal advices, the Justice had reluctantly felt bound to impose a penalty of £1000. The Appeal Court hoped that in future suitable guidance would be given to prosecutors and that DVLA would reconsider the terms of their letters.

Sections 11–14 of the Act cover the issue and use of trade licences to be taken out by a motor trader or vehicle tester. Both are defined in s 62(1) of the Act.

A 'motor trader' is defined in s 62(1) as (a) a manufacturer or repairer of, or dealer in, vehicles, or (b) any other description of person who carries on a business of such description as may be prescribed by regulations made by the Secretary of State and a person is treated as a dealer in vehicles if he carries on a business consisting wholly or mainly of collecting and delivering vehicles, and not including any other activities except activities as a manufacturer or repairer of, or dealer in, vehicles.

A 'vehicle tester' means a person, other than a motor trader, who regularly in the course of his business engages in the testing on roads of vehicles belonging to other persons.

The vehicles covered by a trade licence are set out in ss 11(2)–(4). In the case of a motor trader who manufactures vehicles, this means all mechanically propelled vehicles which are from time to time temporarily in his possession in the course of his business as a motor trader, all vehicles kept and used by him solely for purposes of conducting research and development in the course of his business as such a manufacturer, and all vehicles which are from time to time submitted to him by other manufacturers for testing on roads in the course of that business. For other motor traders a trade licence covers all mechanically propelled vehicles which are from time to time temporarily in his possession in the course of his business as a motor trader.

1   *Melville v Thomson* 2006 SCCR 663, 2006 SLT1017.

In the case of a vehicle tester, the licence covers all mechanically propelled vehicles which are from time to time submitted to him for testing in the course of his business as a vehicle tester.

In all these circumstances, however, only one vehicle may be used under a trade licence at any one time, and the vehicles so covered may not be kept on the road – see s 12. In addition to the provisions of ss 11–14, reference must be made to regs 35–42 of the Road Vehicles (Registration and Licensing) Regulations 2002.[1]

A motor trader or vehicle tester who has had an application for a trade licence refused may require the Secretary of State to review the decision in terms of s 14 of the Act.

If a vehicle is registered in terms of a particular class of duty because of its nature and composition but thereafter its nature and composition are altered, this may bring the vehicle into another class of duty which the keeper is obliged to pay.[2] Sections 15A and 17 (as amended) provide exceptions. See also 8.15.11 below.

Section 66 of the Road Traffic Act 1988 allows the Secretary of State to make regulations prohibiting the grant of excise licences for certain vehicles except in compliance with certain conditions.

8.16.7 Registration and registration numbers

Part II of the Vehicle Excise and Registration Act provides for the registration of vehicles and the issue of registration marks and numbers. These numbers must be clearly fixed on a vehicle and legible, and be readily distinguishable by day or by night.[3] Failure to fix a registration mark, or to have one that is obscured or rendered indistinguishable, is an offence punishable up to level 3.[4]

The regulation of registration plate suppliers in terms of the Vehicles (Crime) Act 2001 has been amended and extended to Scotland by ss 44–46 of the Roads Safety Act 2006.

Section 47 of the 2006 Act also allows for the amendment of ss 7 and 22 of VERA to allow prescription of the particulars of both the vehicle and the keeper that will be held in the register of vehicles. This provision is not yet in force.

1   Road Vehicles (Registration and Licensing) Regulations 2002 (SI 2002/2742) as regularly amended.
2   VERA 1994, s 15; *Blaikie v Morrison* 1957 JC 46; 1957 SLT 290 and *Blue Band Motors Ltd v Kyle* 1972 SLT 250.
3   Section 23 of VERA 1994.
4   See ss 42 and 43 of VERA 1994.

Section 49 of the 2006 Act allows for disclosure of registration information to foreign authorities. Sections 49A and 49B concern disclosure and use of information relating to foreign-registered vehicles.

8.16.8 Forgery or fraud

In terms of s 44 of the Vehicle Excise and Registration Act 1994, it is an offence to forge, or fraudulently to alter or use, or fraudulently lend or allow to be used by any other person any registration mark, trade plate or registration document. In terms of s 45 it is an offence to make a false or misleading statement in respect of any application for a licence or registration mark, or in respect of a requirement to furnish particulars relating to a vehicle or the keeper thereof.

By virtue of ss 46 and 46A (as amended) of the Act any person who is the registered keeper of a vehicle or any other person in a position to do so, or the alleged user of an unlicensed vehicle, is obliged to give such information as he may be required on behalf of a Chief Officer of Police or the Secretary of State as to the identity of the person or persons involved in an alleged offence of using or keeping a motor vehicle on a road without a licence or in contravention of the requirements in respect of trade plates, or in respect of a vehicle alleged to have been altered so that a different rate of duty applies. It is an offence to fail to comply with any of these requirements. The institution and conduct of proceedings in Scotland relative to licensing matters is dealt with in s 48, including prosecution outwith the normal time limits, but when the prosecution was taken within six months of sufficient information coming to the notice of the person instituting proceedings.

8.16.9 Evidence

Section 52 of the Vehicle Excise and Registration Act 1994[1] provides for the admission of records as evidence.

The section states *inter alia*:

'(1) A statement to which this section applies is admissible in any proceedings as evidence (or, in Scotland, sufficient evidence) of any fact stated in it with respect to matters prescribed by regulations made by the Secretary of State to the same extent as oral evidence of that fact is admissible in the proceedings.

(2) This section applies in a statement in a document purporting to be: –

---

1   As amended by the Finance Act 1995, s 19 and Sch 4 para 38.

(a)   a part of the records maintained by the Secretary of State in connection with any functions exercisable by him under or in terms of this Act,

(b)   a copy of a document forming part of those records, or

(c)   a note of any information contained in those records, and to be authenticated by a person authorised to do so by the Secretary of State.

(4)   In this section as it has effect in Scotland, "document" and "statement" have the same meanings as in section 17(3) of the Law Reform (Miscellaneous Provisions) (Scotland) Act 1968, and the reference to a copy of a document shall be construed in accordance with section 17(4) of that Act.

(6)   Nothing in subsection (4) limits to civil proceedings the references to proceedings in subsection (1).'

The Vehicle and Driving Licences Records (Evidence) Regulations 1970[1] are made in terms of s 52 (1) of VERA.

In *Cardle v Wilkinson*,[2] a statement contained in a document as described in sub-s (1) and authenticated by a rubber stamp signature was held to be admissible in evidence.

8.16.10 Change of ownership

The Road Vehicles (Registration and Licensing) Regulations 2002,[3] regs 22–24 provide for changes of the registered keeper of a vehicle in two categories: change of keeper where the new keeper is not a vehicle trader (reg 22) and change of keeper where the new keeper is a vehicle trader (reg 23). In both situations the keeper must notify the Secretary of State 'forthwith' of the details of the change, the date it occurred and then both old and new keeper must sign a declaration confirming the details as correct. For vehicle traders there are particular obligations set out in reg 24. These reflect a three-month grace period in which the motor dealer may simply pass any part of the vehicle registration document he holds if the vehicle is passed onto another motor dealer. Otherwise, or if the vehicle is passed onto another person, he must notify the Secretary of State of the details of the transfer or, 'forthwith', details of any new keeper.

---

1   Vehicle and Driving Licences Records (Evidence) Regulations 1970 (SI 1970/1997).

2   *Cardle v Wilkinson* 1982 SLT 315, 1982 SCCR 33, 1982 CO Circulars A/3.

3   Road Vehicles (Registration and Licensing) Regulations 2002 (SI 2002/2742).

An offence under s 59 of VERA occurs if this notification of change of ownership is not made 'forthwith' and can be punished by a fine up to level 3. What this means will be a matter of fact and circumstances in each case; in *A & C McLellan (Blairgowrie) Ltd v McMillan*,[1] a prosecution for failure to make proper notification failed because it had not been embarked upon within a six-month period after it could be reasonably said that the former owner had failed to make notification as soon as possible. Further, under reg 18 the registered keeper of any vehicle must intimate any change of name or address to the Secretary of State. In terms of regs 17 and 17A, the owner of a vehicle must notify the Secretary of State when a vehicle has been sent permanently out of the country or destroyed.

The requirement of statutory off-road notification is set out in reg 26 and Sch 4.

A cherished number plate may be transferred from one vehicle to another on payment of the appropriate fee. Provisions as to the content, position and sizing of registration marks are set out in the Road Vehicles (Display of Registration Marks) Regulations 2001 (SI 2001/561 as amended). Breaches of the regulations are prosecuted in terms of s 59 of VERA 1994.

8.16.11 Alteration of vehicle

In terms of reg 16 of the Road Vehicles (Registration and Licensing) Regulations 2002 and s 15 of VERA, where a vehicle licence has been taken out for a vehicle at a rate of duty specified in the legislation and the vehicle is at any time used in an altered condition, or in a manner or for a purpose which brings it under the description of vehicle to which a higher rate of duty applies in accordance with s 15 of the Act, the owner of the vehicle is under a duty to furnish the prescribed particulars to the Secretary of State and must send those details to him together with the licence and the additional duty chargeable.

8.16.12 Registration documents

In association with the issue of a licence in respect of a mechanically propelled vehicle, the Secretary of State also issued a registration document giving details of the vehicle and its owner, in terms of the Road Vehicles (Registration and Licensing) Regulations 2002,[2] reg 10 (as

---

1   *A & C McLellan (Blairgowrie) Ltd v McMillan* 1964 SLT 2.
2   Road Vehicles (Registration and Licensing) Regulations 2002 (SI 2002/2742).

amended). Although the document is associated with the vehicle rather than the driver, the owner must produce the document for inspection if he is required to do so by a police officer at any reasonable time or by anyone acting on behalf of the Secretary of State (reg 12). Mutilation or alteration of the document except under the procedure provided for on a change of ownership is an offence.

8.17 TEST CERTIFICATES (MOT CERTIFICATES)

In terms of ss 45–48 of the Road Traffic Act 1988,[1] any motor vehicle other than a goods vehicle used on the road must have a valid and current test certificate, unless exempted. The requirements for goods vehicles are dealt with in ch 9. It is an offence for a vehicle which must have a certificate not to have one. It is submitted that a vehicle which is parked on a road is normally being 'used' in terms of s 47; however, in the case of *Tudhope v Every*[2] it was held that a vehicle which had been immobilised could not be 'used' in this sense of the word.

The requirement to have a test certificate applies to all vehicles not less than three years old (Road Traffic Act 1988, s 47). The three-year period follows on the date of the first registration of the vehicle. Small passenger coaches, taxis and ambulances need a certificate after one year.[3] The Motor Vehicles (Test) Regulations 1981,[4] provide exemptions including vehicles being taken to or being retrieved from a prearranged test.[5] The regulations made by the Secretary of State in respect of the requirements of construction and condition of such vehicles and for the issue of the relevant certificates in all matters relating thereto are provided for in the foregoing regulations as amended by numerous detailed amendment regulations from 1982 onwards. The MOT became stricter as from May 2018 with particular emphasis on diesel emissions, as well as introducing new categories of defect: dangerous, major and minor.

The examination of vehicles for the purpose of issuing a test certificate has to be carried out by duly appointed inspectors who receive their commission from the Secretary of State, and further such tests must be carried out in approved stations with approved apparatus.[6]

---

1   As amended by the RTA 1991, Sch 4 paras 52 and 53.
2   *Tudhope v Every* 1976 JC 42, 1977 SLT 2.
3   RTA 1988, s 47(3).
4   Motor Vehicles (Test) Regulations 1981 (SI 1981/1694).
5   Regulation 6(2).
6   RTA 1988, s 45.

Chapter 9

Public service vehicles and carriage of goods by road

PART 1
PUBLIC SERVICE VEHICLES

9.1 TRAFFIC AREAS AND TRAFFIC COMMISSIONERS

The United Kingdom is split into 11 traffic areas and the Scottish traffic area serves as a single authority for the whole of Scotland.[1] There is a single Traffic Commissioner for each such area who is appointed by and acts under the general directions of the Secretary of State.[2] There is a single Traffic Commissioner for Scotland who can act in England in relation to reserved matters within the meaning of the Scotland Act 1998. Likewise, Traffic Commissioners in England and Wales can act in Scotland in relation to reserved matters.[3] There is also provision for the appointment of deputy Traffic Commissioners for the Scottish Traffic

1   Public Passenger Vehicles Act 1981 (c14), s 3(1) as amended.
2   PPVA1981, s 4(1) as amended by the Transport Act 1985, s 3, as amended by Local Transport Act 2008 (c 26).
3   Sections 4(3A) and (B) as introduced by Local Transport Act 2008 (c 26), Pt 1, s 2(4) (3 July 2013).

Area under paragraph 3 or 4 of Schedule 2 to the Act. Deployment of Traffic Commissioners is a matter for the Senior Traffic Commissioner, a post introduced under s 4A of the Act, with powers set out in ss 4B and C. In terms of guidance these only relate, in Scotland, to reserved matters.[1]

The Traffic Commissioners are obliged to publish information in respect of their activities in terms of regulations made under s 5 of the Public Passenger Vehicles Act 1981.[2] The Traffic Commissioner's office is a part of the Department of Transport. In practice, the Traffic Commissioner uses that title when dealing with passenger vehicle matters, and is known as the 'licensing authority' when dealing with matters concerning goods vehicles. The commissioners have widespread responsibilities in respect of the licensing of large goods vehicles and passenger carrying vehicle drivers, and also for operators' licences for public service and transport of goods operations. The commissioners also have duties in respect of the supervision of public service and freight operations. A commissioner may hold an inquiry into any matter as he thinks fit in connection with the exercise of his functions.[3] Each Commissioner must report annually to the Secretary of State[4] and keep a record of all licences granted by his office.[5]

The Traffic Commissioner discharges some of his responsibilities in practice through vehicle examiners. Like the police, examiners are entitled to carry out roadside tests and to require particular vehicles to undergo weight testing. The Driver and Vehicle Standards Agency (DVSA), an executive agency of the Department of Transport, has day-to-day responsibility for the authorisation of MOT garages and mechanics; the testing and plating of goods vehicles; the licensing by certificates of initial fitness or certificates of conformity of public service vehicles and their annual testing; and the notifiable alterations for both public service vehicles and goods vehicles.

9.2 DEFINITIONS

9.2.1 'Public service vehicle'

In terms of s 1 of the Public Passenger Vehicles Act 1981 (and subject to the whole provisions of the section) 'a public service vehicle' means –

1   Introduced by the Local Transport Act 2008, Pt 1, s 3.
2   As amended by the Transport Act 1985, s 3(2).
3   PPVA 1981, s 54, as amended.
4   PPVA 1981, s 55, as amended.
5   PPVA 1981, s 56, as amended.

'a motor vehicle (other than a tramcar) which –

(a)   being a vehicle adapted to carry more than eight passengers, is used for carrying passengers for hire or reward; or

(b)   being a vehicle not so adapted, is used for carrying passengers for hire or reward at separate fares in the course of a business of carrying passengers.'

9.2.2 General

The phrase 'adapted to carry more than eight passengers' depends on the circumstances of the case and the number of passengers carried is only one factor. In England a stretched limousine actually carrying nine passengers was not a public service vehicle given its normal use and lay out.[1] The phrase 'for hire or reward' is defined in s 1(5) and (6) of the Public Passenger Vehicles Act 1981; see also *Hawthorn v Knight*.[2] The phrase 'separate fares' means payment by individual passengers in respect of any journey or journeys, whether the payments are made in terms of a fixed tariff imposed by the operator or under an arrangement between the passenger and the carrier.[3] For the purposes of the Act, a vehicle is deemed to be in use until that use has been permanently discontinued.[4] Section 1(3) provides exceptions for vehicles carrying passengers at separate fares in the course of a business of carrying passengers, under certain circumstances described in Pts 1 and 3 of Sch 1 to the Act, unless the vehicle is adapted to carry more than eight passengers. Further, in terms of s 1(4) private motorists are allowed to make car-share arrangements, for a fare or for a consideration. A 'fare' need not be paid only to the driver or owner of the vehicle.[5]

9.3 PUBLIC PASSENGER SERVICE REQUIREMENTS

9.3.1 General

In respect of any such operation of public passenger service, there must be a certificate of initial fitness in respect of the public service vehicles which are used for the purpose of the service; the person or company who is the operator of the service must have a public service vehicles operator's licence; and the driver of the vehicle must have a public service vehicle

---

1   *VOSA v Johnson* EWHC 2003 (2003 167 JP 497).
2   *Hawthorn v Knight* 1962 JC 31, 1962 SLT 69.
3   *Aitken v Hamilton* 1964 SLT 125.
4   PPVA 1981, s 1(2).
5   *Hawthorn v Knight* 1962 JC 31, 1962 SLT 69.

driver's licence (see 9.5 below). In addition, the drivers of certain kinds of passenger carrying vehicle are subject to the legislation on drivers' hours and records of work.

9.3.2 Deregulation

Under the previous system, a public passenger service operation required a road service licence for what were called stage carriage services, (in addition to an operator's licence), in terms of ss 2 and 30–37 of the Public Passenger Vehicles Act 1981. These sections were repealed by ss 1 and 139(3) of and Sch 8 to the Transport Act 1985 which came into force on 26 October 1986 in terms of the Transport Act 1985 (Commencement No 6) Order 1986.[1] As a result of the repeal of ss 30–37 of the 1981 Act, such services were deregulated. In the place of the former road service licences, additional conditions may now be imposed by the Traffic Commissioner on the licences issued to public service vehicle operators in respect of what are now termed local services and which are defined in s 2 of the Transport Act 1985. The commissioner's powers to impose these conditions in respect of registration and traffic regulation are found in ss 6–9 of the 1985 Act as amended, with further amendment yet to come into force.

9.3.3 Certificates of fitness of public service vehicles

In terms of s 6[2] of the Public Passenger Vehicles Act 1981, any public service vehicle adapted to carry more than eight passengers cannot be used on a road unless there is in force in respect of such a vehicle a certificate of initial fitness or its equivalent (which is a certificate of conformity under a type approval scheme: see 9.3.3 below). Such a certificate may not provide a defence to a civil claim based on a failure to supply employees with safe equipment.[3] Such certificates of fitness are issued by a vehicle examiner under s 66A[4] of the Road Traffic Act 1988. The powers of inspection and testing available to such examiners are described at 7.14 above, and such officials have the right of inspection of all public vehicles by virtue of s 68 of the Road Traffic Act 1988.[5] They have the power to issue fixed penalties.

---

1   Transport Act 1985 (Commencement No 6) Order 1986 (SI 1986/1794).
2   As amended by the Road Vehicles (Approval) (Consequential Amendments) Regulations 2009 (SI 2009/818).
3   *Donnelly v Glasgow Corporation* 1953 SC 107, 1953 SLT 161; but see also *Sullivan v Gallagher and Craig* 1959 SC 243, 1960 SLT 70.
4   As amended by the Road Vehicles (Powers to Stop) Regulations 2011 (SI 2011/996).
5   As amended by RTA 1991, s 12.

A public service vehicle may not ply for hire generally.[1] Certain exemptions are given to school buses used in certain circumstances by a local education authority in terms of s 46(1) of the Public Passenger Vehicles Act 1981.

By virtue of ss 6(1)(b), (d) and 10 of the Public Passenger Vehicles Act 1981, the approval by the Secretary of State of a vehicle as a type vehicle or a certificate of type of approval, may be treated as an equivalent to a certificate of fitness or as a certificate of initial fitness.[2]

9.4 PUBLIC SERVICE VEHICLE OPERATORS' LICENCES

9.4.1 General

In addition to certificates of fitness or equivalents relating to vehicles, the operator of any public service vehicle operation must have a licence granted to him in accordance with the relevant statutory provisions.[3] The term 'operator' is defined in s 81 of the Public Passenger Vehicles Act 1981. In terms of s 46, exemption may be granted to a school bus used by an education authority. The licence relates to the operator rather than the vehicle and is granted by the Traffic Commissioner for the relevant area in which are situated the operating centre or centres of the vehicles used in the operation.[4] The power of the Traffic Commissioners to grant licences is contained in s 4(3) and the procedure to be followed by the commissioner is dealt with in ss 14, 14ZA–14ZC[5] and 14A.[6] The commissioner also regulates the fees in respect of the issue of licences and must report annually to the Secretary of State and keep records of all licences issued.[7] Only one public service vehicle licence can be held by any one person in a particular area but there is no restriction on such a person holding such licences in other traffic areas.[8]

---

1   Transport Act 1985, s 30.
2   See also RTA 1988, s 54ff, and the relevant regulations.
3   PPVA 1981, s 12, as amended by Transport Act 1985, Sch 1 para 4.
4   PPVA 1981, s 12(2).
5   As substituted for s 14 by the Road Transport Operator Regulations 2011 (SI 2011/2632).
6   Introduced by TA 1985, s 25.
7   PPVA 1981, s 56, as amended by TA 1985, s 3(5) and Sch 2, Pt II.
8   PPVA 1981, s 12(3).

Licences can either be standard or restricted.[1] There is a limit imposed on the number of vehicles that may be used under a restricted licence.[2] In terms of s 14ZA of the 1981 Act, the commissioner must be satisfied that the applicant for a licence is of good repute, of appropriate financial standing and of the requisite professional competence. For a restricted licence the last of these qualifications is not required.[3] Schedule 3 to the Act gives further details in respect of such applications. By virtue of s 14ZC the applicant must also demonstrate that he has sufficient facilities or arrangements for maintaining the vehicles which are to be operated in terms of the licences in a fit and serviceable condition and that he can provide suitably for observing the requirements of the legislation governing the driving and operation of such vehicles. Provisions in respect of the conditions that may be applied to such licences are dealt with in ss 26 and 27 of the Transport Act 1985. The Chief Constable of the area or the local authority may object to the grant of such licences by virtue of s 14A.[4] The powers of the Traffic Commissioner to disqualify operators from holding a licence are described in s 28 of the 1985 Act.

The licence specifies the date it comes into force and, subject to its revocation or termination under any other statutory provision, continues indefinitely.[5] The previous duration of five years was dispensed with by the Deregulation and Contracting Out Act 1994, s 61. Further, the licence normally indicates the maximum number of vehicles which may be operated, together with further conditions where they are prescribed or otherwise;[6] the same section allows the commissioner to designate stops and include undertakings in the licence, and these can all be revoked or varied; and a description of the prescribed conditions to be attached to a licence is provided in the Public Service Vehicles (Operators Licences) Regulations 1995.[7] By virtue of s 17(1) and (5) of the Public Passenger Vehicles Act 1981 as amended the commissioner has the power to revoke, suspend or vary the conditions on a licence at any time. If the commissioner wishes to revoke a licence on the ground that the operator no longer satisfies the requirement of being of good repute or having the appropriate financial standing, or being professionally competent, a public

---

1   PPVA 1981, s 13.
2   PPVA 1981, s 16 as amended by TA 1985.
3   PPVA 1981, s 14ZB.
4   Inserted by TA 1985, s 25.
5   PPVA 1981, s 15.
6   PPVA 1981, s 16.
7   Public Service Vehicles (Operators Licences) Regulations 1995 (SI 1995/2869).

hearing must first be held if the operator requires. The commissioner may appoint assessors in terms of s 17A.[1]

By virtue of s 18,[2] the operator has a duty to exhibit on each vehicle covered by the licence an appropriate disc issued by the commissioner. This disc gives particulars of the operator of the vehicle, his operator's licence and its date of expiry, but no details of the vehicle itself. Current regulations are the Public Service Vehicles (Operator's Licences) Regulations 1995.[3]

The operator must inform the Secretary of State of any relevant criminal convictions, or of any incident or damage relating to any of the vehicles covered by the licence, which might have a bearing on public safety.[4]

Exemption from some of the foregoing requirements is available to local education authorities in respect of school buses carrying fare-paying passengers.[5] Community bus services exempted from some operator and driver licensing requirements under a system of permits are dealt with under ss 22 and 23 of the Transport Act 1985 together with other regulations and in general, reference should be made to ss 18–23A of the Transport Act 1985 in respect of these exemptions.

By virtue of s 57 of the 1981 Act, an operator's licence is not assignable and ceases to be valid on the death, bankruptcy, sequestration or mental incapacity of the holder, or in respect of any other event described in the licence by the commissioner. Deferment of termination may be granted in certain circumstances. The regulations covering the procedure for applications for such licences come in terms of s 59; and reference should be made to the Public Service Vehicles (Operators' Licences) Regulations 1995[6] and Sch 3 of the 1981 Act.

It is an offence to forge or alter any licence, disc, certificate or document, or to make a false statement in any application connected with an operator's licence.[7] The registered keeper of a public service vehicle has a duty to disclose the identity of the driver of that vehicle at any given time.[8]

---

1   Introduced by TA 1985, s 5.
2   As amended by the Deregulation and Contracting Out Act 1994, ss 63 and 68 and Sch 14 para 6.
3   Public Service Vehicles (Operator's Licences) Regulations 1995 (SI 1995/2908).
4   PPVA 1981, ss 19 and 20, as amended by TA 1985, s 29 and s 7 of the Road Safety Act 2006 in relation to fixed penalties.
5   PPVA 1981, s 46.
6   Public Service Vehicles (Operators' Licences) Regulations 1995 (SI 1995/2908).
7   PPVA 1981, ss 65 and 66, as amended.
8   PPVA 1981, s 70.

Section 74 of the Road Traffic Act 1988 imposes duties on the operator to inspect his vehicles and keep records of such inspections.

9.4.2 Appeals

In the event of a Traffic Commissioner refusing an application for a public service vehicle operator's licence, or if a condition is imported into the licence which has not been included in the application, the appellant has the right to appeal to the Upper Tribunal.[1] Under previous legislation, the decision of the Secretary of State could be appealed on a point of law to the Court of Session.[2] Such an appeal is no longer specifically provided for but is not necessarily unavailable, for example by means of the process of judicial review. In such appeals the Traffic Commissioner has no locus to appear but the Secretary of State has if he has been represented before the Tribunal. If not he may do so with the leave of the Court in appropriate cases.[3]

Further, a person who has had an application for a certificate of initial fitness in terms of s 6 of the Public Passenger Vehicles Act 1981, or a type vehicle certificate in terms of s 10, refused, may appeal to the Secretary of State under s 51.[4] Section 49A[5] allows the commissioner to vary or revoke his own decisions.

9.5 PUBLIC SERVICE VEHICLES DRIVERS' LICENCES

Drivers of public service vehicles (now called passenger carrying vehicles or PCVs) and of heavy goods vehicles (now called large goods vehicles or LGVs) no longer require the issue of a separate licence. The licensing of PCV or LGV drivers is now incorporated in the ordinary driving licence, but the additional authorisations are under the control of the Traffic Commissioners. The legislation governing these matters is found in the Road Traffic (Driver Licensing and Information Systems) Act 1989, ss 1–5 and Sch 2, which extensively alters Pt IV of the Road Traffic Act 1988 and in particular ss 110–121 thereof. Section 121 of the 1988 Act contains

---

1   PPVA 1981, s 50, as substituted by Transfer of Functions (Transport Tribunal and Appeal Panel) Order 2009 (SI 2009/1885).

2   See, for example, *Strathclyde Passenger Executive v McGill's Bus Service* 1984 SLT 377.

3   *Coakley v Secretary of State for Transport* 2003 SLT 1367.

4   As amended by the Transport Act 1985, s 31 and the RTA 1991, ss 48 and 83, Sch 4 para 16 and Sch 8.

5   Added by the Deregulation and Contracting Out Act 1994, s 65(1).

definitions of passenger carrying vehicles. The holder of a licence entitling the driver to drive a passenger carrying vehicle is therefore subject to the general rules that apply to the holder of a driving licence;[1] for example, it is an offence to cause or permit another to drive a passenger carrying vehicle without a licence allowing him to drive a vehicle of the class.[2] Appropriate provision is made for the earlier form of licence to remain in effect.

Regulations may be made to govern the conduct of drivers, conductors and inspectors of public service vehicles, and also to regulate the conduct of passengers, by virtue of ss 24 and 25 of the Public Passengers Vehicles Act 1981. The regulations currently in force are the Public Service Vehicles (Conduct of Drivers, Inspectors, Conductors and Passengers) Regulations 1990 as amended.[3] Breaches of the regulations can be dealt with under both ss 24 and 25 by a fine not exceeding level 2 and level 3 respectively on the standard scale. For offences involving drivers, they may be added to the person's driving record.

A special driving test must be taken (see 9.12.2 below). The regulations, *inter alia*, impose duties of care on the drivers of buses only in respect of persons entitled to board the bus and not in respect of anyone attempting to board while it is in motion.[4] These sections and regulations do not apply to trolley buses, but do apply to trams.

The Motor Vehicle (Driving Licences) Regulations 1999[5] make detailed provision for categories of entitlement, age limits, licence applications, tests of competence to drive and other matters concerning goods and passenger carrying vehicles.

9.6 LOCAL AUTHORITY SERVICES

By virtue of s 101(1) of the Road Traffic Act 1930, as amended by the Transport Act 1968, ss 31 and 37, a local authority may run public service vehicles on any road inside or outside its district as part of any operation of tramways, light railways, trolley vehicles or omnibuses which it undertakes in terms of a local Act or order.

---

1   See RTA 1988, Ch 8 and Pt III.
2   RTA 1988, s 87(2).
3   Public Service Vehicles (Conduct of Drivers, Inspectors, Conductors and Passengers) Regulations 1990 (SI 1990/1020).
4   *Reid v MacNicol* 1958 SLT 42.
5   Motor Vehicle (Driving Licences) Regulations 1999 (SI 1999/2864).

9.7 PASSENGER TRANSPORT AUTHORITIES AND EXECUTIVES

The function of passenger transport authorities is to make general policy in respect of any unmet demand for public transport service in the area. The function of the Passenger Transport Executive is to secure services which will comply with that policy. How this is achieved varies from area to area. The detailed provisions for these functions, and in respect of local authority bus operations, are found in Pt IV of the Transport Act 1985. The consequent financial provisions including those relating to travel concession schemes, are dealt with in Pt V of the Act. Part V covers general miscellaneous matters including questions of competition law, travel concession schemes, the reconstitution of the Transport Tribunal, the provision by British Rail of substitution road services and the constitution of the Disabled Persons Transport Advisory Committee. Both are now subject to amendment by the Scottish Parliament and regard should be had, for example, to the Transport (Scotland) Act 2005 (asp 12).

9.8 TRAVEL CONCESSIONS

The local authority may make travel concessions to certain qualified persons who travel on its vehicles, by introducing either free travel or reduced fares. Persons who qualify for these concessions may be those over 60 years of age; children under 16; persons between the minimum school leaving age and 18 who are undergoing full-time education; blind persons; disabled persons; and others the Secretary of State may specify. Those provisions are contained generally in the Transport Act 1985, ss 93ff as amended by the Local Government in Scotland Act 2003 (asp 1), Pt 8, s 44(1).

9.9 INTERNATIONAL CARRIAGE OF PASSENGERS AND LUGGAGE BY ROAD

Reference should be made to the Road Transport (International Passenger Services) Regulations 1984 (SI 1984/748), as amended. These control services, whether regular or occasional, by vehicles registered in the United Kingdom whether regulated by the Community or ASOR states ('ASOR' is the Agreement on the International Carriage of Passengers by Road by means of Occasional Coach and Bus Services) or not. They impact on the provisions of both the Public Passenger Vehicles Act 1981 and the Transport Act 1985.

PART 2
CARRIAGE OF GOODS BY ROAD

9.10 GOODS VEHICLES

The legislation imposes certain requirements on the operation of commercial goods vehicles and the carriage of goods on the roads for hire or reward. The principal considerations met with in practice are the requirement that anyone operating a goods vehicle should have an operator's licence, the need for the driver to have a licence authorising him to drive the vehicle in question, and the qualification of the amount of hours of work that a driver of a commercial vehicle is entitled to do and the records which he must keep in respect of that work.

9.11 GOODS VEHICLES OPERATORS' LICENCES

9.11.1 General

The Goods Vehicle (Licensing of Operators) Act 1995 provides that it is an offence to use a goods vehicle on a road for the carriage of goods for hire or reward, or for in connection with any trade or businesses carried on by the operator except under an operator's licence.[1] This is subject to a number of exceptions, including relating to the use of small goods vehicles, s 2(1B) and s 2(1C), and the use of a goods vehicle for international carriage by a haulier established in a member state other than the United Kingdom and not established in the United Kingdom, or a haulier established in Northern Ireland and not established in Great Britain, s 2(2).

The licensing authority is the Traffic Commissioner.[2] A description of the phrase 'hire or reward' is given at 9.2.2 above. A vehicle is used for reward where a payment is made, even although there is no legal obligation on the payer to make such payment.[3] For further definitions of the phrase 'hire or reward', reference should be made to the cases of *Wurzel v Houghton Main Home Delivery Service Ltd*[4] and *Albert v Motor Insurers Bureau*.[5]

---

1 GV(LO)A 1995, s 2, as amended by the Road Transport Operator Regulations 2011 (SI 2011/2632).
2 GV(LO)A 1995, s 1.
3 *Aitken v Hamilton* 1964 SLT 125.
4 *Wurzel v Houghton Main Home Delivery Service Ltd* [1937] 1 KB 380.
5 *Albert v Motor Insurers Bureau* [1972] AC 301.

The licensing authority may specify in the operator's licence what vehicles the operator is authorised to use in terms of the licence.[1] Applications for licences, their issue and duration, their conditions, suspension, curtailment and variation, and the disqualification and revocation of licences are dealt with in ss 8–34 of the 1995 Act. Schedule 2 provides the qualifications expected of applicants for operators' licences. Reference should also be made to the Goods Vehicles (Licensing of Operators) Regulations 1995.[2] The power of Traffic Commissioners to hold inquiries (which are wide-ranging) and review and appeals procedure are provided for in ss 35–37. In order to secure that the conditions of an operator's licence are being observed, authorised examiners have powers of entry and inspection.[3] Operators' licences are not transferable.[4] All these sections have been subject to amendment in detail including s 6 of the Road Safety Act 2006 in relation to notification of fixed penalties.

Operators' licences may be standard, which allow the vehicles to be used both for hire or reward, and in connection with the trade or business, and for international transport operations or national transport operations only. Alternatively, licences may be restricted, which allows the vehicles covered by the licence to be used in respect of the operator's trade or business only. The nature of these licences, relevant conditions, exceptions and the qualifications which have to be met by an operator before a licence is granted to him are contained in the Goods Vehicles (Licensing of Operators) Regulations 1995.[5] Reference needs also to be made to the Schedules of the Act. For more detailed and practical advice on the licensing of the operators of goods vehicles, the Traffic Commissioner's Office issues, in association with the Department of Transport, a number of useful booklets and guides on the subject.

9.11.2 Operators' licences: inspection and evidence

The operator of a goods vehicle has a duty to inspect the vehicle and a further duty to keep records of that inspection.[6] In any proceedings for a failure to observe regulations under s 74 of the Road Traffic Act 1988 or a

---

1   GV(LO)A 1995, s 5.
2   Goods Vehicles (Licensing of Operators) Regulations 1995 (SI 1995/2869).
3   GV(LO)A 1995, s 40–42.
4   GV(LO)A 1995, s 48.
5   Goods Vehicles (Licensing of Operators) Regulations 1995 (SI 1995/2869).
6   RTA 1988, s 74, as amended by the RTA 1991, Sch 4 para 57.

failure to observe the construction and use regulations, such records are sufficient evidence of the matters stated therein.[1]

9.12 GOODS VEHICLES DRIVERS' LICENCES

9.12.1 General

Drivers of heavy goods vehicles (now called large goods vehicles or LGVs) no longer need to obtain a separate licence. The entitlement to drive various classes of commercial vehicle is incorporated in the ordinary driving licence. The additional authorisations are under the control of the Traffic Commissioners. The legislation governing these matters is found in Pt IV of the Road Traffic Act 1988 and in particular ss 110–121 thereof. The holder of a licence authorising the driver to drive a large goods vehicle is therefore subject to the general rules that apply to any other holder of a driving licence.[2] It is not only persons who have actual knowledge of the absence of an appropriate licence on the part of the driver who can be found guilty of causing or permitting the driver to commit an offence; constructive or imputed knowledge of the lack of such a licence may lead to conviction.[3]

A large goods vehicle is defined in s 121 of the Road Traffic Act 1988 (as amended) as:

> 'a motor vehicle (not being a medium sized vehicle within the meaning of Part III of this Act) which is constructed or adapted to carry or haul goods and the permissible maximum weight of which exceeds 7.5 tonnes'.

An appeal against the refusal by the Secretary of State to grant a licence is available in terms of s 119 of the Road Traffic Act 1988[4] (see also 9.12.2 below).

In terms of the definition of the term 'permissible maximum weight' contained in s 108 of the Road Traffic Act 1988, a rigid or articulated vehicle drawing a trailer may bring a vehicle into the category of LGV licensing if the total weight of the combination exceeds 7.5 tonnes.

---

1   RTOA 1988, s 14, as amended by RTA 1991, Sch 4 para 86; see also Good Vehicles (Licensing of Operators) Act 1995, s 43.
2   See RTA 1988, Ch 8 and Pt III.
3   *MacPhail v Allan and Day* 1980 SLT (Sh Ct) 136.
4   Introduced by the Road Traffic (Driver Licensing and Information Systems) Act 1989, s 2(1).

9.12.2 Application for, and nature of, licence

An application for a licence is made to the Traffic Commissioner for the area in which the applicant resides.[1] Generally, the principal requirements and conditions of such licences are found in Pt IV of the Act, but there are also a number of important statutory instruments.[2] Again, the Traffic Commissioner issues booklets in respect of applications for such licences. In particular an applicant must pass a special driving test.[3] Reference should also be made to the Motor Vehicles (Driving Licences) Regulations 1999.[4]

The licensing authority has power to revoke or suspend a licence.[5] Considerations which may result in revocation and disqualification are the driver's conduct, his failure to keep records or a physical disability.[6] The disqualification may be indefinite or for such period as the licensing authority considers to be appropriate. The revocation of a licence by a Traffic Commissioner results in disqualification from driving the prescribed classes of vehicle.[7]

If the test of competency to drive is alleged to have been unfairly conducted, or was not conducted properly in terms of the relevant regulations, the applicant may appeal by way of application to the sheriff for the area where he resides.[8] An appeal to the sheriff is also available in respect of any refusal, revocation or curtailment of a licence.

9.13 GOODS VEHICLES PLATING AND TESTING CERTIFICATES

9.13.1 General

Sections 45 and 49 of the Road Traffic Act 1988,[9] and Pt IV of that Act generally provide that all goods vehicles which are used on the roads

---

1   RTA 1988, s 111, as amended.
2   Eg the Driving Licences (Community Driving Licence) Regulations 1996 (SI 1996/1974), and the Motor Vehicles (Driving Licences) Regulations 1999 (SI 1999/2864).
3   RTA 1988, ss 89 and 89A, as amended by the Road Traffic (Driver Licensing and Information System) Act 1989 etc.
4   Motor Vehicles (Driving Licences) Regulations 1999 (SI 1999/2864).
5   RTA 1988, s 115, as amended.
6   See *Warrender v Scottish Traffic Area Licensing Authority* 1976 SLT (Sh Ct) 76.
7   RTA 1988, s 117.
8   RTA 1988, s 119, as amended; see, eg, *Crawford v Scottish Traffic Area Licensing Authority* 1974 SLT (Sh Ct) 11.
9   As amended by the RTA 1991, Sch 4 paras 52 and 54.

must have both a plating certificate and a test certificate, and provision is also made for the testing of goods vehicles. A plating certificate contains the plated particulars (including the plated weight) which are prescribed. The test certificate relates to requirements of construction and use. The Goods Vehicles (Plating and Testing) Regulations 1988[1] make provision in respect of both types of certificate. Reference should also be made to Pt III of the Road Vehicles (Construction and Use) Regulations 1986,[2] in respect of plating requirements, testing and inspection. Test certificates have to be renewed periodically. Section 48 of the Road Safety Act 2006 amends s 49 and introduces a new s 49A which requires the Secretary of State to maintain a record of vehicle testing and that the details kept therein may be used to verify records kept for the purposes of vehicles excise and registration. Neither provision is yet in force as at the time of writing. See also 7.12.8 above.

9.13.2 Type approval schemes

The plating and testing certificates are required for all goods vehicles that are manufactured or produced and used. For practical reasons, they are implemented by means of type approval schemes. Manufacturers may submit to the Secretary of State a type vehicle for approval. The approval is intended to cover all matters of design, construction, equipment and marking. The Secretary of State then issues a type approval certificate, and this enables the manufacturer to provide other vehicles with a certificate of conformity to the effect that all such further vehicles conform to the type vehicle submitted to the Secretary of State. The plated particulars must be indicated on every vehicle. The principle of the scheme is extended to vehicle parts. There are a number of statutory instruments which implement the schemes in detail. A discussion of these details is not within the scope of this book.

9.13.3 Inspection

Authorised examiners have extensive powers of test and inspection of all kinds of motor vehicles. Sections 9–15 of the Road Traffic Act 1991 replace or amend various sections in the Public Passengers Vehicles Act 1981 and the Road Traffic Act 1988. In effect, the previous categories of certifying officers, examiners of goods vehicles and public service examiners are replaced by a single class of vehicle examiners. Such

---

1   Goods Vehicles (Plating and Testing) Regulations 1988 (SI 1988/1478) (as regularly amended).
2   Road Vehicles (Construction and Use) Regulations 1986 (SI 1986/1078).

examiners are appointed and authorised by the Secretary of State. Most of such examiners will be members of the DVSA, but there is provision for police officers also to be appointed and authorised.

By virtue of ss 9–15, the following provisions are made for vehicle examination. Section 66A of the Road Traffic Act 1988 allows the Secretary of State to appoint vehicle examiners.

In addition, the Road Vehicles (Powers to Stop) Regulations[1] introduced new ss 66B and 66C to the Road Traffic Act 1988, as well as amending s 67 and the Road Traffic Offenders Act 1988. These provisions provide for 'Stopping officers'. Their powers are introduced by s 66B and associated offences by s 66C. These officers are to be used for checks of commercial vehicles, both domestic and EC, involving licencing and other matters.

Section 67 of the Act provides that vehicles may be tested on roads to check that they comply with all aspects of the construction and use regulations (including lighting) and includes the power of the examiner to drive the vehicle in question, and to require the driver to comply with his instructions. Section 68 provides specifically for the inspection of public passenger vehicles and goods vehicles, and gives the examiner the power to drive the vehicle, as well as the power to enter premises to inspect the vehicle or detain it for the purpose of testing it. It is an offence intentionally to obstruct an examiner in his pursuit of any of these powers. Further, an examiner or a police officer in uniform may direct the driver to drive his vehicle to a testing station not more than five miles distant from where the vehicle is stopped. Section 69, subject to s 69A, gives the examiner the power to prohibit the driving of any unfit vehicle (not only PCVs or LGVs). Section 70 allows the prohibition of overloaded passenger or goods vehicles, and ss 71 and 72 create offences and allow for removal of prohibitions respectively. Section 74 imposes inspection duties on the operator.

Prosecution for overloading or dangerous vehicles is dealt with at 7.12.6, 7.12.7 and 7.12.15 above.

As noted already, since s 5 and Sch 1 to the Road Safety Act 2006 came into force in 2009, the fixed penalty scheme has extended to include the issuing of fixed penalties by vehicle examiners. Schedule 1 details the required amendments to Pt III of the Road Traffic Offenders Act 1998.

---

1   Road Vehicles (Powers to Stop) Regulations 2011 (SI 2011/996).

9.14 DRIVERS' HOURS AND RECORDS OF WORK

9.14.1 General

Section 95 of the Transport Act 1968 (as substantially amended) provides that drivers engaged in the road transport industry, whether engaged in the carriage of passengers or of goods, must observe certain restrictions in the hours worked. It should be noticed that the term 'working' used throughout this part of the legislation is not necessarily exclusively confined to 'driving'. The basic idea is that no driver of any vehicle engaged in the carriage of passengers or goods should drive for longer than certain periods,[1] and such vehicles should have installed and use prescribed recording equipment ('the tachograph').[2] Accordingly, the legislation makes provision for two sorts of offences: those concerned with maximum permitted driving hours and rest periods and breaks, and those concerned with the fitting and use of tachographs. It should be emphasised from the outset that this is a particularly complex field of law, and adequate coverage of the topic is not within the scope of this book.

The purpose of these restrictions and provisions is specifically described as a protection of the public against the risks which arise when drivers are suffering from fatigue. The Secretary of State has extensive power to make regulations in respect of these matters and, in practice, makes regulations to take account of any requirement imposed by the rules of the European Union. Numerous regulations have been made in terms of s 95. Part VI of the Act outlines the general framework of the scheme. Broadly speaking, there are two kinds of rules: those which apply to national and international driving, and those which, exempted from the first category, apply to what is called domestic driving. The international and national rules apply to most goods vehicles over 3.5 tonnes maximum weight. There are various exceptions from these requirements provided for in the regulations. Significant changes were introduced by the Goods Vehicles (Recording Equipment) Regulations[3] which introduced new ss 99ZA–99ZF and which also reflect the introduction of digital tachographs.

Generally, the requirements of international and national driving are at present as follows. The rules apply to all goods vehicles which exceed 3.5 tonnes permissible maximum weight and to all passenger vehicles carrying more than nine persons including the driver (see 9.14.4 below).

1   Transport Act 1968, s 96(2).
2   TA 1968, s 97, as amended.
3   Goods Vehicles (Recording Equipment) Regulations 2005 (SI 2005/1904).

The permitted hours of driving are complex and are now contained in Regulation (EC) 561/2006 which took effect from 11 April 2007 and replaced Council Regulation (EEC) 3820/85. A very approximate general survey of the new rules now follows.

A driver must not drive for more than nine hours in a day. This may be extended to 10 hours twice a week. After four and a half hours of driving a driver must take a break of at least 45 minutes unless he takes a rest period. This break may be replaced by a break of at least 15 minutes followed by a break of at least 30 minutes each distributed over the period in such a way as to comply with the general principle. Weekly rest periods must be taken after six consecutive daily driving periods. The total period of driving per fortnight must not exceed 90 hours. A driver must have a minimum daily rest of eleven consecutive hours which may be reduced in certain circumstances. These general rules are subject to extensive exceptions and revision. Vehicles not subject to these rules may be required to observe the requirements in Pt VI of the Transport Act 1968, which contains other rules of a like kind. Statutory defences of both sets of regulation offences are found in s 96(11) and (11B) of the 1968 Act.[1]

Journeys to some European countries outside the European Union are subject to an international agreement on drivers' hours. These agreements (the AETR Rules) may also have to be observed. Further, if a country is neither in the European Union nor subject to the AETR Rules (eg Switzerland) the domestic rules of that country have to be observed.

Certain operations are exempted from the international and national drivers' hours and tachograph rules when they are engaged in specific operations. In such cases, drivers of goods vehicles which are so exempted are subject to certain domestic rules. These are that no driver may drive for more than ten hours in a day or be on duty for more than 11 hours on any working day. There are also special considerations given to mixed domestic and EU driving and there are certain exemptions even from the domestic rules. Drivers governed by domestic rules do not have to install and use the tachograph.

9.14.2 Offences

In respect of offences in terms of these regulations, any record produced by recording equipment tendered by drivers as correct which show that driving has occurred for longer than the permitted hours are in themselves sufficient, in the absence of any definite and further evidence,

---

1   See also *Lees v Styles* 1997 SLT (Sh Ct) 11.

to constitute the offence.[1] However, evidence that the weekly rest period has not been taken has to be established by demonstrating the number of hours worked.[2] The onus is on the driver to show that he is entitled to any of the statutory exceptions.[3] In determining whether an offence has been committed, hours of driving outside the United Kingdom can properly be taken into account.[4]

Tachographs must be kept inspected every two years and calibrated every six years.

There can be difficulties of jurisdiction in respect of offences libelled because of the terms of s 103(7) of the Transport Act 1968; and practitioners may encounter some difficulty in discovering what might be the appropriate penalties for some tachograph offences. A useful summary is found in *Wilkinson Road Traffic Offences* Vol 1 (Text), 28th Edition, at paras 14.201 and 202.

9.14.3 Keeping of records

There are numerous requirements relating to the keeping of records in terms of Pt VI of the Transport Act 1968 both in terms of paper records and data download. Employers have a duty to provide their drivers with record charts of an approved type that can be used in the tachograph. The driver is obliged to enter certain information on the chart before inserting it into the tachograph. It is the driver's responsibility to see that recording by the tachograph takes place properly. Drivers are then obliged to return their charts to their employers who must keep them for a year. Only those drivers whose driving is governed by these EC Rules are required to operate the tachograph; other drivers are merely constrained by the domestic driving rules. However, the provision of the tachograph requirements as indicated above is complex and there are a number of exceptions.

The basic regulations are the Passenger and Goods Vehicles (Recording Equipment) Regulations 2005,[5] the Passenger and Goods

---

1   Transport Act 1968, s 97(B), as amended by Passenger and Goods Vehicles (Recording Equipment) Regulations 2005 (SI 2005/1904), reg 3 and Passenger and Goods Vehicles (Tachographs) (Amendment) Regulations 2016/248, *Adair v Craighouse Cabinet Works Ltd* 1937 JC 89, 1937 SLT 499.
2   *Douglas v Glass* 1990 SCCR 445.
3   *Lees v Styles* 1997 SLT (Sh Ct) 11.
4   *Fox v Lawson* [1974] AC 803, [1974] 2 WLR 247.
5   Passenger and Goods Vehicles (Recording Equipment) Regulations 2005 (SI 2005/1904).

Vehicles (Recording Equipment) (Downloading and Retention of Data) Regulations 2008[1], and the Drivers Hours (Goods Vehicles) (Keeping of Records) Regulations 1987.[2]

Any entry on a record sheet made by a crew member can be sufficient evidence of the matters appearing therein.[3] However, in any prosecution the Crown must prove the number of hours worked when the driver was engaged in both regulated and unregulated driving.[4] It is recommended that practitioners involved in this detailed and continually changing subject should consult a specialist work on the subject for further information on this matter.

9.14.4 Exemptions

Certain exemptions are granted in respect of both drivers' hours and the installation and use of the tachograph in respect of certain vehicles. For example, certain passenger and public authority vehicles; ambulances; breakdown vehicles; vehicles in restricted use in agricultural, forestry and fishing enterprises; vehicles carrying animal carcases and waste unfit for human consumption are exempted.[5] Also exempted are vehicles in respect of operations carried out by specialised vehicles;[6] this exemption applies to the operations which are carried out (such as door-to-door selling) rather than the vehicles themselves.[7] Police officers and other appropriate persons – for example, examiners appointed under s 66A of the RTA 1988 – have an extensive power of inspection in respect of tachograph

1   Passenger and Goods Vehicles (Recording Equipment) (Downloading and Retention of Data) Regulations 2008 (SI 2008/198).
2   Drivers Hours (Goods Vehicles) (Keeping of Records) Regulations 1987 (SI 1987/1421).
3   Transport Act 1968, ss 97 and 97B, as amended by Passenger and Goods Vehicles (Recording Equipment) Regulations 2005 (SI 2005/1904) reg 3 and the Passenger and Goods Vehicles (Recording Equipment) (Tachograph Card) Regulations 2006 (SI 2006/1937).
4   *Douglas v Glass* 1990 SCCR 445.
5   See Regulation (EC) 561/2006 and the Community Drivers' Hours and Recording Equipment Regulations 2007 (SI 2007/1819), and the Schedule thereto; see also *Ross-Taylor v Houston* 1986 SCCR 210 (exemption for transport of livestock to local markets or slaughterhouses); *Weir v Tudhope* 1987 SCCR 307 (exemption for specialised breakdown vehicles).
6   See Regulation (EC) 561/2006, art 3 and art 13.
7   *Struthers (Lochwinnoch) v Tudhope* 1982 SLT 393, 1981 SCCR 329; *Stewart v Richmond* 1983 SLT 62, 1982 SCCR 383; *Baron Meats Ltd v Lockhart* 1993 SLT 279, 1991 SCCR 537; *Reith v Skinner* 1996 SCCR 506.

operations[1] and exemption from all these requirements is given to the police and fire brigade and to armed service vehicles, but not to vehicles in the public service of the Crown.[2] Reference should also be made to the Community Drivers' Hours and Recording Equipment Regulations 2007;[3] and the Drivers' Hours (Harmonisation with Community Rules) Regulations 1986.[4]

Regulation (EC) 561/2006 provides[5] for similar exemptions in the equivalent EC legislation. In particular, arts 3(d) and (e), and 13(1)(c) appear to extend the exemption to ambulance-type vehicles, while the UK regulations do not. It is suggested that ambulances are exempt in terms of reg 2 of the Drivers' Hours (Goods Vehicles) (Exemptions) Regulations 1986.[6]

9.15 FOREIGN GOODS VEHICLES AND PUBLIC SERVICE VEHICLES

9.15.1 General

By virtue of s 1 of the Road Traffic (Foreign Vehicles) Act 1972 (as amended), appointed examiners are entitled to inspect foreign goods vehicles and foreign public service vehicles, to satisfy themselves that the relevant provisions of domestic road traffic legislation are being observed. If necessary they may prohibit driving of the vehicle either absolutely or for a specified time.

9.15.2 International carriage of goods by road

The Goods Vehicles (Community Licences) Regulations 2011[7] make provision for a Community licence allowing goods vehicles access to the market in the carriage of goods by road between Member States and for a driver attestation where the driver is a third country national.

---

1   Transport Act 1968, s 99 as amended
2   TA 1968, s 102, as amended by the Road Traffic (Consequential Provisions) Act 1988, Sch 3 para 6.
3   Community Drivers' Hours and Recording Equipment Regulations 2007 (SI 2007/1819).
4   Drivers' Hours (Harmonisation with Community Rules) Regulations 1986 (SI 1986/1458).
5   Regulation (EC) 561/2006, art 3.
6   Drivers' Hours (Goods Vehicles) (Exemptions) Regulations 1986 (SI 1986/1492).
7   Goods Vehicles (Community Licences) Regulations 2011 (SI 2011/2633).

The competent authority for the community licence is a Traffic Commissioner and, for driver attestation, the Secretary of State, in terms of reg 5.

Failure to comply with the requirement to possess a Community licence is a summary offence in terms of reg 4 and is met with a penalty of up to a level 4 fine.

Stopping Officers, introduced by s 66B of the Road Traffic Act 1988, as amended, have the power to stop vehicles to check whether any offence under reg 4 has occurred.

Appendix A

Tables

SHORTEST STOPPING DISTANCES IN OPTIMUM CONDITIONS FOR MOTOR CARS

Miles per hour	Thinking distance		Braking distance		Total	
	Feet	Metres	Feet	Metres	Feet	Metres
20	20	6	20	6	40	12
30	30	9	45	14	75	23
40	40	12	80	24	120	36
50	50	15	125	38	175	53
60	60	18	180	55	240	73
70	70	21	245	75	315	96
80	80	24	320	98	400	122
90	90	27	405	124	495	151
100	100	29	500	153	600	182

Regard must be had to the fact that these represent braking in optimum conditions. Equally, it should be noted that these figures were derived from testing a Ford Anglia in the 1960s. Modern brakes might produce very different results in all conditions.

APPROXIMATE SPEED-DISTANCE TABLE

Miles per hour	Yards per second	Metres per minute
20	10	530
30	15	805
40	20	1 080
50	25	1 335
60	30	1 610
70	35	1 885
80	40	2 140
90	45	2 425
100	50	2 670

APPROXIMATE RATE OF ABSORPTION IN BREATH ANALYSIS CASES (AVERAGE OF 6.5g PER 100ml PER HOUR)

Breath reading	30 min	60 min	90 min	120 min
30	29	23	20	17
35	32	28	25	22
40	37	33	30	27
45	42	38	35	32
50	47	43	40	37
60	57	53	50	47
70	67	63	60	57
80	77	73	70	67
90	87	83	80	77
100	97	93	90	87
110	107	103	100	97
120	117	113	110	107
130	127	123	120	117
140	137	133	130	127
150	147	143	140	137

APPROXIMATE RATE OF ABSORPTION IN BLOOD ANALYSIS CASES (AVERAGE OF 15g PER 100ml PER HOUR)

Breath reading	30 min	60 min	90 min	120 min
80	72	65	57	50
90	82	75	67	60
100	92	85	77	70
110	102	95	87	80
120	112	105	97	90
130	122	115	107	100
140	132	125	117	110
150	142	135	127	120
160	152	145	137	130
170	162	155	147	140
180	172	165	157	150
190	182	175	167	160
200	192	185	177	170

Appendix B

Endorsement offence codes

Aiding, abetting, counselling or procuring offences
For these offences, the codes are similar, but with the number 0 on the code changed to 2. For example, code LC20 (driving otherwise than in accordance with a licence) becomes code LC22 on your licence if you have helped someone to do this.

Causing or permitting offences
For these offences, the codes are similar, but with the number 0 on the code changed to 4. For example, LC20 (driving otherwise than in accordance with a licence) becomes LC24 on your licence if you've caused or permitted someone to do this.

Inciting offences
For these offences, the codes are similar, but with the number 0 on the code changed to 6. For example, DD40 (dangerous driving) becomes DD46 on your licence if you have incited someone to do this.

Code	Offence	Points
	Accident Offences	
	These codes must stay on a driving licence for four years from the date of the offence.	
AC10	Failing to stop after an accident	5 to 10
AC20	Failing to give particulars or report an accident within 24 hours	5 to 10
AC30	Undefined accident offences	4 to 9
	Disqualified driver	
	These codes must stay on a driving licence for four years from the date of the offence	
BA10	Driving while disqualified by order of court	6
BA30	Attempting to drive while disqualified by order of court	6
	These codes must stay on a driving licence for four years from the date of the conviction	
BA40	Causing death by driving while disqualified	3–11
BA60	Causing serious injury by driving while disqualified	3–11

Code	Offence	Points
	Careless Driving	
	Codes CD10 to CD30 must stay on a driving licence for four years from the date of the offence.	
CD10	Driving without due care and attention	3 to 9
CD20	Driving without reasonable consideration for other road users	3 to 9
CD30	Driving without due care and attention or without reasonable consideration for other road users	3 to 9
	Codes CD40 to CD70 must stay on a driving licence for 11 years from the date of the conviction.	
CD40	Causing death through careless driving when unfit through drink	3 to 11
CD50	Causing death by careless driving when unfit through drugs	3 to 11
CD60	Causing death by careless driving with alcohol level above the limit	3 to 11
CD70	Causing death by careless driving then failing to supply a specimen for alcohol analysis	3 to 11
	Codes CD80 and CD90 must stay on a driving licence for four years from the date of the conviction.	
CD80	Causing death by careless, or inconsiderate, driving	3 to 11
CD90	Causing death by driving: unlicensed, disqualified or uninsured drivers	3 to 11
	Construction and Use Offences	
	These codes must stay on a driving licence for four years from the date of the offence.	
CU10	Using a vehicle with defective brakes	3
CU20	Causing or likely to cause danger by reason of use of unsuitable vehicle or using a vehicle with parts or accessories (excluding brakes, steering or tyres) in a dangerous condition	3
CU30	Using a vehicle with defective tyre(s)	3
CU40	Using a vehicle with defective steering	3
CU50	Causing or likely to cause danger by reason of load or passengers	3
CU80	Breach of requirements as to control of the vehicle, mobile telephone etc	3–6
	Reckless/Dangerous Driving	
	These codes must stay on a driving licence for four years from the date of the conviction.	

Code	Offence	Points
DD10	Causing serious injury by dangerous driving	3 to 11
DD40	Dangerous driving	3 to 11
DD60	Manslaughter or culpable homicide while driving a vehicle	3 to 11
DD80	Causing death by dangerous driving	3 to 11
DD90	Furious driving	3 to 9

Drink

Codes DR10 to DR61 must stay on a driving licence for 11 years from the date of the conviction.

Code	Offence	Points
DR10	Driving or attempting to drive with alcohol level above limit	3 to 11
DR20	Driving or attempting to drive while unfit through drink	3 to 11
DR30	Driving or attempting to drive then failing to supply a specimen for analysis	3 to 11
DR31	Driving or attempting to drive then refusing to give permission for analysis of a blood sample that was taken without consent due to incapacity	3 to 11
DR61	Refusing to give permission for analysis of a blood sample that was taken without consent due to incapacity in circumstances other than driving or attempting to drive	10

Codes DR40 to DR70 must stay on a driving licence for four years from the date of the offence.

Code	Offence	Points
DR40	In charge of a vehicle while alcohol level above limit	10
DR50	In charge of a vehicle while unfit through drink	10
DR60	Failure to provide a specimen for analysis in circumstances other than driving or attempting to drive	10
DR70	Failing to provide specimen for breath test	4

Drugs

These codes must stay on a driving record for 11 years from the date of the conviction.

Code	Offence	Points
DG10	Driving or attempting to drive with drug level above the specified limit	3 to 11
DG60	Causing death by careless driving with drug level above the limit	3 to 11
DR80	Driving or attempting to drive when unfit through drugs	3 to 11

These codes must stay on a driving record for four years from the date of the offence or four years from date of conviction where a disqualification is imposed.

Code	Offence	Points
DG40	In charge of a vehicle while drug level above specified limit	10
DR90	In charge of a vehicle when unfit through drugs	10

Insurance Offences

Code IN10 must stay on a driving licence for four years from the date of the offence.

IN10	Using a vehicle uninsured against third party risks	6 to 8

Licence Offences

These codes must stay on a driving licence for four years from the date of the offence.

LC20	Driving otherwise than in accordance with a licence	3 to 6
LC30	Driving after making a false declaration about fitness when applying for a licence	3 to 6
LC40	Driving a vehicle having failed to notify a disability	3 to 6
LC50	Driving after a licence has been revoked or refused on medical grounds	3 to 6

Miscellaneous Offences

These codes must stay on a driving licence for four years from the date of the offence.

MS10	Leaving a vehicle in a dangerous position	3
MS20	Unlawful pillion riding	3
MS30	Play street offences	2
MS50	Motor racing on the highway	3 to 11
MS60	Offences not covered by other codes (including offences relating to breach of requirements as to control of vehicle)	3
MS70	Driving with uncorrected defective eyesight	3
MS80	Refusing to submit to an eyesight test	3
MS90	Failure to give information as to identity of driver etc	6

Motorway Offences

Code MW10 must stay on a driving licence for four years from the date of the offence.

MW10	Contravention of special roads regulations (excluding speed limits)	3

Code	Offence	Points

Pedestrian Crossings

These codes must stay on a driving licence for four years from the date of the offence.

PC10	Undefined contravention of pedestrian crossing regulations	3
PC20	Contravention of pedestrian crossing regulations with moving vehicle	3
PC30	Contravention of pedestrian crossing regulations with stationary vehicle	3

Speeding Offences

These codes must stay on a driving licence for four years from the date of the offence.

SP10	Exceeding goods vehicle speed limits	3 to 6
SP20	Exceeding speed limit for type of vehicle (excluding goods or passenger vehicles)	3 to 6
SP30	Exceeding statutory speed limit on a public road	3 to 6
SP40	Exceeding passenger vehicle speed limit	3 to 6
SP50	Exceeding speed limit on a motorway	3 to 6

Traffic Directions and Signs

These codes must stay on a driving licence for four years from the date of the offence.

TS10	Failing to comply with traffic light signals	3
TS20	Failing to comply with double white lines	3
TS30	Failing to comply with 'stop' sign	3
TS40	Failing to comply with direction of a constable/warden	3
TS50	Failing to comply with traffic sign (excluding 'stop' signs, traffic lights or double white lines)	3
TS60	Failing to comply with a school crossing patrol sign	3
TS70	Undefined failure to comply with a traffic direction sign	3

Theft or Unauthorised Taking

Code UT50 must stay on a driving licence for four years from the date of the offence.

UT50	Aggravated taking of a vehicle	3 to 11

Special Codes

TT99	To signify a disqualification under 'totting-up' procedure. Code TT99 must stay on a driving licence for four years from the date of conviction.	

Code	Offence	Points
	'Mutual recognition' codes	MR code
	You will get an 'MR' code on your licence if you are disqualified while driving in Northern Ireland, Isle of Man or the Republic of Ireland. Your disqualification period will also be valid in GB and will stay on your licence for four years from the date of conviction.	
MR09	Reckless or dangerous driving (whether or not resulting in death, injury or serious risk)	MR09
MR19	Wilful failure to carry out the obligation placed on driver after being involved in a road accident (hit or run)	MR19
MR29	Driving a vehicle while under the influence of alcohol or other substance affecting or diminishing the mental and physical abilities of a driver	MR29
MR39	Driving a vehicle faster than the permitted speed	MR39
MR49	Driving a vehicle whilst disqualified	MR49
MR59	Other conduct constituting an offence for which a driving disqualification has been imposed by the State of Offence	MR59

Appendix C

Expert scientific evidence in statutory defences and special reasons

by the late Professor J K Mason[1] – re-edited by Professor Anthony Busuttil

Although there have been changes to the relevant legislation in Scotland,[2] there are still three main situations in which 'scientific' evidence may be needed to satisfy a statutory defence. Firstly, there is the post-accident drinking defence, established by the Road Traffic Offenders Act 1988, s 15(3) to charges brought under Road Traffic Act 1988, s 3A(1)(b) or 5(1); the latter constitutes the most commonly invoked defence and provides the template for all the relevant calculations. Secondly, there is the defence provided in Road Traffic Act 1988, s 5(2) that a person accused of being in charge of a vehicle with a tissue alcohol level above the prescribed limit was not going to drive so long as his or her tissue level exceeded the limit; in contrast to the s 15 defence, there is nothing in s 5(2) that insists on substantiating 'scientific' evidence. The third situation is not, strictly speaking, a defence but is one in which the accused pleads 'special reasons' for non-disqualification; almost invariably this depends on the drinks having been 'laced' with excess alcohol but, occasionally, the accused may plead that he was served drinks having an alcoholic concentration different from that ordered. There is some suggestion – certainly in England – that expert evidence is not always required on this point;[3] the situation in Scotland is considered below.

The word 'scientific' has been apostrophised above. This is to emphasise that the calculations involved in these defences cannot be regarded as scientific in the sense that their accuracy satisfies scientific criteria. There are so many variables involved in a biological situation that any calculation is in the nature of an approximation. Since it is

---

1   Both, successively, Regius Professor (Emeritus) of Forensic Medicine at the University of Edinburgh. The views expressed in Appendix C are those of the authors and do not necessarily represent those of the editor.
2   Drink-drive limit in Scotland – https://www.mygov.scot.
3   *Pugsley v Hunter* [1973] RTR 284; *DPP v Younas* [1990] RTR 22.

impossible to cover all these in a single equation, it is easier – and more honest – to use very simple data and, having admitted the limitations of the method, to make any necessary adjustments on an empirical basis. For these reasons, it is probably best to eschew the sophisticated and complex analyses that have appeared from time to time[1] and to rely instead on the Tables prepared by the British Medical Association in 1960;[2] these have not been challenged in court and have the merit of public judicial approval.[3] A resumé of the Tables, amended to include breath equivalents, is given in Annexe 1.

There are several major impediments to rigorous scientific accuracy in this field. The first lies in the individual's metabolic rate for alcohol (or the rate at which alcohol is broken down in the body) which is unknown and <u>unknowable</u> – for any later experimental assessment gives only the metabolic rate at the time of the experiment, not at the time of the offence. The rate of absorption of alcohol is a further complication. Such experimental assessment is not within the realms of possibility either in general medical practice or in hospital practice This is slowed by food in the upper gastro-intestinal tract but the extent of this is variable; reasonable practice based on the majority of experimental protocols, is to allow 30 minutes before assuming that *some* alcohol is available in the blood stream for metabolism. More problematic is the time taken for *all* the alcohol ingested to have been absorbed and, here, it is only possible to say that liquid contents of the stomach are *likely* to have been absorbed in the upper small intestine within two hours but, clearly, it could be less and the total volume will be a major influence – indeed, the general empirical evidence is that the alcohol in beer is absorbed more slowly than is that in spirits or wine. The problem arises particularly when an impossible result is obtained (see below). Perhaps more importantly, a proportion of ingested alcohol is destroyed by the gastric enzyme *alcohol dehydrogenase*, the quantity and power of which is, again, a biological variable; the significance is, of course, that alcohol destroyed in this way

1   See, for example, AWR Forrest 'The estimation of Widmark's factor' (1986) 26 *Journal of the Forensic Science Society*, 249.

2   British Medical Association, *'The Relation of Alcohol to Road Accidents'* (1960) London: BMA, Appendix A.

3   *R v Somers* [1963] 3 All ER 808.

will *never* reach the blood stream.[1] The final 'scientific' variable depends upon the body's weight and configuration; the significance of these is discussed below. The absorption, metabolism and excretion of alcohol is discussed in several scientific publications.[2]

Of the other, non-specific, imponderables, the accused's memory is likely to be of major importance. Here, it has to be noted that the s 15(3) defence is not, as it is frequently and pejoratively described in the English courts, a 'hip-flask' defence. The majority of cases arise from the accused not appreciating that he is likely to be breathalysed and legitimately taking a restorative drink in his home after a stressful experience. The man who can quantitate with great accuracy what alcohol he consumed in such circumstances is, possibly, less credible than one who has no more than a fair idea. In this connection, the decision in *Hassan*,[3] which allows the court to accept a good approximation, is to be welcomed as a corrective of the earlier draconian decisions.[4] Even so, if the post-incident drinking has taken place at home, it is essential that a marked glass [the same or one identical to that from which alcohol had been consumed on the day in question, indelibly marked from memory and retained as a potential eventual production in court] be produced for measurement; in practice, most people know the approximate size of drinks they pour for themselves and both the court and the expert witness are working in a vacuum without such an estimate. In other instances, a marked consumption from a bottle and the residual amounts in it have to be considered. A further problem arose as to whether the accused's evidence must be corroborated in Scots law; it was determined in *King v Lees*[5] that this was not necessary – thereby eliminating a source of discrimination

1   RJK Julkunen et al 'First pass metabolism of ethanol: an important determinant of blood levels after alcohol consumption' (1985) 2 *Alcohol*, 437. For the same reason, a person who has had a gastrectomy is likely to have a higher tissue alcohol level than anticipated: J Caballeria, M Frezza, R Hernández-Muñoz et al 'Gastric origin of the first-pass metabolism of ethanol in humans: effect of gastrectomy' (1989) 97 *Gastroenterology*, 1205.
2   Alcohol metabolism: general aspects. Ghazali R, Patel V B in *Molecular aspects of alcohol and nutrition, 2016*; Cederbaum A L Alcohol Metabolism. *Clinics in Liver Disease.* 2012; v 16 iss 4 pp 667–685. Ramchandani V A, Kwo PY, Li T K Effect of food and food consumption on alcohol elimination rates in healthy mem and women. *J Clin Pharmacology* Dec 2001; v 41{2} pp 1345–1350.
3   *Hassan v Scott* 1989 SCCR 49.
4   Eg *Sutherland v Aitchison* 1979 SLT 37; *Ferns v Tudhope* 1979 SLT 23; *Campbell v Mackenzie* 1981 SCCR 341.
5   *King v Lees* 1993 JC 19. For discussion, see D Sheldon, 'Hip flasks and burdens' 1992 SLT 33.

against the single person. Another complication that is often ignored in precognition is the effect of vomiting; in practice, this may be of great significance in limiting the amount of alcohol available for absorption.

THE SECTION 15(3) DEFENCE

The section is directed in sub-section (a) to credibility and in sub-section (b) to scientific corroboration; it is the latter with which we are concerned here. Theoretically, the method is simple. The gross 'value' of the post-incident drink is calculated from the tables using a correction factor based on the formula 154/W where W is the person's weight at the time of the incident in lbs or more routinely nowadays 70/w – when w is the weight in kilograms, the rationale of this is discussed below. Knowing both the time the person started drinking after the incident and the time of the definitive breath analysis – and allowing 30 minutes for effective absorption to occur – the amount metabolised prior to testing can be estimated on the assumption that the rate is 8.2 micrograms [µ] /100 ml breath /hour, or 18 mg alcohol/100 ml blood/hour. This immediately introduces an uncertainty into the calculations because the *actual* metabolic rate, as discussed more fully under the s 5(2) defence below, can be taken to vary between 5.0 and 11.4 g/100ml of breath/hour or 11.4 and 26.1 mg alcohol/100 ml breath/hour; since the precise value within this bracket is unknown, the only fair compromise is to use the mean value.[1] [2] Deducting this figure from the gross value gives the net value for the post-incident consumption (N). The defence under s 15(3)(b) is established if O [the observed value on the Intoximeter print-out] – N is less than 22 µg alcohol/100 ml breath or 50 mg alcohol/100ml blood.

To give an example: a man weighing 72 kg and who has not had any alcohol during the day, is involved in an incident; he subsequently drinks 100 millilitres of whisky starting at 22:30 and, at 02:00, he provides a specimen of breath which contains 33 µg alcohol/100 ml. Calculated breath alcohol is 70/72 × 100/28.4 [3] × 9.63 – ie 32.9 µg of alcohol per 100 millilitres of breath; thus, his defence is feasible, and the slight discrepancy can be

---

1   The figures, converted from blood levels, are taken from *Gumbley v Cunningham* [1989] RTR 49. For background analysis, see MJ Lewis 'Blood alcohol: The concentration-time curve and retrospective estimation of level' (1986) 26 *Journal of the Forensic Science Society* 95.

2   *Elimination rates of breath alcohol.* Pavlic M, Grubweiser P, Libiseller K, Rabi W. *Forensic Science International* v 171, iss.1, 24 August 2007 pp 16–21.

3   One fluid oz is 28.4 ml or cc and the old BMA tables did not use the metric system.

easily be accounted by imprecise timings and variations in metabolic/excretory rates for alcohol.

The credibility factor

It is submitted that the wording of the Act is such that the *only* calculation needed for the defence is the value of O – N, and there is some English precedent which suggests that this interpretation is correct.[1] The matter has not been tested in the courts but it is probable that the Scottish preference would be to admit any evidence relevant to establishing the alcohol level at the time of driving.[2] It is clear from what has been said that 'back-calculation' is subject to considerable potential error and medical scientists have persistently advised that it should not be attempted.[3] Nonetheless, the mere existence of s 15(3)(b) indicates that the legislature anticipated its use and the expert must make the best of what is, admittedly, a bad job in assisting the court. Thus, in Scotland at least, the expert will almost certainly be asked to evaluate the contribution of any pre-incident drinking and, as a consequence, a credibility gap may well appear. To revert to the example given above: the calculated post-incident value certainly satisfies the subsection so long as the accused had no drink before. But, suppose he admitted to, say, 10 µg's 'worth' of pre-incident drinking? When this is taken into account, it will throw the calculations out of kilter and the expert cannot confirm the feasibility of the defence being offered. The courts, in fact, are left with little option but to reject the defence offered.

Nonetheless, the problem is raised as to what constitutes an unreasonable discrepancy in the *expert's* mind – and this is impossible to answer. One can say that one 'likes to get within one drink' of the anticipated result but there are so many variables which alter with the circumstances that this can be no more than a rule of thumb. A specific area which needs clarification is the 'impossible' or 'minus' result which occurs when the supposed post-incident value exceeds the observed value. This can, often, impair credibility but, in many cases, the conditions are such as to cast serious doubt on whether the whole 'alcohol dose' was absorbed at the time of breath analysis. Again, this is a biological variable which the expert should take into account but cannot quantitate with scientific accuracy; the proposition becomes increasingly tenable not only as the interval between the last drink and the test shortens but also

1 *Millard v DPP* [1990] RTR 201.
2 *Tudhope v Williamson* 1976 JC 16.
3 And there are good reasons for supporting this view: JK Mason 'Conversion on the Road to Auchtermuchty' 1996 SLT 33.

as the amount of alcohol drunk within a short time of the Intoximeter test increases.

The effect of body weight

Once absorbed, the alcohol in the body should be distributed equally throughout the body water.[1] It has to be assumed that the body water represents a fixed proportion of the body weight – and this is allowed for in the Tables; accordingly, we can say that the tissue (or water) concentration will depend upon the total body weight which is a directly measurable variable. The Tables indicate that a further correction factor of 6/5 should be applied in the case of women, this being said to reflect the different fat/water content in men and women and hence, a differing body water/ weight distribution. A moment's thought will show, however, that there is no such thing as a 'standard' man or woman – some are fat, some are thin, some are more muscular than others and it is wrong to generalise. Experience has shown, for example, that the correction factor applied to women often appears to exaggerate the tissue level calculated from a stated intake but, as would be expected, the degree of deviation varies considerably.

The 'Widmark factor'

In an attempt to get round this problem, many laboratories apply the so-called Widmark equation when correlating alcoholic intake and distribution.[2] This is based on the simplified assumption $a = bwr/100$ where a = the amount of alcohol ingested measured in grams, b = the blood alcohol concentration in mg/100ml, w = the body weight in kg and r = the 'Widmark factor' which is, essentially, the ratio of the total body water to the blood water. Using this method, it is conventional to regard r = 0.6 for men and 0.5 for women

---

1   The water miscibility of alcohol explains the difference between blood and urine levels. Alcohol is not concentrated in the urine; the difference merely reflects the fact that, whereas urine is almost pure fluid, blood contains a considerable proportion of solid material. This results in relatively standard urine: blood alcohol ratio of 1.33:1. Alcohol is promptly distributed equally through all body water compartments without modification by the action of he heart with an early equilibrium being achieved. It passively comes of blood within the lungs into the immediately surrounding {alveolar air}. The use of micro[μ]grams reflects the smaller concentration in expired air.
2   Based on the work of EMP Widmark, a German physiologist who published his findings in 1932.

It is apparent that this introduces yet another uncertainty to the calculations. Whatever figure is chosen from whatever published results, it is bound to be an average which may be far removed from the individual's actual status[1] – and it will be seen that relatively minor deviations will have considerable effect on the end result. Many efforts have been made to overcome these, and related, difficulties, such as applying different distribution factors to differing body configurations but, ultimately, these involve idiosyncratic decisions which impart a sense of accuracy which may be spurious; they are better avoided.

Variations in alcohol content of alcoholic drinks

It is clear that one cannot, nowadays, speak in terms of 'beer' or 'spirits'; there are wide variations in alcoholic concentration in all generic alcoholic drinks and these must be accommodated when making the necessary calculations.

The BMA Tables are based on a 40% v/v alcoholic concentration for spirits but not all are of this strength – proof is not a system which is in current use.[2] Most vodkas and gins are 37.5% by volume v/v; the strength of wine generally varies between 8–12% v/v. It is convenient to convert the intake to fluid ounces and to use the tables for spirits with a correction factor of: × w/40 – where w is the alcoholic concentration of the wine drunk. It is therefore essential that, in addition to volumes consumed, the strength of the drinks is known as well, in order to attempt to render the calculations more accurate.

The Tables relate to beers of a strength of 3.2% alcohol v/v.[3] Normally, a correction factor of × b/3.2 would be used where b is the concentration v/v of alcohol in the beer or cider actually drunk and this holds for small amounts of such drinks. However, experience has, again shown that the tables do not allow for the fact that large volumes of fluid remain in the

1   The r factor is estimated as varying between 0.55 and 0.9 for men.
2   Since 1 January 1980, the United Kingdom has used the ABV standard to measure alcohol content, as prescribed by the European Union. In common with other EU countries, on 1 January 1980, Britain adopted the system of measurement recommended by the International Organisation of Legal Metrology (OIML), a body with most major nations among its members. The OIML system measures alcohol strength as a percentage of alcohol by volume at a temperature of 20°C. It replaced the Sikes system of measuring the proof strength of spirits, which had been used in Britain for over 160 years.
3   Ie volume/volume. Ethanol has a specific gravity of 0.8; the strength of an alcoholic drink would, therefore, appear lower if expressed as weight/weight rather than as v/v.

stomach longer than do, say, measures of spirits. As a consequence, gastric alcohol dehydrogenase has longer to operate and relatively less 'beer alcohol' is available for absorption by comparison with 'spirit alcohol' Some authors allow for this by altering the r factor[1] (see above) but it is submitted that this is illogical – the body water distribution cannot alter with oral intake and the effect must alter with the quantity as well as the nature of the drink. This problem of gastric destruction of alcohol can be circumvented, somewhat empirically, by using a correction factor of b/4 for moderate quantities of beer (2–3 pints) and b/5 for larger amounts.

Some useful volumetric equivalents are given in Annexe 2.

DEFENCE TO CHARGES UNDER ROAD TRAFFIC ACT 1988, S 3A

The principles behind the defence to charges under s 3A are obviously similar to those under s 5(1)(a) save that s 3A(1)(a) specifically refers to the tissue alcohol concentration at the time of driving while s 3A(1)(c) allows for a compulsory test within 18 hours of that time. The result is to put the stamp of parliamentary approval on 'back calculation'. This introduces some additional problems.

It is difficult to see why the legislature specifically introduced an 18 hour limit. As an end-point, it is virtually meaningless. To show *any* alcohol in the breath at this point in time, the breath concentration at the time of the incident must have been in the region of 120 mg alcohol/100 ml – or a blood level of 270 mg/100 ml – at which point, it is at least unlikely that a person would have been capable of driving a car. In practice, the effect of the wide variation in individual metabolic rates becomes so great after 8 hours as to discredit any 'probability' of a *true* back-calculation. The best that could be done would be to provide theoretical limits based on the figures that were not disputed in *Gumbley v Cunningham* (see below).

Rather more concern lies in the terms of the constituting evidence in s 3A cases. It is at least arguable that a report based on back calculation can only be valid if the resulting figure is qualified by 'provided no further alcohol was drunk between the incident and the test'. That being so, it would follow that *any* alcohol taken would invalidate the evidence. A defence would be established under s 15(3)(a) of the Road Traffic Offenders Act 1988 (the 'credibility limb') without necessary recourse to the expert evidence required under s 15(3)(b) – the situation would revert

---

1   Eg LA King 'Alcohol concentrations with quantity of alcohol consumed' (1993) 23 Journal of the Forensic Science Society, 213.

to that in England prior to *Rowlands v Hamilton*.[1] The proposition has not, however, been tested in the courts.

Finally, the question has to be asked whether the license to back calculate is particular to s 3A or whether it can be extrapolated to s 5(1) offences. The only apposite case still leaves the general question of back calculation in doubt.[2]

THE SECTION 5(2) DEFENCE

There is no statutory requirement for expert evidence to sustain this defence but it is reasonably certain that the courts will seek such evidence unless the circumstances are absolutely clear;[3] the same considerations would apply as in 'laced drinks' cases (see below). On the other hand, since there can be virtually no opinion evidence in what is almost entirely a matter of mathematics, the expert's report cries out for a minute of admission. This generalisation is, however, subject to an interesting ethical point as to the presentation of the evidence. The relevant question can be put to the expert in two ways:

(a) At what time would the accused have been fit to drive? or

(b) Would the accused have been fit to drive at [a certain time]?

The former construction clearly allows for deception on the part of the accused – he can formulate his story according to the answer given; the latter, by contrast, limits the expert evidence to corroborating or disproving the accused's unbiased statement. It is suggested that the former may well be an improper formulation and the prosecution are entitled to elicit how the expert evidence was sought.

Such considerations aside, however, the 'scientific' defence *ought* to be simply established. Given a knowledge of how much was drunk from what time and of the time and reading of the Intoximeter test, the accused's *actual* metabolic rate (R) should be given by the formula $(V - C)/t$ where V is the 'value' of the drink taken, C is the Intoximeter reading and t is the time in hours between starting to drink (+ the arbitrary 30 minutes for effective absorption) and the Intoximeter test. It can then be said that he would be fit to drive in s 5(1) terms in $(C - 35)/R$ hours.

1   *Rowlands v Hamilton* [1971] RTR 153.
2   *Hain v Ruxton* 1999 SCCR 243. For discussion, see J K Mason 'Back-calculation and the Crown Agents' letters' (2000) 5 SLPQ 25.
3   In England, a distinction is to be made between prosecutions under s 4(2) (unfit to drive) and s 5(1)(b) (exceeding the prescribed limit): *DPP v Frost* [1989] RTR 11 The latter requires expert evidence to establish a defence.

This deceptively simple calculation does not, however, always work out in practice. In the first place, there is no reason why those accused in this situation should know their consumption with any accuracy; secondly, and more pragmatically, it is hard to convince them that it is in their interests to be as truthful as possible. The majority greatly underestimate their intake and the result is an impossibly low calculated metabolic rate; this inevitably reacts against credibility – a particularly unfortunate matter as the defence, essentially, stands or falls on the question of credibility. The error may, however, be genuine and, for this reason, it is very much fairer to both sides to stay clear of the difficulties associated with the precise circumstances and to concentrate on the certainties offered by *Gumbley v Cunningham*.[1]

SPECIAL REASONS FOR NON-DISQUALIFICATION

The fact that the accused drank alcohol unknowingly has been accepted as a special reason for non-disqualification in both Scotland[2] and England.[3] Although the courts tend to look on the plea with some scepticism, it is nevertheless frequently accepted. The conditions for acceptance have appeared, at times, to be very severe in England[4] but many of the recorded decisions are inconsistent; as one English judge put it: 'Cases in this particular branch of the law are not always easy to reconcile'.[5] Much of the problem may stem from the nature of the act. 'Lacing' drinks is dangerous and selfish – and the perpetrator is probably unable to appreciate that he is laying himself open to a charge of abetting a criminal offence.[6] Consequently, the main evidence as to credibility is likely to be of poor quality and, as a corollary, the scientific evidence must be founded on a doubtful basis. The very limited Scottish precedents indicate that expert evidence must be led unless the circumstances are clear and obvious to the court[7] (see paragraph 8.5.4).

The method follows that for the s 15(3)(b) defence. The 'value' of the added alcohol is deducted from the Intoximeter reading and the conditions

---

1   *Gumbley v Cunningham* [1989] AC 281.
2   *Skinner v Ayton* 1977 SLT (Sh Ct) 48.
3   *Pugsley v Hunter* [1973] RTR 284; *Alexander v Latter* [1972] RTR 441; *R v Krebs* [1977] RTR 406.
4   *Adams v Bradley* [1975] RTR 233.
5   *Beauchamp-Thompson v DPP* [1989] RTR 54 per Hutchison J at 61.
6   In England, Attorney General's Reference (No 1 of 1975) [1975] QB 773; *DPP v Anderson* [1990] RTR 269.
7   See note 15 above. For England, see *DPP v O'Connor and allied cases* [1992] RTR 66.

for acceptance of the plea are established if the resultant figure is less than 22 µg/100 ml breath. It will be apparent, however, that the effect of metabolism must be calculated on a proportional basis as described above unless the accused was an intended teetotaller. Aside from the court's almost inevitable suspicion of collusion, the plea commonly breaks down not so much on the calculations as on the anticipated effect on the target of the 'lacing' – 'surely', it will be said, 'he ought to have appreciated that something was wrong and he was feeling intoxicated when he should not have been, or indeed more intoxicated than expected, and he should not have driven?'

This is not an easy question to answer for the effects of alcohol depend almost as much on psychological as on pharmacological factors. It is, for example, a nice point to decide whether a teetotaller will be disproportionately affected because of a lack of habituation or whether he will be quite unable to understand his symptoms and to refer them to a substance of which he has no general or immediate knowledge. It is clear, however, that the higher the Intoximeter reading, the less likely is it that 'special reasons' will be accepted.

FURTHER POSSIBLE DEFENCES

It would be inappropriate here to try to detail the defences which might be founded on the presumption that the breath alcohol level was apparently, but falsely, raised. A few notes must suffice.

A defence which was commonly put forward is by the uncontrolled diabetic who maintains that the reading is due to acetone rather than alcohol in the breath. The Intoximeter provides a very high degree of discrimination against possible interference by substances other than ethanol. It seems likely that such a defence could be considered only if the subject was so affected as to be close to diabetic coma – and, in that case, he would be unlikely to be driving a car or, indeed, to be out drinking.

A number of defences have relied on accidental inhalation of the fumes of alcohol or other contaminating solvents when, say, at work. Experiments have shown that it is not possible to raise the tissue alcohol level significantly by inhaling alcohol[1] and exposure to industrial solvents

---

1   JK Mason, and DJ Blackmore, 'Experimental inhalation of ethanol vapour' (1972) 12 *Medicine, Science and the Law*, 205. See also MJ Lewis, 'A theoretical treatment for the estimation of blood alcohol concentrations arising from inhalation of ethanol vapour' (1985) 25 *Journal of the Forensic Science Society*, 11.

would be unlikely to affect the analysis within the usual time parameters of testing.[1]

A 'petrol defence' – generally involving a supposed remainder in the mouth following syphoning of petrol – has often been invoked but experimental data indicate that such a residue is eliminated within some 15–20 minutes. Instances of successful defences based on the application of, say, spirits of camphor to the lips or the use of mouth washes containing alcohol to a level of 1% have been reported; experimentation has shown that the alcohol in such preparations may give rise to a high reading but that this is dissipated within minutes.

A very similar defence is based on the presence of mouth alcohol following the normal ingestion of an alcoholic drink. It is important to appreciate that this does not involve a claim that the residual alcohol is, of itself, sufficient to raise the tissue alcohol. The rationale is that the mouth is acting as if it were a calibrating cell in the old Camic machine in which air was drawn over a standard solution of alcohol. Since the solution which will give a recording of 35 mg alcohol/100ml air consisted of .0893% alcohol, it is clear that the remains of a whisky can be diluted several hundred times in the saliva and still produce a positive result. Once again, however, any effect of mouth alcohol wears off within minutes[2] and, for this reason, it is standard practice for the police to be advised to delay testing for 20 minutes if the subject claims he has only recently had an alcoholic drink – something which, in practice, will apply only to the roadside test. In fact, the modern versions of the Intoximeter are able to distinguish mouth alcohol; if mouth alcohol is detected, the machine does not calibrate and give a result.

To complete the picture, the frequent contention that the Intoximeter is faulty and is giving an impossibly high reading must be considered. Any mechanical apparatus is liable to breakdown; but, once again, it is difficult, if not impossible, to see how such a claim can be supported in the face of a positive roadside test and in the absence of any supporting evidence of malfunction. The machine calibrates before each of the two tests and purges in between.

The question of medication remains. Since alcohol is a central nervous depressant, a large number of medicines with similar properties will potentiate the *effects* of alcohol and are, therefore, important in respect

---

1   RC Denney, 'Solvent inhalation and "apparent" alcohol studies on the Lion Intoximeter 3000' (1990) 30 *Journal of the Forensic Science Society*, 357.
2   SDA Franklin and A Stephens 'Can wine tasting be used as a defence to a charge of excess alcohol?' (2000) 40 *Science and Justice*, 39.

of charges under s 4. They will **not**, however, affect the Intoximeter reading and are, thus, irrelevant in the great majority of s 5 prosecutions. An exception may, however, lie in the so-called H2 receptor antagonist group of drugs that are used in treatment of peptic ulceration and other intestinal complaints. Some work has indicated that these drugs, by inhibiting the action of gastric alcohol dehydrogenase, will lead to a higher tissue alcohol than would normally be achieved by a given intake.[1] The evidence is sufficient for the Danish authorities to have imposed the placing of a warning on containers of the drug cimetidine.[2] Experimental work, however, relates to relatively low alcoholic intake and it has to be said that the findings are not universally accepted – even so, the possibility remains. Were such an effect shown to be significant at social drinking levels, it would give rise to a plea of special reasons for non-disqualification rather than defence to a charge under s 5(1). It is of interest that there is no evidence of a similar reaction using the more modern drugs of the 'proton pump inhibitor' group.

It is inappropriate to include in this section a full discussion of defences based on physical incapacity to provide a specimen (ss 6(4) and 7(6)). These are multiple and range from an inability to activate the Intoximeter to a fear of needles. Whether or not the latter condition constitutes a 'reasonable excuse' is a matter of fact and outwith the province of the expert witness.[3]

CONCLUSION

It is obvious that the expert will not agree to give evidence on behalf of the accused unless his calculations indicate that a defence is available; as many as 40% of cases may fall at this first hurdle. It is impossible to predict the outcome of a trial simply on the basis of the relevant figures. The inference must be that the courts are, in general, willing to accept the scientific element of the evidence once it is seen as providing a valid defence. But, at the same time, it is appreciated that the expert is working only from information provided by the accused; whether or not a defence is successful then depends entirely on the court's assessment of the credibility of that information.

1   C DiPadova, R Roine, M Frezza et al 'Effects of Ranitidine on blood alcohol levels after ethanol ingestion' (1992) 267 *Journal of the American Medical Association*, 83.
2   M Andersen and JS Schou 'Are H2 receptor antagonists safe over-the-counter drugs?' (1994) 309 *British Medical Journal*, 493.
3   *DPP v Warren* [1993] AC 319 as interpreted in *DPP v Jackson* (Failure to provide specimen) [1999] 1 AC 406.

ANNEXE 1

TISSUE ALCOHOL EQUIVALENTS
OF ALCOHOLIC DRINKS

(Based on the Tables prepared by the British Medical Association
'The Relationship of Alcohol to Road Accidents' (1960))

(a) Beers, lagers, ciders etc

Intake in pints	Breath mg/100ml	Blood mg/100ml	Urine mg/100ml
0.5	8	18	24
1	16	37	49
1.5	24	55	73
2	32	73	97
3	48	110	147
4	64	147	195
5	80	183	244
6	96	220	293
7	112	257	343
8	129	295	391
9	144	329	439
10	160	366	488

(b) Standard spirits

Intake in fl oz mg/100ml	Breath mg/100ml	Blood mg/100ml	Urine
1	9.63	22	30
2	20	45	60
3	29	67	90
4	39	90	120
5	49	112	150
6	59	135	180
7	69	157	210
8	79	180	240
9	88	202	270
10	98	225	300
13.3	131	300	400
26.7	262	600	800

Note 1.   All figures are reduced to the nearest whole number – the
accuracy of the method does not justify the use of decimal points.

Note 2.   All values must be multiplied by 154/W where W is the weight of the man in lbs or 70/w where w is weight in kilograms. The stated correction factor for women is 154/W 6/5. The rationale is discussed in the text.

Note 3.   For spirits other than those of standard strength, the value must be multiplied by c/40 where c is the alcoholic concentration v/v. Thus, the correction factor for ordinary vodka is 0.94.

Note 4.   Regulations now state that single measures will be dispensed in 25ml amounts.

ANNEXE 2

SOME USEFUL EQUIVALENTS

1 fluid ounce	=	28.4 ml
1 gill	=	5 fl oz
1 pint	=	568 ml
	=	20 fl oz
	=	4 gills
1 gallon	=	4.55 litres
1 litre	=	35.2 fl oz
	=	1.76 pints
Standard bottle of spirits	=	26.7 fl oz
	=	750 ml
Standard bottle of wine	=	700 ml

ALCOHOLIC CONTENT (V/V) OF SOME BEERS, LAGERS AND CIDERS COMMONLY DRUNK IN SCOTLAND

Youngers Tartan	3.5	Tennent's lager	4.0
McEwan's Export	4.2	McEwan's lager	3.8
Tetley Bitter	3.6	Holsten Pils	5.8
Tennent's/McEwan's 70/–	3.5(d)	Beck's Bier	5.0
Tennent's/McEwan's 80/–	4.2(d)	Elephant	7.5
Guinness (stout)	4.1(d)	Carlsberg Special Brew	8.5
Newcastle Brown	4.5	Old Peculiar	5.6(d)
Alloa Export	4.2(d)	Tennent's Superlager	9.0
Caledonian Deuchars IPA	3.8(d)	Red Stripe	4.8
Tiger Bitter	4.0	Stella Artois	5.0
Kronenbourg	5.5	Budweiser & Coors Light & Heineken	5.0
Carling	4.0	A number of Polish, Italian and Eastern beers are also on the UK market	

Ciders (%)

Strongbow	5.3
Woodpecker	3.5
Scrumpy Jack	6.0
Diamond White	8.2

Note: There are minor variations according to whether the product is sold in cans, kegs or draught. The values above are for cans or bottles except were marked (d).

ANNEXE 3

MINIMUM REQUIREMENTS FOR DEFENCE CALCULATIONS

(a) RTOA 1988, s 15(3)(b)

In addition to a copy of the complaint, the summary of evidence of the police and a copy of the Intoximeter print-out, the following information will always be required:

(a)   The time the accused started drinking (if applicable);

(b)   How much was consumed before the accident/incident;

(c)   The time of the accident/incident;

(d)   The time the accused started drinking after the accident/incident;

(e)   The amount drunk between then and the Intoximeter test;

(f)   The time of the Intoximeter test;

(g)   The result of the Intoximeter test;

(h)   The accused's weight at the relevant time;

(i)   The *precise* type of beer, wine etc drunk.

(b) RTA 1988, s 5(2)

In most cases, the defence depends upon the accepted limits of metabolism. In this case, all that is needed is:

1   The time of the Intoximeter test;

2   The result of the Intoximeter test;

3   The expert *ought* to know the time when the accused intended to drive again (see text for discussion of this point).

It is, however, often desirable to work out the accused's actual metabolic rate – and the higher the Intoximeter reading, the more important this is. More information is then needed:

(a)   The time the accused started to drink;

(b)   The amount drunk – accuracy is imperative here;

(c)   The specific type of alcohol drunk;

(d)   The time drinking stopped;

(e) The time of the Intoximeter test;

(f) The result of the Intoximeter test;

(g) The accused's weight.

(c) Plea of 'Special Reasons'

The essential information is:

(a) The time the 'lacing' started;

(b) The precise quality and quantity of the 'lacing' material;

(c) The time and result of the Intoximeter test;

(d) The accused's weight at the time.

These cases, however, depend a great deal on credibility, for which the following additional information will be needed:

(e) The time the accused thought he started drinking;

(f) Precisely what he thought he was drinking;

(g) How much he drank voluntarily.

Appendix D

Drugged driving

by Professor A Busuttil[1]

Increasingly, evidence has accumulated world-wide that certain drugs, whether prescribed medically or acquired illegally, can influence brain function, ie have psychoactive effect. Thus they may cause problems with the co-ordination of the complex physical and mental activities that are required for safe and careful driving of mechanically propelled vehicles. Research commissioned by the Department of Transport and published in 2001 showed that one in six of the bodies of dead drivers – 18% – and 16% of dead motorcyclists had illegal drugs at post-mortem examination.[2] In 2005, 17% of 1,396 randomly tested drivers in Glasgow had taken at least one illegal drug, with ecstasy [MDMA] and cannabis being the most prevalent.[3] In 2010 Sir Peter North QC published his review and a House of Commons Transport Select Committee concluded that drug screening of drivers should be introduced as soon as practically possible.[4] Drugs have been shown in both simulated and actual performance testing to alter reaction time, information processing, sustained attention, speed estimation, short-term memory, judgement, learning comprehension, decision-making and the response to multiple stimuli.[5,6]

1   Regius Professor of Forensic Medicine at the University of Edinburgh – Emeritus. The views expressed in Appendix D are those of the author and do not necessarily represent those of Andrew Brown QC.
2   Department of Transport 2001. Reported road casualties in Great Britain- https://www.tri.co.uk/reports-publications/report 2650.
3   Assum T, Mathhijssen R, Houwing S, Buttress S C, Sexton B, Tunbridge RJ, Oliver J, 2005. The prevalence of drug driving and relative risk estimations. A study conducted in the Netherlands, Norway and United Kingdom. Final programme. Report- http://www.transport.
4   Sir Peter North, June 2010. Report of the Review of Drink and Driving Law. http://webarchive.nationalarchives.gov.uk/20100921035225/http:/northreview.independant.gov.uk/docs/NorthReview Report.
5   Hindmarch I, Gudgeon AC, 'The effects of clobazam and lorazepam on aspects of psychomotor performance and car handling ability' (1980) *British J Clin Pharmacology*, 26; 10: 45.
6   Hindmarch I, Kerr JS, Sherwood A, 'The effects of alcohol and other drugs on psychomotor performance and cognitive function' (1991) *Alcohol Alcoholism*, 26; 71.

The UK Government's Crime and Courts Act 2013 devolved powers to Scottish Ministers to introduce a drug-driving offence and the power to specify the limits that should apply for different drug types. This followed powers over setting the drink-driving limit being devolved to Scotland through the Scotland Act 2012. On 21 April 2017, the then Cabinet Secretary for Justice in Scotland, Michael Matheson, announced that drug-driving limits and roadside testing will be introduced in Scotland. It is illegal, and indeed a long-standing offence, to drive while impaired by drugs, and this offence will continue to operate meanwhile; but the Scottish Government plans to introduce new drug-driving limits that will allow prosecutions where different drug types are detected above specified levels.[1] This should mean that it will be easier to hold drug-drivers to account, as there will no longer be a requirement to prove that someone was driving in an impaired manner, as is to date the case: specifically, trained police officers can currently carry out roadside impairment tests and then have their conclusion confirmed by a medical examination. Under the new offence, evidence of impaired driving will not be required, with law enforcement agencies instead being able to investigate and prosecute on the basis of a driver being shown to be above the specified limits for individual drug types. The Scottish Government is involved in on-going discussions with Police Scotland, the Scottish Police Authority and the Crown Office & Procurator Fiscal Service on the operational requirements, including how roadside testing can be put in place. Ministers intend to lay down regulations for approval by MSPs, with implementation, including the need to have the necessary testing equipment in place, expected in 2019.

The Department of Transport in July 2014 laid down guidelines for health care professionals on drug driving in relation to prescribed drugs.[2]

DRUNK DRIVING AND DRUGGED DRIVING

The relationship between alcohol and driving has been used as a model for drugged driving by some. However, this is not a good analogy, as when compared with ethanol even very small quantities of drugs within the body may lead to defective driving capacity. Unlike alcohol, drugs are not distributed evenly throughout the body water compartments but may be bound to fat and protein, and then gradually released therefrom.

---

1   http://news.gov.scotland/news/new-curbs-againsr-drug-drivig. 21 April 2017.
2   8 Guidance for healthcare professionals on drug driving – gov.uk.https://www.gov.uk/government/uploads/...data/.../healthcare-profs-drug-driving.pdf. 1 July 2014.

TABLE 1

Drug	Time to peak in hours	Per cent protein binding	Elimination half-life in hours
Morphine	0.1–0.3	26–30 %	1.3–3.4
Methadone	4.0	60–87 %	18–97
Cocaine	0.75–1.5		0.75–1.25

Furthermore drugs, unlike alcohol, are not broken down by body ferments or enzymes, which are located mostly within the liver, to innocuous compounds; but their break-down products or metabolites may still be active per se and indeed may last longer within the body than the parent drug, and will thus continue to affect driving capabilities for an inordinately lengthy period. This is usually referred to as the elimination half-life of the drug – namely, the amount of time which would be required for the body to lose or inactivate half the amount of the drug that has found its way into the body into pharmacologically active metabolites. Diazepam has an elimination half-life of 92 to 99 hours; desmethyldiazepam an elimination half-life of up to 98 hours.

Drugs may also have more than one (first) peak of action with an effect on driving soon after ingestion, and a second peak several minutes or hours after the drug enters the body. Thus, with cannabis there is a peak of its psychotropic effects on the brain within 20 minutes, and another peak of less marked activity about one and a half to two hours later, when some of the drug, formerly bound to fat and lipids in the body, is released back into the main circulation.

It is also a well-established fact that different individuals because of their genetic make-up or for other reasons, such as variations in liver function, hyperactive breakdown enzymes (due to so-called acceleration or induction of activity thereof by other drugs, eg anticonvulsants, will produce a certain effect on a person on one occasion, and a slightly different effect on another person or on the same person on another occasion. What is certain is that certain levels of drugs will invariably have a deleterious effect on driving skills and the new legislation will take this into account.

With drugs, with the passage of time, and the continuous use of the same compound over a period, an element of habituation arises in the subject and there is a development of a decreased or altered effect from the taking of drugs resulting in larger doses being required by the addict to obtain the same effects therefrom. The latter phenomenon is often referred to as tolerance to a drug, and in some cases the effects derived from a large dose of a drug may be similar in a chronic addict to the effect of a much smaller quantity of the drug in a novice or naive user of the same drug.

Drugs also interact with one another giving an addictive effect. This addictive effect may sometimes be synergistic, namely that the sum of the effects of two drugs may be more than that would be expected from a simple arithmetic summing up of the effects derived from the use of each drug individually and separately.

Furthermore, all drugs that may affect the brain may interact with alcohol, another depressant of the central nervous system even when this is concomitantly present in small doses within the body,[1,2,3,4] Thus a person who has consumed alcohol as well as such drugs may appear to a lay person much more inebriated than would be expected for a given amount of alcohol, simply because together with the alcohol, he has also taken a drug which has an effect on the brain and mental activities.

The doctor and the medical examination

Currently a medical practitioner is invariably asked to attend by the police in a so-called 'section 4' procedure. This procedure is laid out in step-by-step sequential forms that are available in policed offices and should be followed to the letter by the arresting police officers. These forms take on board all the recommendations laid out in *Reid v Nixon; Dumigan v Brown* 1948 J C 68, 1948 SLT 295 as follows:

1.   Before being examined the person arrested should be cautioned in the usual manner before being asked to submit to a medical examination by a doctor who will be selected and called out by the police.

1   Kerr JS, Hindmarch I, 'The effect of alcohol alone and in combination with other drugs on information processing, task performance and subjective responses' (1998) *Human Psychopharmacology*, 13: 1.

2   Morland J, Setchleiv J, Haffner JF et al, 'Combined effects of diazepam and ethanol on mental and psychomotor functions' (1974) *Acta Pharmacologica Toxicologica* (Copenhagen), 34: 5.

3   Manno JE, Kipinger GF, Scholz N, Forney RB, 'The influence of alcohol and marihuana on motor and mental performance' (1971) *Clin Pharmacol Thera*, 12: 202.

4   Linnoila M, Hakkinen S, 'Effects of diazepam and codeine alone and in combination with ethanol, on simulated driving' (1974) *Clin Pharmacol Thera*, 15: 368.

2.   The person arrested should be formally informed of his right to summon a doctor of his own choosing and afforded facilities to do so, although the clinical examination by a police doctor need not be delayed until this second medical practitioner arrives.

3.   If consent to a medical examination is not forthcoming, this fact is recorded; then even if a doctor is called out, he can only visually observe the person detained. This is done from a distance. No form of medical examination or testing can be carried out. The doctor can only make notes as to the appearance, demeanour, gait and speech of the arrested driver which to some extent may reinforce the observations made by the police.

4.   If a medical practitioner is called out, he should be briefed fully about the circumstances of the arrest. The actual examination normally proceeds outwith the physical presence and the earshot of police officers, unless they are required as a chaperone in an examination of a person of the opposite sex to that of the doctor or if the person to be examined appears to be showing violence towards the doctor.

5.   Any interviewing of this person in relation to recent events should be directed solely to testing his memory, coherence and orientation, and not directed towards obtaining information about his possible guilt. It is however legitimate to ask about prescribed medication.

If such procedures are not followed, it is possible that the evidence collected by the doctor may be deemed to be inadmissible.

Information about the taking of drugs or prescribed medication may already have been volunteered to the police by the persons arrested. The police may also have discovered powders, tablets or other substances within the vehicle or in the clothing, which suggest that the accused had recent access to drugs. It is also often the case that a so-called field test is carried out on such substances. Solvents and the paraphernalia used to inhale these, cannabis 'reefers' or 'joints' and other objects may be found in the vehicle which may alert police to the possible use of such substances.

The detained driver will already have been asked at the roadside to provide a sample of breath for alcohol analysis, and if this roadside test is positive, samples of breath for testing in the static, legally approved device for assaying breath alcohol would also have been asked for. Some alcohol may be present, but this would be below the legally prescribed level.

As from 1 April 2001, a national standardised form was introduced by the Association of Chief Police Officers aiming to assist police officers to record the results of roadside tests to see if drivers' performance is impaired by drugs. This would serve as preliminary assessment of the drivers and will be referred to as 'field impairment testing'. In these tests the police will assess the size of the drivers' pupils, comparing them to a gauge held to the side of the face. Watering of the eyes or reddening will also be recorded. Motorists will also be asked by the police to stand with feet together, tilting the head back and counting to 30 seconds. Excessive movement or sway is recorded by the officers. Other tests which will be carried out will be to have the subjects walk along a straight line and turn, stand on one leg, and touch the tip of their noses with the tip of the index finger.

Medical confidentiality

It is important that the medical practitioner establishes his role in such instances with the persons to be examined. It is essential that the examinee knows and appreciates that the medical examination is carried out primarily to establish whether there is impairment to drive due to the taking of drugs and the results of this examination will be held in confidence but fully disclosed to the police at the time, in reports and at subsequent judicial proceedings. The rule of medical confidentiality does not hold in such specific examinations.

Scope of the medical examination

The clinical examination that is carried out has two principal aims: to determine any physical and neurological changes consistent with producing an impairment to drive that can be because of drugs, and to differentially diagnose these from medical or other complaints. The actual examination can follow the various stages listed in the form produced by the Faculty of Forensic & Legal Medicine of the Royal College of Physicians of London, which acts both as an aide-memoir and as a means of recording the medical findings.[1] This form need not be used at all, but the police should always obtain a full written report from the medical practitioner which should include the results of all the tests carried out and a declaration that at the time of the examination the ability of the persons examined to drive a mechanically propelled vehicle was impaired through drink or drugs. Contemporaneous notes should always be made by the medical practitioner and be available for scrutiny.

---

1   Publications – Faculty of Forensic & Legal Medicine.

This examination, which should last for about 20 minutes, must be carried out in such a way that vital functions are assessed and measured. It is not necessary to take the body temperature or to examine the eardrums on all occasions but an examination of the eyes, of pulse and blood pressure, and tests of orientation to time, place and person, and of co-ordination of neuromuscular functions are essential in all cases.

In general, the clinical investigations that should be carried out are those shown in Table 3.

TABLE 3

Function tested	*Clinical Investigation*
Level of consciousness	Glasgow Coma Scale (maximum 15)
Orientation	Time, place, person
Speech	Ability to participate in normal conversation, speech changes
Drowsiness	Drooping, swollen eyelids
Attention span	Backward counting
Heart rate	
Size of pupils reaction to light and accommodation	Excessive dilation with stimulants and pin point size with opioid and opiates
Conjunctiva changes	Injection (prominent blood vessels) of the conjunctiva with cannabis smoking
Eye movements on lateral and upward gaze	Nystagmus (spontaneous pendular eye movement)
Tongue changes and smell in the mouth	Alcohol (congeners), marihuana, volatile hydrocarbons
Gait	Performance over a short distance
Balance	Ability to stand unaided on both or either foot = Romberg's test
Co-ordination tests	Finger-nose pointing, collecting an object from the floor, alternate clapping on the back of the hand, opening buttons, tying shoe laces
Mood	Elation, euphoria, depression
Psychotic symptoms	Hallucinations, delusions
Cognitive performance	Obeying simple commands, remembering an item of information, e.g. an address given a few minutes previously.

Which drugs affect driving?

Different drugs are known to be associated with different clinical findings[1] [2] [3] but in the presence of several drugs in combination there may be an absence of or a change in the expected findings. The drug groups[4] which are known to cause driving impairment are:

1.   benzodiazepine drugs (such as diazepam, temazepam, lorazepam, chlordiazepoxide, etc) used as tranquillisers, anxiolytics and hypnotics;[5]

2.   cannabis;[6] [7] [8]

3.   opioids (eg diamorphine, heroin codeine, methadone);[9]

4.   amphetamines and related drugs (eg 'ecstasy');[10]

5.   cocaine;[11]

6.   antihistaminic (used in allergy prevention and treatment)[12];

7.   antidepressants[13];

1   Pickworth WB, Rohner MS, Fant RV, 'Effects of abused drugs on psychomotor performance' (1997) *Experimental & Clinical Psychopharmacology*, 5: 235.
2   Seppala T, Linnoila M, Mattila MJ, 'Drugs, alcohol and driving' (1979) *Drugs*, 17: 398.
3   Zacny JP, A review of the effect of opioids on pschyomotor and cognitive functioning in humans' (1997) *Experimental & Clinical Psychopharmacology*, 3: 432.
4   *Medical Aspects of Fitness to Drive – A Guide for Medical Practitioners* (1995, Medical Commission on Accident Prevention), chs 12 and 13.
5   O'Hanlon J F, Vermereen A et al, 'Anxiolytics' effects on the actual driving performance of patients and healthy volunteers in a standarised test' An integration of three studies (1995) *Neuropsychobiology*, 31; 81.
6   Moskowitz H 'Marihuana and driving' (1985) *Accid Anal Prev, 17*: 323.
7   Hartman B L, Brown TL, Milavetz G *et al*. 'Cannabis effects on driving lateral control with or without alcohol'. *Drug Alcohol Dependence*. 2015, 154:25–37
8   Hartman R L, Huestis M A 'Cannabis effects on driving skills' *Clin Chem* 2013:59 (3), 478–492.
9   Zancy JP, 'A review of the effects of opioids on psychomotor and cognitive functioning in humans' (1995) *Exp Clin Psychopharmacol*, 3: 432.
10   Hurst PM, 'Amphetamines & driving' (1987) *Alcohol, Drugs & Driving*, 3: 13.
11   Siegel RK, 'Cocaine use and driving behaviour' (1989) *Alcohol, Drugs & Driving*, 3: 1.
12   Verster J C, Volkerts E R. *Annals of Allergy, Asthma & Immunology*. 93 (3) March 2004, pp 294–301.
13   Ramaekers J 2017 http://www.sciennce.direct.com/science, articles.

8.   other psychotropic drugs used to treat mental conditions such as schizophrenia [1];

9.   hallucinogens (eg LSD).

Impairment

No recognised tight definition of 'impairment' is available and thus its diagnosis is one of subjective and personal deduction by the individual doctor, which depends on the results of the tests carried out and the level of experience in similar cases. A good rule of thumb is that if it is felt that it would be safe for the examinee to be given the keys of a car and to drive, then he would not be impaired.

Once a conclusion has been reached at the end of this clinical examination the examinee should be informed of what conclusions the doctor has reached in terms of the impairment. The two police officers involved in this arrest should be informed of the decision. A signed 'Soul and Conscience' certificate is to be issued to the procurator fiscal in a sealed envelope handed to the police; a pre-prepared form is available in the police offices for this purpose. As in all medical examinations the medical practitioner must be aware of the potential differential diagnoses. These include:

1)   acute anxiety state;

2)   withdrawal from drugs rather than their acute effects;

3)   sleep deprivation;

4)   medical conditions, eg Parkinson's, Disseminated Sclerosis;

5)   complications of diabetes (hypoglycaemia, ketosis);

6)   head injury.

Sampling of blood and urine

Although the medical opinion is sufficient on its own to indicate to the courts the presence of impairment to drive, the police will then be entitled to ask for a sample of blood or urine, the actual choice of sample being theirs. If the doctor feels that the state of the peripheral veins due to previous abuse is such that it would be well-nigh impossible to obtain blood from the examinee, the doctor should express his medical opinion on this to the police. To require the arrested driver either to provide a sample while waiting for the doctor or prior to the examination is inappropriate;

1   Ravera E Brit. *J Clin Pharmacol* 72(3), 505–513, 2011.

the sample should only be requested after the medical practitioner had diagnosed impairment.

A sealed 'drugs kit' is provided for this purpose. It must be ensured that this is well within its expiry date. This kit contains all the requirements for venepuncture, two containers with integral anticoagulant and preservative and two sets of labels. It is important that the seal of the envelope containing this kit is broken in full sight of the detained driver. Only such kits should be used and about 20 millilitres of blood withdrawn and divided out between the two sample bottles, which are then sealed and labelled. The driver can choose his sample of the two and this is then placed in the envelope provided which is further sealed.

If a urine sample is requested by the police, the appropriate kit and the method used in procedures set out in s 5 of the Road Traffic Act 1988 should be followed in this instance. If the driver wishes to take his sample, he should sign for it; if he does not want it this should preferably be retained by the police as a production to indicate that the procedure had been followed through appropriately.

In due course a copy of the toxicology report, which is both qualitative and quantitative, should be made available to the driver or his legal agents, and to the medical practitioner who carried out the medical examination. It is essential that the doctor is aware of the findings as it would be rather embarrassing if indeed it is found that he has pronounced on the presence of impairment, and in an appropriate analysis, no drugs are found in the blood-stream or urine of the driver.

The expert for the defence

If an expert is instructed on behalf of the defence in such cases, it will be his role to carry out the following checks on the papers and statements provided:

1. Was the procedure undertaken by the police in accordance with the stipulations and regulations for such a procedure?

2. Was the clinical examination carried out comprehensively and appropriately?

3. Was the conclusion reached appropriate given the results of the clinical tests carried out on the driver? (Forms used and any contemporaneous notes made by the doctor and his subsequent report may be necessary to give an opinion on this specific matter.)

4. Was the toxicological testing carried out appropriately?

5. Were the laboratory analytical findings in conformity with the medical opinion reached at the end of the examination?

Appendix E

Sentencing Guidelines Council: Causing Death by Driving

Definitive Guideline

Foreword

In accordance with section 170(9) of the Criminal Justice Act (CJA) 2003, the Sentencing Guidelines Council issues this guideline as a definitive guideline.

By virtue of section 172 of the CJA 2003, every court must have regard to a relevant guideline. This guideline applies to the sentencing of offenders convicted of any of the offences dealt with herein who are sentenced on or after 4 August 2008.

This guideline applies only to the sentencing of offenders aged 18 and older. The legislative provisions relating to the sentencing of youths are different; the younger the age, the greater the difference. A separate guideline setting out general principles relating to the sentencing of youths is planned.

The Council has appreciated the work of the Sentencing Advisory Panel in preparing the advice on which this guideline is based and is grateful to those who responded to the consultation of both the Panel and Council.

The advice and this guideline are available on www.sentencing-guidelines.gov.uk or can be obtained from the Sentencing Guidelines Secretariat at 4th Floor, 8–10 Great George Street, London SW1P 3AE.

A summary of the responses to the Council's consultation also appears on the website.

Chairman of the Council

July 2008

Foreword

Introduction

A. Assessing seriousness

    (I)   DETERMINANTS OF SERIOUSNESS
- Awareness of risk
- Effect of alcohol or drugs
- Inappropriate speed of vehicle
- Seriously culpable behaviour of offender
- Victim
  - (a) Alcohol/drugs
  - (b) Avoidable distractions
  - (c) Vulnerable road users

    (II) AGGRAVATING AND MITIGATING FACTORS
- (a) More than one person killed
- (b) Effect on offender
- (c) Actions of others
- (d) Offender's age/lack of driving experience

    (III) PERSONAL MITIGATION
- (a) Good driving record
- (b) Conduct after the offence
  - Giving assistance at the scene
  - Remorse
- (c) Summary

B   Ancillary orders

    (I)   DISQUALIFICATION FOR DRIVING
    (II) DEPRIVATION ORDER

C. Sentencing ranges and starting points
THE DECISION MAKING PROCESS

D. Offence guidelines

- CAUSING DEATH BY DANGEROUS DRIVING
- CAUSING DEATH BY CARELESS DRIVING WHEN UNDER THE INFLUENCE OF DRINK OR DRUGS ETC.
- CAUSING DEATH BY CARELESS OR INCONSIDERATE DRIVING
- CAUSING DEATH BY DRIVING: UNLICENSED, DISQUALIFIED OR UNINSURED DRIVERS

Annex A Dangerous and careless driving – definitions
Introduction

1.   This guideline applies to the four offences of *causing death by dangerous driving, causing death by driving under the influence of alcohol or drugs, causing death by careless driving and causing death by driving: unlicensed, disqualified or uninsured drivers.*

2.   The Crown Prosecution Service's *Policy for Prosecuting Cases of Bad Driving* sets out the approach for prosecutors when considering the appropriate charge based on an assessment of the standard of the offender's driving. This has been taken into account when formulating this guideline. **Annex A** sets out the statutory definitions for dangerous, careless and inconsiderate driving together with examples of the types of driving behaviour likely to result in the charge of one offence rather than another.

3.   Because the principal harm done by these offences (the death of a person) is an element of the offence, the factor that primarily determines the starting point for sentence is the culpability of the offender. Accordingly, for all offences other than *causing death by driving: unlicensed, disqualified or uninsured drivers*, the central feature should be an evaluation of the quality of the driving involved and the degree of danger that it foreseeably created. These guidelines draw a distinction between those factors of an offence that are intrinsic to the quality of driving (referred to as "determinants of seriousness") and those which, while they aggravate the offence, are not.

4.   The levels of seriousness in the guidelines for those offences based on dangerous or careless driving alone have been determined by reference only to determinants of seriousness. Aggravating factors will have the effect of either increasing the starting point within the sentencing range provided or, in certain circumstances, of moving the offence up to the next sentencing range.[1] The outcome will depend on both the number of aggravating factors present and the potency of those factors. Thus, the same outcome could follow from the presence of one particularly bad aggravating factor or two or more less serious factors.

5.   The determinants of seriousness likely to be relevant in relation to *causing death by careless driving under the influence* are both the degree of carelessness and the level of intoxication. The guideline sets out an approach to assessing both those aspects but giving greater weight to the

---

1   See Section C below for a description of the meaning of range, starting point etc in the context of these guidelines.

degree of intoxication since Parliament has provided for a maximum of 14 years imprisonment rather than the maximum of 5 years where the death is caused by careless driving only.

6.   Since there will be no allegation of bad driving, the guideline for *causing death by driving; unlicensed, disqualified or uninsured drivers* links the assessment of offender culpability to the nature of the prohibition on the offender's driving and includes a list of factors that may aggravate an offence.

7.   The degree to which an aggravating factor is present (and its interaction with any other aggravating and mitigating factors) will be immensely variable and the court is best placed to judge the appropriate impact on sentence. Clear identification of those factors relating to the standard of driving as the initial determinants of offence seriousness is intended to assist the adoption of a common approach.

A.   Assessing seriousness

(i)   Determinants of seriousness

8.   There are five factors that may be regarded as determinants of offence seriousness, each of which can be demonstrated in a number of ways. Common examples of each of the determinants are set out below and key issues are discussed in the text that follows in paragraphs 10–18.

Examples of the determinants are:

- **Awareness of risk**

  (a)   a prolonged, persistent and deliberate course of very bad driving

- **Effect of alcohol or drugs**

  (b)   consumption of alcohol above the legal limit

  (c)   consumption of alcohol at or below the legal limit where this impaired the offender's ability to drive

  (d)   failure to supply a specimen for analysis

  (e)   consumption of illegal drugs, where this impaired the offender's ability to drive

  (f)   consumption of legal drugs or medication where this impaired the offender's ability to drive (including legal medication known to cause drowsiness) where the driver knew, or should have known, about the likelihood of impairment

- **Inappropriate speed of vehicle**

  (g) greatly excessive speed; racing; competitive driving against another vehicle

  (h) driving above the speed limit

  (i) driving at a speed that is inappropriate for the prevailing road or weather conditions

  (j) driving a PSV, HGV or other goods vehicle at a speed that is inappropriate either because of the nature of the vehicle or its load, especially when carrying passengers

- **Seriously culpable behaviour of offender**

  (k) aggressive driving (such as driving much too close to the vehicle in front, persistent inappropriate attempts to overtake, or cutting in after overtaking)

  (l) driving while using a hand-held mobile phone

  (m) driving whilst the driver's attention is avoidably distracted, for example by reading or adjusting the controls of electronic equipment such as a radio, hands-free mobile phone or satellite navigation equipment

  (n) driving when knowingly suffering from a medical or physical condition that significantly impairs the offender's driving skills, including failure to take prescribed medication

  (o) driving when knowingly deprived of adequate sleep or rest, especially where commercial concerns had a bearing on the commission of the offence

  (p) driving a poorly maintained or dangerously loaded vehicle, especially where commercial concerns had a bearing on the commission of the offence

- **Victim**

  (q) failing to have proper regard to vulnerable road users

9. Issues relating to the determinants of seriousness are considered below.

(a) Alcohol/drugs

10. For those offences where the presence of alcohol or drugs is not an element of the offence, where there is sufficient evidence of driving

impairment attributable to alcohol or drugs, the consumption of alcohol or drugs prior to driving will make an offence more serious. Where the drugs were legally purchased or prescribed, the offence will only be regarded as more serious if the offender knew or should have known that the drugs were likely to impair driving ability.

11.   Unless inherent in the offence or charged separately, failure to provide a specimen for analysis (or to allow a blood specimen taken without consent to be analysed) should be regarded as a determinant of offence seriousness.

12.   Where it is established to the satisfaction of the court that an offender had consumed alcohol or drugs unwittingly before driving, that may be regarded as a mitigating factor. However, consideration should be given to the circumstances in which the offender decided to drive or continue to drive when driving ability was impaired.

(b)   Avoidable distractions

13.   A distinction has been drawn between **ordinary** avoidable distractions and those that are more significant because they divert the attention of the driver for longer periods or to a greater extent; in this guideline these are referred to as a gross avoidable distraction. The guideline for *causing death by dangerous driving* provides for a gross avoidable distraction to place the offence in a higher level of seriousness.

14.   Any avoidable distraction will make an offence more serious but the degree to which an offender's driving will be impaired will vary. Where the reaction to the distraction is significant, it may be the factor that determines whether the offence is based on *dangerous* driving or on *careless* driving; in those circumstances, care must be taken to avoid "double counting".

15.   Using a hand-held mobile phone when driving is, in itself, an unlawful act; the fact that an offender was avoidably distracted by using a hand-held mobile phone when a causing death by driving offence was committed will always make an offence more serious. Reading or composing text messages *over a period of time* will be a *gross* avoidable distraction and is likely to result in an offence of causing death by dangerous driving being in a higher level of seriousness.

16.   Where it is proved that an offender was briefly distracted by reading a text message or adjusting a hands-free set or its controls at the time of the collision, this would be on a par with consulting a map or adjusting a radio or satellite navigation equipment, activities that would be considered an avoidable distraction.

(c)   Vulnerable road users

17.   Cyclists, motorbike riders, horse riders, pedestrians and those working in the road are vulnerable road users and a driver is expected to take extra care when driving near them. Driving too close to a bike or horse; allowing a vehicle to mount the pavement; driving into a cycle lane; and driving without the care needed in the vicinity of a pedestrian crossing, hospital, school or residential home, are all examples of factors that should be taken into account when determining the seriousness of an offence. See paragraph 24 below for the approach where the actions of another person contributed to the collision.

18.   The fact that the victim of a causing death by driving offence was a particularly vulnerable road user is a factor that should be taken into account when determining the seriousness of an offence.

(ii)   Aggravating and mitigating factors

(a)   More than one person killed

19.   The seriousness of any offence included in these guidelines will generally be greater where more than one person is killed since it is inevitable that the degree of harm will be greater. In relation to the assessment of culpability, whilst there will be circumstances in which a driver could reasonably anticipate the possible death of more than one person (for example, the driver of a vehicle with passengers (whether that is a bus, taxi or private car) or a person driving badly in an area where there are many people), there will be many circumstances where the driver could not anticipate the number of people who would be killed.

20.   The greater obligation on those responsible for driving other people is not an element essential to the quality of the driving and so has not been included amongst the determinants of seriousness that affect the choice of sentencing range. In practical terms, separate charges are likely to be brought in relation to each death caused. Although concurrent sentences are likely to be imposed (in recognition of the fact that the charges relate to one episode of offending behaviour), each individual sentence is likely to be higher because the offence is aggravated by the fact that more than one death has been caused.

21.   Where more than one person is killed, that will aggravate the seriousness of the offence because of the increase in harm. Where the number of people killed is high and that was reasonably foreseeable, the number of deaths is likely to provide sufficient justification for moving an offence into the next highest sentencing band.

(b)   Effect on offender

22.   Injury to the offender may be a mitigating factor when the offender has suffered very serious injuries. In most circumstances, the weighting it is given will be dictated by the circumstances of the offence and the effect should bear a direct relationship to the extent to which the offender's driving was at fault – the greater the fault, the less the effect on mitigation; this distinction will be of particular relevance where an offence did not involve any fault in the offender's standard of driving.

23.   Where one or more of the victims was in a close personal or family relationship with the offender, this may be a mitigating factor. In line with the approach where the offender is very seriously injured, the degree to which the relationship influences the sentence should be linked to offender culpability in relation to the commission of the offence; mitigation for this reason is likely to have less effect where the culpability of the driver is particularly high.

(c)   Actions of others

24.   Where the actions of the victim or a third party contributed to the commission of an offence, this should be acknowledged and taken into account as a mitigating factor.

(d)   Offender's age/lack of driving experience

25.   The Council guideline *Overarching Principles: Seriousness*[1] includes a generic mitigating factor *"youth or age, where it affects the responsibility of the individual defendant"*. There is a great deal of difference between recklessness or irresponsibility – which may be due to youth – and inexperience in dealing with prevailing conditions or an unexpected or unusual situation that presents itself – which may be present regardless of the age of the offender. The fact that an offender's lack of driving experience contributed to the commission of an offence should be treated as a mitigating factor; in this regard, the age of the offender is not relevant.

(iii)   Personal mitigation

(a)   Good driving record

26.   This is not a factor that automatically should be treated as a mitigating factor, especially now that the presence of previous convictions is a statutory aggravating factor. However, any evidence to show that

1   *Overarching Principles: Seriousness*, paragraph 1.25, published 16 December 2004, www.sentencing-guidelines.gov.uk.

an offender has previously been an exemplary driver, for example having driven an ambulance, police vehicle, bus, taxi or similar vehicle conscientiously and without incident for many years, is a fact that the courts may well wish to take into account by way of personal mitigation. This is likely to have even greater effect where the driver is driving on public duty (for example, on ambulance, fire services or police duties) and was responding to an emergency.

(b) Conduct after the offence

– Giving assistance at the scene

27.   There may be many reasons why an offender does not offer help to the victims at the scene – the offender may be injured, traumatised by shock, afraid of causing further injury or simply have no idea what action to take – and it would be inappropriate to assess the offence as more serious on this ground (and so increase the level of sentence). However, where an offender gave direct, positive, assistance to victim(s) at the scene of a collision, this should be regarded as personal mitigation.

– Remorse

28.   Whilst it can be expected that anyone who has caused death by driving would be expected to feel remorseful, this cannot undermine its importance for sentencing purposes. Remorse is identified as personal mitigation in the Council guideline[1] and the Council can see no reason for it to be treated differently for this group of offences. It is for the court to determine whether an expression of remorse is genuine; where it is, this should be taken into account as personal mitigation.

(c)   Summary

29.   Evidence that an offender is normally a careful and conscientious driver, giving direct, positive assistance to a victim and genuine remorse may be taken into account as personal mitigation and may justify a reduction in sentence.

B.   Ancillary orders

(i)   Disqualification for driving

30.   For each offence, disqualification is a mandatory part of the sentence (subject to the usual (very limited) exceptions), and therefore an important

---

1 Ibid, paragraph 1.27.

element of the overall punishment for the offence. In addition, an order that the disqualification continues until the offender passes an extended driving test order is compulsory[1] for those convicted of causing death by dangerous driving or by careless driving when under the influence, and discretionary[2] in relation to the two other offences.

31. Any disqualification is effective from the date on which it is imposed. When ordering disqualification from driving, the duration of the order should allow for the length of any custodial period in order to ensure that the disqualification has the desired impact. In principle, the minimum period of disqualification should either equate to the length of the custodial sentence imposed (in the knowledge that the offender is likely to be released having served half of that term), or the relevant statutory minimum disqualification period, whichever results in the longer period of disqualification.

(ii) Deprivation order

32. A general sentencing power exists which enables courts to deprive an offender of property used for the purposes of committing an offence.[3] A vehicle used to commit an offence included in this guideline can be regarded as being used for the purposes of committing the offence.

C. Sentencing ranges and starting points

1. Typically, a guideline will apply to an offence that can be committed in a variety of circumstances with different levels of seriousness. It will apply to a *"first time offender"* who has been **convicted after a trial**. Within the guidelines, a *"first time offender"* is a person who does not have a conviction which, by virtue of section 143(2) of the Criminal Justice Act 2003, must be treated as an aggravating factor.

2. As an aid to consistency of approach, the guideline describes a number of levels or types of activity which would fall within the broad definition of the offence.

3. The expected approach is for a court to identify the description that most nearly matches the particular facts of the offence for which sentence is being imposed. This will identify a **starting point** from which the sentencer can depart to reflect aggravating or mitigating factors affecting

---

1   Road Traffic Offenders Act 1988, s 36(1).
2   Ibid, s 36(4).
3   Powers of Criminal Courts (Sentencing) Act 2000, s 143.

the seriousness of the offence (beyond those contained within the column describing the nature of the offence) to reach a **provisional sentence**.

4.   The **sentencing range** is the bracket into which the provisional sentence will normally fall after having regard to factors which aggravate or mitigate the seriousness of the offence. The particular circumstances may, however, make it appropriate that the provisional sentence falls outside the range.

5.   Where the offender has previous convictions which aggravate the seriousness of the current offence, that may take the provisional sentence beyond the range given particularly where there are significant other aggravating factors present.

6.   Once the provisional sentence has been identified by reference to those factors affecting the seriousness of the offence, the court will take into account any relevant factors of personal mitigation, which may take the sentence beyond the range given.

7.   Where there has been a guilty plea, any reduction attributable to that plea will be applied to the sentence at this stage. This reduction may take the sentence below the range provided.

8.   A court must give its reasons for imposing a sentence of a different kind or outside the range provided in the guidelines.

The decision making process

The process set out below is intended to show that the sentencing approach for offences of causing death by driving is fluid and requires the structured exercise of discretion.

1.   Identify Dangerous Offenders

Offences under s 1 and s 3A of the Road Traffic Act 1988 are specified offences for the purposes of the public protection provisions in the 2003 Act (as amended). The court must determine whether there is a significant risk of serious harm by the commission of a further specified offence. The starting points in the guidelines are (a) for offenders for whom a sentence under the public protection provisions is not appropriate and (b) as the basis for the setting of a minimum term within an indeterminate sentence under those provisions.

2.   Identify the appropriate starting point

Identify the level or description that most nearly matches the particular facts of the offence for which sentence is being imposed.

3.   Consider relevant aggravating factors, both general and those specific to the type of offence

This may result in a sentence level being identified that is higher than the suggested starting point, sometimes substantially so.

4.   Consider mitigating factors and personal mitigation

There may be general or offence specific mitigating factors and matters of personal mitigation which could result in a sentence that is lower than the suggested starting point (possibly substantially so), or a sentence of a different type.

5.   Reduction for guilty plea

The court will then apply any reduction for a guilty plea following the approach set out in the Council's Guideline "Reduction in Sentence for a Guilty Plea" (revised July 2007).

6.   Consider ancillary orders

The court should consider whether ancillary orders are appropriate or necessary.

7.   The totality principle

The court should review the total sentence to ensure that it is proportionate to the offending behaviour and properly balanced.

8.   Reasons

When a court moves from the suggested starting points and sentencing ranges identified in the guidelines, it should explain its reasons for doing so.

D.   Offence guidelines

Causing death by dangerous driving

Factors to take into consideration

1.   The following guideline applies to a *"first-time offender"* aged 18 or over convicted after trial (see Section C above), who has *not* been assessed as a dangerous offender requiring a sentence under ss 224–228 Criminal Justice Act 2003 (as amended).

2. When assessing the seriousness of any offence, the court must always refer to the full list of aggravating and mitigating factors in the Council guideline on Seriousness[1] as well as those set out in the adjacent table as being particularly relevant to this type of offending behaviour.

3. **Levels of seriousness**

The 3 levels are distinguished by factors related predominantly to the standard of driving; the general description of the degree of risk is complemented by examples of the type of bad driving arising. The presence of aggravating factors or combinations of a small number of determinants of seriousness will increase the starting point within the range. Where there is a larger group of determinants of seriousness and/or aggravating factors, this may justify moving the starting point to the next level.

Level 1 – The most serious offences encompassing driving that involved a deliberate decision to ignore (or a flagrant disregard for) the rules of the road and an apparent disregard for the great danger being caused to others. Such offences are likely to be characterised by:

- A prolonged, persistent and deliberate course of very bad driving **AND/OR**

- Consumption of substantial amounts of alcohol or drugs leading to gross impairment **AND/OR**

- A group of determinants of seriousness which in isolation or smaller number would place the offence in level 2

Level 1 is that for which the increase in maximum penalty was aimed primarily. Where an offence involves both of the determinants of seriousness identified, particularly if accompanied by aggravating factors such as multiple deaths or injuries, or a very bad driving record, this may move an offence towards the top of the sentencing range.

Level 2 – This is driving that created a *substantial* risk of danger and is likely to be characterised by:

- Greatly excessive speed, racing or competitive driving against another driver **OR**

- Gross avoidable distraction such as reading or composing text messages over a period of time **OR**

---

1   *Overarching Principles: Seriousness*, published 16 December 2004, www.sentencing-guidelines.gov.uk.

- Driving whilst ability to drive is impaired as a result of consumption of alcohol or drugs, failing to take prescribed medication or as a result of a known medical condition **OR**

- A group of determinants of seriousness which in isolation or smaller number would place the offence in level 3

Level 3 – This is driving that created a *significant* risk of danger and is likely to be characterised by:

- Driving above the speed limit/at a speed that is inappropriate for the prevailing conditions **OR**

- Driving when knowingly deprived of adequate sleep or rest or knowing that the vehicle has a dangerous defect or is poorly maintained or is dangerously loaded **OR**

- A brief but obvious danger arising from a seriously dangerous manoeuvre **OR**

- Driving whilst avoidably distracted **OR**

- Failing to have proper regard to vulnerable road users

The starting point and range overlap with Level 2 is to allow the breadth of discretion necessary to accommodate circumstances where there are significant aggravating factors.

4. Sentencers should take into account relevant matters of personal mitigation; see in particular guidance on **good driving record, giving assistance at the scene and remorse** in paragraphs 26–29 above.

Causing death by dangerous driving

Road Traffic Act 1988 (section 1)

THIS IS A SERIOUS OFFENCE FOR THE PURPOSES OF SECTION 224 CRIMINAL JUSTICE ACT 2003

Maximum penalty: 14 years imprisonment

Minimum disqualification of 2 years with compulsory extended re-test

Nature of offence	Starting point	Sentencing range
Level 1 The most serious offences encompassing driving that involved a deliberate decision to ignore (or a flagrant disregard for) the rules of the road and an apparent disregard for the great danger being caused to others	**8 years** custody	**7–14 years custody**
Level 2 Driving that created a substantial risk of danger	**5 years** custody	**4–7 years custody**
Level 3 Driving that created a significant risk of danger [*Where the driving is markedly less culpable than for this level, reference should be made to the starting point and range for the most serious level of causing death by careless driving*]	**3 years** custody	**2–5 years custody**

Additional aggravating factors	Additional mitigating factors
1. Previous convictions for motoring offences, particularly offences that involve bad driving or the consumption of excessive alcohol or drugs before driving 2. More than one person killed as a result of the offence 3. Serious injury to one or more victims, in addition to the death(s) 4. Disregard of warnings 5. Other offences committed at the same time, such as driving other than in accordance with the terms of a valid licence; driving while disqualified; driving without insurance; taking a vehicle without consent; driving a stolen vehicle 6. The offender's irresponsible behaviour such as failing to stop, falsely claiming that one of the victims was responsible for the collision, or trying to throw the victim off the car by swerving in order to escape 7. Driving off in an attempt to avoid detection or apprehension	1. Alcohol or drugs consumed unwittingly 2. Offender was seriously injured in the collision 3. The victim was a close friend or relative 4. Actions of the victim or a third party contributed significantly to the likelihood of a collision occurring and/or death resulting 5. The offender's lack of driving experience contributed to the commission of the offence 6. The driving was in response to a proven and genuine emergency falling short of a defence

Causing death by careless driving when under the influence of drink or drugs or having failed without reasonable excuse either to provide a specimen for analysis or to permit the analysis of a blood sample

Factors to take into consideration

1. The following guideline applies to a *"first-time offender"* aged 18 or over convicted after trial (see page 8 above), who has not been assessed as a dangerous offender requiring a sentence under ss 224–228 Criminal Justice Act 2003 (as amended).

2. When assessing the seriousness of any offence, the court must always refer to the full list of aggravating and mitigating factors in the Council guideline on Seriousness[1] as well as those set out on the facing page as being particularly relevant to this type of offending behaviour.

3. This offence can be committed through:

(i)   being unfit to drive through drink or drugs;

(ii) having consumed so much alcohol as to be over the prescribed limit;

(iii) failing without reasonable excuse to provide a specimen for analysis within the timescale allowed; or

(iv) failing without reasonable excuse to permit the analysis of a blood sample taken when incapable of giving consent.

4. In comparison with *causing death by dangerous driving*, the level of culpability in the actual manner of driving is lower but that culpability is increased in all cases by the fact that the offender has driven after consuming drugs or an excessive amount of alcohol. Accordingly, there is considerable parity in the levels of seriousness with the deliberate decision to drive after consuming alcohol or drugs aggravating the *careless* standard of driving onto a par with *dangerous* driving.

5. The fact that the offender was under the influence of drink or drugs is an inherent element of this offence. For discussion on the significance of driving after having consumed drink or drugs, see paragraphs 10–12 above.

6. The guideline is based both on the level of alcohol or drug consumption and on the degree of carelessness.

---

1   *Overarching Principles: Seriousness*, published 16 December 2004, www. sentencing-guidelines.gov.uk.

7. The increase in sentence is more marked where there is an increase in the level of intoxication than where there is an increase in the degree of carelessness reflecting the 14 year imprisonment maximum for this offence compared with a 5 year maximum for causing death by careless or inconsiderate driving alone.

8. A refusal to supply a specimen for analysis may be a calculated step by an offender to avoid prosecution for driving when having consumed in excess of the prescribed amount of alcohol, with a view to seeking to persuade the court that the amount consumed was relatively small. A court is entitled to draw adverse inferences from a refusal to supply a specimen without reasonable excuse and should treat with caution any attempt to persuade the court that only a limited amount of alcohol had been consumed.[1] The three levels of seriousness where the offence has been committed in this way derive from the classification in the Magistrates' Court Sentencing Guidelines.

9. Sentencers should take into account relevant matters of personal mitigation; see in particular guidance on **good driving record, giving assistance at the scene and remorse** in paragraphs 26–29 above.

---

1   *Attorney-General's Reference No. 21 of 2000* [2001] 1 Cr App R (S) 173.

Causing death by careless driving when under the influence of drink or drugs or having failed either to provide a specimen for analysis or to permit analysis of a blood sample

Road Traffic Act 1988 (section 3A)

THIS IS A SERIOUS OFFENCE FOR THE PURPOSES OF SECTION 224 CRIMINAL JUSTICE ACT 2003

Maximum penalty: 14 years imprisonment

Minimum disqualification of 2 years with compulsory extended re-test

The legal limit of alcohol is 35µg breath (80mg in blood and 107mg in urine)	Careless/ inconsiderate driving arising from momentary inattention with no aggravating factors	Other cases of careless/ inconsiderate driving	Careless/ inconsiderate driving falling not far short of dangerousness
71µ or above of alcohol/ high quantity of drugs OR deliberate non-provision of specimen where evidence of serious impairment	**Starting point:** 6 years custody	**Starting point:** 7 years custody	**Starting point:** 8 years custody
	Sentencing range: 5–10 years custody	**Sentencing range:** 6–12 years custody	**Sentencing range:** 7–14 years custody
51–70 µg of alcohol/ moderate quantity of drugs OR deliberate non-provision of specimen	**Starting point:** 4 years custody	**Starting point:** 5 years custody	**Starting point:** 6 years custody
	Sentencing range: 3–7 years custody	**Sentencing range:** 4–8 years custody	**Sentencing range:** 5–9 years custody
35–50 µg of alcohol/ minimum quantity of drugs OR test refused because of honestly held but unreasonable belief	**Starting point:** 18 months custody	**Starting point:** 3 years custody	**Starting point:** 4 years custody
	Sentencing range: 26 weeks–4 years custody	**Sentencing range:** 2–5 years custody	**Sentencing range:** 3–6 years custody

Additional aggravating factors	Additional mitigating factors
1. Other offences committed at the same time, such as driving other than in accordance with the terms of a valid licence; driving while disqualified; driving without insurance; taking a vehicle without consent; driving a stolen vehicle	1. Alcohol or drugs consumed unwittingly
	2. Offender was seriously injured in the collision
	3. The victim was a close friend or relative
2. Previous convictions for motoring offences, particularly offences that involve bad driving or the consumption of excessive alcohol before driving	4. The actions of the victim or a third party contributed significantly to the likelihood of a collision occurring and/or death resulting
3. More than one person was killed as a result of the offence	
4. Serious injury to one or more persons in addition to the death(s)	5. The driving was in response to a proven and genuine emergency falling short of a defence
5. Irresponsible behaviour such as failing to stop or falsely claiming that one of the victims was responsible for the collision	

Causing death by careless or inconsiderate driving

Factors to take into consideration

1.   The following guideline applies to a *"first-time offender"* aged 18 or over convicted after trial (see Section C above).

2.   When assessing the seriousness of any offence, the court must always refer to the full list of aggravating and mitigating factors in the Council guideline on Seriousness[1] as well as those set out in the table below as being particularly relevant to this type of offending behaviour.

3.   The maximum penalty on indictment is 5 years imprisonment. The offence is triable either way and, in a magistrates' court, statute provides that the maximum sentence is 12 months imprisonment; this will be revised to 6 months imprisonment until such time as the statutory provisions increasing the sentencing powers of a magistrates' court are implemented.[2]

4.   Disqualification of the offender from driving and endorsement of the offender's driving licence are mandatory, and the offence carries between 3 and 11 penalty points when the court finds special reasons for

1   *Overarching Principles: Seriousness*, published 16 December 2004, www.sentencing-guidelines.gov.uk.
2   Criminal Justice Act 2003, ss 154(1) and 282; Road Safety Act 2006, s 61(5),

not imposing disqualification. There is a discretionary power[1] to order an extended driving test where a person is convicted of this offence.

5.   Since the maximum sentence has been set at 5 years imprisonment, the sentence ranges are generally lower for this offence than for the offences of *causing death by dangerous driving* or *causing death by careless driving under the influence*, for which the maximum sentence is 14 years imprisonment. However, it is unavoidable that some cases will be on the borderline between *dangerous* and *careless* driving, or may involve a number of factors that significantly increase the seriousness of an offence. As a result, the guideline for this offence identifies three levels of seriousness, the range for the highest of which overlaps with ranges for the lowest level of seriousness for *causing death by dangerous driving*.

6.   The three levels of seriousness are defined by the degree of carelessness involved in the standard of driving. The most serious level for this offence is where the offender's driving *fell not that far short of dangerous*. The least serious group of offences relates to those cases where the level of culpability is low – for example in a case involving an offender who misjudges the speed of another vehicle, or turns without seeing an oncoming vehicle because of restricted visibility. Other cases will fall into the intermediate level.

7.   The starting point for the most serious offence of *causing death by careless driving* is lower than that for the least serious offence of *causing death by dangerous driving* in recognition of the different standards of driving behaviour. However, the range still leaves scope, within the 5 year maximum, to impose longer sentences where the case is particularly serious.

8.   Where the level of carelessness is low and there are no aggravating factors, even the fact that death was caused is not sufficient to justify a prison sentence.

9.   A fine is unlikely to be an appropriate sentence for this offence; where a non-custodial sentence is considered appropriate, this should be a community order. The nature of the requirements will be determined by the purpose[2] identified by the court as of primary importance. Requirements most likely to be relevant include unpaid work requirement, activity requirement, programme requirement and curfew requirement.

1   Road Traffic Offenders Act 1988, s 36(4),
2   Criminal Justice Act 2003, s 142(1).

10. Sentencers should take into account relevant matters of personal mitigation; see in particular guidance on good driving record, giving assistance at the scene and remorse in paragraphs 26–29 above.

Causing death by careless or inconsiderate driving

Road Traffic Act 1988 (section 2B)

Maximum penalty: 5 years imprisonment

Minimum disqualification of 12 months, discretionary re-test

Nature of offence	Starting Point	Sentencing range
Careless or inconsiderate driving falling not far short of dangerous driving	**15 months custody**	**36 weeks–3 years custody**
Other cases of careless or inconsiderate driving	**36 weeks custody**	**Community order (HIGH)–2 years custody**
Careless or inconsiderate driving arising from momentary inattention with no aggravating factors	**Community order (MEDIUM)**	**Community order (LOW)– Community order (HIGH)**

Additional aggravating factors	Additional mitigating factors
1. Other offences committed at the same time, such as driving other than in accordance with the terms of a valid licence; driving while disqualified; driving without insurance; taking a vehicle without consent; driving a stolen vehicle	1. Offender was seriously injured in the collision
2. Previous convictions for motoring offences, particularly offences that involve bad driving	2. The victim was a close friend or relative
3. More than one person was killed as a result of the offence	3. The actions of the victim or a third party contributed to the commission of the offence
4. Serious injury to one or more persons in addition to the death(s)	4. The offender's lack of driving experience contributed significantly to the likelihood of a collision occurring and/or death resulting
5. Irresponsible behaviour, such as failing to stop or falsely claiming that one of the victims was responsible for the collision	5. The driving was in response to a proven and genuine emergency falling short of a defence

Causing death by driving: unlicensed, disqualified or uninsured drivers

Factors to take into consideration

1. The following guideline applies to a *"first-time offender"* aged 18 or over convicted after trial (see page 8 above). An offender convicted of causing death by driving whilst disqualified will always have at least one relevant previous conviction for the offence that resulted in the disqualification. The starting point and range take this into account; any other previous convictions should be considered in the usual way.

2. When assessing the seriousness of any offence, the court must always refer to the full list of aggravating and mitigating factors in the Council guideline on Seriousness[1] as well as those set out in the table below as being particularly relevant to this type of offending behaviour.

3. This offence has a maximum penalty of 2 years imprisonment and is triable either way. In a magistrates' court, statute provides that the maximum sentence is 12 months imprisonment; this will be revised to 6 months imprisonment until such time as the statutory provisions increasing the sentencing powers of a magistrates' court are implemented.[2]

4. Disqualification of the offender from driving and endorsement of the offender's driving licence are mandatory, and the offence carries between 3 and 11 penalty points when the court finds special reasons for not imposing disqualification. There is a discretionary power[3] to order an extended driving test where a person is convicted of this offence.

5. Culpability arises from the offender driving a vehicle on a road or other public place when, by law, not allowed to do so; the offence does not require proof of any fault in the standard of driving.

6. Because of the significantly lower maximum penalty, the sentencing ranges are considerably lower than for the other three offences covered in this guideline; many cases may be sentenced in a magistrates' court, particularly where there is an early guilty plea.

7. A fine is unlikely to be an appropriate sentence for this offence; where a non-custodial sentence is considered appropriate, this should be a community order.

8. Since driving whilst disqualified is more culpable than driving whilst unlicensed or uninsured, a higher starting point is proposed when the offender was disqualified from driving at the time of the offence.

1   *Overarching Principles: Seriousness*, published 16 December 2004, www.sentencing-guidelines.gov.uk.
2   Criminal Justice Act 2003, ss 154(1) and 282; Road Safety Act 2006, s 61(5).
3   Road Traffic Offenders Act 1988, s 36(4).

9.   Being uninsured, unlicensed or disqualified are the only determinants of seriousness for this offence, as there are no factors relating to the standard of driving. The list of aggravating factors identified is slightly different as the emphasis is on the decision to drive by an offender who is not permitted by law to do so.

10.   In some cases, the extreme circumstances that led an offender to drive whilst unlicensed, disqualified or uninsured may result in a successful defence of 'duress of circumstances.'[1] In less extreme circumstances, where the *decision to drive was brought about by a genuine and proven emergency*, that may mitigate offence seriousness and so it is included as an additional mitigating factor.

11.   A driver may hold a reasonable belief in relation to the validity of insurance (for example having just missed a renewal date or relied on a third party to make an application) and also the validity of a licence (for example incorrectly believing that a licence covered a particular category of vehicle). In light of this, an additional mitigating factor covers those situations where an offender genuinely believed that there was valid insurance or a valid licence.

12.   Sentencers should take into account relevant matters of personal mitigation; see in particular guidance on good driving record, giving assistance at the scene and remorse in paragraphs 26–29 above.

1   In *DPP v Mullally* [2006] EWHC 3448 the Divisional Court held that the defence of necessity must be strictly controlled and that it must be proved that the actions of the defendant were reasonable in the given circumstances. See also *Hasan* [2005] UKHL 22.

Causing death by driving: unlicensed, disqualified or uninsured drivers

Road Traffic Act 1988 (section 3ZB)

Maximum penalty: 2 years imprisonment

Minimum disqualification of 12 months, discretionary re-test

Nature of offence	Starting point	Sentencing range
The offender was disqualified from driving **OR** The offender was unlicensed or uninsured plus 2 or more aggravating factors from the list below	**12 months custody**	**36 weeks–2 years custody**
The offender was unlicensed or uninsured plus at least 1 aggravating factor from the list below	**26 weeks custody**	**Community order (HIGH)–36 weeks custody**
The offender was unlicensed or uninsured – no aggravating factors	**Community order (MEDIUM)**	**Community order (LOW)– Community order (HIGH)**

Additional aggravating factors	Additional mitigating factors
1.　Previous convictions for motoring offences, whether involving bad driving or involving an offence of the same kind that forms part of the present conviction (i.e. unlicensed, disqualified or uninsured driving)	1.　The decision to drive was brought about by a proven and genuine emergency falling short of a defence
2.　More than one person was killed as a result of the offence	2.　The offender genuinely believed that he or she was insured or licensed to drive
3.　Serious injury to one or more persons in addition to the death(s)	3.　The offender was seriously injured as a result of the collision
4.　Irresponsible behaviour such as failing to stop or falsely claiming that someone else was driving	4.　The victim was a close friend or relative

Annex A:

DANGEROUS AND CARELESS DRIVING

Statutory definitions and examples

Dangerous driving

A person is to be regarded as driving dangerously if the standard of driving falls *far below* what would be expected of a competent and careful driver and it would be obvious to a competent and careful driver that driving in that way would be dangerous.

Examples of the types of driving behaviour likely to result in this offence being charged include:

- Aggressive driving (such as sudden lane changes or cutting into a line of vehicles) **or** Racing or competitive driving **or** Speed that is highly inappropriate for the prevailing road or traffic conditions

- Disregard of traffic lights and other road signs which, on an objective analysis, would appear to be deliberate

- Driving a vehicle knowing it has a dangerous defect or with a load which presents a danger to other road users

- Using a hand-held mobile phone or other hand-held electronic equipment when the driver was avoidably and dangerously distracted by that use

- Driving when too tired to stay awake or where the driver is suffering from impaired ability such as having an arm or leg in plaster, or impaired eyesight

Careless driving

Careless driving is driving that "falls *below* what would be expected of a competent and careful driver" and a person is to be regarded as driving without reasonable consideration for other persons "only if those persons are inconvenienced by his driving".[1]

---

1   1988 Act, s 3ZA as inserted by the Road Safety Act 2006.

Examples of the types of driving behaviour likely to result in an offence of *causing death by careless or inconsiderate driving* being charged are:

(i)   Careless Driving

- overtaking on the inside or driving inappropriately close to another vehicle

- inadvertent mistakes such as driving through a red light or emerging from a side road into the path of another vehicle

- short distractions such as tuning a car radio

(ii)   Inconsiderate Driving

- flashing of lights to force other drivers in front to give way

- misuse of any lane to avoid queuing or gain some other advantage over other drivers

- driving that inconveniences other road users or causes unnecessary hazards such as unnecessarily remaining in an overtaking lane, unnecessarily slow driving or braking without good cause, driving with un-dipped headlights which dazzle oncoming drivers or driving through a puddle causing pedestrians to be splashed

Depending on the circumstances, it is possible that some of the examples listed above could be classified as *dangerous* driving (see the revised CPS guidance). However, experience shows that these types of behaviour predominantly result in prosecution for *careless* driving.

A typical piece of *careless* driving may be that it is a momentary negligent error of judgement or a single negligent manoeuvre, so long as neither falls so far below the standard of the competent and careful driver as to amount to *dangerous* driving.

Published by the Sentencing Guidelines Council, © Crown Copyright, 2008

Index

[all references are to paragraph number]